Blockchain across Oracle

Understand the details and implications of the Blockchain for
Oracle developers and customers

Robert van Mölken

BIRMINGHAM - MUMBAI

Blockchain across Oracle

Acquisition Editor: Dominic Shakeshaft
Project Editor: Kishor Rit
Content Development Editor: Gary Schwartz
Technical Editor: Saby D'silva, Gaurav Gavas
Proofreader: Safis Editing
Indexer: Pratik Shirodkar
Graphics: Tom Scaria
Production Coordinator: Sandip Tadge

First published: October 2018

Production reference: 1121018

Published by Packt Publishing Ltd.
Livery Place
35 Livery Street
Birmingham
B3 2PB, UK.

ISBN 978-1-78847-429-0

www.packtpub.com

`mapt.io`

Mapt is an online digital library that gives you full access to over 5,000 books and videos, as well as industry leading tools to help you plan your personal development and advance your career. For more information, please visit our website.

Why subscribe?

- Spend less time learning and more time coding with practical eBooks and Videos from over 4,000 industry professionals

- Improve your learning with Skill Plans built especially for you

- Get a free eBook or video every month

- Mapt is fully searchable

- Copy and paste, print, and bookmark content

Packt.com

Did you know that Packt offers eBook versions of every book published, with PDF and ePub files available? You can upgrade to the eBook version at `www.packt.com` and as a print book customer, you are entitled to a discount on the eBook copy. Get in touch with us at `customercare@packtpub.com` for more details.

At `www.packt.com`, you can also read a collection of free technical articles, sign up for a range of free newsletters, and receive exclusive discounts and offers on Packt books and eBooks.

Contributors

About the author

Robert van Mölken lives in Utrecht, the Netherlands, and he studied Computer Science at the University of Applied Sciences in Utrecht and received his BCS in 2007. He started his professional career as a graphic designer and web developer, but soon shifted his focus to Fusion Middleware. Robert is now a Senior Application Integration Specialist and one of the expertise leads on Integration, Internet of Things, and cloud at AMIS with over 11 years of IT experience.

Robert's transition from building service-oriented business processes using Fusion Middleware 12c, toward connecting the physical world with the world of IoT using Oracle Cloud offerings and open source solutions has helped him become a leader in this emerging technology. His fascination for using the latest technology led to the research of blockchain to replace the currently used B2B and B2C patterns and tooling. Besides this book, Robert is also the co-author of the first Oracle PaaS book, *Implementing Oracle Integration Cloud Service*, which was published by Packt in 2017.

Robert is also heavily involved in the Oracle developer community. He is an international speaker at conferences, author/blogger on the AMIS Technology blog, the Oracle Technology Network, and participates in OTN ArchBeat Podcasts. Robert is a member of the board of the Dutch Oracle User Group (nlOUG) and organizes meetups. He works closely with several Oracle Product Management teams participating in Beta programs and takes what he learns and applies it to new presentations, blog posts, and community engagement.

Robert was awarded Oracle ACE (Acknowledged Community Expert) Associate in 2015, Oracle ACE in 2016, and Developer Champion in 2017. As his designations expanded, so have his areas of expertise.

> *First of all I would like to express my utmost gratitude to my family and friends who supported me in the past one and a half year it took to write this book. It has been an exciting journey with some stressful times that consumed most of my free time, but in the end it was worth it.*

I also would like to thank the people who helped me over the years to shape my professional career, especially my colleagues at AMIS that gave me the chances to excel in my career. Without you I wouldn't came this far.

Lastly, I would like to thank the Product Management team at Oracle responsible for the Blockchain Cloud Service to have given me early access to the software to be able to write the implementation chapters.

About the reviewers

Sven Bernhardt is a Software Architect with over 10 years of experience in planning, designing, implementing, and deploying individual software solutions for different customers from different industries. From a technology perspective, Sven is an Oracle technology expert and has meaningful knowledge about leading open source technologies. He also has significant experience as Technology Coach and Trainer.

Sven works as Senior Solution Architect for OPITZ CONSULTING Deutschland GmbH, a German Oracle Platinum Partner. He's one of the company's lead architects, who follows his passion for designing and building future-oriented, robust enterprise applications based on pioneering technologies and new, innovative concepts. In his role, Sven is involved in diverse projects dealing with challenges in the area of modern software architectures and digital transformation. In this area, he's always looking for solutions where existing and new approaches can be meaningfully combined with each other—since in most of the cases, software projects don't start on a greenfield.

Besides his work as a Software Architect in customer projects, Sven is a frequent speaker at numerous IT conferences and an author of blogs as well as articles in diverse magazines. In addition, he's an active member of the Oracle Developer Community and currently has the status of an Oracle ACE.

Arturo Viveros is an outstanding Mexican IT Professional currently based in Oslo, Norway. He is a certified Cloud Integration Architect with over 12 years of experience in the design, development, and delivery of software for a variety of customers and industries. Arturo is also a Developer Champion, Oracle ACE, and a published technology writer both in English and in Spanish; he also strives constantly to be involved with and support developer communities/user groups that focus on technologies such as Oracle, Java, DevOps, cloud, software architecture, open source, and blockchain. In his spare time, Arturo enjoys family life, reading, hiking, traveling, playing guitar, and practicing sports such as tennis, football, and skiing.

Thanks to Robert and the Packt crew for having me be a part of this awesome project; special thanks to my employer Sysco for supporting this kind of endeavor and particularly to my department manager Jon Petter who is always in my corner. As always, all my efforts are dedicated to my lovely wife Jessica and my beautiful family Luly, Arturo, and Dany.

Packt is searching for authors like you

If you're interested in becoming an author for Packt, please visit authors.packtpub.com and apply today. We have worked with thousands of developers and tech professionals, just like you, to help them share their insight with the global tech community. You can make a general application, apply for a specific hot topic that we are recruiting an author for, or submit your own idea.

Table of Contents

Preface

Since you are reading this book, I will assume that you are interested in learning more about blockchain technology in the context of using it in an Oracle environment. In this book, I will try my best to provide you with this knowledge. This book will guide you through the concepts and terminology behind blockchain and how these affect Oracle developers and customers. The chapters in this book examine real-world use cases for several major industries. Apart from these informative chapters, this book also provides a sample implementation of setting up and running a private blockchain on the Oracle cloud.

When speaking about blockchain, we mean a distributed (key-value) database that enables a group of entities to share a unified digital ledger and conduct transactions rapidly and safely with each other without having to go through a central authority. Each entity controls its assets via a private key and independently verifies all transactions. Blockchains have no single point of failure, so entities can appear, disappear, or malfunction without affecting the group as a whole.

Before taking a deep dive into blockchain, we'll begin with a presentation of the broad history of blockchain and where it came from.

History of Blockchain

Originally, blockchain was conceived as the underlying technology for **Bitcoin** by **Satoshi Nakamoto** (an alias for the unknown inventor(s)?) in October 2008. This was not the first time; however, the idea of cryptographically securing a chain of data blocks had been described. There were multiple publications throughout the 1990s by several authors, sometimes in parallel. In the late 1990s and at beginning of 2000, the first publications arose which talked about a decentralized digital currency and a theory of cryptographically secured chains. Two important names generally acknowledged for inventing the intellectual precursors of the technology are Wei Dai and Nick Szabo.

It wasn't until 2008, however, when these concepts resulted in the creation of the first blockchain. It was accomplished in the publication of the white paper *Bitcoin: A Peer-to-Peer Electronics Cash System*, by Satoshi Nakamoto, which can still be obtained at `http://www.bitcoin.org/bitcoin.pdf`. This white paper describes the concept behind the underlying technology that eventually became the blockchain.

Just three months after the publication of the white paper, the code for Bitcoin was released in a freely available, open source format, on January 9, 2009.

The Bitcoin network itself started on January 3, 2009, when Satoshi Nakamoto used the code to "mine" the first Bitcoins. A few days later, the first transaction took place. In the months that followed, the Bitcoin network gained more and more attention and membership, which led to the first official currency rate on October 5, 2009. At that time, one Bitcoin (or BTC) was worth about $ 0.76 (USD), which was based on an equation that included the electricity cost that a computer node required to generate a Bitcoin. At the time of this writing, June 7, 2018, a Bitcoin is worth about 7,693.50 USD, but its all time high has been 19,783.06 USD. Finally, on February 6, 2010, individuals could buy and sell bitcoins using the newly established dollar currency exchange. In that same year, the market cap exceeded $1 M USD because of increased member participation, and within three years' time, the market cap surpassed $ 1B USD. A more detailed history can be found at http://www.historyofbitcoin.org.

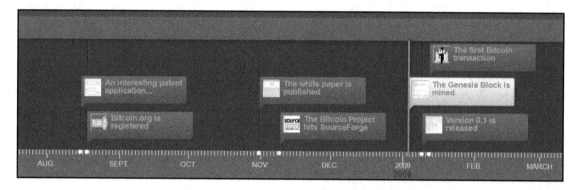

The timeline of the history of Bitcoin and blockchain

Remember, this book is not solely about Bitcoins, but rather about the technology behind it. If we fast forward in time, we will see the rise of many alternative blockchain-based currencies. Because the Bitcoin core code is open source, any knowledgeable individual can start a new coin by changing this code. Thus, you can understand why there are a number of alternative coins, but the one that stands out is Litecoin (https://litecoin.org).

Litecoin is one of the initial cryptocurrencies that followed Bitcoin and was introduced on October 7, 2011. It also is open sourced. It is a fork of the Bitcoin core code, meaning an alteration of the current code (or protocol) to change the rules–released by Charlie Lee, a former Google employee. Litecoin can be viewed as the silver to Bitcoin's gold, as the overall volume is higher and the price is lower. Litecoin is primarily distinguished from Bitcoin by a decreased block generation time (2.5 instead of 10 minutes), an increased maximum number of coins, and a different hashing algorithm. Don't worry if you do not understand these concepts yet, because I will touch on all of them in the upcoming chapters.

Some other honorable mentions include **Dash**, **Zcash**, and **Ripple**. Dash (`https://dash.org`) defined itself as being the more secretive version of Bitcoin, as it offers greater anonymity by making transactions through its decentralized network almost untraceable. Zcash (`z.cash`), on the other hand, claims to provide security and/or privacy based on the selective transparency of transactions by making such details as sender, recipient, and amount, private. All of these cryptocurrencies are adaptations of the original Bitcoin core code, or they take the concepts behind this code and create something totally new. Ripple (`https://ripple.com`), technically a public blockchain, stands out the most as it specifically focuses on banks. It is an interesting example, as though it is a publicly based platform, it is privately controlled through central ownership and the code is closed sourced. This enables banks to settle cross-border payments in real time and at a lower cost.

Once again, we will move forward in time to the year 2015. Starting then, several start-ups appeared that researched the use of the blockchain for very different purposes. One of the most well-known is **Ethereum**, which is an open source, public blockchain-based platform for distributed computing. One of the distinguishing features of Ethereum are smart contracts. A **smart contract** is a (scripting) functionality designed to facilitate contractual agreements using a Turing-complete virtual machine. This means that it has conditional branching (for example, "if" and "goto" statements, or a "branch if zero" instruction). Because Ethereum is still a public blockchain, it provides its own cryptocurrency called "Ether" to compensate participants who help perform computations on the platform. In `Chapter 5`, *Blockchain 101 - Security, Privacy, and Smart Contracts*, we will go through these agreements in great detail.

Some of the well-known cryptocurrencies and platforms based on blockchain code

Up until this point, I have only discussed public blockchains. After 2015, this changed, as numerous software was made publicly available to run your own private blockchain network. Public blockchains, such as Bitcoin and Ethereum, are terrible when it comes to exchanging information because of the high transaction cost. Private blockchains were introduced to solve the problems related to these costs. Moreover, they are designed to provide more privacy and openness by managing the blockchain user permissions.

A private blockchain performs the following:

- Ensuring that activity on the blockchain is only visible to chosen participants
- Introducing control over permissions to manage which transactions are allowed
- Enabling verification (mining) of transactions without the costs associated with the **proof of work (PoW)**

There are a couple of private blockchains, some are cloud-based while others run on-premises. There are companies, such as Deloitte's Rubix and Eris Industries' Monax, which sell turnkey solutions for private blockchains directly to businesses. Monax, for example, offers out-of-the-box SDKs for the Finance, Insurance, and Logistics industries. Other companies, such as Microsoft and IBM, offer **Blockchain as a Service (BaaS)** on their own cloud infrastructure. Both run **Hyperledger Fabric** (hyperledger.org). Microsoft runs Ethereum as well. Microsoft also offers private blockchain nodes packaged as Azure Quickstart Templates (azure.microsoft.com/en-us/resources/templates/?term=blockchain).

Since 2016, the number of vendors that provide open source software to run your own private blockchain has increased. One that is already mentioned is Hyperledger Fabric. It is part of the umbrella project Hyperledger, which was originally started by the Linux Foundation in early 2016. The project offers multiple open source blockchains and tools from different contributors, each providing different mechanisms and features. The available tools include a composer (package management) and an explorer (analytics). Blockchains within Hyperledger Fabric are built to run on Linux, but they can also run on macOS and Windows, using Docker (docker.com).

A strong competitor of Hyperledger is **MultiChain** (multichain.com). MultiChain goes the desktop route, deploying a private blockchain on a desktop, even in a Windows environment. It is also open source and allows rapid design, deployment, and operation of private blockchains according to your custom specification. With MultiChain, it is possible to create multiple types of data streams including key-value or identity databases.

For the implementation of our blockchain, we will look more closely at two private blockchains in `Chapter 8`, *Ethereum Versus Hyperledger*, and what makes them different from each other.

Major companies such as Visa, Capital One, NASDAQ, and Philips are now investing in the various available blockchain platforms and implementing them in their daily businesses. The following figure shows the highlights in the history of blockchain:

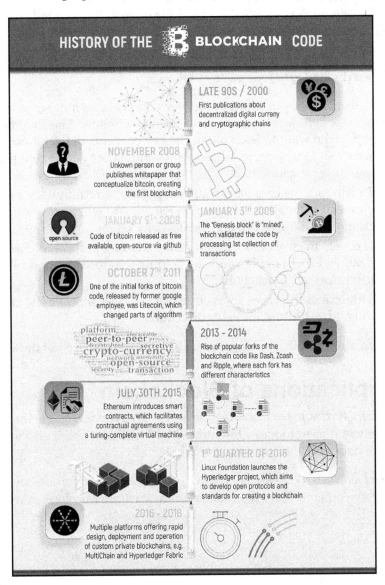

What this book covers

The book's goal is to illustrate the capabilities of the blockchain and show how these can be applied across the Oracle Red Stack. The book will introduce concepts and technologies that will allow you to implement your own blockchain in an Oracle environment. It will not go into the technical details of implementing and setting up your own private blockchain, but it will touch upon the basics. The book also covers five major industries, and it will provide examples of how the blockchain is used for projects in these industries. It will also help guide you as to where more information can be found, as a single volume can't possibly cover every aspect of the technology behind blockchain.

The book has been divided into four parts as follows:

- *Part I* covers the implications of the blockchain across industries that use Oracle and serve as high-level overviews of what is to follow. The chapters in *Part I* are for people who want to learn about the key concepts of the blockchain, how it affects current Oracle projects, and which industries will benefit the most from implementing the blockchain.
- *Part II* addresses the core blockchain concepts and terminology in detail. By the time you read through the chapters in *Part II,* you will have a solid understanding of the technology behind blockchain.
- *Part III* covers the use of blockchain as a replacement for tradition cross-organizational (B2B) applications by helping you to set up and run your own consortium/private blockchain.
- *Part IV* describes use cases across five major industries. The last chapter of this part will address future industry directions.

The following is a more detailed explanation of each chapter in each of these parts.

Part I: Implications of Blockchain

Chapter 1, *An Introduction to the Blockchain*, serves as an overview of the ideas and terminology that you'll need to know to work with blockchain, and it also introduces common characteristics of working with blockchain.

Chapter 2, *How Blockchain Will Disrupt Your Organization,* is an overview of the affects the blockchain can have on your daily workload and the customer projects in which you're involved.

Part II: Blockchain Core Concepts and Terminology

Chapter 3, *Blockchain 101 - Assets, Transactions, and Hashes*, covers the concepts of hashing, blocks, (distributed) blockchains, and the mining process.

Chapter 4, *Blockchain 101 - Blocks, Chains, and Consensus*, builds on the previous chapter and continues exposing the technical details of different kind of assets, how transactions work, and how consensus is reached among entities in a blockchain.

Chapter 5, *Blockchain 101 - Security, Privacy, and Smart Contracts*, shows that with blockchain, trust is everything. It also talks about how to know that your assets in a blockchain are secure. In addition to security, it covers how blockchain protects your privacy. Finally, this chapter covers smart contracts for conditional transactions.

Chapter 6, *Understanding the Blockchain Data Flow*, takes a look at how the discussed technical aspects of blockchain come together. Running through the flow of a few transactions helps to make sense off it all.

Chapter 7, *Public Versus Private Blockchains and their Providers*, discusses the exact differences between public and private/consortium blockchains. It is important to know that you don't have to build the blockchain yourself—there are plenty of providers.

Part III: Implementing a Permissioned Blockchain

Chapter 8, *Ethereum Versus Hyperledger*, covers two major private blockchains that you can run yourselves: Ethereum and Hyperledger. Based on the story we have woven so far, you should be ready to implement your own blockchain. This chapter also details the differences between these platforms and discusses which one is more suited to implementing a consortium blockchain.

Chapter 9, *Building a Next-Generation Oracle B2B Platform*, takes a look at blockchain concepts and reflects on where blockchain can replace certain parts of the Oracle middleware. The chapter proposes an insurance and claim process example and shows how a traditional cross-organizational application can be rebuild using blockchain to overcome current inefficiencies.

Chapter 10, *Introducing the Oracle Blockchain Cloud Service*, explores Oracle's answer for running a consortium blockchain, which uses Hyperledger Fabric as its core. The chapter answers questions on Oracle's strategy and what they offer as a cloud service on top of Fabric.

Chapter 11, *Setting Up Your Permissioned Blockchain,* will walk you through the steps involved for setting up our own permissioned blockchain for our real-world use-case described in Chapter 9, *Building a Next-Generation Oracle B2B Platform,* now that we know what the Oracle Blockchain Cloud Service is capable of.

Chapter 12, *Designing and Developing Your First Smart Contract,* helps you design and develop our first smart contract that we can later deploy and test on the Oracle Blockchain Cloud Service. In the process, we will also set up a development environment.

Chapter 13, *Deploying and Testing Your First Smart Contract,* enables you to deploy and test our smart contract (developed based on the use-case described in Chapter 9, *Building a Next-Generation Oracle B2B Platform*) on the Oracle Blockchain Cloud Service and test its functions using the REST proxy.

Chapter 14, *Configuring, Extending and Monitoring Your Network,* (the last implementation chapter) helps extend our blockchain network we have set up in Chapter 10, *Introducing the Oracle Blockchain Cloud Service,* by adding an external Hyperledger Fabric participant. This new member organizations will join the existing network and install the same smart contract.

Part IV: Real-World Industry Case Studies

Chapter 15, *Blockchain Across the Financial Services Industry,* explores real-word use/study cases in the financial services industry. We look at what the impact of blockchain is on this industry, and which day-to-day operations are already being transformed.

Chapter 16, *Blockchain Across the Transportation Industry,* covers real-world examples in the transportation industry, what is the impact of blockchain, and why is it a viable technology for this industry. We explore how blockchain has transformed freight/fleet tracking and international shipping (supply chain).

Chapter 17, *Blockchain Across the Healthcare Industry,* provides insights into what types of healthcare use-cases work great when running on a blockchain; think about secure electronic patient records, drug supply chain, fraud detection, and advanced clinical trials.

Chapter 18, *Future Industry and Technology Directions,* finally, looks at future directions of blockchain across other industries, such as energy and agriculture, and why it have taken longer for these industries to transform. We also look at the future of the blockchain technology itself in the next 5 years.

How I have approached this book

The approach I have adopted in this book is worth explaining. If you read the section about the target audience, you'll note that I'm not only aiming at the developer community, but at a wider customer audience that uses Oracle. To help me do this, I have set up some parameters to help you understand why things have been done a particular way. Note the following:

1. The book is split into multiple parts: *Part I* serves as an management overview of the blockchain. *Part II* goes into greater detail about blockchain core concepts and terminology. *Part III* addresses how to implement a permissioned blockchain. Finally, *Part IV* provides practical examples of blockchain implementations across several industries. You can read the parts as you wish in order to get the most value out of the book in the time you have available.

2. I have dedicated *Part III* of this book to developers implementing blockchain using the Oracle Blockchain Cloud Service. In this part, we go through the setup and running of a blockchain on the Oracle Cloud in great detail, but the smart contract code can also be deployed on other vendors.

3. I have tried to build the examples around plausible ideas to which anyone can relate. To achieve this, I have drawn on the idea of implementing a blockchain in projects on which I have previously worked professionally.

4. I have endeavored to convey the ideas and concepts in a way that places best practice over being a purist.

5. I have tried not to get caught up in any unnecessary complexities that can arise in order to ensure everybody understands the flow of data within a blockchain. All of the examples should work from your home or work computer without needing to speak with your internet provider or network manager about IP addresses.

6. The book uses tools that the entire target audience can use and understand—"nice" software and tools are not necessarily used in this book. The software and tools that are discussed represent those that are most popular and commonly used.

Who this book is for

This book seeks to support a broad range of readers, from line-of-business managers to software architects and developers. The first two chapters are especially useful for individuals who want to know what might be the effects of the blockchain on their business. Besides the high-level overview at the start, the book covers technical aspects of the blockchain such as the building blocks of a typical blockchain network.

Together, we will explore the impact of adding a blockchain to your current IT architecture. Finally, this book is intended for developers, and I will go through the process of setting up and running your own blockchain on the Oracle Autonomous Cloud Service and extend by connecting to an on-premises blockchain network. The implementation part is mostly done on the cloud service available on the Oracle Cloud, but the smart contract we develop can be deployed on any Hyperledger Fabric blockchain network.

To get the most out of this book

For most parts of the book, you don't need anything beyond what is mentioned in this section. It goes through all of the things that you'll need to implement a blockchain yourself. I have taken the approach of using free services and tools wherever possible. I will explain in greater detail the different tools and services throughout the book, but let's start by introducing what is needed at minimum:

- For implementing a blockchain smart contract, we will use software from Hyperledger Fabric (`https://www.hyperledger.org/projects/fabric`).
- Our blockchain will run on Oracle Autonomous Blockchain Cloud Service, but you can also run the Fabric blockchain on-premises using Docker images. To run on-premises, you need to download and install the pre-requirements (`https://hyperledger-fabric.readthedocs.io/en/release-1.1/install.html`).
- Oracle Cloud Account: A trial of the Blockchain Cloud Service will be sufficient for most things (as long as you have try running the blockchain within the trial period).
- We also make use of Postman (`https://www.getpostman.com`) as a tool to talk with the APIs supplied by the blockchain software. Postman is a free download.

Download the example code files

You can download the example code files for this book from your account at `www.packt.com`. If you purchased this book elsewhere, you can visit `www.packt.com/support` and register to have the files emailed directly to you.

You can download the code files by following these steps:

1. Log in or register at `www.packt.com`.
2. Select the **SUPPORT** tab.
3. Click on **Code Downloads & Errata**.
4. Enter the name of the book in the **Search** box and follow the onscreen instructions.

Once the file is downloaded, please make sure that you unzip or extract the folder using the latest version of:

- WinRAR/7-Zip for Windows
- Zipeg/iZip/UnRarX for Mac
- 7-Zip/PeaZip for Linux

The code bundle for the book is also hosted on GitHub at `https://github.com/packtpublishing/blockchain-across-oracle`. In case there's an update to the code, it will be updated on the existing GitHub repository.

We also have other code bundles from our rich catalog of books and videos available at `https://github.com/PacktPublishing/`. Check them out!

Download the color images

We also provide a PDF file that has color images of the screenshots/diagrams used in this book. You can download it here: `https://www.packtpub.com/sites/default/files/downloads/9781788474290_ColorImages.pdf`.

Conventions used

There are a number of text conventions used throughout this book.

`CodeInText`: Indicates code words in text, database table names, folder names, filenames, file extensions, pathnames, dummy URLs, user input, and Twitter handles. Here is an example: "Mount the downloaded `WebStorm-10*.dmg` disk image file as another disk in your system."

A block of code is set as follows:

```
func main() {
  err := shim.Start(new(InsuranceChaincode))
  if err != nil {
    fmt.Printf("Error starting chaincode - %s", err)
  }
}
```

When we wish to draw your attention to a particular part of a code block, the relevant lines or items are set in bold:

```
[default]
exten => s,1,Dial(Zap/1|30)
exten => s,2,Voicemail(u100)
```

```
exten => s,102,Voicemail(b100)
exten => i,1,Voicemail(s0)
```

Any command-line input or output is written as follows:

```
$> curl -sSL https://goo.gl/6wtTN5 | bash -s 1.1.0
$> sudo dpkg -i ~/Downloads/code_*.deb; sudo apt -f install -y
```

Bold: Indicates a new term, an important word, or words that you see onscreen. For example, words in menus or dialog boxes appear in the text like this. Here is an example: "Select **System info** from the **Administration** panel."

Warnings or important notes appear like this.

Tips and tricks appear like this.

Get in touch

Feedback from our readers is always welcome.

General feedback: If you have questions about any aspect of this book, mention the book title in the subject of your message and email us at customercare@packtpub.com.

Errata: Although we have taken every care to ensure the accuracy of our content, mistakes do happen. If you have found a mistake in this book, we would be grateful if you would report this to us. Please visit www.packt.com/submit-errata, selecting your book, clicking on the Errata Submission Form link, and entering the details.

Piracy: If you come across any illegal copies of our works in any form on the Internet, we would be grateful if you would provide us with the location address or website name. Please contact us at copyright@packt.com with a link to the material.

If you are interested in becoming an author: If there is a topic that you have expertise in and you are interested in either writing or contributing to a book, please visit authors.packtpub.com.

Reviews

Please leave a review. Once you have read and used this book, why not leave a review on the site that you purchased it from? Potential readers can then see and use your unbiased opinion to make purchase decisions, we at Packt can understand what you think about our products, and our authors can see your feedback on their book. Thank you!

For more information about Packt, please visit `packt.com`.

Part I

Implications of the Blockchain

1
An Introduction to the Blockchain

This chapter serves as an introduction to the blockchain and its underlying technology. It requires minimal technical knowledge. It summarizes the content that you can expect to encounter in the upcoming chapters that go into greater depth. In this chapter, I will explain the blockchain technology is on a more architectural level, rather than describing every detail of each component or layer.

When you ask 10 people what they think the term *blockchain* means, you might not be surprised to get 10 different and conflicting answers, as use of the term blockchain can be a bit confusing. A lot of people connect it to Bitcoin (`https://bitcoin.org/`) or other virtual (crypto) currencies. Some people talk about the **Ethereum** Application Platform (`https://ethereum.org`), some about smart contracts (executable code), but most of the time, blockchain is explained as a distributed, shared ledger.

In essence, a blockchain is a system of maintaining digitally-distributed ledgers in a way that allows individuals who do not fully trust each other to agree on updates to the shared ledger. Blockchains use peer-to-peer protocols rather than a central authority or third party to distribute and verify transactions between entities. There is no single point of failure, so entities can appear, disappear, or malfunction without affecting the group.

In this chapter, you will learn about the following topics:

- What is a blockchain and how does it work?
- What is the architecture behind the blockchain ecosystem?
- What are the differences between public and private blockchains?
- How secure is a blockchain, and what about an individual's privacy?
- What kind of applications can run on a blockchain?

What is a blockchain?

When talking about blockchains, we always refer to it as a **distributed ledger technology** (**DLT**) that established the underlying, open source technology behind Bitcoin. A blockchain is a digital system of recording transactions of assets in a list that is replicated across available nodes in a network, rather than being stored in a central data store, as is the case with traditional databases.

In a distributed ledger such as a blockchain, the data is distributed to all nodes in a trustless manner (meaning without a trusted third party such as VISA, MasterCard, or your bank) using a peer-to-peer protocol in near real time. Each node individually processes and verifies every transaction redundantly, bundles the verified transactions into a block, and broadcasts them to all other nodes in the network. Through a consensus mechanism, the block of transactions is validated by other nodes in which the majority has to approve the block before it becomes final and is added to the blockchain. The blockchain uses a combination of digital signatures and cryptography to prove your identity and authenticity and to enforce read/write and execute permissions (access rights). This makes it possible to permit write access for certain participants and read access to other participants, or even to a wider audience; that is, everybody.

If you loosely compare a blockchain to a traditional database, a blockchain is a system that contains an ordinary database and some extra software that corroborates that submitted records conform to previously agreed-upon rules before adding the new records to the database. This extra software listens and broadcasts new records to all nodes, or *peers*, participating in the network, ensuring that each peer has the same data in its database. The following diagram is an overview of the capabilities that make up blockchain technology:

Blockchain Technology			
Digital Ledger	Smart Contract	APIs	Digital Identity
Consensus	Incentives	Data Distribution	Digital Signatures
Data Storage	Participants	Cryptographic Protocol & Hash Functions	

The major technologies used by the blockchain are divided into five groups, each representing a different layer in the architecture

Technically, a blockchain is a new method of data storage. It is actually just a file with a predefined data structure (that is, how the data is logically put together). It can be compared with other data structures, such as relational databases (tables, columns, and rows), XML files, **comma-separated values** (**csv**), Excel database files, and binary files (images and videos). An analogy that I often use is that blocks in a chain are the same as pages in a book. Each page in a book, just like this one, has a bunch of *text* structured in *paragraphs*, and *information* about its *context* (also called metadata), such as the chapter number, chapter title, and page number. Similarly, in a blockchain, each block consists of a collection of content, for example, the list of transactions, and a header, which contains technical information about the block, a reference to the previous block, and a digital signature (hash) of the data contained in the block.

A blockchain, where blocks are linked to each other to make a chain, is analogous to pages in a book. Pages use sequential numbering that makes it easy to know their order. If pages were to be pulled out of the book and thrown into a pile, it would be easy to put them back in order. A blockchain, though, is cleverer. The following diagram shows that each block links back to the previous block via the block's fingerprint. The fingerprint is determined by the individual block's content and the fingerprint of the previous block, as demonstrated in the following diagram:

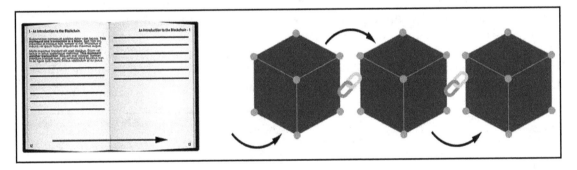

Each block in the chain links back to its previous block, like page numbers in a book

In a book, the ordering of pages is implicitly built on a page whose number is one less; that is, page 13 follows page 12 (13-1), whereas blocks are represented by fingerprints or hashes that are built upon each other. For example, block 3 with hash 8ec6cc0 is determined by hashing its data together with hash 9a59c5f of the previous block. By using a fingerprint that is determined based on the previous one, it can be used for validating the internal consistency of the data.

This scenario is shown in the following screenshot:

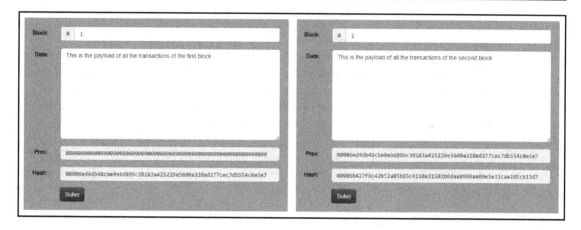

Two blocks are linked together by their hashed fingerprints. The fingerprint of block #2 is based on its data and the fingerprint of block #1.

You can check whether the data is consistent within a block by generating the fingerprint yourself and comparing it to the one that is part of the block's header. If someone wants to change the information stored in one of the earlier blocks, they need to regenerate all of the fingerprints from that point until the end of the chain. However, the blockchain will appear to be altered, and it is instantly noticeable by others. Depending on the consensus method used, the creation of these fingerprints can be a very difficult and slow process, which makes it very problematic to rewrite the blockchain. Furthermore, the number of blocks already present in the blockchain can be huge, for example, for Bitcoin (June 3, 2018: 512253 blocks with a size of 156 GB). The following screenshot shows that when changing the data, the hash is also changed and the block becomes invalid:

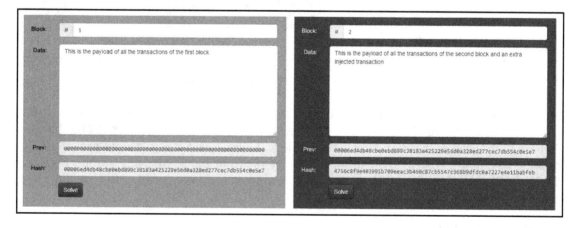

The data in block #2 is changed, and it generates a different fingerprint than before

How does a blockchain work?

The technology (that is, the architecture, mechanisms, security, and so forth) behind the blockchain can be seen both as the backbone for future accounting and as an engine for a modern message transport system. So how does a blockchain actually work during runtime?

The following diagram shows how blockchain systems must follow a specific flow of actions in order to consistently maintain a distributed ledger of facts (a key-value database with the current state of assets) and a separate history of their updates (distributed transaction log). The transactions that you submit are stored and verified without the involvement of a governing central authority using advanced mathematics and computer science, that is, cryptographic hash functions.

The blockchain not only secures these transactions but also protects their integrity (and anonymity). This demonstrated in the following diagram:

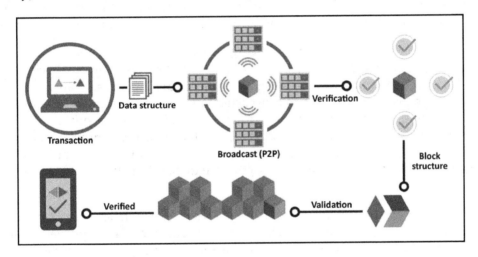

The flow that a transaction follows from submission to being verified by the majority of networks

Now let's take a closer look at the preceding diagram that describes the flow of transactions in a blockchain. When you want to exchange data with someone else on the blockchain, you do this by submitting a transaction in which you propose your changes.
A **Transaction** usually contains the context (action) in which it should be executed and any asset that can be described in digital form, such as currency, contracts, and incident and medical records. The **Data structure** of proposed changes to an asset can be both structured and unstructured, but often it is represented as **JSON (JavaScript Object Notation)**, which is a human-readable text format for data objects.

A typical blockchain provides client APIs to interact with the transaction, but generally you would use a web application that calls the API with which you would submit your transaction to one of the active nodes (peers) in the network.

Depending on the network's capabilities, the transaction is either locally validated or directly *broadcast* to all active nodes in the network using the **peer-to-peer network** (P2P). When locally validated, your transaction is only broadcast after validation, based on a set of network rules. Each node that receives your transaction will, depending on network rules, either verify it instantly or transcribe it into a secure record and place it in a queue of pending transactions. In this case, nodes, in other words, the participating computers or servers in the network, *verify* whether your transaction is valid based on a set of rules to which the network has agreed.

For example, your transaction can trigger participating nodes to execute business logic (such as a smart contract) and follow the consensus protocol to verify the results. Some consensus protocols require you to pay a transaction fee to get your transaction verified. The amount you pay is part of your transaction, and it determines the time it takes to get verified. Some nodes that create blocks only verify transactions that have a higher reward.

Depending on the rules defined by the network's protocol, validating nodes *combine transactions* into a block and digitally fingerprint the result so that they can be validated by other nodes in the network. Just like transactions, blocks are broadcast to all active nodes using the peer-to-peer network. When consensus is reached, depending on the network' rules, participating nodes either batch the transactions and store the results as a cryptographically secured, immutable data block, or they take the approved block and append it to their ledger. Consensus protocols may include a reward system for nodes that create a block or require you to pay a transaction fee to distribute the currency to the rightful recipient.

Following the consensus mechanisms and network rules, it may take several blocks until you can be certain that your transaction is verified and not part of an orphaned chain. It is possible for multiple peers to create a block at the same time or just a few seconds apart from each other. This can produce a **fork** in the chain. Both blocks are initially accepted by the majority of the network, creating two chains. For any block of transactions, however, there is only one way to the **genesis block** (that is, first created in the chain), and blocks that are part of the smaller chain are eventually rejected.

In the following diagram, you can see that the longest chain survives and that smaller chains are rejected:

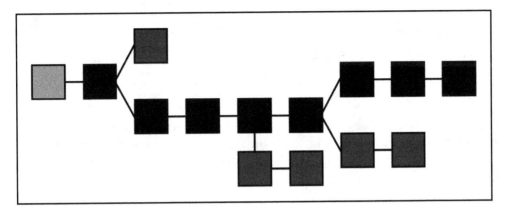

The genesis block is shown in green. The main chain is shown in black and the orphaned/rejected chain appears in red.

Those transactions that are part of the rejected block(s) are added back to the pool of queued transactions and will eventually be included in another block. With blockchains that use an incentive model, the reward that someone receives for solving an orphaned block is practically lost.

What is the architecture behind the blockchain?

As I mentioned earlier, the blockchain is not just a distributed database; it includes advanced software and security techniques to create a network of nodes (peers) that are always in sync, where each node validates and verifies transactions and blocks redundantly in order to reach consensus, and it provides a platform to run decentralized applications. To achieve this, the blockchain or digital ledger technology is built upon a layered architecture. In most cases, this contains four or five layers, namely the data layer, network layer, consensus layer, incentive layer, and application layer.

The data layer

At the bottom layer of the stack is the data layer, which deals with the data structure and the physical storage of data in the blockchain.

The following diagram shows the common capabilities that are part of this layer:

Data Layer			
Transaction	Chain Structure	Digital Signature	Merkle Tree
Data Model	Participants	Cryptographic Protocol and Hash Functions	

The capabilities of the data layer, such as cryptographic protocols, hash functions, digital signatures, and others

The data layer includes capabilities that describe the transaction and data model, the type of participants that can connect and use the blockchain (that is, the permissions model), the structure of the chain and its blocks, and the cryptography and hash functions to secure data and generate digital signatures.

Data model, transactions, and chain structure

The first two capabilities, data model and transactions, are closely related to each other. This is where the data model describes the type of assets available on the network and its data structure. Transactions trigger actions to modify asset data and transact assets between participants. The data model can be very simple and contain just one asset, such as a cryptocurrency like Bitcoin, or a more complex model with multiple assets that can even have relationships between them. The same applies to the transactions available on the network.

An asset(s) can be created or referenced in a *transaction*, which in essence transfers the asset(s) between two parties who wish to exchange the data, for example, processing a payment between two parties, placing an order on an online store, registering an automobile, tracking diamonds around the world, or sharing your digital identity. More background will be provided on these two capabilities in Chapter 3, *Blockchain 101 - Assets, Transactions, and Hashes*.

The chain structure is also related to transaction data. It describes the data structure in which individual transactions are combined into a block and how these blocks are chained to each other. The structure is usually different across blockchain platforms, since it is used to run on a specific platform. When comparing blockchains, you will notice that more advanced platforms have more complex structures; that is, they contain more information. For reference, the minimum size of a block on the Bitcoin blockchain is around 100 bytes, whereas the minimum size of a block on the Ethereum blockchain is around 525 bytes. The chain structure also describes the maximum size of a block, how blocks are chained together, and how incentives are paid out to participants. More information will be provided about this capability in Chapter 4, *Blockchain 101 - Blocks, Chains, and Consensus*.

Cryptographic protocol, hash functions, and digital signatures

These three capabilities—cryptographic protocols, hash functions, and digital signatures—secure and digitally sign the data in the blockchain. A cryptographic protocol performs a security-related function by applying cryptographic methods, and it describes the algorithms such as hash functions should be used. The protocol used by a blockchain usually incorporates at least these aspects:

- Entity authentication
- Public/private key cryptography
- Secured application-level data transport
- Fingerprint/signature generation
- Data encryption methods

To prove that the data on the blockchain has not been tampered with, transactions, blocks, and participating nodes are signed by generating digital signatures (or *fingerprints*) on the content of the data using hash functions. A hash function takes any *input data* and produces an *output*, which, based on the algorithm in use, has a different fixed length. The output of a hash function is always a string, for example, an SHA256 hash is a 256-bit (32 byte) string of the input data. However, the input could be a list of transactions, and the output would be the digital signature that is placed on the block so that the content of the block (transactions) can be easily validated by others. In the given example, **SHA** stands for **Secure Hash Algorithms**, which are a family of cryptographic hash functions published by the National Institute of Standards and Technology.

Merkle tree

In the cryptography used in a blockchain, there is a fourth capability that ensures that the data is still valid, and that is a **Merkle tree**. The Merkle tree, or **hash tree**, is a tree of data blocks in which every leaf node is labeled by a hash or digital signature, and every non-leaf node (for example, the top of the tree) is labelled with the cryptographic hash of all of the digital signatures of its child nodes as its input. The hash tree is used by the blockchain to verify all data that is stored, processed, and transferred between nodes in the network. It can ensure that the blocks received from other nodes (peers) in the network are undamaged and unaltered, and it can verify that other peers do not send malicious data blocks and lie about their content. More details about these capabilities will be presented in Chapter 3, *Blockchain 101 - Assets, Transactions, and Hashes*.

Participants

A blockchain network is nothing without its participants. A public blockchain can have an infinite number of participants, since anyone can join the network. On the other hand, a blockchain network for business is a collectively-owned, peer-to-peer network operated by a group of identifiable participants. With either network, participants can be individuals or legal entities, such as a business, university, or hospital. The data layer describes the rules for joining the network and the permissions model for accessing and writing the data.

As the blockchain will become more relevant, powerful, and useful in direct proportion to the number of participants, this paradoxically raises one of the biggest concerns, which is the processing power needed to maintain and operate a huge blockchain over time. Solving this challenge is paramount from an architectural perspective and probably key for blockchain applications to become 100% viable in relation to a ton of use cases and eventually positioning themselves as mainstream technology.

The network layer

The second layer up on the stack, just above the data layer, is the network layer. This layer deals with the propagation or broadcast of transactions and block data among available peers in the network, the reliability of the network, and local validation of data. The following diagram shows the common capabilities that are part of this layer:

The capabilities of the network layer include a peer-to-peer network to broadcast transactions

Peer-to-peer network and broadcast of data

You may have heard of *BitTorrent*, a peer-to-peer network where users share files among each other without a central server having control over the data. The network layer of a blockchain is similar to this, and it is also managed by a peer-to-peer network, which is an architecture for distributing data in a network. In the case of blockchain, it is a network in which nodes (peers) are interconnected and share data or tasks (resources) among each other. This is different to a traditional client-server model, where the centralized server holds 100% of the data and the client needs to trust that the data is legitimate.

A peer-to-peer network runs without the use of a centralized administration system to coordinate transactions. Rather, it sends or broadcasts transactions to each connected party in the network. Nodes can join or leave when they want. When a node joins or rejoins the network, all active nodes will then share all of the updates required to be in sync. These peers commonly find each other through a central index server, or by seeking other participants that use the same software through the internet. When a transaction is published to one of the peers in the network, that peer broadcasts the transaction and its data to all connected nodes in order to ensure that everyone is in sync with each other. Besides transactions, peers periodically generate blocks of verified transactions, which is part of the consensus mechanism, and they are broadcast in the same way.

A peer-to-peer network is, in some ways, less efficient than the client-server model, as the data is distributed and redundantly processed. However, each peer can operate independently, which makes the peer-to-peer network more scalable and robust. Since no central server controls the flow of data, it is harder to close down the network. Additional detail regarding this capability is presented in Chapter 3, *Blockchain 101 – Assets, Transactions, and Hashes*.

Relay network

When running a big-scale blockchain across multiple continents, it is sometimes required, due to legal or performance reasons, for example, that these continents' systems can run separately for each other. Each continent can have its own network of nodes running independently, but they are all connected to each other through trusted node(s) that relay validated blocks of transactions to and from each continent's network. More information about this capability is presented in Chapter 4, *Blockchain 101 - Blocks, Chains, and Consensus*.

Local validation

Platforms that support smart contracts often support local validation. As the name suggests, this capability allows a peer to validate a transaction locally before it broadcasts the transaction to the rest of the network. The peer to which the transaction is submitted will validate and execute the transaction and smart contract rules. Only if no exceptions occur will the transaction be broadcast, else the transaction is canceled. More information regarding this capability is presented in Chapter 6, *Understanding the Blockchain Data Flow*.

The consensus layer

The third layer of the stack is the consensus layer. This layer deals with the enforcement of network rules that describe what nodes within the network should do to reach consensus about the broadcasted transactions. It also deals with the generation and verification of blocks. The following diagram shows the common capabilities that are part of this layer:

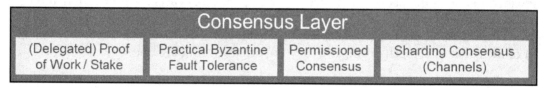

The capabilities of the consensus layer include the different consensus mechanisms that are available

The consensus layer includes capabilities that describe the rules for reaching consensus. The rules that need to be enforced depend on the consensus mechanism that is chosen when the network is initially set up.

When we speak about consensus, we mean the collaborative process that participating nodes of the network use to agree that a transaction is valid and to keep the distributed ledger synchronized at all times. These consensus mechanisms lower the risk of malicious (or fraudulent) transactions because they would have to occur (or be executed) across many locations at the same time, or else the tampering will be noticed almost immediately by other nodes. To reach consensus, the majority of the participants need to agree that the transaction is valid before it is permanently recorded in the ledger.

Once a transaction is permanent, no one, not even a system administrator, can delete the transaction from the ledger. The cost and time needed to reach consensus depends on the mechanism in place and the number of nodes participating in the consensus. A permissionless, or public, blockchain has relatively higher costs as compared to a trusted network of participants (permissioned or private blockchain). A wide variety of consensus mechanisms exist and are available to choose from in order to run an enterprise blockchain. When trust is high between nodes, a simple consensus mechanism, such as a majority vote, may be all that is needed. Alternatively, the network may choose to use a more hardened method.

The following example mechanisms and capabilities demonstrate how a network can reach consensus. The available consensus mechanisms can be categorized in to two groups: sophisticated and lightweight consensus mechanisms. Where the trust between participants is limited or non-existent, you will usually see one of the following more advanced consensus methods being used.

Sophisticated consensus mechanisms

In the world of Bitcoins and Altcoins (cryptocurrencies based on the blockchain developed by the Bitcoin core team), the **Proof of Work (PoW)** mechanism is used for consensus. PoW was originally a protocol developed with the primary goal of preventing cyber attacks, such as a DDOS attack. The idea behind PoW was first published in 1993 by Cynthia Dwork and Moni Naor, and used in the Bitcoin white paper as it allows for *trustless* and *distributed* consensus. This protocol requires participating nodes to perform an intensive form of calculations (also called mining) in order to create a new group (or block) of trustless transactions on the blockchain. The mining of transactions is necessary for two reasons:

1. Verifying the legitimacy of transactions
2. Creating new digital currency to reward miners for executing the first reason

To verify these transactions, the miners need to solve a mathematical problem (or puzzle). The first miner that solves this puzzle gets the reward (in the form of new cryptocurrency) and a transaction fee amount supplied by the transaction owners. Verified blocks of transactions are permanently added to the public blockchain ledger, and with every new block, the puzzle gets a bit more difficult. This requires miners to work more efficiently over time. Miners who can deliver more computing power are usually the ones that solve the puzzle the quickest.

Luckily, there are other ways to verify transactions. A mechanism known as **Proof of Stake (PoS)** is an algorithm with the same end goal as PoW. However, the way it achieves the objective is different. The main difference between PoW and PoS is that with the latter, participation is restricted to the participants that have a legitimate stake (wealth) in the blockchain. Instead of all participants (or stakeholders) trying to confirm the validity of the information submitted, this consensus method chooses an individual to approve it by running a type a lottery. The chance of your being chosen is calculated based on your proportional stake (wealth) in the network. For each X amount of stake a participant holds, they get a lottery ticket. When it is time to verify and create a new block of transactions, the network chooses a lucky winner to announce their conclusions. Where a PoW-based blockchain rewards a miner for solving (mining) the mathematical puzzle to create a new block, a PoS-based blockchain does not reward an individual for creating a new block. Rather, the individual receives compensation (in the form of collected transaction fees). Thus, the term *mining* is replaced with the term **forging**, where a block is forged rather than mined.

This is demonstrated in the following diagram:

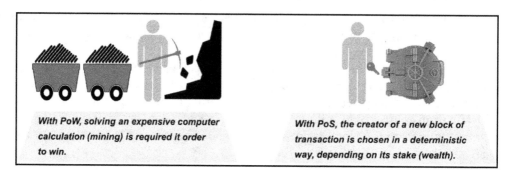

With PoW, solving an expensive computer calculation (mining) is required it order to win.

With PoS, the creator of a new block of transaction is chosen in a deterministic way, depending on its stake (wealth).

PoW requires expensive computer calculations to create a new block of transactions, which can be done by anyone.
With PoS, the creator of a new block of transactions is chosen based on their stake (wealth).

The preceding diagram shows the main difference between the two consensus methods. The PoS consensus method has advantages over the PoW method, as it does not perform useless calculations in order to create a block. This prevents a lot of energy from being wasted and is more cost efficient. Also, the PoW protocol is sensitive to a 51% *attack*, where an individual controls a minimum of 51 percent of the total computational power available in the entire network. With the PoS protocol in place, it is much harder to execute this type of attack because an individual needs to own 51 percent of the total amount of wealth (assets/coins), which is very unlikely.

The PoS protocol also has a variant called the **delegated proof of stake (DPoS)**. The main difference between the two is analogous to the difference between a direct democracy, where you vote for a specific person, and a representative democracy, where you select a group of voters who then collectively vote on a specific person. With a DPoS, the participants choose an entity to represent their collective stake in the blockchain. Thus, you decide which entity, also called a **delegate node**, will represent your stake in the blockchain. This allows you to join a team in order to magnify your stake. This helps balance out the power of large stakeholders. In `Chapter 4`, *Blockchain 101 - Blocks, Chains, and Consensus*, I will address these protocols in more detail.

Lightweight consensus mechanisms

In a business environment, where trust between participants is high or at least partially present, you can come across one of the following more lightweight consensus methods. One of the most well-known consensus mechanisms, besides PoW and (delegated) PoS, is the **practical byzantine fault tolerance (PBFT)** method. It is used by many enterprise blockchain providers.

The difference between the previously-discussed sophisticated methods and PBFT is that this protocol is much more lightweight, since it does not require nodes to perform computations in order to create and verify blocks of transactions. With PBFT, every peer in the network maintains its own internal state, or their view on the current plan of actions. Transactions that are submitted to the network reach the validating peers at different times, so the order of transactions received doesn't have to be the same. In a given time period, peers that are fully in sync *vote* for a validating leader who chooses the sequence of transactions. The other peers use this sequence, in conjunction with their internal state, to perform a computation until they have the same sequence and consensus.

The following diagram shows you visually how this consensus mechanism works:

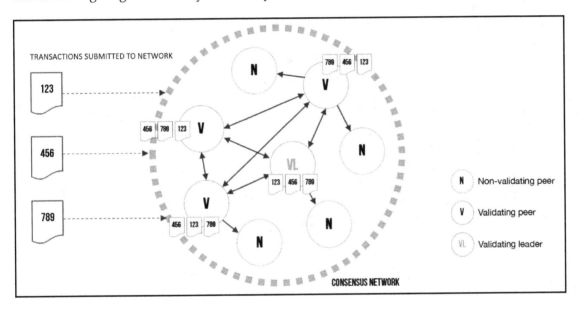

With PBFT, each peer might receive the same transactions in a different order, but broadcast their sequence to all other peers in order for validating peers to vote regarding the correct order

With PBFT, a consensus is reached based on the total number of decisions submitted by all peers. The consensus does not operate on the principle requiring that the majority of peers agree on a single decision submitted by a validating peer, but every decision that is sent. For every block, one of the validating pears is chosen as the leader, which will ultimately decide the final order of the transactions. So, if participant *A* sends one result sequence to participant *B*, and a different result sequence to participant *C*, then participant *C* would send this different result to participant *B*, who concludes that participant *A* has sent two different sequences. I will discuss the PBFT in more detail in Chapter 4, *Blockchain 101 - Blocks, Chains, and Consensus*.

Another similar consensus mechanism is the **federated Byzantine agreement (FBA)**. It assumes that participants in a network know each other, and they can distinguish which participants are important to them and which are not. In contrast to PBFT, instead of listening to all votes coming in for a certain sequence, a validating peer waits for the majority of the nodes it considers to be important to agree on a transaction before it agrees to the transaction. The same goes for the other validating peers in the network. A transaction is considered verified once enough peers considered important by enough nodes have agreed on its legality.

Another up-and-coming consensus mechanism is called the **Tangle** protocol. It works a bit differently than the ones I have explained up until now, and it is not considered a blockchain. When you submit a transaction with the Tangle protocol, it is confirmed by the network if and when two other peers in the network have proofed your transaction. Therefore, it is different from the others since, at any given time, no single node helps maintain the entire ledger. Each node helps by adding or editing two transactions at a time. The protocol also stores the transactions on a **directed acyclic graph (DAG)** (`https://en.wikipedia.org/wiki/Directed_acyclic_graph`) rather than on a linked list. In short, a DAG is a graph without a directed cycle, such that there is no way to start at any vertex v and follow a consistently-directed sequence of edges that eventually loops back to v again, as shown in the following diagram:

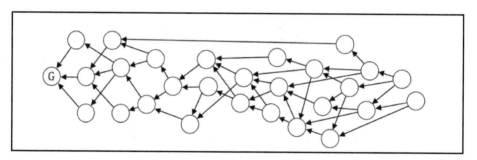

Transactions connected into a DAG. Arrows are drawn from the child to the parent. G is the genesis transaction.

The Tangle protocol does not know the concept of miners either. Since each edge holds only one transaction, other users can easily perform validation and PoW. Thus, there are no fees or rewards for confirming transactions in the ledger, but in order to submit your own transaction, you need to proof two other transactions first.

Permissioned consensus

When setting up a private or consortium blockchain between well-trusted entities, you might not need a full-blown consensus protocol.

It might be sufficient to work with a permissions-only consensus. This capability describes a consensus method in which there is no PoW to be done to verify transactions. Rather, it is based on the authorization and granted permissions that a user has on the data. If a user has write privileges on a certain entity, then they are allowed to modify that entity's data. Some users might have all permissions on a system, whereas others only have read permissions on a specific type of entity. This consensus model is more in line with permission models used by a traditional database or web application.

Sharding consensus

A number of blockchain platforms currently available support a capability called sharding consensus. Sharding is a type of data partitioning that separates large databases into smaller, faster, and more manageable parts called **shards**. Some blockchains try to use sharding consensus to make the blockchain faster and more efficient by not having every validating peer validate the same data blocks. With sharding consensus, a validating peer is assigned to one of the partitions and is only responsible for validating transactions that are part of that partition. Other blockchains implement this capability by allowing participants to create private channels or *subnets* between specific peers in the network for the purpose of conducting private and confidential transactions, meaning peers can exchange transactions on a *global* ledger and exchange private transactions with other peers on a private channel. Participants who want to form a channel must be explicitly authenticated and authorized on that channel to transact and share updates on the ledger. Each channel has its own shared digital ledger and transactions log, and it must coexist in the same blockchain.

The incentive layer

The fourth layer of the stack is the optional incentive layer. This layer deals with the distribution of rewards that are earned by nodes in the network for the work they do to reach consensus. Whether this layer is implemented or not depends on the consensus mechanism in use. The following diagram shows the common capabilities that are part of this layer:

Incentive Layer	
Rewards Distribution	Transaction Fees

The capabilities of the incentive layer, including the distribution of rewards and transaction fees

The incentive layer include capabilities that describe what kinds of incentives are given by the network, when and how incentives can be earned by nodes, and the minimum amount of transaction fees needed to perform actions on the blockchain.

Rewards distribution and transaction fees

To run a successful public blockchain, there needs to be some kind of incentive program for individuals to join the network and to participate in the validation of transactions. As explained in the section on the consensus layer, what kind of work needs to be performed to reach consensus depends on the mechanism chosen by the network originator: the more difficult the PoW, the more elaborate the rewards distribution system.

A blockchain that uses PoW rewards the node (or miner) who solves the mathematical puzzle first when creating a new block. The node receives an amount of cryptocurrency in return. For example, Bitcoin currently has a block rewards of 12.5 coins, which halves every 210,000 blocks. With 144 blocks mined each day, it halves on average every four years. The miner that mines the block also receives all of the transaction fees. The total amount of transaction fees that the miner receives depends on the kind of transactions included in the block. The individual fee of a transaction is based on its size (in bytes), the age of its inputs (how long ago the coins spent were received), and the speed at which you want your transaction to be validated and verified. Thus, to submit a transaction successfully, you need to calculate the amount of the fee you need to pay in order for your transaction to be included by a miner in one of the next blocks. The higher the fee you must pay, the quicker your transaction is validated and verified. For example, in Bitcoin, the transaction fee for the next block can range between $5 and $35 USD.

A blockchain that uses PoS does not have a reward system for mining, or, in this case, forging a block of transactions. All of the digital currency is created in the beginning and can, for example, be bought and sold through exchanges and may also distributed as transaction fees. The node that does the proofing of the transactions will only receive the transaction fees included by the original submitters of the transactions. The amount of transaction fee the forger receives depends on the complexity of each individual transaction and the fuel needed to execute it. So, to submit a transaction successfully, once again you need to calculate the amount of the fee you need to pay in order for your transaction to be validated and verified in one of the upcoming blocks. When the amount is too low, it is possible that your transaction will remain in a pending status for a long time. You can then choose whether to resend it with a higher fee. Some blockchains, such as Ethereum, in addition to the transaction fee, also use a *gas* fee for the execution of the transaction, and when this is too low, your transaction will fail and you will lose the gas fee to the forger.

There are also consensus mechanisms that combine the two systems, such as **Proof of Activity (PoA)**. With PoA, miners first have to solve a cryptographic puzzle to create a block. The winner then receives a block reward. This block, however, does not contain transactions—it only contains the address of the winner. Next, a group of validating nodes (forgers) is chosen to verify the transaction that will be added, and they receive a reward for validating transactions.

The application layer

The fifth and final (top) layer of the stack is called the application layer. This layer deals with providing the interfaces to access, program, and use the blockchain. The following diagram shows the common capabilities that are part of this layer:

Application Layer			
Digital Ledger	Smart Contract	APIs	Decentralized Applications

The capabilities of the application layer, including the programmable smart contracts and APIs

The application layer includes capabilities that provide application interfaces on top of the blockchain, both out-of-the-box functionality and custom implementations. The capabilities describe how the digital ledger is implemented and exposed to the world, how smart contracts can be built and run on the blockchain, and how third-party applications can interact with the digital ledger and smart contracts.

Digital ledger

One of the core capabilities of the blockchain is the digital ledger, a type of database or system of records, which is distributed (shared, replicated, and synchronized) by the network layer among the participants in the network. The digital ledger records the transactions, such as the transfer of assets or data, from one participant to another, or among multiple participants in the network. Commonly, a key/value data structure is used to record these transactions and its assets. More advanced digital ledgers, such as the one used by Ethereum, NEO, and Hyperledger, also record smart contract code in the ledger as its own asset. Some digital ledgers have the ability to save the current state separately from the transactions log, which allows third-party applications to query the data easily without needing to replay the entire transaction log.

Smart contract

Another capability that is indispensable in a modern blockchain is smart contracts. A smart contract, also known as a *cryptographic contract*, governs interactions with the digital ledger, and it allows agreements between network participants to be executed automatically. Smart contracts can act as a complement, or substitute, for legal agreements. It is computer code that directly controls certain aspects of transactions under certain conditions. A smart contract not only defines the terms and conditions (rules and penalties) of an agreement, but it is also capable of automatically facilitating, executing, and enforcing the negotiation or performance of an agreement. A smart contract does this by taking the input, putting that input through the rules set out in the smart contract, and executing the required actions defined by those contractual clauses. For example, a smart contract could stipulate the pay-out on a shipping of perishables depending on when the shipment arrives. Shipments that arrive later than agreed to by both parties are free; otherwise, the importer automatically pays the grower the unit price × the number of units in the shipment.

RESTful and command-line APIs

For external clients and applications to interact with the blockchain, its ledger, and smart contracts, most platforms offer both a **CLI** (**command-line interface**) and a RESTful **API** (**application programming interface**). Such interfaces define a set of functions that developers can use to perform certain actions on the blockchain and receive responses via the HTTP protocol using the GET and POST method. The two interfaces differ in terms of functions supported. For example, you can use the command-line interface to control the settings of your node, whereas RESTful APIs can be used to invoke and query data on the blockchain. More advanced blockchain platforms also offer **SDKs** (**Software Development Kits**) for specific programming languages that are an abstraction layer on top of these APIs.

Decentralized applications

A capability that is still a very new concept is a decentralized application. A **decentralized application (dApp)** is a blockchain-enabled website that runs independently on every node of the peer-to-peer network, rather than on a single serve. They are comprised of both a frontend (web) application and a backend application, where the smart contract (backend application) allows it to connect to the blockchain. For example, a decentralized application includes the data model it uses (participants, assets, and transactions), an authorization and permissions model, smart contracts (backend), and a frontend web application. One public blockchain platform that supports this capability is **Blockstack** (http://blockstack.org).

Differences between public and private blockchains

When starting to develop applications to be run on the blockchain, the technologies that you will need depend on whether you will allow anyone to join and write data on your blockchain, or whether only known, (partly) trusted entities will be allowed to join and write data. Generally speaking, there are two kinds of blockchains: **public**, or **permissionless**, and **private**, or **permissioned**. A public blockchain is not specifically owned by anyone, whereas a private blockchain can be owned by a single entity or by a consortium (group of entities). As explained throughout this chapter, both public and private blockchains use the same technologies, but this is where the similarities end.

- **Public blockchains**: When we talk about public blockchains, we generally mean that the distributed ledger is public, and virtually anyone, without having any permissions granted by a central authority, can write and/or read data to the ledger. Since a public blockchain is designed to be trustless (anyone can write to it), and participants don't need anyone's approval to add data to the ledger, it requires advanced mechanisms for arbitrating discrepancies and ways to defend itself against attacks, as there is no authority to decide what happens when someone misbehaves. To secure a public blockchain, anyone can choose to participate in the consensus (validation) process, assisting in validating transactions by determining which ones get added and by verifying the current form and status of the blockchain. Another advantage stemming from the fact that anyone can join a public blockchain (trustless) is that most are secured by crypto-economics, where participants receive economic incentives for the work they do to validate transactions. This makes it more interesting to join, and it creates a fully decentralized network. The downside of a public blockchain is that these mechanisms create more complexity and raise the cost of running this type of blockchain.
- **Private blockchains**: Conversely, in a private blockchain, the distributed ledger is only accessible to participants who are known and trusted. The control over who can read verified transactions, who can submit transactions, and who can verify transactions, is done by a preselected set of nodes. Participants can only join after obtaining an invitation or gaining permission. An invitation can be sent by an existing participant, a certificate authority, or by a decision of the entire consortium.

The private blockchain is mandated when a consortium of parties wish to participate in trading, but sometimes do not fully trust one another, or when some information should only be accessible to some of the trading partners. Many of the mechanisms that a public blockchain needs to keep the data tamper-proof are not needed on a private blockchain, but are regulated by legal contracts. This dramatically impacts the technical decisions and changes the building blocks and mechanisms required to run the blockchain. It leads to lower costs and the faster throughput of data, since there are fewer nodes that need to reach consensus. Due to its controlled-access aspect, private blockchains deliver increased privacy so that mission-critical applications can also run on the blockchain. The downside of a private blockchain is that you have to decide which participants have the power of granting permissions.

I will discuss the differences between public and private blockchains and their advantages and challenges in more detail in `Chapter 7`, *Public Versus Permissioned Blockchains and Their Providers*.

How secure and private are blockchains?

Both public and private blockchains provide a certain level of out-of-the-box security for your data. The consensus mechanism is the main driver behind the security and correctness of the blockchain. With a public blockchain, all users need to abide by the consensus algorithm that verifies all transactions, and when doing so they need to prove that they made a sufficient amount of effort by solving a mathematical problem. In many cases, the first user to solve the problem, or who is chosen to solve the problem, gets rewarded. Each new solution then forms the basis for the next block of transactions to be solved. It becomes almost impossible to manipulate data that is confirmed in an earlier block, since it directly affects the blocks that were created after that block. A private blockchain is even more secure, since you need to have secured permission to participate on the network. Since read and write access needs to be granted explicitly to a participant, it is likely that you know and trust them. The changes on the ledger can be tracked back to an actual person, whereas with a public blockchain, it is only tied to a network address that can be owned by anyone.

Nonetheless, there are still some security risks that the software and the network rules cannot fix for you. Public blockchains, for example, that use cryptocurrencies to fuel their network have also led to black market trading. Since transactions are bound to an address and not a personal identity, it is hard to figure out who is actually trading. Because of this, public blockchains increasingly draw the attention of cybercriminals who steal cryptocurrencies or other available assets. Another security issue relates to the method of reaching consensus.

The most commonly-used means of achieving consensus consume a lot of energy. This may lead to centralization or the possibility of collusion, because the majority of the network nodes are run in countries with cheap electricity, or even within a single country.

This does not mean there are no security concerns when using a private blockchain. With a private blockchain, operators can control who is allowed to connect to the network and operate a node. Some concerns include the fact that a node can restrict the transmission of information or transmit incorrect information. Such nodes must be identified and bypassed in order to maintain the integrity of the system.

Besides security, you need to think about the participant's privacy on the blockchain. Privacy is much more nuanced, and addressing this issue can lead to uncomfortable questions. What needs to be kept private? Why? From whom? When looking into maintaining privacy, there are solutions that can be easily implemented in some cases, while in others it may be much harder. Many of these solutions are compatible with the currently existing blockchains, but it depends on what you want to achieve as to whether they will prove satisfactory. Technologies that allow users to do absolutely everything on blockchain without the possibility of being tracked are more difficult to create.

To secure private data on a public blockchain, you can look into the following methods:

- Cryptographic obfuscation
- Secure multi-party computation
- Zero-knowledge proofs

In short, **cryptographic obfuscation** is a way of turning your application into a *black box* version (or its equivalent). The application still has the same underlying logic, and it also returns the same outputs for the given inputs. However, because the data is encrypted along the way, it's impossible to determine any details of how it works.

Secure multi-party computation is a type of cryptographic system where parties jointly compute a function over their inputs while keeping those inputs private. Each party initially receives access to a share of the input by the sender and computes a function over that share. The outputs are returned to the sender, who can assemble the final output without any party knowing more than their initial share.

Another powerful technology is **zero-knowledge proofs**. This allows you to construct a mathematical proof that, when executing a given program on some input by the user, returns a particular output without revealing any other information. One zero-knowledge proof that can easily be implemented uses a digital signature showing that you know the value of a private key, which, when processed by the smart contract, can be converted into a particular public output.

When using a private or permissioned blockchain, it is much easier to secure the privacy of the data in the blockchain because participants and operators can limit read and write permissions on shared data (assets) and the execution of transactions. Even though you might think you're losing the decentralization of the network, there is still some degree of decentralization maintained in their structure. This is done by allowing participants to grant read/write permissions to other participants, which leads to a *partially decentralized* design.

I will discuss the security risks and the privacy methods of both public and private blockchains in more detail in Chapter 5, *Blockchain 101 - Security, Privacy, and Smart Contracts*.

What kind of applications can I run on blockchains?

I want to conclude this chapter by going over some of the applications that you can imagine running on some of the public or private blockchains currently available. The most widely-used or anticipated public blockchain platforms on which to run your own decentralized application are Ethereum and Blockstack.

- **Ethereum**: One of the longest standing platforms in existence is Ethereum, an open platform that lets you build, run, and use decentralized applications using the blockchain technology. This decentralized platform runs applications in the form of smart contracts; that is, applications that run exactly as programmed without censorship, fraud, or interference by a third party. These smart contracts consist of computer code that can facilitate the exchange of anything of value, such as currency, content, property, or shares. Because of the decentralized nature of the platform, there is no possibility of downtime.
- **Blockstack**: One upcoming public platform is Blockstack, which aims to be the new internet of decentralized applications. With Blockstack, users own their data and maintain their privacy, security, and freedom, instead of the application provider. In addition to the platform, Blockstack also has its own browser in which you can access the available apps. It uses the already existing lower level of the public internet, but applications are serverless and decentralized. Blockstack also provides a decentralized **domain name system (DNS)**, decentralized public key distribution system, and registry for apps and user identities.

Either of these platforms lets you build applications. Ethereum is more basic and broadly accepted, but it only supports smart contracts (backend code). Blockstack, on the other hand, is a platform for decentralized applications that contains both frontend (web application) and backend (smart contracts).

Other decentralized applications

Examples of decentralized applications that don't necessarily use these platforms are *Storj*, *UjoMusic*, and *OpenBazaar*.

Storj (pronounced: storage) is a decentralized cloud storage platform that uses the blockchain technology and end-to-end cryptography to secure your files in a decentralized manner. Storj protects your data by encrypting your files client-side, shredding them into little chunks called *shards*, and storing these pieces in a decentralized network of computers. Because the files are shredded into little pieces, nobody has a complete copy of your encrypted files. Beyond serving as a platform, it is also a cryptocurrency and a suite of decentralized applications. The applications can be used to store your files on the network or rent out your hard drive space. The cryptocurrency called **Storj Token** is given in return to nodes that share their hard drive space. More information about the platform can be found on their website at `https://storj.io/`.

Personally, I like to listen to great music and always hope that the artists I listen to get paid for their work from the monthly subscription fees that I pay. One platform that tries to address the issue of ownership (creator's identity) and music licensing is UjoMusic. The platform provides a portal where the artist can own their creative works, and the use of those works always remains in the control of the artist. It uses Ethereum, so it is no longer necessary to register a copyright and sign with a publisher in order to ensure that an artist gets paid when somebody uses or listens to their creation. UjoMusic uses a decentralized and distributed file storage system (Swarm, the decentralized storage branch of Ethereum) to enable redundant copies of the data that are fault-tolerant, resilient, censorship-resistant, and self-sustaining due to the built-in incentive systems. UjoMusic also uses COALA IP (`https://www.coalaip.org/`), which is a blockchain-ready intellectual property and licensing protocol so that they can build an open, global database of rights, holders and their works. More information about the UjoMusic platform can be found on their website at `https://ujomusic.com/`.

Who hasn't bought something online from Amazon, eBay, or Alibaba? These companies offer a marketplace where you can buy goods from sellers worldwide. Instead of directly interacting with the seller to conduct a transaction, the data is owned by the online service, and the payment goes through a provider such as VISA or MasterCard.

The blockchain project OpenBazaar aims to cut out the middleman. It still provides a platform for e-commerce, but it uses a different approach. It uses the blockchain technology to put the power back into the customer's hands. Instead of buyers and sellers needing to go through a centralized service like Amazon and using a credit card to make a purchase, OpenBazaar connects buyers and sellers directly. To use OpenBazaar, you download the client application. With this application, a seller can create a new product listing, including the details that you would normally see on an e-commerce website. When you publish the listing, it becomes accessible and is distributed over a peer-to-peer network to other users. Anyone can search for the item based on the keywords you applied. If someone buys your item, they pay with a cryptocurrency, like Bitcoin, and, when purchased, the client application creates a contract between the buyer and the seller with both digital signatures. Payments are sent into an escrow account for holding. Once the seller has sent the item to the buyer and they are satisfied with it, the buyer releases the funds and the seller receives the cryptocurrency (for example, Bitcoins). Surely it can all go wrong, just like any other marketplace? A buyer can receive something totally different from what they ordered or receive nothing at all. In this case, OpenBazaar offers the use of moderators (also users of the network), who both the buyer and seller trust, to resolve the issue, and they only release the funds if they sign the transaction. More information about this platform can be found at `https://www.openbazaar.org/`.

The last three examples discussed were of public applications that could be used by anyone. In some cases, however, you don't want to build and run a decentralized application that is accessible to everyone in the world. Certainly, with enterprise or mission-critical applications, you want to control access and secure the privacy of the data on the blockchain. If you want to run these kinds of decentralized applications, it is better to look at private or permissioned blockchain platforms, such as Hyperledger (Fabric) and R3/Corda.

- **Hyperledger Fabric**: Hyperledger, and specifically the Hyperledger Fabric project, is one of the most commonly-used permissioned blockchains, and it is endorsed by several large IT vendors, including IBM, Oracle, and Microsoft. It is a blockchain framework implementation, a combination of a **digital ledger technology** (**DLT**) and a smart contract engine. Hyperledger Fabric is a platform with a modular architecture that can be used for all kinds of distributed ledger solutions. It aims to deliver a high degree of confidentiality, resiliency, flexibility, and scalability. The architecture is designed so that it supports pluggable implementations of different components and accommodates the changes in the blockchain/digital ledger ecosystem.

- **R3/Corda**: Some private or consortium blockchains focus on specific markers. Corda is one of these, and it is a distributed/shared ledger platform specifically designed for recording and processing financial and legal agreements by regulated financial institutions. The platform supports smart contracts, which, in Corda's case, is an agreement whose execution can both be automated through computer code along with human input and control, and whose rights and obligations, as expressed in legal prose, are legally enforceable. Corda links the business logic and data of the smart contract with associated legal prose in order to ensure that the financial agreement(s) follow the law and can be enforced.

You can build applications on both platforms. Whereas R3/Corda is specific to financial and legal applications on which you can execute and enforce smart contracts linked to legal contracts, Hyperledger Fabric is a platform that lets you create and control your own blockchain and the applications running on its network. One example of a permissioned, decentralized application that uses the Hyperledger Fabric project is **Medicalchain**.

This is one blockchain that I currently follow with much interest. It uses the blockchain technology to store patients, medical/health records securely. Instead of different organizations having their own copy of these records, it maintains a single version of the truth. If organizations such as doctors, hospitals, laboratories, pharmacists, and health insurers want access to a patient's record, they can request permission for this purpose and record additional transactions on the distributed ledger. The platform creates a user-focused electronic health record, and it stores and shares this record securely in the blockchain. Medicalchain empowers and enables patients and users to give healthcare professionals explicit access to their data, and it records all interactions with the data in an auditable, transparent, and secure way. The platform offers users two applications: a doctor-to-patient telemedicine application, and a health data marketplace application. The telemedicine application enables users to consult with a doctor remotely (using their mobile phone, for example) for a small fee that can be paid directly to the doctor within the application. The platform also offers organizations the ability to build custom, decentralized applications to improve the (localized) user experience and put these applications on the marketplace. Users are able to use their medical data to power these applications and other services running on the platform. Besides Hyperledger Fabric, they can also use the public Ethereum blockchain for its cryptocurrency, which can then be used to pay for services on the platform. More information about this platform can be found at `https://medicalchain.com`, or by reading their white paper at `https://medicalchain.com/Medicalchain-Whitepaper-EN.pdf`.

Another similar example in which a private or permissioned blockchain such as Hyperledger Fabric can be used is for vehicle insurance. Imagine a consortium of drivers, insurers, emergency services, and vehicle repair shops.

Together, they operate a blockchain and run a decentralized application that can record the insurance policy, driver reports, and driving records, allowing an **Internet of Things (IoT)**-equipped vehicle to execute a claim automatically when it is involved in an accident. The application could automate claim processing, verification, fraud detection, and payment. Such an application would eliminate duplicate reports and enable the sharing of all data in a transparent way so that repair shops wouldn't have to contact the insurance company first before repairing the car, as they have already been informed that they are allowed to do the repairs.

I will discuss some of the available blockchain providers and how you work with them to develop your own applications in greater detail in `Chapter 7`, *Public Versus Permissioned Blockchains and their Providers*.

Summary

This chapter served as an introduction to the technology behind blockchain. The chapter started by explaining that a blockchain is a digital system of recording transactions of assets in a list that is replicated across available nodes in the network. A block in the chain is somewhat analogous to pages in a book.

The chapter continued by answering the question of how a blockchain works, and it described the flow of data in a blockchain once a transaction is submitted, from the broadcast of transactions to all other nodes using a peer-to-peer network to the verification steps in the consensus protocol. I reviewed each step in the flow of data, its purpose, and the changes that occur to the data.

In the next section, you learned what the architecture behind the blockchain technology looks like, as well as the architectural layers and capabilities of a typical blockchain. I described the purpose of each layer, namely the data layer, network layer, consensus layer, incentive layer, and application layer, and, for each capability, additional details about what you can do with it were provided.

After explaining the technology in more detail, you learned about the similarities and differences between public and private blockchains, how each secures the data and ensures your privacy, and what kinds of applications can run on public and private blockchains.

In the next chapter, *How Blockchain Will Disrupt Your Clients and Customers*, I will talk about Oracle's vision for using the blockchain in everyday applications, how it will affect Oracle developers, and the possibilities for end users/customers.

2
How Blockchain Will Disrupt Your Organization

The previous chapter summarized the technology behind blockchain and the platforms on which you can run your own decentralized applications. Since this book focuses on the usability of the blockchain in the context of Oracle (that is, its application stack and the industries and companies using Oracle software), this chapter will focus on the disruptive effects the blockchain is going to have on you and your clients and customers. This chapter represents a somewhat condensed preview of the upcoming, in-depth, hands-on content to be presented in chapters 8 to 14.

Most of these chapters are related to Oracle, since that is the primary demographic upon which this book will focus. This is not a surprise in that Oracle announced the **Autonomous Blockchain Cloud Service (ABCS)** in October 2017. ABCS is a **PaaS (Platform-as-a-Service)** offering for running your own blockchain. This chapter explains Oracle's strategy behind the announcement of this new cloud service, introduces the platform being offered, and discusses how it will affect Oracle developers and customers, such as yourself.

In this chapter, you will learn about the following topics:

- Why is blockchain a disruptive technology?
- What is Oracle's strategy when it comes to blockchain?
- How is Oracle involved in developing the future of blockchain?
- What is included in the Autonomous Blockchain Cloud Service?
- What are Oracle's competitors doing in this arena?
- What are the disruptive effects of the blockchain for you?

Why is blockchain a disruptive technology?

In the previous chapter, you learned what exactly constitutes a blockchain, how it works, and what are the architecture and ecosystems behind the technologies. But why is this technology in the news so often, and why are most IT-driven companies saying it is the most disruptive technology in decades?

Blockchain is going to celebrate its tenth birthday in 2018. Originally developed to support Bitcoin, it has gone beyond the world of cryptocurrencies and into the world of business IT. What started as a shared ledger that can process and settle financial payments in near real time (minutes) using cryptographic computer algorithms, without the need for a third party to verify transactions, has since evolved as an open source technology that can be used by many other applications that need the support of a distributed ledger—from finance to insurance to health care. The technology has the potential to be as disruptive to these industries, and to global financial services in particular, as Amazon was for the retail industry. For example, banks can move away from paper-based financial and legal contracts to smart and secure contracts to manage transactions from loan entry to final settlement.

What truly makes blockchain disruptive is that, in essence, it's a trustless system. It is a system where there is no requirement for trust, since the consensus protocol serves this purpose. Trust is built in to the blockchain through different entities validating transactions redundantly and distributing their results to all other nodes in order to verify that transactions are real and can be performed. The way that the blockchain and the consensus mechanisms work, as explained in the previous chapter, makes the technology *very secure* and is a major factor in its adoption. It is nearly impossible for anyone to tamper with transactions or ledger records that are present in blockchain. Blocks are digitally secured with a fingerprint that is based on its data, and when someone tampers with that data, the fingerprint will be different and easily recognized by other nodes.

Since blockchain started as an open source technology, no single vendor or corporation owns the basic technology and can patent its design and implementation. The further development of the technology is carried out by the open source community, which includes large vendors such as Oracle, IBM, and Microsoft. There are other kinds of distributed ledger technologies from vendors that are patented, but they work differently and don't contain the core concepts of blockchain. This means that blockchain technology can easily adjust when future needs arise, which is another powerful aspect of blockchain.

Instead of a traditional system of records having a centralized database, blockchain functions as a distributed network model in which transactions are broadcast to and stored in all nodes of that network. There is *no single point of failure*, so nodes can *appear*, *disappear*, or *malfunction* without affecting the group as a whole. Operations happen in real time on the blockchain, and whenever a transaction occurs, it is broadcast to all validating nodes. One of the nodes validates the transaction and adds it to the blockchain. With many of the consensus protocols out there, the node that creates the block gets a compensation for the work performed. Thus, when some of the validating nodes go offline, they do not impact real-time operations because other nodes can validate the transaction. Inherent in its distributed model, the blockchain is very scalable. Blockchain follows an architecture in which each node (or *peer*) in the network can run independently of others by having its own processing and storage capability.

The blockchain serves as the underlying engine of your platform. It can support many other applications that require digital and distributed ledger types of operations. For example, road or fire accidents can be registered in a decentralized platform using this technology. Besides using a digital ledger, the more evolved blockchains are programmable. Using programmable IF-THEN-ELSE rules called smart contracts, which can replace financial and legal contracts, you can extend the blockchain by running your backend application directly on it. This creates the opportunity to run your own business models by implementing proprietary customizations.

Blockchain is here to stay, and with every passing day, the interest in this technology is growing. It has been adopted by major companies and investors from banking and non-banking sectors, and it has been endorsed as a primary future technology for banking, insurance, healthcare, and others.

What is Oracle's strategy?

Oracle is always looking into leveraging (disruptive) emerging technologies. They are currently investing in cloud and mobile integration, artificial intelligence (data analytics, conversational AI/chatbots, machine learning), and the **Internet of Things** (**IoT**). In the summer of 2017, Oracle cemented their interest in Blockchain, but as you will learn in a moment, they actually started investing in it at the beginning of 2016.

On May 31, 2016, a U.S. patent application under the registration number US 15/169,622 was filed by Maurice P. Herlihy and Mark S. Moir of Oracle Labs with the title *Accountability and Trust in Distributed Ledger Systems*. This was published on August 17, 2017 under number US20170236120 A1. The patent can be found at `https://www.google.com/patents/US20170236120`. The patent describes a distributed ledger system for enhanced accountability and trust. It is based on the ideas behind the open source consensus protocol **Tendermint** (`https://tendermint.com/`), which itself is based on the previously explained PBFT consensus. The following quote is a reference to sections *0056* to *0058* of the patent:

> *[0056] This section gives an overview of extensions to a ledger protocol such as Tendermint that may be implemented in embodiments of a distributed ledger system. The following section titled Enhanced Distributed Ledger System—Details presents further details of these embodiments.*

> *[0057] Ideally, a proposer should not be able to (1) pretend it has not received a transaction that it received, (2) control which received transactions to include in its proposed block, (3) control their order in the block, or (4) inject transactions ahead of those it has received. Any such attempt should result in undeniable proof of misbehavior, or at least produce evidence that can be accumulated and analyzed after-the-fact.*

> *[0058] In some embodiments, fairness violations may be made much more difficult to achieve without detection by imposing deterministic rules governing the order in which transactions are propagated (making "missing" transactions apparent), which transactions are included in each proposed block, and the order in which they appear. This may be achieved by requiring nodes to regularly disclose auditable state information.*

Just one week before the patent was published, on August 10, 2017, Oracle announced on their corporate blog that they had joined the **Hyperledger** consortium (`https://blogs.oracle.com/cloud-platform/oracle-joins-hyperledger-consortium`). Hyperledger is an open source global collaboration project hosted by the Linux foundation at `https://hyperledger.org/`. Its objective is to create advanced cross-industry blockchain technologies. The consortium includes leaders in finance, banking, technology (including the IoT), supply chain, and manufacturing. Oracle joined because they see the potential in the approach of the consortium in building blockchain technology using open source collaboration, modular architecture, horizontal/cross-industry technology support, and support for enterprise needs.

One of the projects developed by the consortium is **Hyperledger Fabric**. It is one of the blockchain framework implementations, and it can be used as a foundation for developing applications or solutions with a modular architecture. Fabric permits pluggable (plug-and-play) components, such as the consensus protocol and membership services, so your network can easily adjust to new technologies. Hyperledger Fabric leverages container technology to host smart contracts, the application logic of the system, called **chaincode**. Oracle is using it as the backbone for their own PAAS offering, **Autonomous Blockchain Cloud Service (ABCS)**. Oracle's goal is to offer a more advanced and enterprise-level distributed ledger cloud platform that will differentiate it from its competitors. The platform might be an interesting offer for customers who are seeking to build new blockchain-based applications and/or extend their current SaaS, PaaS, IaaS, and on-premises applications. Oracle's focus is to strengthen the fundamental technology foundations of distributed ledgers, simplify and accelerate deployment of blockchains, and support customer use cases.

One of the main reasons why Oracle is investing in blockchain technology, and why I became interested in the technology in 2016, is due to the problems it can solve through cross-enterprise transactions. Some of these challenges that we need to deal with include the following:

1. The lack of real-time information visibility within a trading ecosystem
2. Error-prone information exchange and processes across enterprise boundaries
3. The high cost and delays associated with offline reconciliations
4. The high risk and costs associated with fraud in cross-company transactions

These issues can lead to a higher risk of legal settlements due to a poor ability to audit records and the accountability for actions owing to cross-ERP discrepancies. Normally, to avoid this, a trusted intermediary is used as a message broker to enable trust in peer-to-peer transactions, which, in return, brings about extra costs and the risk of data leakage.

From my personal experience with traditional B2B transactions and software used to perform such transactions, for example, *Axway*, I recognize these challenges and I'm convinced that blockchain can help overcome them. Traditional B2B transactions use a trusted intermediary to act as a message broker. This increases the challenge, since that broker can also make mistakes when routing messages. When messages get lost, you need to do manual research to determine what went wrong and why a message was not received or was rejected. So, instead of every entity having its own B2B gateway and point of truth for incoming and outgoing transactions, with blockchain you have one distributed ledger that holds a single point of truth that provides complete visibility and real-time information across your company's ecosystem.

Oracle's strategy is to build an easy-to-use **DLT** (**Distributed Ledger Technology**) cloud platform by pursuing the following objectives:

1. It offers an industry-neutral and enterprise-ready permissioned, highly secure blockchain platform with built-in privacy and confidentiality to address needs including scalability, robustness, and performance. It also provides built-in backups and recoverability of the data.

2. The platform makes it easy for you to deploy, configure, manage, and monitor your blockchain and reduce the cost of deploying and running an enterprise blockchain. The platform is a preassembled and ready-to-use, managed PaaS cloud solution, so that you, or any of your developers, can focus on the business logic behind the transactions.

3. The platform provides tools and templates to start developing applications within minutes, which should accelerate the development and integration of blockchain applications by supporting API-driven development and facilitating quick experimentation of new business processes.

4. It enables you to extend your enterprise ERP, SCM, and other business processes, including trade and accounting, to share data and conduct distributed transactions in a secure fashion with other organizations. The platform also offers built-in integrations with SaaS, PaaS, and on-premises applications, and can interact with other blockchain networks.

More information about Hyperledger Fabric can be found in Chapter 8, *Ethereum Versus Hyperledger,* or visit the Hyperledger website at https://hyperledger.org/projects/fabric.

What is the blockchain cloud service?

As previously mentioned, Oracle announced their answer to the objectives stated in the preceding strategy at Oracle Open World in the fall of 2017, namely, the ABCS. ABCS is a distributed ledger cloud platform that is preassembled and aims to be production-ready, highly secure, cost effective, and scalable. It is designed to be developer friendly, can integrate with existing enterprise applications, and interact with other blockchain networks.

With ABCS, you can create a trusted network for the exchange of B2B transactions and extend your operations beyond your business enterprise. Because of real-time information visibility across your company's ecosystem, ABCS allows you to optimize your business decisions. Due to the use of a trusted shared ledger of information, it eliminates the cumbersome offline reconciliations and accelerates transactions between participants in your network.

The underlying peer-to-peer network eliminates intermediaries and their related costs, the possible single points of failure (for example, what happens when the intermediary goes down?), and delays before a transaction is delivered to a receiving participant. ABCS provides you with the security of knowing that business-critical records are tamperproof via the mechanism of securely replicated, cryptographically-linked blocks that protect against single points of failure and insider tampering. The following diagram shows the components of the Oracle Autonomous Blockchain Cloud Service:

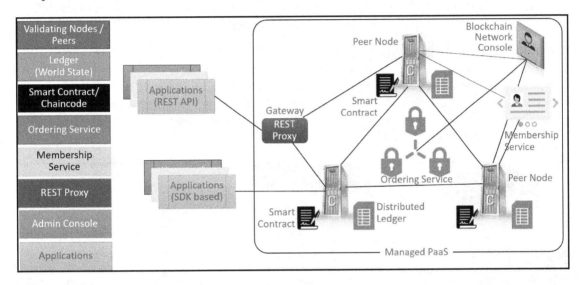

Components include validation nodes, distributed ledger, smart contracts, ordering and membership service, REST proxy, and an admin console

In short, the Oracle Autonomous Blockchain Cloud Service is a PaaS that offers a distributed ledger platform running in the cloud (and on-premises in the future), and consists of a (preassembled) network of validating nodes (or *peers*) that validate and update the ledger upon receiving transactions and responds to queries on the data by executing smart contracts; that is, code representing the business logic that runs on the blockchain. The number of validating nodes can be chosen by the user when setting up the network. External applications can interact with the blockchain by invoking transactions or run queries through client SDKs and REST API calls, which prompts the selected (validator) peers to run the corresponding smart contracts.

The validating nodes digitally sign the results, which are then verified by each other and sent to the ordering service. After consensus is reached on the order of transactions using PBFT voting, the transaction results are grouped into a tamperproof data block by cryptographically securing the contents. These data blocks are sent to all peer nodes in the network to be validated and appended to the ledger. Besides peers and selected validator peers, every business network has administrators for all participating partners. Service administrators can use the web console of the ABCS to configure the blockchain network (including nodes and other participants), deploy and initiate smart contacts, publish REST API access to external applications, and monitor its operations.

What differentiates the Oracle Autonomous Blockchain Cloud Service from other platforms is that it does not require any assembly to build a trusted network. It comes with a set of infrastructure and embedded resources, such as compute (virtual machine), containers (docker), storage, identity management, and event streaming, so that you can quickly set up and run your production-ready blockchain. The following diagram shows the assigned resources used for each of the blockchain components:

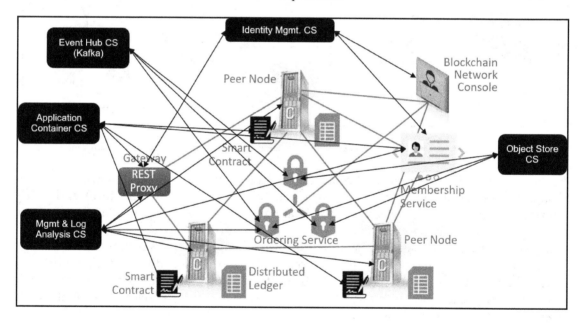

You can easily create your own instance of the cloud service by submitting a simple setup form and specifying a few parameters. After submitting the provisioning form (shown as follows), Oracle provisions the underlying infrastructure with the required blockchain network components (including membership, peer nodes, and ordering service), REST proxy, and an administration console. It is also possible to add partners easily in a geographic location. A partner can provision their own service instance in the Oracle Public or Private Cloud using the administration console and complete the certificate exchange (export/import process) to gain access. It is also possible to build hybrid networks and join partners already running Hyperledger Fabric outside the Oracle cloud by importing the organization's certificate into your ABCS instance (network founder).

Form containing the provisioning steps for creating a new instance of the Blockchain Cloud Service

Since the platform is built on top of Hyperledger Fabric, it lets you automate business logic by creating smart contracts. Smart contracts, also called chaincode, can be created to check conditions such as matching purchase orders, invoices, and shipping information prior to triggering payment, and updating the ledger. It also has support for event notification, a capability to publish custom events from smart contracts that trigger notifications for client SDKs, which enables applications to execute actions based on the payload of an event. With ABCS, you can define an endorsement policy when deploying a smart contract in which you can specify how many peers must endorse the result, and you can even define specific organizations' whose endorsements are required.

Another differentiator to justify using ABCS over its competitors is the integration of blockchain transactions in applications and especially in Oracle's own product portfolio. You can simply integrate existing application by invoking the available REST APIs to run transactions or queries synchronously and receive an immediate response. Using the REST API or the SDK, you can extend SaaS applications to use Oracle BCS through PaaS-for-SaaS, or build new applications in Oracle Java, Application Container, Mobile, Application Builder, Integration, or SOA Cloud Services. Oracle also offers out-of-the-box support for the ABCS through their Oracle Digital Innovation Platform for open banking and Netsuite Cloud Platform.

The final BCS differentiator as compared to running Hyperledger Fabric on your own datacenter is the ability to administer and monitor your blockchain using just a web browser. With the administration console provided, you can view the status of your network directly from the dashboard, or, by selecting among various tabs, you can navigate to view and manage the components of the blockchain (nodes, channels, and chaincodes). The following screenshot shows the operational dashboard of a Blockchain Cloud Service Instance:

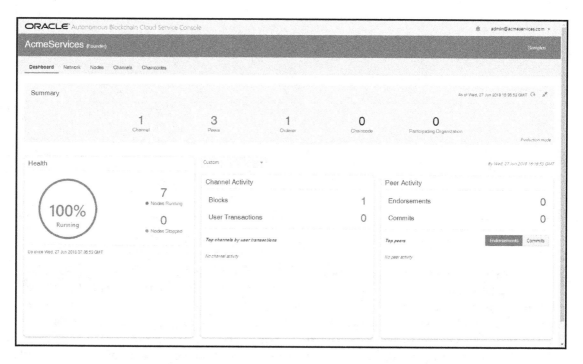

Operational Dashboard of the Oracle Blockchain Cloud Service showing blockchain health and transaction execution statistics

You can dynamically change the configuration and easily manage your network, its peers, orders, and membership services on the fly. You can configure private channels and set permissions policies. Using the dashboard, you can monitor all network components and view channel, ledger metrics, and node logs for troubleshooting. When hosting your own Hyperledger Fabric network or node, you have to use the REST APIs or command-line tools to monitor and configure your network. In the case of ABCS, the administration console is the abstraction layer on top of these APIs since the core blockchain functionality uses Hyperledger Fabric.

What are Oracle's competitors doing?

Now that we have established that Oracle is heavily investing in blockchain, you might wonder what Oracle's competitors are doing with this technology. The competition is not standing still either, so let's take a look at the hosted blockchain offerings, also called **Blockchain-as-a-Service (BaaS)**, from the usual suspects including IBM, Microsoft, and **Amazon Web Services (AWS)**, and newcomers like R3, Ethereum, and Blockstack. The following comparison is derived from a report prepared by 451 Research (`https://cloud.oracle.com/opc/paas/ebooks/451_Reprint_Oracle_02OCT2017.pdf`).

IBM offers a blockchain platform that runs on its *Bluemix*-powered cloud. The platform is based on the Hyperledger Fabric v1.0 framework, just like Oracle, and Hyperledger Composer, a rapid development tool for blockchain applications. It enables organizations to provision and operate their own secure blockchain-enabled business network quickly and develop and govern decentralized applications. Currently, it does not offer an administration console in any form. It runs the Hyperledger Fabric docker images in the cloud by executing the available scripts.

Amazon's AWS currently does not offer a specific blockchain service itself, but it invests in blockchain technology through its partner community. You can find offerings by partners in the AWS Marketplace, such as those that provide VM images that provision blockchain networks from different vendors. AWS did partner with the investment firm **Digital Currency Group (DCG)** to facilitate an experimentation environment for enterprises including financial institutions, insurance companies, and enterprise technology companies in order to spur innovation.

Microsoft also offers Blockchain-as-a-Service, but instead of one flavor, they provide multiple options. At the time of writing, I can find three solutions from Microsoft and 16 other solutions available through their partners, such as **BlockApps**, on its Azure Marketplace. Microsoft offers both Ethereum and Hyperledger Fabric as an option for their Azure Blockchain service and the choice of a single (Ethereum and Hyperledger Fabric) or multi-node network (Ethereum only). The single node service is designed for quick and easy development. For the multi-node network, Microsoft Azure Cloud provides an administration console for provisioning and configuring your network and minimalistic status pages where you can monitor the health of each node. The following screenshot shows the step where you define the size of your network:

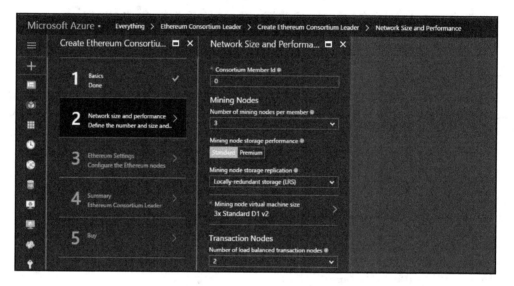

Provisioning steps for creating a multi-node Ethereum network

Microsoft's offerings will change in the near future, as they announced their Coco framework in the fall of 2017. Coco is an open source system that enables high-scale, confidential blockchain networks. Its goal is to reduce the complicated development techniques needed to meet the operational and security needs of enterprises. Coco is not a standalone blockchain protocol, but rather a foundation that delivers efficient consensus algorithms and flexible confidentiality schemes. It implements a consistent, distributed, and persistent store (such as a key-value store) replicated across a trusted network of nodes, provides secure node-to-node and application-to-node communication, and delivers a codified governance model to support arbitrary, distributed policy management. More information about the Coco framework can be found on GitHub at `https://github.com/Azure/coco-framework`.

R3 is a distributed database technology company, and it leads a consortium of over 80 of the largest financial institutions to design and deliver distributed ledger technologies to global financial markets. It collaborates with its partners on research, experimentation, design, and engineering to bring the users of blockchain technology into the design and production process. Corda, the consortium's joint effort in creating an open source distributed ledger platform, is specifically designed to record and manage agreements between financial institutions. In the long term, R3 envisions a *global ledger* with which all economic actors will interact and that will allow any parties to record and manage agreements among themselves in a secure, consistent, reliable, private, and authoritative manner. More information about R3's Corda platform can be found at `https://docs.corda.net/`.

Ethereum is a public platform that supports programmable smart contracts, and decentralized applications can be built and deployed on top of it. Start-ups frequently use Ethereum as a foundation for their solutions or for crowdfunding (by minting a new cryptocurrency). In addition to Microsoft supporting Ethereum by offering it as part of its Azure Blockchain Service, in 2017, large banks such as JPMorgan Chase and ING, technology giants such as Intel, and 30 other organizations, formed the **Enterprise Ethereum Alliance** in order to focus on enterprise uses of Ethereum.

Blockstack is a new, decentralized internet where users can manage their own data and apps. This decentralized application platform provides services in the field of identity control and storage without any party having central authority. Blockstack technology protects information through the use of the blockchain and provides an open, interoperable system that transcends borders and organizations. Decentralized applications built for Blockstack run in a browser in which users give explicit read/write permissions to their data. Information is encrypted and stored on users' personal devices. There are no intermediaries, no passwords, and no massive data silos to breach.

What are the disruptive effects on individuals?

Now that you know the disruptive effects of blockchain technology, Oracle's strategy behind leveraging the technology, and its PaaS offering, the Blockchain Cloud Service, let's look at the disruptive effects the technology has on individuals. The following effects are speculative, based on common sense, and some future thinking. My approach here is to review certain job roles and explain the effects the technology can have on each.

Database administrator

Blockchain will definitely have an impact on database technologies as it replaces the trusted third party that normally mediates any data transactions. Instead of a centralized database that records transactions, and authenticates and authorizes each user, blockchain allows transactions and identities to be validated by any of the nodes in the network, which can exist at different physical locations. Each transaction needs to be confirmed by multiple nodes before being committed to the database. Rather than having a centralized database, blockchains arguably represent a new sort of shared distributed database. Yes, there are database systems that use the dynamo model (`https://en.wikipedia.org/wiki/Dynamo_ (storage_system)`) to distribute data redundantly between multiple database locations. Blockchain, however, represents a paradigm shift in how we manage permissions within the database.

In traditional databases, the database owner has absolute control over the data stored in the database, but in a blockchain system, the ownership of the data is maintained by its creator. This allows companies to switch to using a blockchain database because of certain out-of-the-box capabilities:

- It can be run on commodity hardware
- It enables fast data distribution
- It supports shared consensus and permission models
- It offers no single points of failure or data corruption

Beyond these capabilities, the blockchain has the potential to disrupt a wide range of business models, such as the management of global identities (passports, ID cards, and birth/death certificates), financial services (transfer of money), health and patient data, voting, and many more transactional data applications. It is likely that databases that maintain records of these types of transactions may soon become obsolete.

Application integration developer

For many years, I served as an integration specialist in Oracle Fusion Middleware. My day-to-day job consisted of developing web service integrations between cloud and/or on-premises applications, and creating business applications that processed B2B transactions. Blockchain will definitely affect integration developers who work on the latter. To sketch you a picture from my experience, with traditional B2B transactions, the majority run through a trusted third-party gateway instead of a direct peer-to-peer connection. One reason for this is that a message needs to be routed to multiple partners.

This means that the transaction or message goes through multiple B2B clients in which the trusted third party receiving the message routes the message, using an enterprise service bus, to multiple receiving B2B clients. The following diagram illustrates this pattern:

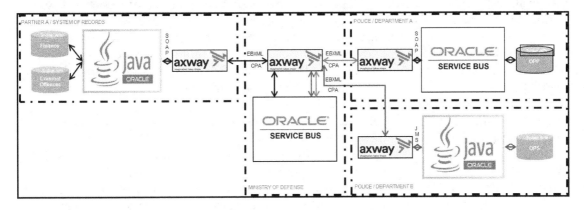

Multiple B2B partners exchanging data through a trusted third party. Each party has its own B2B client, for example, Axway, that secures the connections and can send and receive messages.

The problem with this scenario is that, as a partner, you don't have end-to-end visibility of the transaction. If you send a message and expect a response in return but do not receive one, you will probably contact the receiving party first, and in case they did not receive anything, you will then need to contact the trusted third party. A lot of things can happen in the transport of your message. For example, the routing of messages to multiple partners can result in unexpected errors. Since everybody uses their own B2B gateway, you can forget about end-to-end visibility on a transaction, because each gateway holds its own state (transaction log) that is not shared. So, how do you know in an instant what happened to the transaction?

Also, when using traditional B2B gateways, such as **Axway**, you need to define a contract between partners (called a **CPA**) to configure the permissions (for example, what kind of operations and messages each can send/receive) and connection metadata. These contracts need to be duplicated and mirrored between partnering gateways. This maintains a trusted and secure connection between the two peers, but it can bring with it a lot of overhead. Certainly, when multiple partners want to interact with each other in the same conversation, then the administrative tasks can become annoying (such as duplicating contracts on each node for each participating party).

These types of transactions is where blockchain can be very disruptive (in a good way). Blockchain can provide one single point of truth that is distributed to each of the B2B partners in the same network. Every transaction that a partner submits to the network is visible almost instantly to other nodes in the network. All partners can process the data within the transaction into their own backend system, but this is done based on the same data. You can even go so far as applications being built directly on top of the blockchain database instead of in a separate data store. This means that as an integration developer, it has an impact on how you handle B2B transactions. Instead of calling an API provided by the B2B gateway, you submit your transaction and the data directly to the API of the blockchain database. The node with which you are communicating can be one of many nodes available to you, but it will usually be a local node. Depending on the blockchain platform used, transactions will be locally validated, so instead of waiting for an acknowledgment from the receiving B2B partner, you know that your transaction is valid once accepted by this node. Since the blockchain has its own database, your process does not have to listen to an (asynchronous) response, but it can issue a query whenever it wants to check to current state of the data. A platform like Hyperledger Fabric also supports an event architecture, so your process can be notified when data has changed. Thus, there is no need for long-running processes. In `Chapter 9`, *Building a Next-Generation Oracle B2B Platform*, I will focus on these disruptive effects in more detail.

Frontend developer

When thinking of a blockchain, you might not relate to it immediately because it feels more like a backend system for distributing data. An evolved blockchain platform can do so much more, for example, running a decentralized web application. Instead of your web application running on a central server with APIs querying a centralized database, it also runs on the blockchain. Your web application is distributed to all nodes in the network and this makes it easily available to local markets, which brings with it low-latency speeds. Whereas, with a traditional web application, you would use REST APIs to authenticate, obtain authorization of data, and query and submit data, a decentralized application receives permission from the user to access their data. Your application still uses lightweight REST APIs, but they run in the same application container as the web application since they run on the same blockchain. What you have to remember is that you don't have to deal with the privacy and security of the data any longer, since the user gives you the permission to do so. If they choose not to do so, they might not be able to (partially) use you web application. As a frontend developer, you need to deal with this fact and understand the implications.

Summary

In this chapter, which served as a preview of the hands-on content to be presented in chapters 8 to 12, I explained the disruptive effects of the blockchain and pointed out that the main reason for this is that blockchain is a trustless system that employs a consensus protocol to validate transactions. This makes it *very secure* and is a major factor in its adoption. Blockchain is not owned by a single vendor or corporation, which makes it easy for anyone to develop the technology further. Because of the distributed network model, there is *no single point of failure,* so nodes can *appear, disappear,* or *malfunction* without affecting the group as a whole. Operations happen in *real time* on the blockchain, and whenever a transaction occurs, it is broadcast to all validating nodes. Then, one of the nodes validates the transaction and adds it to the blockchain. Inherent in its distributed model is that it is very *scalable.* A blockchain is highly programmable and so advanced that it can run full-blown decentralized applications.

I continued by answering the question about Oracle's strategy regarding this technology; how they are involved in the future development of the Hyperledger Fabric framework and what their plans are surrounding their own PaaS offering, the ABCS.

In the next section, I introduced Oracle's Autonomous Blockchain Cloud Service and described the feature set it offers compared to Hyperledger Fabric, the underlying framework of ABCS. I explained that BCS is a PaaS offering that makes it easy to provision, build, and develop your own blockchain business network. However, Oracle is not the only one investing in blockchain technology. We also took a look at what Oracle's competitors, including IBM, Microsoft, and AWS are doing in the blockchain space.

Finally, I reviewed some of the disruptive effects the blockchain technology might have on your business. Many roles, such as architects and business analysts, will be affected. This will be covered in greater depth in Chapter 9, *Building a Next-Generation Oracle B2B Platform.*

In the next part of the book, *Blockchain Core Concepts and Terminology,* we will start exploring the technology behind the blockchain in more detail. In Chapter 3, *Blockchain 101 - Assets, Transactions, and Hashes,* I will explain what we mean by assets, what is included in a typical transaction, how assets are distributed to all nodes in the network, and how transactions are secured by hashes.

Part II

Blockchain Core Concepts and Terminology

3
Blockchain 101 - Assets, Transactions, and Hashes

In the previous chapters, you read two executive summaries that introduced the world of blockchain and the effects that it can have on you as an Oracle developer or customer. In Part II, we will cover the architectural building blocks of a blockchain.

In this chapter, we will look at the fundamentals that make up the blockchain technology, which include assets, transactions, and hashes. You will learn about the following topics:

- What are transactions, and how does a blockchain deal with transactions?
- How are transactions managed in a blockchain network?
- What is the general structure of a transaction, and how can we send them?
- How are transactions signed so that we can assume they are not compromised?
- Which hash functions are used by a typical blockchain?

Assets

When it comes to a blockchain the things that are transacted between individuals or organizations are called digital assets. An asset can be a financial product. One of the most well-known blockchain assets are a type of digital currency (also known as tokens), and sometimes they represent stakes in a particular project or company. Cryptocurrency tokens exist conceptually as entries on a ledger (a blockchain). These *tokens* belong to you because you own a key that lets you create a new entry on the ledger and transfer the ownership to someone else. A token is not something you actually store on your computer; you store the keys that let you transfer the quantity.

Between organizations, assets more commonly include financial and legal contracts, digital twins of physical objects, records of ownership, and business documents (insurance policies, birth certificates, and so forth).

Transactions

Every second, transactions take place between parties everywhere around the world. In the context of blockchain, you will most likely think of transactions like processing a payment between two parties, placing an order on an online store, or keeping track of accounts. But if you think outside the box, there are so many more kinds of transactions that you, as an Oracle developer or customer, can imagine. For example, the registration of vehicles, tracking diamonds around the world, keeping medical records, sharing documents, and getting access to your favorite online service all involve transactions. In most cases, each participant keeps track of these transactions by recording and securing them in a ledger (for example, a database, spreadsheet, or computerized record tracking system), thus holding their version of the truth. As you can understand, this is a perfect recipe for human error, or possibly even fraud when using multiple ledgers.

Transactions can definitely be complex, especially if they rely on intermediaries for validation. Doing so can create inefficiencies and eventually result in delays and potential losses for all parties. The following diagram shows the complexity of a financial transaction when buying something on, for example, Amazon, and paying by credit card:

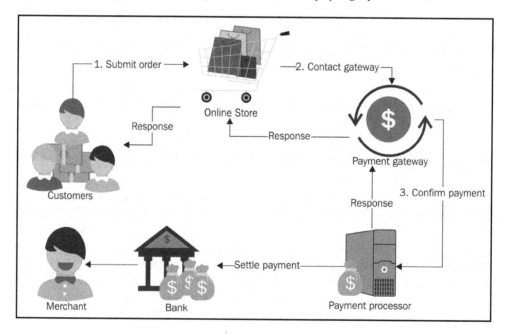

Example of a complex financial transaction when buying something on Amazon

One of the goals of blockchain is to secure and be able to view the end-to-end transaction by reducing those vulnerabilities. Functionally, a **blockchain** is an open, shared ledger for recording the history of transactions between two parties in an efficient, verifiable, and permanent way. The ledger is shared with everybody who has a transaction recorded in it. This ledger can also be programmed to trigger transactions automatically. Technically speaking, a blockchain can be seen or understood as a distributed database that records a continuously growing list of transactions. Commonly, a key/value data structure is used to record these transactions and their assets, as shown in the following diagram:

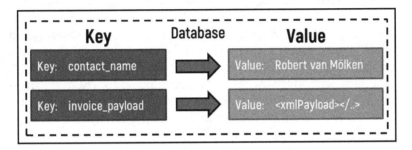

Example of a key/value structure used to record transactions and their assets

Managed by a peer-to-peer network

When you use a traditional ledger, you record the transaction and transfer its assets manually, for example, if you're keeping track of the transaction in an Excel document or using an APEX application running on an Oracle database. Typically, a blockchain is managed by a peer-to-peer network, and transactions are sent to each party using this network. A **peer-to-peer** (**P2P**) network is the architecture used for distributed computing/applications and, in the case of blockchains, it is a network in which nodes ("peers") are interconnected and share data or tasks ("resources") among themselves. Within the network, each peer makes a portion of their resources, for example, network bandwidth, processing power, and disk storage, available to other participants in the network. The network runs without the use of a centralized administration system to coordinate transactions.

Peer-to-peer network architecture in a nutshell

The architecture of a peer-to-peer network is designed around nodes or "peers", which function as both client and server simultaneously to any other node on the network. This means that it differs from the traditional client-server model, where a node usually communicates through a central server, such as when transferring a file using an **FTP (File Transfer Protocol)** service. In a P2P network, however, all nodes communicate with each other, for example, when file sharing using BitTorrent.

Peers in a P2P network can connect in two ways. The most common way is to connect to a central server, but the server's only purpose is to index all users who are currently online and connected. The software that runs on a node will query the index server to know to whom it can connect. The second way is that the node seeks out other participants on the internet, such as other nodes running the same software.

In the context of blockchain, there is no central server to which to connect. The software that you run on your machine will need to connect to the IP address of at least one of the active participants. With a public blockchain like Bitcoin or Ethereum, there are seeds that hold a list of active participants, for example, `bitseed.xf2.org`. The client software that you are running can use these seeds to connect to the network. However, depending on the client, it includes a list of semi-permanent nodes compiled in the code. During runtime, it usually keeps a database of all of the nodes to which it ever connected so that it can easily recover after a reconnect. With a private blockchain, an IP address would usually be provided to you by the regulator or one of the participants, which you can add manually to the client.

As explained, assets transacted on the blockchain come in all types, but usually they have a financial value. Assets that are transferred from you to another entity are recorded in a transaction; for example, cryptocurrency transactions like bitcoins are sent to and from *electronic wallets*. Wallets are used to sign the transactions digitally for security. I will explain this in more detail later on in this chapter.

With cryptocurrencies, the assets that are transferred are not part of the blockchain transaction—only the metadata of the transaction is recorded. Thus, cryptocurrencies such as Bitcoin, Litecoin, Dash, and Zcash don't exist anywhere–not even in your electronic wallet. They are not physical objects that you can hold, nor do they represent a digital file. Compare this with your bank account, which holds pounds, euros, or dollars. They do not represent a physical object until you exchange them as well. Every peer that joins the network has a particular address, but there are no digital assets held within it.

Instead, the blockchain only holds records of transactions between different addresses, where the balance increases or decreases. If you want to know the current balance of an address, you must reconstruct it by querying the blockchain. For example, client software iterates through all blocks of the blockchain to get the information to construct the balance.

What is a blockchain address?

An address, such as a Bitcoin address, is a simple identifier that has a length of 26 to 35 alphanumeric characters. These addresses represent a possible destination. Unlike an e-mail address, however, one person tends to have many different addresses. With some blockchains like Bitcoin, a unique address is used for each transaction. In other blockchains, however, the address represents one specific entity that stays the same over time.

When looking at a Bitcoin address, the format commonly starts with a 1, for example, 1BvBMSEYstWetqTFn5Au4m4GFg7xJaNVN2.

An address is case-sensitive and very precise. A typo can result in your transaction being rejected due to an incorrect address. The probability is very low that if you mistype the address, the transaction will be accepted, so I recommend that you always do a copy and paste procedure using your computer's clipboard.

As I mentioned at the beginning of this chapter, the goal of this book is not to look at these cryptocurrencies in great detail, but rather to focus on applications of the blockchain with which you, as Oracle developers, will work and that customers may request. For instance, the kinds of data streams that can be transferred within these applications are totally different to those used for cryptocurrencies. Whereas cryptocurrencies only hold metadata of a payment, the applications you will learn about in this book can hold megabytes of binary data in a single transaction. Think of full XML or JSON documents versus references to actual documents saved in a document store.

What does a transaction look like?

If a company (Packt Publishing, for example) is sending assets to one of its developers, such as yourself, with a contract to be signed for payment in Bitcoins, that transaction contain three pieces of information: an input, an asset (amount) to transfer, and an output.

In the context of Bitcoins, the transaction contains the following information:

- The address used to receive the Bitcoins from someone else, or that was created when buying Bitcoins from a currency exchange
- The number of Bitcoins that Packt is sending to you for your work
- The Bitcoin address where you want to receive the Bitcoins

A major misconception is that the input address represents your wallet address, but it actually represents the address where the Bitcoins were last sent. The input to a transaction can include multiple "last-sent-from" addresses. Due to the way Bitcoin transactions work with addresses, it is not that easy to use as an everyday payment currency because it is so technical in nature.

Example of a bitcoin transaction

When looking at the structure of a bitcoin transaction from a technical point of view, it looks like the following:

Input:
```
Previous tx:
f5d8ee39a430901c91a5917b9f2dc19d6d1a0e9cea205b009ca
73dd04470b9a6
Index: 0
scriptSig:
304502206e21798a42fae0e854281abd38bacd1aeed3ee3738d9e
1446618c4571d10
90db022100e2ac980643b0b82c0e88ffdfec6b64e3e6ba35e7ba5fdd7
d5d6cc8
d25c6b241501
```

Output:
```
Value: 1000000000
scriptPubKey: OP_DUP OP_HASH160
404371705fa9bd789a2fcd52d2c580b6
5d35549d
OP_EQUALVERIFY OP_CHECKSIG
```

In this example, the input uses the previous transaction `f5d8`... to import the needed 10 BTC the sender wants to transact by referencing the previous output at index #0. The output sends the 10 BTC, whose value is represented by the number of Satoshi (`1 BTC = 100,000,000 Satoshi`), to the Bitcoin address `40437`... When recipients want to spend the Bitcoins, they will again reference the same output index #0 of this new transaction as the input for their own transaction. The `scriptSig` and `scriptPubKey` parts of a transaction are used for the verification process.

Where cryptocurrency transactions supply a token/asset value as the payload of the transaction, a more business transaction-driven blockchain will commonly transact more complex structures. In the context of other applications, like sending a contract or an invoice, the transaction contains the following information:

- The address of the peer in the (private) blockchain network held by Packt
- The binary payment, which can hold any key/value data structure, including a reference to a digital document
- The address of the peer in the (private) blockchain network held by you

How can you send a transaction?

Let's return to the previous example where the address represents the destination of a specific peer. If you want to send/receive assets yourself, you need two things: an address where the sender can reach you and a private key. The address is randomly generated when you join the blockchain, and it contains a simple sequence of letters and numbers. The address is based on the private key that you supply. The two are paired together. Your private key should be kept secret, and it, too, is a simple sequence of letters and numbers. Both elements will comprise your wallet. Losing your private key also means losing access to all of the assets within your wallet. With blockchain, transactions and assets can be viewed by all peers that join the network. Think of it as a glass safe: everyone can see what's inside, but you can only put something into it or take something out of it if you have the key.

The following diagram shows how the public-key cryptography used by a blockchain works:

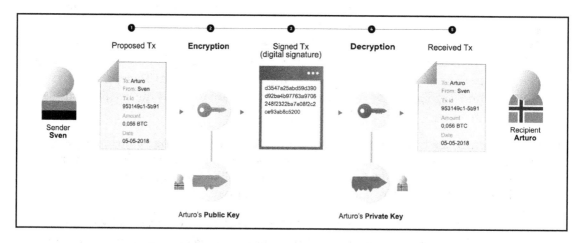

Sven sends a transaction to Arturo. The transaction is encrypted and signed with the public key of Arturo, resulting in a digital signature that can easily be checked by others. Arturo receives the transaction and can view the data using its private key.

The private key is used when you are sending something to another peer. You use your private key to sign the transaction. When the message is signed, it is sent out to the wider network to be verified by what are called **miners**. I will go into more detail on this subject in the next chapter, where we will examine the verification and consensus mechanisms.

Hashes

Until now, we have explored the concepts that make up a transaction and how you can send transactions yourself. One of these concepts is that transactions are signed. When a transaction is signed, it generates a hash or digital signature that is based on the content of the transaction. The hash verifies that the data sent in a transaction is not compromised or has not changed during its travel.

A hash is calculated by executing a **hash function**, which is called *hashing*. Before I go into the detail of the hash functions that are used within different blockchains, I'm first going to take you through the concept of such functions. A hash function takes any **input data**, and produces an **output**, which, based on the algorithm used, has a different fixed length.

Dissecting a hash

A hash has a fixed length, which, in terms of computer data, is represented in bits. A **bit** is the smallest possible data type, and it can be either a 0 or a 1. Think of it as a light bulb, where the light bulb can either be on (1) or off (0). Computer data can be represented as a series of light bulbs that have different patterns. Each pattern represents different data. A series of 8 bits or light bulbs form 1 byte or row, so a 256-bit string has 32 rows of 8 or 16-by-16 light bulbs.

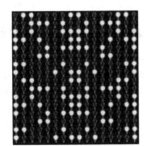
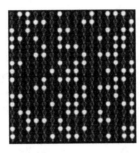
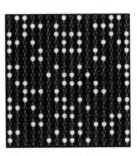

A computer's memory can store billions or even trillions of these light bulbs. Nevertheless, a 256-bit string is more than enough for hashing since the number of mathematical possibilities is 2^{256}, which is an astronomical number.

The output of a hash function is always a string, for example, an **MD5 hash** is a 128-bit (16-byte) string of the input data. The following example is an MD5 hash that is commonly used to check whether a file has been compromised:

```
echo "<Order xmlns='urn:hash'><id>123</id></Order>" | md5sum
168be32ad9a5c7c5764bc6e73690f2d9
```

This function takes the input string, an XML message, and it produces an output, in this case a sequence of random letters and numbers – 168be32ad9a5c7c5764bc6e73690f2d9. This hash is known as the *digital fingerprint* of the input string, and it is referred to as the *message digest*. The message digest for this input string is always the same, but if one character changes, the hash will be completely different:

```
echo "<Order xmlns='urn:hash'><id>223</id></Order>" | md5sum
e729cddd99382c3426b78ba749abaf0c
```

All good hash functions are one-way only, and to find the same hash, all combinations of inputs need to be executed until the correct input is hashed. The output of hash functions should be random. As in the previous example, changing a single character will lead to a different hash, or else guessing it would be very easy. When comparing the message digests of two proclaimed versions and they match, you can be sure that you received the same version that the sender sent to you. Also, a hash function should be collision-resistant, which means that two different inputs can't lead to the same output. The importance of these properties will be more evident when we look at the hash functions that are used in the context of blockchain.

The types of hash functions used by blockchain

In the world of hash functions, there are a lot of different types, as can be found at `http://www.wikiwand.com/en/List_of_hash_functions`. In the context of blockchain, the main hash functions involved include RIPEMD-160, SHA(2)-256, and KECCAK-256. Both RIPEMD-160 and SHA(2)-256 are used by the original blockchain, Bitcoin core code for hashing, but with a slight twist; that is, it defines its own hash functions as follows:

```
hash160(privateKey) = RIPEMD-160(SHA-256(privateKey))
hash256(byteArray) = SHA-256(SHA-256(byteArray))
```

The first function is used for identifying a destination, otherwise called the address, and it is computed by hashing your private key first with SHA-256 and then immediately after with the RIPEMD-160 hash function. The second function is used for hashing two core entities: **transactions** and **blocks**. The hash function is used to generate a transactionId or a blockId by hashing the data using SHA-256 and then hashing the 256-bit output again using SHA-256. We will explore the concept behind blocks later in this chapter.

How do SHA2/Merkle-Damgård hash functions work?

Hash functions, such as MD5, RIPEMD-160, and SHA-256, fall under a class of hash algorithms called Merkle–Damgård. These form a construction or method of building cryptographic hash functions that are collision resistant from collision-resistant, one-way compression functions.

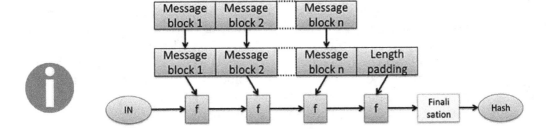

In the preceding diagram, the function receives an input, which first applies a left-padding function to create a result with a size that is a multiple of a fixed number (such as 512 or 1024). The function then breaks the result up into blocks of that fixed number and processes one block of data at a time with the compression function. Each time the new block inputted, it is combined with the result of the previous round. To make the result more secure, the last block is padded with zeros as needed and bits that represent the length of the entire message. Sometimes, the function serves as a finalization function to harden the hash.

As I mentioned, other, often newer, blockchains use different hashing algorithms. For example, Ethereum uses KECCAK-256, a precursor of SHA3-256, to identify an account by hashing the private key. The main reason that Ethereum changed its algorithm is because previously with SHA-2, there were a number of attacks discovered. Thus, there was a growing fear that the secure SHA-2 algorithm would soon be broken. The creators chose KECCAK-256, as it was a totally different algorithm to SHA and AES.

How do SHA3/Sponge hash functions work?

Hash algorithms such as KECCAK-256 and SHA3-x fall into a class of hash functions called Sponge. This is a construction or method of building cryptographic hash functions with a limited internal state. It takes an input stream of bits of any length and produces an output stream of bits of any desired length.

In the following diagram, the function receives an input. When executed, the state memory (**S**) is initialized with 0 bits (**b**). The state memory is divided into two parts (bitrate **r** and capacity **c**). The capacity (**c**) part is always a whole multiple of bitrate (**r**) by padding enough bits. The input is split into blocks P_i of a fixed length, and put into a function (**f**) that permutes or transforms the state memory. After the transformation, the output blocks Z_i are hashed and are combined into an output string:

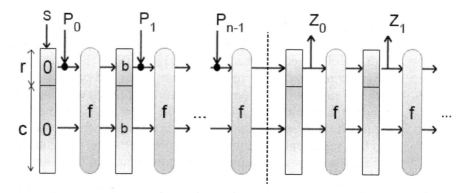

Digital signatures, such as the transactionId, blockId, and address are a fundamental part of blockchains and provide identity validation and hashes, which allows us to keep the integrity of the blockchain, and represent its current (potentially infinite) state. They are more powerful and credible, compared to physically signing a check or contract, because this kind of signature can be highly inconsistent and easily forged, imitated, or supplanted as opposed to the immutable nature of a blockchain hash.

These kinds of signatures are also used to identify transactions. Instead of describing a transaction, for example, as "Packt sends Developer X a total of Y units of currency Z at date and time DT", it is referenced by the unique digital signature or hash. By referring to a hash, it can be used directly to track and trace the transaction, for example, copy and paste the hash in a UI (such as blockchain explorer) to see details of the transaction. Usually, a user interface hides any kind of IDs or serial numbers, but as the use of technologies, such as blockchain, which use cryptographic hash functions become more widespread, showing a hash is often better than displaying a long description.

Summary

In this first chapter of the second part of the book, I have covered three fundamental concepts of a blockchain—*assets, transactions,* and *hashes.* I explained that one of the main purposes of the blockchain is transferring valuable assets using a shared ledger and compared it with the current solution of keeping separate digital records in an Excel of central database.

In the section about transactions, I covered how these assets are transferred from one to another entity using a managed peer-to-peer network. I explained that assets are recorded in a transaction on the blockchain in a digital shared ledger that holds the full history of the assets transferred, and which is distributed to each entity that is part of the blockchain, so that each entity has the same truth.

I went through some examples of transferring assets, including cryptocurrencies such as Bitcoin and Litecoin, but also more interesting assets such as real-world goods, and financial products. I covered how the structure of a transaction appears and how transactions can be sent to and from entities using own digital identities (for example, wallets).

To demonstrate how transactions are secured, I talked about hashes, hash functions and what their importance is when identifying addresses, transactions, and eventually blocks. I covered the hash functions that the core blockchain code uses to create identifying output strings and explained the inner workings of these different hash functions.

In the next chapter, we will look into the building blocks of the blockchain itself. What are blocks and chains and how to do we know that chains are valid and not broken?

4
Blockchain 101 - Blocks, Chains, and Consensus

In the previous chapter, we looked at the three fundamental concepts of the blockchain: *assets*, *transactions*, and *hashes*. Assets are a digital representation of the things we transact on a blockchain through a transaction, which holds information about the assets that are transferred from one entity to another. You learned about the underlying transaction mechanism, what structure is used by a transaction, and how you can send transactions to another entity in the network. Besides transactions, we touched upon the concept of hashes, which allows us to create a secure signature that can be used to verify a transaction.

In this chapter, we will look into the building blocks of the blockchain itself: *blocks, chains,* and *consensus*. Using a step-by-step approach, I will explain how single blocks of transactions can create a stack that can be secured in such a way that it creates a chain surrounding these blocks, also called a blockchain. When transactions are submitted to the blockchain, there is a mechanism in place to ensure that the transaction is valid. Designated "peers" in the network validate the transaction, and when they reach consensus, or general agreement, the transactions are added to the blockchain as a new block.

In this chapter, you will learn about the following topics:

- What are the fundamental building blocks of the blockchain?
- What is stored in a block, and when is a block created?
- How does a block become part of the blockchain?
- How does the blockchain reach consensus regarding its transactions?

Blocks

In Chapter 3, *Blockchain 101 - Assets, Transactions, and Hashes,* I explained that when assets are transferred from one entity to another, they are recorded as a transaction. A blockchain sees a great deal of transaction activity, so instead of recording every transaction separately, the transactions executed during a given period of time are permanently recorded in a **block**. Each block is made up of a list of transactions. Think of it as a paper ledger or notebook where an individual page holds multiple records. In this case, each page represents a block.

How many transactions each block can hold depends on the configured block size of the blockchain and the payload size of the combined transactions. It does not mean that a block always has to reach its maximum block size in order to be verified, as a block can also hold as little as one transaction. In essence, a block records some or all of the most recent transactions that have not yet been processed, as shown in the following diagram:

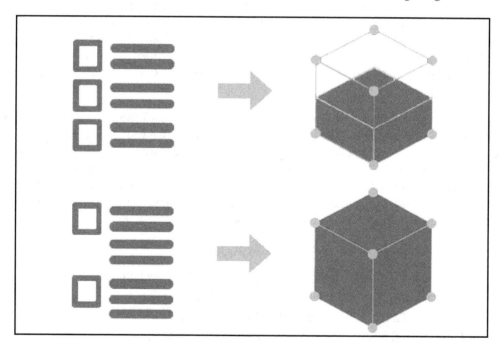

Blocks can include new transactions until the maximum block size is reached

Breaking down blocks

As mentioned previously, a block is a permanent store of the transaction recorded and validated during a given time period. Technically, the transaction data is written to a read-only file called a block. When we look into the details of a block, it represents the *present* and contains transactions that have been recorded recently, as well as a reference to the past. Each time a block is finalized, it becomes part of the past and cannot be altered or removed. The blockchain works in a cycle where new transactions are stored in the next block with a reference to the preceding block. The structure of a block depends on the blockchain.

The following table shows the structure of a block used in the bitcoin core code:

Bytes	Field Name	Description
4	Magic number	Value is always 0xD9B4BEF9.
4	Block size	Number of bytes following up to the end of the block.
80	Block header	Consists of six items used to give the block context.
1-9	Transaction counter	Positive integer indicating the number of transactions.
V_b	Transactions	Non-empty list of transactions.

V_b stands for variable bytes

When comparing this with the structure of an Ethereum block, we see in the following table that the block header field can be much larger:

Bytes	Field Name	Description
>508	Block header	Consists of 15 items used to give the block context.
V_b	Transaction list	Non-empty list of transactions.
V_b	Ommer list	List of ommer blocks that helped with the proof-of-work.

V_b stands for variable bytes

In blockchains, every block also contains a header, which, like an HTTP request, gives context to the block. The structure of the header depends on the implementation of the blockchain; for example, bitcoin implements a serialized 80-byte format string, whereas Ethereum has a format with a variable length of at least 508 bytes. The header is constructed when finalized and used to create the **proof-of-work**, or **POW**, which I will discuss in more detail later on in this chapter.

The format used for the block header by a blockchain based on the Bitcoin core code is described in the following table:

Bytes	Field Name	Description
4	Version	The block version number indicates which set of block validation rules to follow.
32	Previous block hash	A hash of the previous block's header. This hash ensures that no previous block can be changed.
32	Merkle root hash	A hash of the root of the Merkle tree (`https://en.bitcoin.it/wiki/Protocol_documentation#Merkle_Trees`) derived from the transactions included in the block. This hash ensures that none of those transactions can be modified without modifying the header.
4	Timestamp	The timestamp of the block in UNIX epoch time. This timestamp is determined by the verifier when starting to hash the header. Blocks with a timestamp of more than two hours in the future will not be accepted.
4	Difficulty target	The difficulty target threshold of which the block hash must be less than or equal to.
4	Nonce	An arbitrary number used by verifiers to generate a correct hash less than or equal to the target threshold. If all 32-bit values are tested without a correct nonce, the time can be updated or the Coinbase transaction can be changed and the Merkle root updated.

Structure of the block header used by a Bitcoin block

When comparing the format used by a blockchain based on Ethereum, the structure looks a little bit different:

Bytes	Field Name	Description
32	Parent hash	A KECCAK-256 hash of the parent (or previous) block header. This hash ensures that no previous block can be changed.
32	Ommer hash	A KECCAK-256 hash of a list of ommer (or uncles) of the block. Uncles are orphaned blocks that contribute to the security of the main chain. They are not considered the canonical "truth" for that particular chain height.
20	Beneficiary	The address for the fees collected from successful mining.
32	State root	A KECCAK-256 hash of the root of the state tree derived from the transactions executed and finalized in the block. This hash ensures that none of those transactions can be modified.
32	Transaction root	A KECCAK-256 hash of the root node of the transaction tree.
32	Receipt root	A KECCAK-256 hash of the root node of the transaction receipt tree.
32	Logs bloom	Bloom filter from indexable (logger address and log topics) information in each log entry from the receipts.
V_b	Difficulty	Big int scalar value corresponding to the difficulty level of the block.

Bytes	Field Name	Description
V_b	Number	Big int scalar value equal to the number of ancestor blocks.
V_b	Gas limit	Big int scalar value equal to the current limit of gas expenditure per block.
V_b	Gas used	Big int scalar value equal to the total gas used in transactions in the block.
V_b	Timestamp	Big int scalar value equal to the timestamp of the block at inception in UNIX epoch time.
32	Extra data	Arbitrary byte array containing data relevant to the block.
32	Mix hash	A KECCAK-256 hash which, combined with the nonce, proves that enough computations are executed on the block.
8	Nonce	A 64-bit hash used by verifiers to prove that enough computations are executed on the block.

Structure of the block header used by a Bitcoin block

Hashing a block

Before a block can be finalized, meaning creating the block and its header structure, designated participants (sometimes called miners, forgers, or endorsers) in the peer-to-peer network need to approve the transactions, for example, by solving a mathematical problem in the case of Bitcoin. This answer, an arbitrary integer called a nonce, is then distributed to other participants that validate the answer. To understand the nonce, let's look at the following example. Let's say that we have a JSON payload of a transport order:

```
{
    "transportOrder": {
        "shippingDate": "2017-7-31T18:00:34.011Z",
        "originWarehouse": 12,
        "destStore": 3,
        "products": [{
                "eanCode": "8806088280486",
                "productName": "Samsung UE40K5600",
                "productCode":  "UE40K5600AWXXN",
                "amount": 4
            },
            {}
        ]
    }
}
```

If the payload is hashed with the SHA(2)-256 hash algorithm, the outcome would be as follows:

```
93eec6bc317252e5682f9201831c087c1e25ee5b9d84215a2e64fca0909c9696
```

Both the transaction and the block are hashed using a hash function, such as SHA-256 or KECCAK-256. However, when hashing a block, there is a little twist. With most public blockchains out there at present, you are rewarded when finalizing a block with a mathematical puzzle that needs to be solved. For example, you need to hash the block in a particular way such that the output hash starts with a (variable) length of zeros. The length of zeros can be based on the current difficulty level. Even if you are not rewarded, it helps with hardening the hash for security reasons.

For example, when the current difficulty level (result of a formula: `https://en.bitcoin.it/wiki/Difficulty`) expects the hash to start with four zeros, then you need an arbitrary number to be added to the blocks, payload in order to generate a valid target hash. In the following screenshot, the nonce is not yet calculated, and the hash does not start with the requisite number of zeros, which makes the hash invalid:

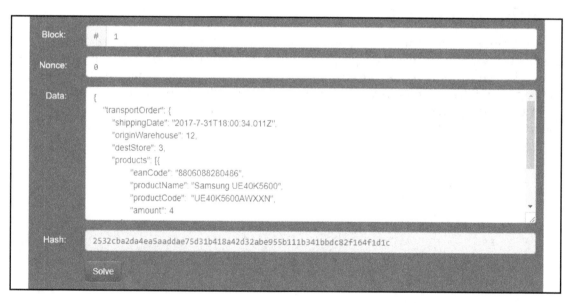

This example calculation can be executed using the blockchain demo at https://anders.com/blockchain

The hash needs to solve a mathematical puzzle to calculate the correct nonce so that the hash starts with four zeros. When executing the mathematical puzzle, it tries integers in sequence. The speed at which these calculations can be executed depends on the amount of computing power that you have available.

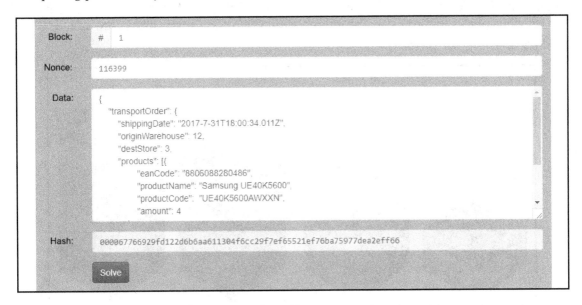

After solving the correct nonce, the block hash is valid since it starts with four zeros

The nonce that resolves to a valid hash becomes part of the block header and is distributed to other participants that can validate the block based on the solution provided.

Chains

Up to this point, you learned that the assets that are transferred between entities are recorded in transactions and that transactions persist in append-only blocks. When a block is finalized, the block header that was created is added to the block that includes the nonce and the hash of the previous block, linking the two. The new block is identified with its own hash or blockId, and is used by the subsequent block, again linking the two.

Blockchain

The word blockchain, originally called block chain, is derived from the link between blocks. Because the hash of one block is based on the hash of the previous block, it is like a chain linking all the way back to the first, or genesis, block. This process confirms the integrity of the previous blocks in the chain. The following diagram shows how blocks are linked together using the previous block hash:

Every block is linked to its previous block through the block hash. The generated hash of a new block uses the hash of the previous block

Because the hash of each new block is based on the hash of the previous block, manipulation of transactions in one of the existing blocks is easily detectable. For example, when a transaction is manipulated, the hash of the block to which it belongs will be different. As with the previously-calculated nonce, the hash would not start with the expected number of zeros. In the following screenshots, you can see the four blocks that are currently part of our blockchain. All the blocks are finalized, or "solved," and have the correct nonce to create a hash that follows the blockchain rules:

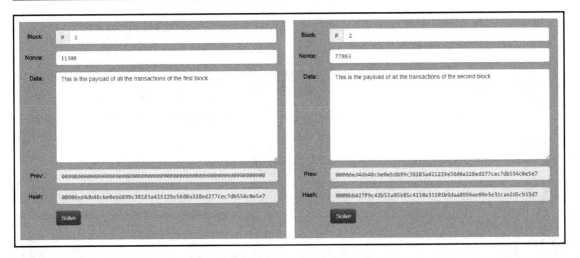

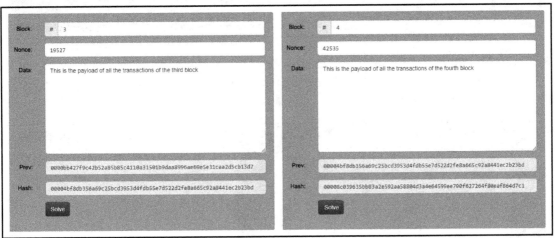

Notice that the nonce is random and not always higher than the nonce of the previous block

When the data in one of these blocks is manipulated, all of the blocks that are linked from that point to the last block in the chain will become invalid. The chain can only become valid when all of the blocks are resolved again.

In the following screenshot, you can see that when the data within the second block is manipulated, it immediately becomes invalid:

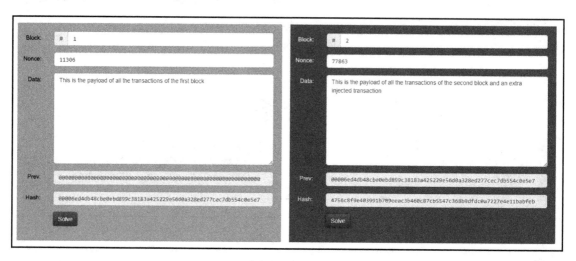

Beyond that, you can see that it immediately invalidates all of the blocks that were created after the one that was manipulated, since the hash and the nonce no longer match, as it can be seen in the following screenshot:

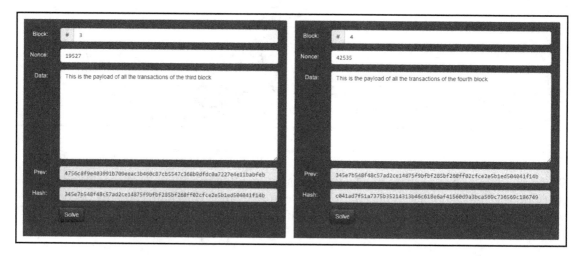

To make the blockchain valid again, all of the blocks need to be revalidated—the longer the chain of blocks, the longer the process to solve the correct hashes takes. Some of the blockchains create a new block every few seconds, which makes this nearly impossible to do. You can see this revalidation (or "mining") process in the following screenshot, where the nonce of the original second block had the value 77863, while it changed to 28460 after resolving the block:

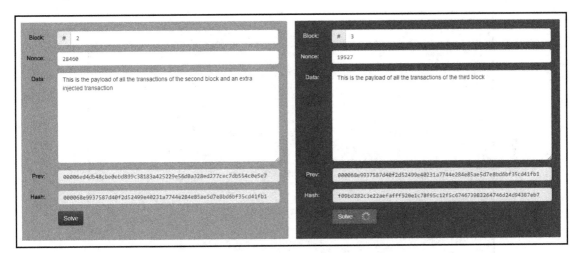

Distributed and decentralized

In the previous chapter, you learned that one of the key properties of the blockchain is that entities (or nodes) that want to transact with each other are part of the same peer-to-peer network. Examples of such networks have existed for years, such as *BitTorrent* and even the older Napster. In the same way that transactions are broadcasted to each node in the network, blocks are also distributed and stored across the network. This eliminates the risk of data being held by a central authority since there is no centralized point that hackers can exploit.

In this decentralized network of computer nodes, every node has a copy of the blockchain. Because there is no central owner (or copy) of the data, the quality of the data is maintained by replication of the database among users. No central owner means that the "trust level" is the same for everybody—there are no special privileges. Since every node has its own copy, when one of the nodes is compromised, that can easily be detected.

This distributed copy of the ledger eliminates the risk of the "double spending" problem, where someone can spend or transact the same asset twice in consecutive transactions. The ledger maintains a chronologically-ordered, time-stamped list of transactions and when a blockchain peer proofs transactions, it can recognize that the ownership of an asset is incorrect and reject the wrongful transaction. In the following example, you can see three peers (A, B, and C) that currently are in sync:

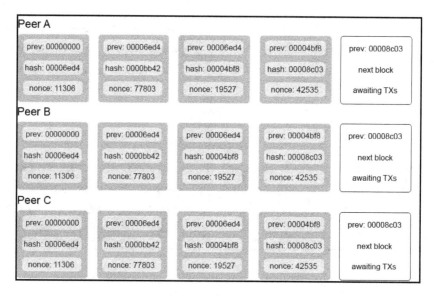

All peers have the same version of the ledger and are in sync with each other

In case the last block of Peer B is compromised, that block will need a different nonce to solve its mathematical puzzle. The compromised block can be revalidated to solve the correct nonce. You can see that this has been done in the following diagram:

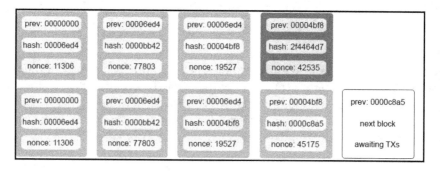

A compromised block is deliberately revalidated by peer B to fix its chain

After the peer has revalidated this last block containing the compromised transaction in the block data, it can create new blocks based on the previous valid block hash. Now the power of the decentralized network comes into play. Other peers validate the blocks that are added to the chain and conclude that the new blocks created by Peer B have a different hash and nonce than the majority of the peers, and the result is that blocks from Peer B are rejected, as demonstrated in the following screenshot:

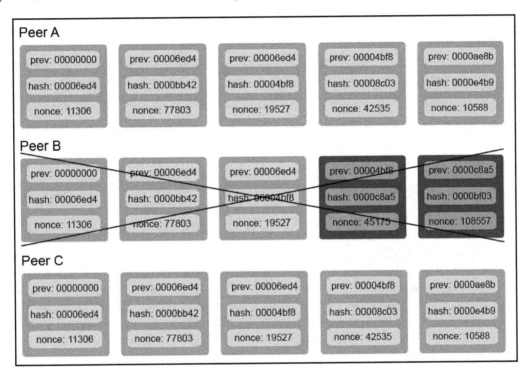

Blocks created on the chain from Peer B are rejected since it's no longer the longest chain

Forks

The process I just described can also happen without someone trying to compromise the data on the blockchain. As the blockchain network grows, it is possible for multiple peers to create a new block at nearly the same time with the same block height (that is, the number of blocks preceding a particular block). This type of event is called an accidental fork. Initially, both blocks are accepted by the majority of the network. However, it is logically resolved when consecutive block(s) are added and one of the chains becomes longer than the alternative(s).

The following diagram shows two of these forks and how they are resolved:

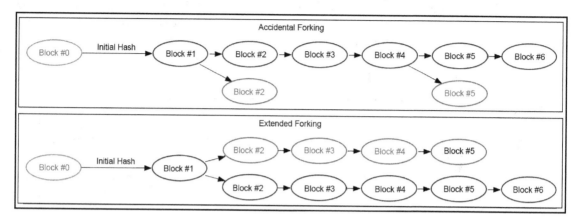

When two or more miners produce a block at nearly same time, it creates a fork in the block chain

Orphaned and stale blocks

For any block in the chain, there is only one path (black blocks) it can have to the genesis block; that is, **block #0** (green block), and the blocks in the smaller chain are eventually rejected. These valid blocks are known as **orphaned blocks** (red blocks) and are not part of the main chain. The transactions that exist within the rejected block(s) are re-added to the pool of queued transactions, and they will eventually be included in another block. With cryptocurrency blockchains, the reward received for solving orphaned blocks is practically lost. When, at any moment, a block is finalized, or "solved," everyone else should stop working on that block and restart their work. If a peer continues to work after that point, the block is known as a **stale block** because it is working on old data and transactions, as demonstrated in the following diagram:

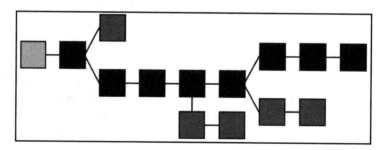

There can only be one valid blockchain (black blocks) connected to the genesis (green) block. Smaller chains of (red) blocks are eventually rejected

Soft fork versus hard fork

There are also forks that are not related to the generation of blocks during normal runtime. A blockchain is still a piece of software, and development of this software can continue. In the traditional sense of software development, a fork means that a different party copies the source code and continues development separate from the original party. In blockchain, a software fork can be divided into two types of forks: **soft forks** and **hard forks**. This may sound contradictory but, in short, a soft fork means that the rules of the blockchain protocol are made tougher (or stricter), whereas a hard fork eases the rules.

Soft fork

A soft fork is a backward-compatible change in the blockchain software where the rules become stricter, and less is permitted than in the situation before. An example of a soft fork would be increasing the generation time of blocks, or reducing the block size from 2 MB to 1 MB. By reducing the block size, the rules are made "tougher," with the result that blocks larger than 1 MB are no longer accepted by nodes that are upgraded to the new code. Older nodes that are not yet upgraded to the new code don't have any problems with blocks created by the upgraded nodes, because the new rules don't conflict with the existing rules. The new block size still fits inside of the old block size. The old nodes don't need to upgrade to the new code immediately, but eventually they will have to. If non-upgraded nodes continue to create blocks, these blocks are not accepted any longer by the upgraded nodes. The downside of a soft fork is that if it is only supported by a minority of the network's power, it can become the shortest chain and be orphaned, or it can even lead to a hard fork because the chain can splinter off. The following diagram shows a comparison between the (non)-compatibility of rules between a soft fork and a hard fork:

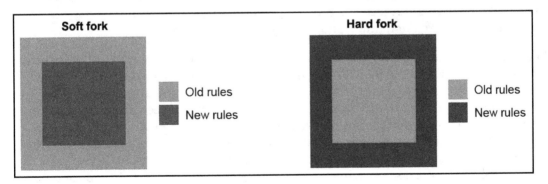

Comparison: soft fork introduces new backward-compatible rules, whereas a hard fork introduces non-compatible rules

Hard fork

When the rules are smoothed, or "weakened," it is known as a hard fork. A hard fork is a non-backward compatible change in the blockchain software that introduces a new rule to the network. For example, the block size can be expanded from 1 MB to 2 MB, which smooths out the rules. When nodes in the network won't update their software, they can't follow the chain any more because the new 2 MB rule conflicts with the maximum block size of 1 MB that they currently accept. If non-upgraded nodes continue their work, they will view the new transactions as invalid.

With a hard fork, all of the nodes in the network need to upgrade. The disadvantage of a hard fork is that if an impasse is reached, a portion of the nodes will not upgrade because they prefer the old rules. In this case, both chains may continue and eventually have their own identity. This happened with Ethereum in 2016, and with the original Bitcoin in August 2017. The latter split up into Bitcoin Cash (new) and Bitcoin (old), because some leaders in the community wanted to expand the block size as it was getting too small to handle the current number of transactions.

Sidechains

As the ecosystem of a blockchain grows in size (transactions) and scale (peers) as time passes, the blockchain also increases in length and storage space. This has led to the concept of a sidechain, which is an independent ledger that is linked directly to the main blockchain without affecting its speed and performance. A sidechain ensures that the main chain is as secure as possible while it makes it possible to explore other options that would never be used on the main chain. Sidechains provide powerful cases such as anonymity, transparency, confirmation times, and Turing-complete options.

Because a blockchain can increase substantially in length and storage space, consequently, it makes it more difficult to manage the network. Thus, most sidechains are developed solely to enhance the scalability of the existing system by forming an interoperable blockchain network, or *pegged sidechain*, without undermining speed and performance. This means that it allows data from one blockchain to be securely used within a completely separate blockchain, but it still can be moved back to the original chain if necessary. Since sidechains are separate systems, they allow innovators to develop new technical and economical applications safely without jeopardizing the main blockchain code and putting valuable data at risk. In the event of a malicious design flaw in a sidechain, the damage is confined just to that particular sidechain.

The underlying mechanism

In technical terms, one of the mechanisms that is commonly used by sidechains is called a *two-way peg*. This mechanism lets you transfer assets to and from sidechains and, in the process, transform *vanilla* assets into all other *flavors* that you can imagine.

Let's look at doing this using the example of cryptocurrencies, where a two-way peg lets us transact Altcoins, such as Litecoin, at a fixed rate. This means that you can take two Bitcoins from the parent or main chain and purchase two Litecoins on the sidechain at a 1:1 fixed rate. Those Litecoins can be sent to someone on that sidechain, and then he or she can redeem them at the same 1:1 rate on the parent chain and receive back two Bitcoins.

This works as follows, and is shown in the following diagram. When a parent chain transfers some assets to sidechain assets, it uses a two-way peg by utilizing a **simple payment verification** (SPV) technique. The parent chain sends the asset to a special SPV-locked output (**1**) on the parent chain. These assets can only be unlocked when an SPV proof of possession (**2**) is performed by the sidechain. While the assets are locked in the main chain, they can be freely transacted (**3**) in the sidechain without losing the identity of the parent chain. However, they can only be transferred back to the same parent chain from which the assets came and not to another parent chain. If you want to exchange the assets back from the sidechain to the parent chain, you need to follow the same process. The assets are transferred to an SPV-locked output (**4**), and they need to produce a sufficient SPV proof of possession (**5, 6**) to unlock the previously locked output on the parent chain:

Example of a two-way peg transaction that allows you to transfer assets between different blockchains

It is in the best interest of both the parent chain and the sidechains that sidechains only transfer the same kind of assets, and that different assets are not interchangeable. A different asset should be treated as a malicious transfer because it can be worthless. We will not focus on the use of sidechains in this book, but keep in mind that they exist and can be useful if you want to develop a different implementation based on existing assets.

Consensus

Now that you know the basic concepts of the blockchain and how blocks are linked together, it is time to look at the mechanism that secures the blockchain and its transactions.

When comparing a blockchain with a traditional database that is based on trust, a traditional database is operated by a single entity, or operator, and it requires a user-controlled access system. Thus, it is crucial for the single entity operating it to be a trustworthy individual. On the other hand, most blockchains (or distributed databases) are operated by unknown entities, which can be an individual, an organization, or even a computer that automatically operates it. So, with this lack of trust, how can we be certain that the data is not compromised?

The trust aspect of the blockchain lies in the way that consensus is reached. In a blockchain, an entity (individual or organization) can submit information that they wish to add to the distributed database. Submitting information results in a transaction, but, compared to a traditional database, it is not immediately committed. As you read previously, a blockchain runs on a peer-to-peer network, and after submission, these transactions are distributed to all nodes in the network. Before transactions can be committed or permanently incorporated into the blockchain, distributed operators, or "miners," who are part of the network need to evaluate and agree on all additions. All transactions must be reviewed and confirmed, so that "consensus" is reached before the transactions are accepted.

Let's review what you have learned up to this point. Transactions represent data or assets that are transferred from one entity, or "peer," to another entity in the network. In a blockchain, this transaction is broadcast to every active node in a peer-to-peer network. These transactions are then validated and put into blocks, where each block represents a page in a ledger. Blocks are then secured by solving a mathematical puzzle, or nonce, which generates the block hash. In a blockchain, you can have nodes dedicated to do the evaluation, or "solving," but in most public blockchains, specifically cryptocurrencies, everybody can help evaluate transactions.

After evaluation, the block hash and nonce become part of the block's header, which also includes the hash of the previous block. When a new block is created, it is just like a transaction and it is broadcast to all active nodes in the network. Other nodes validate the block by checking to see whether the given nonce solves to the correct hash based on the transactions listed in the block's data. Once the majority of the nodes positively validate and accept the block, consensus is reached.

Methods of reaching consensus

In a blockchain, or in any distributed database, there are four common algorithms to reach consensus:

1. **Proof-of-work (PoW)**
2. **Practical Byzantine fault tolerance (PBFT)**
3. **Proof-of-stake (PoS)**
4. **Delegated proof-of-stake (DPoS)**

A good consensus scheme should solve the following questions:

- Who is allowed to append blocks to the chain?
- When do updates happen on the blockchain?
- What transactions should be added to the block?
- How can you permit secure software changes to the blockchain?
- How can attacks or inconsistencies be solved?

Proof-of-work

Let's start with the best-known method of reaching consensus, referred to as the PoW algorithm or scheme. This scheme is used by blockchains built upon the Bitcoin core code. The PoW scheme is the one used in this chapter to explain the core concepts of the blockchain. It uses a system of hash functions to create conditions under which a single participant (individual, organization, or computer) is allowed to submit its conclusions about the broadcast transactions. Those conclusions, in the form of a new block, are broadcast to all other participants who then can independently verify them. If a participant submits false conclusions, the other participants will fail to compute by the rules of the hash function and the conclusions are rejected. The process of searching for the right conclusion is done by finding the valid hash based on the message input and an arbitrary number (or nonce).

The following diagram shows the steps for finding the correct hash:

The process of proofing a new block on the Bitcoin blockchain

In most of the PoW-style blockchains, the node that submits its conclusions the quickest, and which are verified by a group of other participants, is, in turn, rewarded for its participation. In terms of energy and computing resources, this participation designed to solve the correct hash can be costly. The process of solving, or *mining*, in such cases is incentivized by the network by giving the participant currency in return. Naturally, this broadens the participation and, in turn, ensures greater stability of the network and a safer, distributed, and decentralized blockchain.

What is Bitcoin mining?

It is a decentralized computational process that serves two goals:

1. Confirming transactions in a trustful manner when a miner has devoted adequate computational power to proof a block
2. Creating, or issuing, new bitcoins for each block

The miner bundles new transactions in a block and verifies internally whether they are valid. Then it selects the header of the most recent block and inserts its hash into the new block as a reference. Then it tries to solve the PoW problem and, when a solution is found, the block is added to its local chain and broadcast to the network. When accepted, the miner receives the issued bitcoins.

Practical byzantine fault tolerance

The practical byzantine fault tolerance algorithm is based on the story of the Byzantine army, known as **Byzantine Generals' Problem**, and was designed as a solution to the problem that the story presents (reference: `https://www.usenix.org/legacy/events/nsdi09/tech/full_papers/clement/clement.pdf`). The story goes that several divisions of the army are camping outside an enemy city. Each division is commanded by its own general. The generals can't communicate directly with each other—they can only communicate by messenger. They observe the enemy and need to decide on a common plan. However, not all of the generals are loyal and some may try to prevent the group from reaching an agreement. If the generals decide to attack the city, they need the majority of the entire Byzantine army to attack at the same time. To accomplish this goal, the generals need an algorithm or scheme that ensures that:

1. All generals who are loyal can reach a consensus on the same plan of attack
2. A small group of traitors are prevented from causing the loyal generals to adopt a bad plan

The loyal generals will do what the scheme tells them to do; whereas the traitors will do whatever they like. The scheme must guarantee this condition, regardless of the actions of the betrayers. Besides reaching an agreement, it should also be a rational plan. This problem can be complicated when there are a few traitorous generals who always cast a vote for a sub optimal plan, or may do so selectively, for example, when you have an uneven number of generals where two decide to attack and another two decide to retreat. The fifth general can then decide to send a message to the first group to attack and for the other group to retreat. The first group might not be so lucky attacking the enemy. The following diagram shows two of these scenarios:

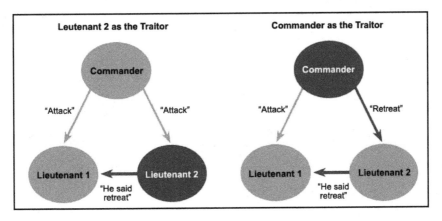

On the left, the 2nd lieutenant is the traitor and on the right, the commander is the traitor

Now let's alter this story so it represents our situation. The generals are the participating entities that run the blockchain, and the messengers are the means of communication across the network. The generals need to decide collectively whether the information submitted or a piece of the plan is valid or not. In our story, a valid piece of information would decide when and where to attack. Loyal generals are participants in the blockchain who ensure the integrity of the blockchain and that only valid information is accepted. The group of traitors are the entities who try to falsify information by submitting incorrect data and send assets that they don't own to other entities on the blockchain.

The PBFT scheme works as follows: Every participant (or general) maintains an internal state that is the specific status of the action plan. When a participant receives a message, or transaction, it is used in conjunction with their internal state to perform a computation. Based on the result of the computation, that participant can then decide what they think about the message and share that decision with the other participants. A consensus is reached based on the total of the decisions submitted by all participants. The consensus does not work by the majority of participants agreeing on only one decision submitted by a general, but that every decision that is sent from one participant to another is broadcast to all other participants in the network. So, if participant A sends a positive vote to participant B and a negative vote to participant C, then participant C would send their negative vote to participant B and conclude that participant A has sent two different votes. Participant B would also send a positive vote to participant C, also resulting in that same conclusion. This type of consensus requires less effort; that is, computing power and energy, but, in turn, it comes at the cost of anonymity because the system knows which decision each participant has sent. This type of consensus is used by blockchains, such as Hyperledger Fabric and Ripple. The following diagram shows the voting process where the Commander sends *A* to all Lieutenants, L1 sends *A* to L2, but L3 sends *B* to L2. From the point of view of Lieutenant 2, the majority of the votes is *A*:

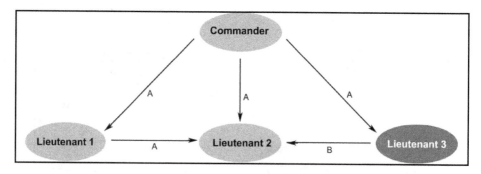

From L2 point of view – Lieutenant 3 is a traitor

Proof-of-stake

The third method that a blockchain might use for reaching consensus is the PoS algorithm or scheme. It is extremely similar to the PoW scheme discussed previously. The main difference between these algorithms is that with PoS, participation is restricted to the entities (individuals or organizations) that have a legitimate stake in the blockchain. An entity needs to have an asset or a smart contract (that is, a programmable asset that can execute code) saved in the blockchain. The blockchain can still be public, but the verification of new transactions and blocks is only done by these entities. The PoS algorithm replaces the calculation of the hash with a digital signature that proves the ownership of the stake. Instead of all stakeholders trying to confirm the validity of the information submitted, the blockchain's network chooses an individual to approve it. The chance of you being chosen is calculated based on your proportional stake (or wealth) in the network. So, instead of all entities in the network attempting to solve the nonce simultaneously to reach a consensus, the network itself runs a lottery to decide who will announce its conclusions—and it might just be you! All system participants with a stake in the network are automatically and exclusively entered into the lottery in proportion to their stake, or the number of lottery tickets.

In a cryptocurrency-based PoS blockchain, the term *mining* is replaced by the term *minting*, where a block is forged rather than mined. Usually, the amount of coins available is determined at the creation of the blockchain and it never changes. The entity that forges or validates the block receives transaction fees, which eventually will grow its stake (or wealth). The following diagram explains the main difference between a PoW and, PoS system:

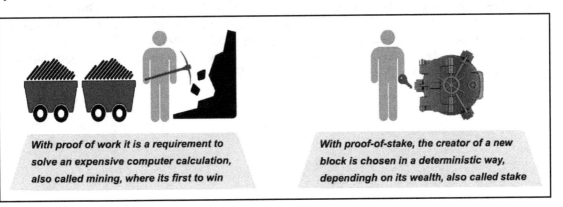

With proof of work it is a requirement to solve an expensive computer calculation, also called mining, where its first to win

With proof-of-stake, the creator of a new block is chosen in a deterministic way, dependingh on its wealth, also called stake

Proof of work versus proof of stake

This system of picking an entity that is already deeply involved in the network, however, can create an increasingly centralized blockchain, certainly if the participant gets an incentive for submitting his or her conclusions. Blockchains that use a PoS system have made modifications to this algorithm in order to ensure that the base of their network remains as broad and as secure as possible. One of these modifications is the prediction of the generator, or "forger," using a randomization formula. The formula looks for the lowest hash value in combination with the size of the stake. Because stakes are public, each participant can predict which account to the right will likely win in order to forge the new block. Another modification is an age-based selection system, where the transaction fees received, or wealth, will only start being part of the participants stake after x amount of days.

The older the received wealth, the greater the chance of getting picked. To control the situation whereby older wealth always has a higher probability of being picked, the age of the wealth is reduced to zero (0) once used in the verification process and it needs to age again to be part of the participant's stake. Also, when the age passes a specific number, the wealth is taken out of the equation. This process secures the network and gradually expands it without consuming significant computation power. A blockchain that uses these methods claims that it makes malicious attacks on the network more difficult because it guarantees fewer centralized pools that forge new blocks. This is the case because having a lot of wealth does not mean that the participant holds 51% of the hashing power, which could provide that power to submit malicious transactions.

In a cryptocurrency-based PoS blockchain, this means that received coins that are unspent, in 30 days, for example, begin to compete for the next block. Thus, older and larger sets of coins have a greater probability of being chosen for signing the next block. Once the coins are used to sign a block, the "coin age" is reduced to zero and needs to age for an additional 30 days to be part of the stake and used for signing another block. If the "coin age" reaches 90 days, for example, the coins are also removed from the equation to prevent very old or large collections of stakes dominating the blockchain.

Delegated proof-of-stake

The final algorithm or schema we'll discuss here is the DPoS. This consensus scheme is claimed to be the most efficient (fastest and decentralized) and most flexible scheme available. The previous schemes are rather basic in the absence of any modifications and can be seen as the most centralized consensus algorithms. The main difference between the regular PoS and the DPoS system is akin to the difference between a direct democracy and a democracy run by representatives. The participating entities (individuals or organizations) choose an entity they trust the most to represent their portion of stake in the blockchain. You decide which entity, also called **delegate node**, will represent your stake in the blockchain. This allows you to join a team to enlarge your stake, which helps to offset and balance out the power of large stakeholders. By changing network settings, such as the block interval, transaction sizes or other more advanced parameter, can be tuned by the power of democracy through the elected delegates. This protects all participants against unwanted changes in the network.

DPoS is claimed to be more efficient. This allows lower transactions fees, fast confirmations, and increased profitability. Critics argue, however, that by consolidating the validation role in fewer hands, it is less decentralized and resilient. Because it employs a "democratic system," it suffers from voter apathy as any such system might. If the majority of the smaller voting block participants fail to vote, the network will exhibit a tendency to be controlled by large stakeholders.

In a cryptocurrency-based PoS blockchain, every entity can perform a "stake," or otherwise participate in the process of validating transactions and earn coins; whereas in a DPoS blockchain, participants who have coins are able to vote for, or join, a delegation. However, the delegation performs the function of validating transactions in order to maintain the blockchain and it is the delegation that profits from the transaction fees received.

Ark is a blockchain that uses DPoS as a consensus scheme. Ark is set of bridged blockchains (or sidechains), and it uses its own token and exchange to deliver an innovative blockchain technology that everyone can use. This blockchain allows all account holders to vote for the top 51 delegates. Everyone can become a delegate. These delegates are allowed to update the blockchain's database. Each account holder votes for a delegate, and these delegates represent all stakeholders of the Ark network.

Within predefined rounds of a given time interval, each delegate has the chance to update the database once by creating a single block round. In each round, the network generates a pseudo random list that denotes when a delegate is allowed to create, or "forge," a block. Transactions are added by a delegate to a block when they are forging it. Like the other consensus methods, Ark uses hash functions to validate the transactions and, once added to a block, participants can check the block to see which transactions have been verified. When the developers of Arc want to update their node software, they put the changes up to a vote. The majority vote decides which version of the software is accepted and used in production. This ensures that the changes that win the vote are in the best interest of the majority of the participants.

The DPoS system can detect inconsistencies and automatically correct them because the version and state of the database is held by the majority of the delegates. The same is also true regarding attacks, where an attacker, for example, would require 51% of all stakes (coins) in order to be able to vote for 26 delegates. If an attacker achieves this, they could do anything they want with these 26 delegates, but it won't be in their best interest to damage the system, since this would diminish the value of the coins.

Summary

In this chapter, I continued covering some of the fundamental building blocks and core concepts of the blockchain—*blocks*, *chains*, and some of the existing *consensus* algorithms.

In the section about blocks, I covered what a block actually is, how it compares with pages in a book, and told what is stored in such a block. You then learned what the structures of different types of blocks are, including its block header, and then studied how blocks are hashed and how the nonce is calculated that is needed to generate the correct target hash.

I continued covering the fundamentals by explaining how blocks are chained together to form the actual blockchain and how these blocks are distributed to all nodes in the decentralized network using a managed peer-to-peer protocol. I went through the process of how nodes can detect that the content of a block is maliciously modified. I explained that this same process can also detect accidental forks in the chain, which happens when multiple block are created with the same block height.

I concluded the section about chains by covering the difference between a soft fork and a hard fork, and how such forks in a chain can occur. Finally, I explained that when your blockchain grows over time, the network may want to try out different rules but not affect the main chain. This can be done using a sidechain (that is, independent ledger). Most sidechains are developed to enhance scalability or transferability among chains. In this section, you studied how the underlying mechanisms of sidechains work.

Finally, you learned about the four main consensus methods that are currently available to validate transactions and create and verify blocks in a blockchain. At the end of the chapter, I reflected back on what was covered and linked all of the pieces together by explaining how consensus solves the trust issue that exists with traditional transactions. For each consensus method or algorithm, I addressed five questions concerning authorization, privacy, and data integrity.

In the next chapter, you will learn about the security and privacy aspects of the blockchain, and how you can use smart contracts to delegate work automatically to participants in the network.

5
Blockchain 101 - Security, Privacy, and Smart Contracts

In previous chapters, I discussed the building blocks which make up the blockchain. In Chapter 3, *Blockchain 101 - Assets, Transactions, and Hashes*, I started with the smallest bits and bytes that flow through the blockchain, whereas in Chapter 4, *Blockchain 101 - Blocks, Chains, and Consensus*, I started by explaining that transactions are added to blocks, and I showed you a few different structures used by the current blockchain in the technology ecosphere. I continued the chapter by describing how blocks are formed and how they are chained together to create a blockchain. Within the lifespan of a blockchain, it is possible to have *forks*. I explained the concept of forks in general and what types of forks exist. I then concluded the chapter by telling you how consensus is reached regarding the trustworthiness of the data in the blockchain and what different methods the blockchain can use to reach it.

In this chapter, I will continue with the topics of security, privacy, and smart contracts, and I will try to make it absolutely clear that a blockchain is not just an ordinary, shared database. This chapter explains how safe blockchain is in reality and what it takes to keep the blockchain safe. Together, we look at the advantages and disadvantages of the blockchain as compared to other shared databases. Whereas security is one side of the story, I also will be touching base on the privacy aspects of the blockchain and how your privacy is not compromised. Finally, I will explain the added value of smart contracts when operating a blockchain, and how they can make automatic decisions based on programmable code.

In this chapter, you will learn about the following topics:

- How secure is the blockchain?
- What kinds of wallets are available to keep data safe?
- Do you have control over your privacy?
- What are smart contracts, and what is their added value?

How secure is the blockchain?

The answer to this question depends on the circumstances. If you listen to some blockchain experts, the technology behind blockchain is going to secure the future of many industries and applications. For example, the technology is the source of **IPFS** (**InterPlanetary File System**, `https://ipfs.io`), a new and more secure internet protocol (replacing http).

It is already revolutionizing the banking industry by delivering secure identity communication and smart contracts (that is, programmable code deployed on the blockchain that act as a complement, or substitute, for legal contracts or complex business transactions), thereby reducing costs by requiring fewer back office employees. Furthermore, it creates distributed ledgers that guarantee the owner of properties. The building blocks are definitely there so that we can say the blockchain itself is secure. However, its security depends on how these building blocks are used by the application layer on top of it.

To explain the security risk inherent in blockchain technology, I will first need to explain the difference between a public and a private blockchain. Some security risks only need to be dealt with when setting up a public blockchain.

Public versus private blockchains

Before I go into the differences between the two types — public versus private blockchains (or, strictly speaking, three types if you count a consortium blockchain separately), let's first review the similarities. Both types use the same underlying peer-to-peer network technology, whereas the shared ledger is replicated to each participant by distribution over the network. These replicas are both maintained and kept in sync through a consensus protocol. Finally, both public and private blockchains provide guarantees that confirmed transactions registered in the shared ledger are immutable (that is, unchangeable) even when there are malicious participants. However, this is where the similarities end. Both types have their own advantages and disadvantages, and both are considered to serve different business cases.

In `Chapter 7`, *Public Versus Permissioned Blockchains and their Providers*, I will explain the advantages and disadvantages in more detail. For the sake of security, let's now take a look at the main differences:

Public Blockchain	Private/Consortium Blockchain
Anyone in the world can read it	Read permissions may be public or restricted
Anyone in the world can send it transactions	Write permissions are kept centralized to one organization or (part of) a consortium
Anyone can see the transactions included if they are valid	Participants can see the transaction in which they participate or have the permission to see all transactions
Anyone can participate in the consensus process	A consortium of selected nodes participates in consensus
It is fully decentralized	It is decentralization based on the number of participants and permissions
3rd-party tools are available to explore the blockchain	Includes database management, auditing, and so on

With a public blockchain, for example, a cryptocurrency, anyone is allowed to read and write transactions into the blockchain. Anyone participating in the blockchain can validate those transactions and publish their findings. In a public blockchain, everybody can verify transactions, but no one is implicitly trusted when doing so. All users need to follow the consensus algorithm that verifies all transactions, and when doing so they need to prove that they have made a sufficient amount of effort by solving a mathematical problem. The first user to solve the problem gets rewarded, whereas each new solution forms the basis for the next block of transactions to be solved. Because of the reward, a lot of people participate in the network and that makes it fully decentralized.

On the other hand, in private or permissioned blockchains, control over who can read verified transactions, who can submit transactions, and who can verify transactions is done by assigned operators. Participants can only join after obtaining an invitation or gaining permission. An invitation can be sent by an existing participant, a certificate authority, or through a decision made by the entire consortium. Sometimes, the application for a private blockchain happens when a consortium of parties wishes to participate in trading but do not fully trust one another, or when some information is made accessible to some of the trading partners but not to others.

Unexpected security risks

Much like cryptocurrencies themselves, one thing that public blockchains have led to is black market trading (reference: https://lifehacker.com/what-to-know-about-monero-the-black-market-cryptocurre-1822558727). Everybody can read and write transactions, and they can do this anonymously. Because transactions are bound to an address and not a personal identity, it is hard to figure out who is actually trading. Public blockchains also increasingly attract the attention of cyber criminals who wish to steal cryptocurrencies or other available assets.

Another security risk associated with a public blockchain is that the commonly-used method of reaching consensus consumes a lot of energy. This may lead to centralization or possible attacks on the network due to collusion, as the majority of the network nodes will be run by countries offering cheap electricity or even a single country that can do so. Changes in electricity pricing policies, or even subsidies, can have a major impact on such networks. The following list shows the average costs to mine one bitcoin around the world (reference: https://www.investopedia.com/news/how-much-does-it-cost-mine-bitcoin-around-world/):

THE COST TO MINE 1 BITCOIN
BASED ON THE AVERAGE ELECTRICITY RATE PER COUNTRY

ALBANIA	$3,894	IRELAND	$11,103	RWANDA	$8,922
AMERICAN SAMOA	$10,706	ISRAEL	$6,087	SAUDI ARABIA	$3,172
ARGENTINA	$4,560	ITALY	$10,310	SERBIA	$3,133
AUSTRALIA	$9,913	JAMAICA	$7,867	SINGAPORE	$5,936
BAHRAIN	$16,773	JAPAN	$8,723	SLOKAVIA	$4,746
BANGLADESH	$2,379	JORDAN	$9,913	SLOVENIA	$7,645
BELARUS	$2,177	KAZAKHSTAN	$2,835	SOLOMON ISLANDS	$16,209
BELGIUM	$13,482	KIRIBATI	$12,966	SOUTH AFRICA	$5,948
BOSNIA AND HERZEGOVINA	$4,084	KOSOVO	$3,133	SOUTH KOREA	$26,170
BRAZIL	$6,741	KUWAIT	$1,983	SPAIN	$11,103
BRUNEI	$4,758	LAOS	$4,845	SRI LANKA	$11,630
BULGARIA	$4,362	LATVIA	$7,122	SURINAM	$2,956
CAMBODIA	$8,327	LIECHTENSTEIN	$8,164	SWEDEN	$4,746
CANADA, ONTARIO	$3,965	LITHUANIA	$5,155	SWITZERLAND	$7,494
CHILE	$9,120	LUXEMBOURG	$7,693	TAHITI	$11,103
CHINA	$3,172	MACEDONIA	$3,914	TAIWAN	$3,774

List of average cost to mine 1 bitcoin of some of the countries. The full list is available on https://www.investopedia.com.

A similar attack allows a pool with a sufficient number of nodes to obtain wealth larger than its actual solving power. This vulnerability allows the colluding group of nodes to force honest nodes into performing wasted computations in a stale fork or branch of the blockchain. During the attack, the honest nodes spend their computation cycles on blocks that eventually will not be part of the blockchain, because they are part of the stale or shortest branch of the blockchain. The colluding group does this by keeping the created blocks private and secretly performing bifurcation of the blockchain.

The colluding group finally reveals the blocks to the public. The honest nodes then need to switch to that branch because they're no longer producing blocks for the dominant/longest chain.

This does not mean that there are no security concerns when using a private blockchain. In a private blockchain, operators can control who is allowed to connect to the network and who can operate a node. One of the concerns of running a private node is that it can restrict the transmission of information, or even transmit incorrect information. Such nodes must be identifiable and bypassed to maintain the integrity of the system. Also, in a private blockchain, all nodes need to use the same method of consensus. Since different nodes can be operated by different parties, there needs to be consensus about the consensus method used by the network, which is commonly reached during a face-to-face meeting with all participating members.

Security starts at the network architecture level

One of the first decisions to make when establishing a blockchain is the choice between a public blockchain and a private blockchain. Do you want to bring your application to the whole world, or do you want only certain parties to be able to join the network? When implementing an application on a public blockchain like Ethereum, there are already tens of thousands of nodes in the network. This means that your solution will be fully decentralized, and nodes can come and go without the need to operate them yourself. By making it explicitly harder or impossible to do certain things by yourself, then others are likely to trust you more and engage with your application sooner. Also, if your blockchain application needs to be *censorship resistant*, a public blockchain can be a viable option. This is the case because if you are pressured by another entity, it is impossible to hand over information even if you wanted to do so.

If your blockchain application is used by (partially) trusted parties, then the application can be implemented on a private blockchain. When implementing an application on a private blockchain such as Hyperledger Fabric, operators have control over the method of consensus, the number of nodes, the available smart contracts, which parties can write and approve new transactions, and other configurations that you normally can't control in a public blockchain.

Private (or permissioned) blockchains, such as Hyperledger Fabric, provide a greater level of privacy. In addition to the main chain, it is also possible to configure dedicated channels where two or more parties can communicate without the involvement of the rest of the network. When running a private blockchain network, operators, usually from multiple participating member organizations, are in control over the number of nodes in the network. When establishing the network architecture, you need to take into account how they should treat uncommunicative, intermittently-active nodes. Nodes can go offline for harmless reasons, but the network must still be resilient in order to function (verifying new transactions and obtaining consensus) without these offline nodes. Thus, the network architecture must define an adequate number of nodes to be able to bring back the offline nodes and get them up to speed quickly when they return.

In the following diagram a centralized ledger (database, excel) is compared to a private and a public blockchain (distributed ledger). It shows how end users (individuals and organizations) interact with the ledger and how it affects the infrastructure architecture of each network:

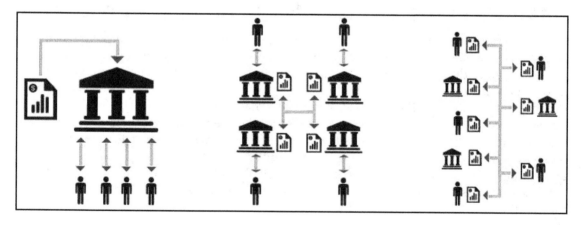

Centralized ledger versus private blockchain versus public blockchain

Importance of the consensus protocol

One of the main mechanisms that make a blockchain secure is the consensus protocol. In `Chapter 4`, *Blockchain 101 - Blocks, Chains, and Consensus*, I explained the four commonly-used consensus protocols. The choice of protocol can determine whether it is best to use a public blockchain for your application. Public blockchains use protocols where all nodes participate in reaching consensus. If you want to be sure that transactions are verified by more than a few nodes, and you don't mind paying these nodes for doing the work, then a public blockchain may be an option for an enterprise blockchain. Usually, public blockchains aren't a good choice for an enterprise blockchain because they are designed to take time, maybe two or five or even 10 minutes before consensus is reached. In addition, transactions are not considered fully verified for about three to six blocks, until the block (including your transaction) has settled deeply enough into the main chain. The delay is both a significant obstacle if your application must deliver near real-time data to the end user and a noteworthy vulnerability when initially, a transaction seems to be verified but is lost later when it is not part of the main chain (that is, part of an orphaned chain or the shortest fork).

In contrast, in a private blockchain, operators can choose the consensus method that they want to use when setting up the blockchain. For example, when using Hyperledger Fabric, as a network starter, you can choose between a few different protocols. You can select the one that suits your cause best and, even better, they are pluggable, which means that you are not stuck with just one. Operators of the blockchain can also choose to deny certain nodes from participating in the consensus. Nodes that do participate are responsible for communicating verified transactions to the rest of the network. The responsibility for determining when and from whom the network can be expanded is a decision made by the same blockchain system operator(s).

Bugs in the blockchain code

With almost every blockchain platform, public or private, the code is open sourced. This is because blockchains use the principles and techniques, and reuse parts of the code, which started the first blockchain. Bitcoin, for example, makes this a requirement. Also, making the code open source means that it can be trusted and no adverse/malicious things can be done with the data sent in a transaction. Because the code is still in its early stages of development, however, it may be subject to unknown security vulnerabilities. For example, the Ethereum smart contract language is relatively new, and it runs in a separate virtual machine. Thus, there may be zero-day attacks that hackers can exploit. Always keep your blockchain node(s) up-to-date and use the most recent software build of the code that is used by the majority of the network.

Manage asset security

Blockchains can store much more data than most public blockchains actually do in practice or allow. The primary use of a blockchain, however, is to exchange assets. For example, cryptocurrencies use a specific payload in every transaction, which holds the amount of that currency that is being exchanged. Similarly, other blockchain systems record the possession of assets. Ownership of assets is demonstrated through the use of a private key (unique string) generated by a hashing algorithm. Assets are stored using the private key in so-called **wallets**. Despite the value of the keys that are stored in wallets, like any data, they can be lost or stolen, just like cash and real-world assets, for example, diamonds. In the case of theft, it is not a failure in the security of a blockchain, but rather personal security has failed by storing the private key insecurely. Of course, these wallets are not only for personal security, but they also provide a robust security framework for (especially public) blockchain implementations. Without it, assets can easily become liabilities and compromise the blockchain's integrity. There are a few ways of storing your assets securely in different kinds of wallets, and they vary in terms of features. Let's look at the available types, so that you know which one suits you best.

Difference between hot and cold wallets

All types of wallets can be classified as either cold or hot. **Hot wallets** refer to any kind of wallet that stores assets online or that is connected to the Internet. These kinds of wallets are usually accessible through a web portal from all over the world, or from an app on your phone, and they are suitable for frequently-accessed or regularly-used funds, for example, for making payments. On the other hand, **cold wallets** refer to any kind of wallet that stores assets offline or that are disconnected from the internet. These kinds of wallets are stored physically on paper or on special hardware, and they're the best strategy for storing large amounts of assets or for long-term holdings.

Software wallets (desktop and mobile)

Software wallets are those that require you to download a software client to create new wallets and use them online. These clients are available for both desktop and mobile platforms. When researching desktop wallets, there are different implementations. For example, clients such as Bitcoin Core (`https://bitcoin.org/en/download`) and Ethereum Geth (`https://geth.ethereum.org/downloads/`) usually require downloading the full blockchain. In bitcoin, this exceeds 145 GB. If you have limited storage space or low internet bandwidth, this can be a real deal breaker.

Luckily, there are also desktop clients that allow you to create, import, and use a wallet without requiring all of the blockchain information. For example, Electrum (`https://electrum.org/`) uses remote servers that handle the most complicated parts of the system. With most of these wallets, you can manage only one specific asset type. Alternatively, Exodus (`https://www.exodus.io/`) offers a desktop client that supports multi-asset wallets. All of these desktop wallets are highly secure and cross-platform, meaning that they are available on Windows, macOS, and Linux.

If you need more easy-to-use software, then you could look into mobile wallets. There are a lot of mobile wallet apps out there that you can download, and that let you create and start using new wallets right away. Copay (`https://copay.io/`) for iOS and Android also offers a desktop counterpart. Alternatively, if you want an app that supports multi-asset wallets, then you might want to look at Multiwallet by Freewallet (`https://freewallet.org/`). Perhaps one of the most useful features of mobile wallets is their capability of making instant payments through the use of QR codes.

Keep in mind that software wallets are only as secure as the computer or mobile device upon which they are stored. The possibility exists that you might see malware that is capable of stealing wallet information in the future. If you have a reasonable level of technical know-how, you can choose to use offline desktop clients that let you encrypt your wallet.

Online or web wallets

Another type of hot wallet is known as **online** or **web wallets**, and for most people, these are the easiest type to use. You can create online wallets as easy as signing up for a new account on `Cryptonator.com`, `BlockChain.info` (Bitcoin), `MyEtherWallet.com` (ether), or any other cryptocurrency service. If you want to use a service that lets you have a multi-asset wallet, `Cryptonator.com` is worth the look. You can log in to these services and your wallet(s) from any device that is connected to the internet. This simplifies access to your assets, although, there are certain tradeoffs. The most important one is trust. Your private keys are stored on another server. If the server is compromised, there is a chance that the hacker has also got hold of your keys. Online wallets should only be used for making small (everyday) transactions. They should not be used for holding a large amount of assets.

Physical or paper wallets

If you want to hold a large amount of assets, for example, in cryptocurrencies, you are better off using a cold wallet, such as a **paper wallet**. A paper wallet is just a term used for printing your public and private keys on a piece of paper, which makes it a more secure wallet than using software or an online wallet. While, if it is stored in a secure place (safe), a paper wallet is more secure than its online counterpart, a piece of paper can suffer water damage, be torn up, or get destroyed in many other ways. Because it is on paper, you can choose to laminate it so that it can handle moisture, preventing any water damage. My advice is to make multiple copies of the piece of paper and keep it stored and safe in several places, for example, in a locker.

Most of the online services and software wallets allow you to print your pre-existing wallet keys. You can also create paper wallets using services such as `BitAddres.com` or `Blockchain.info` in order to create a paper wallet and print the assets stored within. Since a cold wallet is only for long-term storage, you need to add a public-private key combination into an online or software wallet in order to perform transactions.

Hardware wallets

At the present time, the best option for storing a large number of assets is arguably a **hardware wallet**, which is another type of cold wallet. Typically, hardware wallets are standalone USB cold storage devices. Instead of adding the wallet to an online service or software client, you plug it into your computer while making a transaction.

Hardware wallets generate private keys offline, on the device itself, so they are secure from any malware on your computer. Hardware wallets such as KeepKey (`keepkey.com`), TREZOR (`trezor.io`), and the Ledger Wallet (`ledgerwallet.com`) are very easy to understand and convenient to use. They also provide backup options and can combat theft by securing them with a password. So, when making backups of your security tokens and your hardware wallet is lost or broken, your assets will still be safe.

Overall, hardware wallets are the most secure option, as you can carry your private keys along with you at all times, and it is not susceptible to computer malware.

Access control

Most enterprise blockchains are run by a consortium or private entity and are permissioned. As such, you need to define a governance structure in these enterprise blockchains. By defining this structure, you ensure which participants can view, query, or update the blockchain and how they can do it. The predefined rules of governance establish a consensus process that is controlled by a group of preselected nodes. For example, the structure includes the types of participants, their role and permissions, and the number of participants that are required to sign a block in order for it to be valid. The latter rule, for instance, can state that 2/3 of all participants need to sign a block.

While the technology behind blockchain guarantees the integrity of the network and the transactions running over it, security components such as access control and the privacy of data must be overlaid on top of it. So, in a permissioned blockchain, protecting participants from unauthorized access is of utmost importance, and outsiders should not be able to tamper with the ledger. As an administrator of such a permissioned blockchain, you must minimize its attack surface by using policies to protect the traffic to and from participating entities. One policy should always be that the blockchain application is secure. The following diagram shows an example of how such a policy can be implemented using certificates:

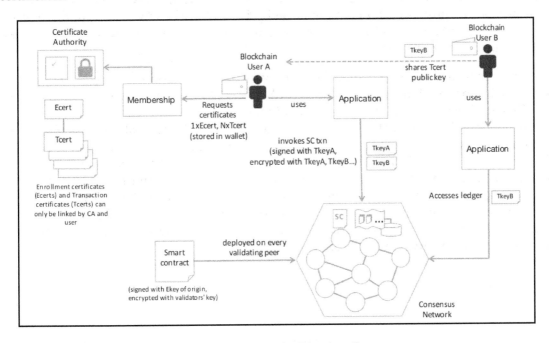

Securing the access to a permissioned ledger using certificates

This requires the secure management of private keys, as a lack of security can heavily impact the integrity and confidentiality of data. Usually, such concerns have already been addressed elsewhere, and the same technologies typically used there should be used to secure these keys as well. You can ensure the protection of these keys using a variety of methods, such as physical and network access control and a key-management solution that does the generation, distribution, storage, backup, and so on.

Reversibility of transactions

In contrast to public blockchains, private blockchains store more data than just the unique text strings associated with the assets being exchanged. Operators therefore must decide how to resolve issues when identification credentials are lost. Owners of a private blockchain need to make a decision as to whether or not verified transactions can be reversed and under what circumstances. For example, they need to decide what happens when data or assets are stolen. Reversing a verified transaction can undermine confidence in the impartiality and fairness of the system. Nonetheless, if it's the result of an exploit or a bug and the system permits it, the blockchain will lose users and it can lead to financial losses. Within a public blockchain, the reversal of transactions may never happen, because there is no owner and it's a controversial process. As a blockchain developer, you should consider the circumstances, for both public and private blockchain networks, under which you would face a similar decision and how you would want to prevent such circumstances from occurring from the very start.

When choosing a blockchain platform to build your application on/against your need to keep one important regulation in mind. As of May 27, 2018, you may need to comply with the **GDPR** (**General Data Protection Regulation**, reference: `https://www.eugdpr.org`). This regulation is a EU law on data protection and privacy for all individuals with the **European Union** (**EU**) and includes one important ruling, which give individuals the right to be forgotten. Any personal data that is put on the blockchain should be able to be deleted, which is nearly impossible with most of the current blockchain platform available, since they all use an immutable transaction log. Blockchain can overcome this easily by creating data checkpoints after x number of blocks and removing the rest of the ledger data. Assets can be updated for example with an empty value, once a new checkpoint is created the old values are permanently removed from the ledger data.

Maintaining privacy on the blockchain

Besides security, you need to think about participants' privacy on the blockchain. Privacy is much more nuanced, and it can lead to uncomfortable questions. What needs to be kept private? Why? And from whom?

Nowadays, in many countries around the world, people trust their governments and other social institutions. The idea of government censorship in such countries seems improbable. Not everyone, however, has this luxury. In all cases, you need a system that is resistant to censorship from any source; one that deters the unwanted prying eyes of snooping individuals and the theft of your identity. When designing your blockchain application, you definitely need to think about this and whether you should run it on a public blockchain or not. For example, electronic medical records can't be shared or modified on a public blockchain without the risk of jeopardizing doctor-patient privilege or confidentiality. Also, many types of trading and lending, identity verification, and credential management can't safely operate on a public ledger.

To explain the privacy inherent in blockchain technology, we will now discuss the different approaches to maintain today's level of privacy, the applications to power a blockchain, and the future of privacy on the blockchain.

Maintaining today's level of privacy

When looking into maintaining privacy, there are some solutions that are easy to implement (others, though, may be much more difficult). Many of these solutions are compatible with currently existing blockchains, but it depends on what you want to achieve as to whether they are adequate. Technologies that allow users to do absolutely everything on a blockchain without the possibility of being tracked are harder to create.

Such technologies can make your application completely privacy-preserving, allowing your users to benefit from the blockchain's security. In addition, the data is encrypted so that the information and its underlying meaning is completely obfuscated (though the information is computed in plain sight). In short, *obfuscation* is way of turning your application into a "black box" version (or its equivalent). The application still has the same underlying logic and also returns the same outputs for given inputs, but because the data is encrypted along the way, it's impossible to determine any details on how the application works.

The most powerful version of this technology is **cryptographically-secure obfuscation**. Think of it as a box filled with wires inside. The wires are encrypted in such a way that the encryption cancels itself out. This means that ultimately, it has no effect on the output. The effect of the type of obfuscation makes it impossible to determine what is happening on the inside. This is demonstrated in the following diagram:

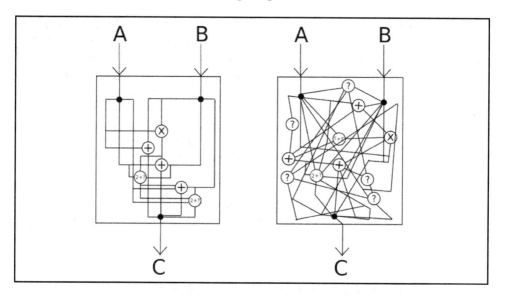

Example of a cryptographically-secure obfuscation

Unfortunately, as it turns out, a perfectly obfuscated black box is mathematically impossible (https://www.iacr.org/archive/crypto2001/21390001.pdf). There is always something that you can extract from an application by looking beyond the outputs, which are a result of a specific set of inputs. There is, however, a more suitable, albeit weaker standard, called **indistinguishability obfuscation** (https://eprint.iacr.org/2013/451.pdf).

It is a rather esoteric property intended for, or likely to be understood by, only a small number of people with specialized knowledge. It is still called "obfuscation," but it is a weaker form of it, so the terminology is a misnomer. The property means that if you can encode a process as a circuit, for example, a piece of code that can be unrolled in such a way that there are several possible distinct circuits that yield the same results, in that case, indistinguishability obfuscation allows the publication of an "obfuscated circuit." Anybody can run the circuit and obtain the result, but an outsider cannot know which of the possible circuits was used internally as the basis for that result.

But how can I use this on a blockchain? you might ask. On an enterprise blockchain, you can use one simple approach; otherwise known as **obfuscated smart contracts**. With this approach, a smart contract contains a private key and accepts invocations that are encrypted with the corresponding public key. In the case of an insurance claim, the contract stores the encrypted information. If the contract needs to read this information from storage, it decrypts the data. Further, if it needs to write data, it encrypts the result before writing it back to storage. If a participant, such as an insurance company, wants to read who's involved in the claim, then they encode the request as a transaction that invokes the contract. The process that executes the obfuscated smart contract will first check to see whether the signature of the participant is entitled to read the information registered in the claim. If so, the contract will return the decrypted information; otherwise, it will result in an error such that the participant can't extract the information. This is demonstrated in the following diagram

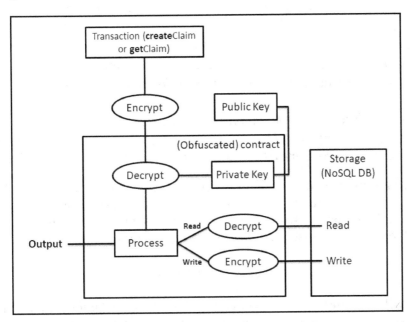

The mechanism of indistinguishability obfuscation, however, is tremendously inefficient. The encryption and decryption process brings with it a lot of overhead, including more CPU power (calculations) and energy to execute the smart contract. You need to set up the contract so that it prevents the reads and writes on small portions of the data, and instead make it always modify large portions of the contract's state. Also, running these kinds of contracts on the blockchain brings this high level of overhead to all nodes running the code, which can lead to the rejection of the contract.

In the context of this book, we are content with using partial solutions and mechanisms that are designed to bring privacy to enterprise-class blockchain applications. Therefore, let's take it a few steps back.

Secure multi-party computation

Instead of the obfuscation of a smart contract, a much lighter solution is **secure multi-party computation** (**sMPC**, reference: `https://en.wikipedia.org/wiki/Secure_multi-party_computation`), which is a type of cryptographic system where parties jointly compute a function encompassing all of their inputs while keeping those private. Each party initially receives access to a share of the inputs by the sender (or dealer) and computes a function over that share. The outputs are sent back to the sender, who can then assemble the final output without any party having knowledge about more than their initial share.

Simplified, sMPC works as follows:

1. A dealer, D, wants to compute a function, F, over an input, I.
2. D selects n parties to the computation by sending each of them a share of the input, si.
3. Each party computes a function over their share $fi(si)$ and reports the result to the dealer, D.
4. The dealer, D, combines these outputs such that $G(f1(s1), f2(s2), ...fn(sn)) = F(I)$

For example, suppose that you have four people working on your team: Alice, James, Bob, and Jessica. You want to find the highest of their four sales scores, with respective inputs *(a, b, c, d)* denoting their monthly score. You wish to do this without revealing their individual scores to each other. This translates to the following function:

$$F(a,b,c,d) = max(a,b,c,d)$$

The goal of sMPC is to design a protocol where all four (Alice, James, Bob, and Jessica) can exchange messages only with each other without relying on a mutual friend; in our example, a dealer who can compute the maximum sales score. Each can still learn $F(a, b, c, d)$ without the protocol revealing who scored what. Each of the parties can only learn what they can conclude from the output and their given input. For example, if the answer is d, then Jessica learns that her score is the highest; whereas Alice (a), James (b), and Bob (c) learn that they don't have the highest score.

A multi-party computation protocol aims to ensure two things: *input privacy* and the *correctness* of the data. The first part ensures that no privately held data can be gathered from the messages sent during the execution of the computation. The only private information that can be deduced is whatever a party can infer by looking at the output of the computation itself. The second part prevents colluding parties, who try to deviate from the instructions during execution, from being able to force honest parties into outputting an incorrect result. The goal here is that honest parties are guaranteed to compute the correct output, or they abort if they find an error.

Practical applications vary from simple computations, such as knowing between two millionaires who is richer, to more complex applications, like electronic voting and auctions.

Zero-knowledge proofs

Another powerful technology designed to preserve privacy is **zero-knowledge proofs**. This technology allows you to construct a mathematical proof that, when executing a given program on some user input, returns a particular output without revealing any other information. One type of zero-knowledge proof that you can easily implement uses a digital signature to show that you know the value of a private key, which, when processed by a smart contract, can be converted into a particular public output.

A fairly easy-to-understand application of zero-knowledge proofs are two-party smart contracts, for example, a financial performance contract between two parties that credits or debits funds based on the performance of an underlying entity (for example, an asset or index). Normally, when you first negotiate the contract, you would write a formula that would credit or debit funds to one party or the other when a certain performance criteria is not met or is exceeded. Instead of writing the formula as a binary option in the contract, such as "If, as a result of an external data source, asset A is used more than X, debit funds from A and send them to B; otherwise, credit the amount of these funds from B to A," you create a hash of the formula and put it in the contract. When the contract is near its end, A and B themselves can compute the amount of funds they need to send or receive from each other. In this case, the zero-knowledge proof is that the correct hash provides the result.

The following diagram shows a transaction is submitted, where the information to spend the output is encrypted with the recipient's public key to a hash and attached to the transaction. The hash can only be used by the recipient to retrieve the funds:

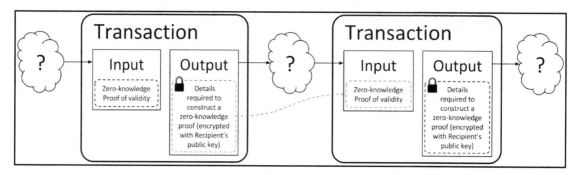

A transaction that uses zero-knowledge proof of validity to encrypt the information in the output

For more detail on zero-knowledge proof technology, visit these sites:

- Keep network: https://backend.keep.network/whitepaper
- SNARKS: https://eprint.iacr.org/2013/507.pdf

Permissioned blockchain

Both sMPC protocols and zero-knowledge proofs are powerful and somewhat complex technologies. They are a bit too much for most enterprise blockchain applications, since you are likely to trust the participating parties. A permissioned blockchain is a more suitable solution in this case.

A **permissioned**, or **consortium blockchain**, is a type of private blockchain. It provides many features designed to preserve participants' privacy, and it provides a hybrid solution between the low-trust public blockchain model and the single (highly) trusted entity private blockchain model. Thus, instead of everybody who has an internet connection participating in the network and its verification process, or allowing a single entity (or company) to have full control, in a permissioned blockchain, a few selected nodes are predetermined for this process.

A permissioned blockchain, as the name suggests, can limit read and write permissions on shared data (assets) and the execution of transactions. For example, imagine a consortium of 15 companies, each operating a warehouse in a supply-chain. If only one company trades and shares track and trace information with three other companies, you can allow permissions only to those companies to read the shared data and no others.

Even though you might think that you're sacrificing the decentralization of the network, it is still maintained to some degree in the permissioned blockchain's structure. This is done by allowing participants to grant read/write permissions to other participants, which leads to a "partially decentralized" design.

Making sense of smart contracts

Up until this point in the chapter, you have learned about the security and privacy that the blockchain provides out of the box and the techniques that enable this to be achieved. In this chapter, I used the words "smart contract" several times. What exactly is a "smart contract," though, what can you use it for, and what technologies are available to create and run smart contracts?

The definition of a smart contract is still fuzzy (that is, it's not yet fully established) and the legal status of smart contracts is also still a little vague. On the other hand, the phrase "smart contracts" was first published way back in 1994 by computer scientist and cryptographer Nick Szabo. This was the same year that web search engines began to appear on the market. Back then, Szabo dubbed smart contracts as the design of electronic commerce protocols between strangers on the Internet created by combining the practices of contract law and related business practices. Szabo's exact description of smart contracts was as follows:

> *A smart contract is a computerized transaction protocol that executes the terms of a contract. The general objectives are to satisfy common contractual conditions (such as payment terms, liens, confidentiality, and even enforcement), minimize exceptions both malicious and accidental, and minimize the need for trusted intermediaries. Related economic goals include lowering fraud loss, arbitrations and enforcement costs, and other transaction costs.*

When reviewing this description, the definition still holds after more than 20 years. However, smart contracts have evolved both in terms of legal construction and from a technology aspect.

What is a smart contract?

Smart contracts are agreements between parties that can act as a complement, or substitute, for legal contracts. They are defined as digital programs, or computer code, that are capable of facilitating, executing, and enforcing the negotiation or performance of an agreement. Contracts will self-execute when the terms of an agreement are met. Also, due to the decentralized consensus architecture, they are tamper-proof and self-enforcing.

Smart contracts diverge from traditional contracts, either verbal or written, being characterized as computer programs built on code. Some smart contracts, however, contain similar logic and characteristics as conventional contracts, whereas others do much more than list contract terms and conditions. For example, a smart contract is capable of collecting external data and processing it according to the contract terms and performing actions based on the data retrieved. The term "smart contract" nowadays is commonly used for much more than simply a formal agreement. It is also used for many other kinds of applications on the blockchain, such as a car auction, digital property, and animal tracking application. The following diagram shows some more examples:

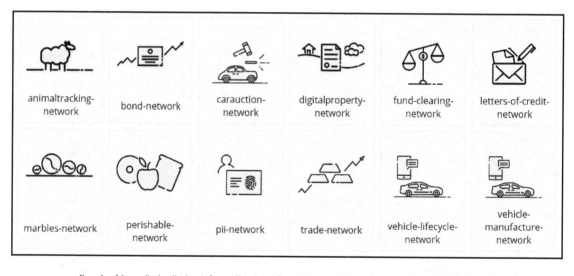

Examples of decentralized applications (reference: Hyperledger Composer playground – https://composer-playground.mybluemix.net)

In the near future, it is unlikely that smart contracts will fully replace traditional legal contracts. However, in some American states, a blockchain smart contract is already legally binding. Nevertheless, they can reduce the complexity and trouble of writing a new contract each time between (new) parties. The technology behind smart contracts can be used to execute the general terms of a traditional contract automatically between two parties and limit the number of exceptions and other errors. Another benefit of smart contracts is that they simultaneously remove the responsibility for checking the accuracy of the process by third parties while simultaneously lowering transaction costs by reducing the amount of fraud since contract terms are automatically implemented.

One common concern I want to highlight though is that not all smart contracts have the same level of quality and security. There are cases where a smart contract was hacked and tens of millions of dollars were lost (reference: `https://www.coindesk.com/understanding-dao-hack-journalists`). Developing a legally binding contract will require a blend of specialties—the expertise of developers and attorneys—to avoid potential legal issues (that is, exploitation of loopholes) with the potential to do even more catastrophic damage to organizations that will eventually rely on smart contract technology.

How smart contracts work

Consider this: A blockchain uses **distributed ledger technology** (**DLT**) in which two parties can share a distribution ledger that governs the process of fabrication, transporting, selling, and management of goods. If those two parties also have shared business logic, they can create a smart contract between themselves to automate the process.

Under a smart contract, you actually define one or more possible actions based on the terms of the physical contract. An action can be executed by an entity (organization or individual) by proposing (submitting) a transaction on the blockchain. Based on the payload, containing the name of the action and required asset data, the corresponding action is executed. The smart contract validates whether the proposed action can be executed successfully with the received data. The proposed transaction and the result of the smart contract execution is sent to other peer(s) to reach consensus about the transaction, for example, by executing the same smart contract and action). Only when there is consensus is the transaction finalized under the terms of the contract. Thus, the contract is evaluated in the same way on both sides since the rules are the same.

Smart contracts are automated programs where the terms of a legal or performance contract are written in programming code, for example, languages such as Java, JavaScript, Python, or Go (also known as Golang). The code that you write defines the transactions (executable functions), the rules (such as if/then/else expressions) and consequences (for example, data manipulation, actions, and events) in the same way a traditional legal document is defined. After submitting a transaction, the code of the relevant function is automatically executed by the distributed ledger system without further onerous input from either party.

Once the contract is digitized and placed on the blockchain, it will perform certain processes and the contract-like characteristics will begin to show when the first asset has been transferred. The first transaction normally transfers (creates) the assets for management on the blockchain, which are transferred or redistributed once again when certain conditions are met. In this stage, another party may join the smart contract by receiving an invite to become a participant. This can initiate automatic execution of other parts of the contract when meeting certain preconditions. This could mean that an action is triggered, such as raising a monthly insurance fee after a car crash or transferring a predetermined amount of cryptocurrency.

Examples of smart contracts

At times, the term "smart contract" can be misleading, for there are several types of smart contracts in existence. The most primitive type of a smart contract can be seen as a vending machine where you can submit transactions based on simple process automation. The vending machine offers X number of items and, after your selection, it returns the price of the asset, accepts your coins, returns any change, and finally hands over the item you bought. The vending machine completes the transaction on its own, without the help of a third party or a system. It delivers the item only after the necessary terms of the transaction are met, for example, after receiving a sufficient amount of money.

In this example, the vending machine (participant A) is the owner of the smart contract, and it knows what is available and what the terms are for each item (asset). Everyone (including you) who has sufficient funds to buy one of the available items can become a participating party (participant B). The smart contract defines the type of assets available, two types of participants, and a minimum of two simple transactions (or actions/methods). One transaction is for receiving the current price of an asset, and one transaction is for buying and handing off the asset. The second transaction receives the given amount of money and the item identification. The smart contract can decline the transaction when the amount of money is not sufficient, or if the asset is no longer available. This concept is illustrated in the following diagram:

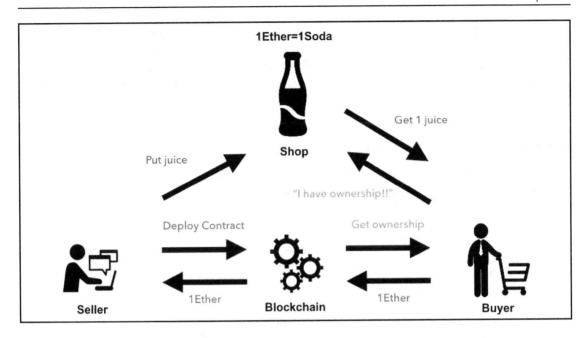

Vending machine smart contract example

You will experience a more complex example in upcoming chapters of this book. Imagine a blockchain network built to register (vehicle) accidents, informing first responders, and submitting accident details to insurance companies. An accident can be registered by a first responder, or, in our case, an **Internet of Things** (**IoT**) device/sensor inside the car. The first responder receives notification of the accident and can examine the data saved in the blockchain. The first responder can then send someone to the crash site who can review the same data and also update the accident report and add participants (including vehicles, drivers (noting their insurance company), injuries, and other damage). The report is then available for a case worker to process by assigning themselves to the case, and, when certain preconditions are met, the report can be shared directly with the insurance companies involved. An insurance company can query the blockchain as to which cases (accident reports) involved them and what is their status. When an insurance company needs to pay out an insurance claim, the contract can withdraw the amount of cryptocurrency representing the insurance claim automatically and send the funds to the receiving party.

In this case, the smart contract has multiple assets defined (such as accident, location, vehicle, and damaged goods), participant types (for example, driver, casualty, responder, case worker, and insurance company), transactions (such as registering the accident, assigning the accident to a case worker, and sending accident details to the insurance company), and even events (for example, the vehicle crash itself).

Multiple participants can interact with the same asset, and a transaction can expand over multiple assets and participants. The smart contract carries a single point of truth about the accident report, no matter who interacts with it. The smart contract knows who can perform (trans)actions on the report, and it can automatically decline certain actions when predefined conditions are not met.

Code example of a smart contract

To give you an idea of what a smart contract looks like from a code perspective, here is a simple example of assigning an accident to a case worker:

```
/**
 * Assign an Case woker to the accident report
 * @param {nl.amis.registry.accidents.AssignToCaseWorker}
assignToCaseWorker - the particular accident that you want to assign to a
responsible case worker
 * @transaction
 */
function AssignToCaseWorker(assignToCaseWorker) {
  if (assignToCaseWorker.accident.status !== 'OPEN')
    throw new Error('Case already assigned to an Case worker.');
  else {
    assignToCaseWorker.accident.status = 'ASSIGNED';
    assignToCaseWorker.accident.assignee = assignToCaseWorker.assignee;
  }
  return getAssetRegistry('nl.amis.registry.accidents.Accident')
  .then(function (assetRegistry) {
    return assetRegistry.update(assignToCaseWorker.accident);
  });
}
```

Summary

In this chapter, we continued our blockchain journey and explored the topics of security, privacy, and smart contracts, making it clear that we are not dealing with just an ordinary shared database. In the security section of this chapter, I explained that the blockchain is actually very secure, but it relies heavily on the way that you set up your network and the choice between a public and a private blockchain. I reviewed the unexpected security risks, the architecture of the network, the importance of the consensus protocol, how to store your assets securely, and how to control access.

In the next section of the chapter on privacy, I described what it takes to secure an individual's privacy on the blockchain. I discussed maintaining today's levels of privacy, from complex obfuscation to a simplified permissioned blockchain. I explained the available options, including cryptographically-secure obfuscation, indistinguishability obfuscation, secure multi-party computation, and zero-knowledge proofs.

Finally, in the last section of the chapter on smart contracts, I described the added value of smart contracts when operating a blockchain and how they can make automatic decisions based on program code. In this section, I explained smart contracts and described how they work. I also provided a few examples of both simple and complex smart contracts.

In the next chapter, I will combine the things that you have learned up to this point and go through the general flow of running a blockchain—from the network architecture to creating an application, submitting a transaction, and verifying transactions.

6
Understanding the Blockchain Data Flow

In Chapter 3, *Blockchain 101 - Assets, Transactions, and Hashes* and Chapter 4, *Blockchain 101 - Blocks, Chains, and Consensus*, I spoke about the building blocks of the blockchain—from assets and transactions to the chain of blocks, forks, and sidechains. I also addressed the way consensus is reached among all participants on the network. In Chapter 5, *Blockchain 101 - Security, Privacy, and Smart Contracts*, I explained what it takes to keep your blockchain and assets secure and introduced smart contracts.

In this chapter, I will combine what you learned about the blockchain previously and go over blockchain data flow and the processing of transactions. Beyond the basic data flow within a blockchain, I will explain the best way to design and set up a blockchain and how you can create, transfer, and manipulate assets.

Depending on the network's parameters, such as stricter validation rules, a blockchain transaction may be processed differently. In this chapter, you will learn about the effects of such parameters on the data flow of a transaction. A simple rule for a balance check will be presented as an example. Other, more complex rules, can be enforced during the execution of the corresponding business function within a smart contract.

In this chapter, you will learn about the following topics:

- What happens during the basic transaction and data flow on a blockchain?
- What are the architecture layers of a blockchain?
- How can you interact with a blockchain and transact assets?
- How and when are single transactions combined into a block?

Overview of the blockchain flow

Let's combine everything that we have learned so far and break down the flow of data and transactions in a blockchain. The technology (that is, the architecture, mechanisms, security, and so forth) behind the blockchain can be seen as the backbone for future accounting and an engine for a modern message transport system.

Basic flow of a transaction

Before going into the details of data flow on the blockchain, let's have a look at the blockchain's basic flow:

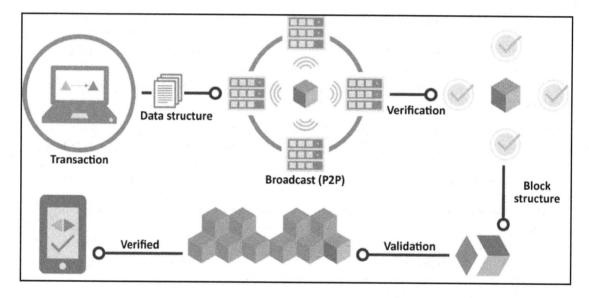

The basic flow allows for the secure management of a shared ledger (database of facts), where transactions are verified and stored on a network without a governing central authority. As I mentioned in the previous chapter, networks come in different forms and shapes, ranging from public open source to private, or permissioned blockchains, which require explicit permissions to read or write certain data or execute transactions. The blockchain is powered by advanced mathematics and computer science in the form of cryptographic hash functions, not just for secure transactions but also for protecting its integrity and anonymity. In the preceding diagram, we can see the following steps:

1. **Transaction**: Two parties want to exchange data that can represent any asset that can be described in digital form, such as money, contracts, deeds, incident or medical records, or vehicle details.

2. **Data structure**: The structure of data within a transaction can be both structured or unstructured. Structured data is often represented as JSON (key/value) documents.

3. **Broadcast** (P2P): The transaction is broadcast to all active nodes that are part of the blockchain network, which is actually a P2P network.

4. **Verification**: Depending on the network's parameters, a blockchain transaction is either verified instantly or transcribed into a secured record and placed in a queue of pending transactions. In the latter case, nodes, that is, the participating computers or servers in the network, determine whether the transactions are valid based on a set of rules to which the network participants have agreed.

5. **Block structure**: Over a certain period of time, verified transactions are combined in a block. Each block is identified by a 256-bit hash using an algorithm agreed upon the network, as I explained in Chapter 3, *Blockchain 101 - Assets, Transactions, and Hashes*. A block also contains a header, including the hash of the previous block, and its hash. The linked sequence of hashes creates a secure, independent, and indestructible chain.

6. **Validation**: Blocks must first be validated to be added to the blockchain. There are many forms of validation, also called consensus methods, as I explained in Chapter 4, *Blockchain 101 - Blocks, Chains, and Consensus*. When we are talking about cryptocurrencies, for example, which are transacted on public blockchains, this is where the "mining" (Proof of Work) or "minting" (Proof of Stake) process would happen. Private or permissioned blockchains use much lighter methods, such as Practical Byzantine Fault Tolerance, or either none or permissioned methods.

7. **Verified chain**: Certain nodes in the network try to solve the mathematical puzzle (for example, mining when using PoW) in order to validate a block. When validated, it is broadcast to all peers in the network and the block is verified by checking the solution. Each node adds the block to the majority (longest) chain of the immutable blockchain. If a malicious peer tries to submit an altered block to the chain, the other nodes can easily detect the changes and reject the block from the majority chain, preventing corruption of the data.

Architecture layers

Now that we have reviewed the basic steps of the data flow of the blockchain, let's translate them into the layered architecture used by a blockchain (or any digital ledger technology). Common architecture consists of the following layers:

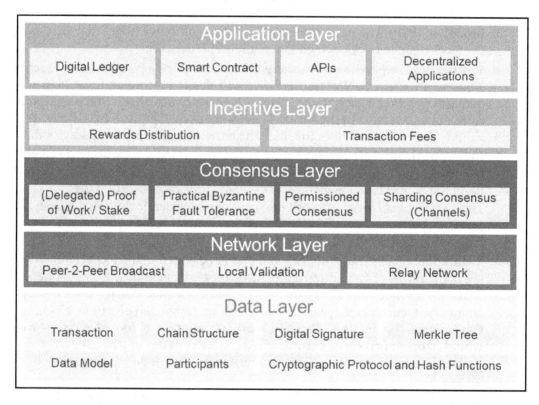

1. **Application layer**: This layer provides application interfaces on top of the blockchain, including smart contracts, a digital ledger, decentralized applications, and APIs. Ethereum, for example, lets you deploy programmable code (also called a smart contract) that can execute complex transactions. Blockstack, on the other hand, even allows you to run a decentralized frontend application.

2. **Incentive layer**: This optional layer distributes rewards or transaction fees earned by participants. Rewards are given in public blockchains to participants who solve a mathematical problem when verifying a block of transactions. Bitcoin, for example, rewards miners when they create a new block and Ethereum distributes received transaction fees.

3. **Consensus layer**: This layer designates a globally accepted set of transactions for processing, and it keeps a total or partial order of these transactions when validating the contents of individual transactions. A consensus method that we haven't seen a lot of to date is sharding. It offers one-to-one/one-to-many private channels, also known as separate chains for specific participating nodes. Ethereum is thinking of implementing sharding as part of their consensus method to overcome scalability issues (reference: `https://github.com/ethereum/EIPs/issues/53`).

4. **Network layer**: This layer propagates, or broadcasts, transactions among available peers in the network. One of the main issues it deals with is how to utilize fully the underlying network bandwidth. A permissioned blockchain, such as Hyperledger Fabric, for example, uses local validation to check that a transaction is not malicious before distributing it to all other nodes on the network.

5. **Data layer**: This layer deals with the data structure and physical storage of the blockchain. The data can be persisted, for example, to a document or NoSQL database in the form of a JSON (key/value) payload. The data structure, for example, allows a smart contract deployed to Ethereum or Hyperledger Fabric to interact with the data on the blockchain.

Architectural thoughts and considerations

To fully understand the basic flow of the data on a blockchain, I will go over the steps in more detail and explain which architectural layers are involved. For each of the steps, I will go over some thoughts and considerations when implementing your own custom blockchain and decentralized application.

Submitting transactions

The first step in the process or data flow is the submission of transactions to the blockchain. This is provided by the application layer. A transaction can be submitted through many different channels, such as web or mobile applications, cloud or SaaS applications, or by any decentralized application or system that can call (internet-connected) REST APIs. This is because most blockchains, or **DLT** (**distributed ledger technology**) software, expose REST or **CLI** (**command line interface**) APIs which these channels can use to interact with the blockchain.

What you will most likely encounter or build yourself is an application that uses these APIs to create and modify assets (for example, participants and data entities) and submit transactions based on a (predefined) data model. Transactions are registered in the distributed ledger, or immutable transaction log, and can lead to the execution of smart contracts (that is, business logic).

A smart contract can itself submit transactions without any user action if certain preconditions are met, for example, when certain data exists, because they run within a background process in a separate engine or virtual machine. In Chapter 12, *Designing and Developing Your First Smart Contract*, I will discuss in great detail how you can submit transactions and execute business logic.

Knowing the data structure

The available transactions, the data model used by these transactions, and the participants involved in the transactions are part of the data layer. When creating your own blockchain application, this is the best place to start. Just like any functional application, you need to start with a design-first approach. In the case of a blockchain application, it is best to start by designing the data model, for example, as shown in this simple UML diagram containing three assets and two participants:

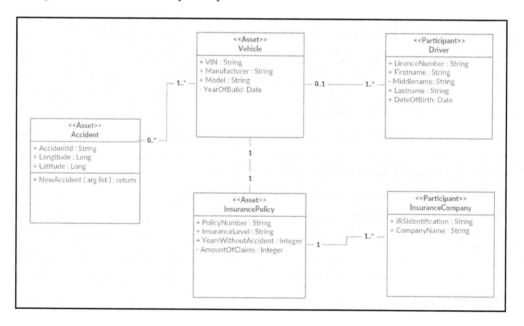

UML model containing the structure of accident and vehicle-related assets and participants

Data can be structured or unstructured, with structured indicating a human-readable document, and unstructured meaning raw, encoded, encrypted, or even binary data. When designing a blockchain application for enterprise use, you will mostly encounter or design a model that uses structured data. When data is privacy-sensitive or should be anonymous, you can choose to encrypt the data before submitting a transaction. However, it would still be structured data before encryption. In many cases, structured data comes in the form of a JSON document or key/value payload.

 A best practice is to design the data model (that is, the structured data objects/assets) from the perspective of the participant or user viewing the data. So, instead of modeling one big asset with all of the information that can ultimately be used by multiple participants, it is better to make smaller assets that are only used or viewed by specific participants. Doing this also makes it a lot easier to set fine-grained permissions.

The following example shows a structured data asset representing a vehicle:

```
{
   "assetType" : "Vehicle",
   "payload" : {
     "vin" : "1FMYU031X7KB97328",
     "manufacturer" : "BMW",
     "model": "M3",
     "yearOfBuild": "2018-10-10"
   }
}
```

The data model you design also includes describing the available transactions. For the preceding example, this might mean that a vehicle transaction needs the vehicle asset structure as its input to create a new asset, or it can reference an existing vehicle by its unique id (for example, its VIN number) when the vehicle is in an accident. In Chapter 8, *Ethereum Versus Hyperledger*, I will discuss how you can model assets, participants, and transactions in various blockchain software frameworks in greater detail.

Broadcasting and verifying data

Once you submit a transaction, which, in our example, includes a new vehicle asset, then the transaction and underlying data is broadcast to all active nodes on the network. The broadcast is provided by the network layer, and uses the peer-to-peer protocol to broadcast the data to the connected nodes. A peer can also relay transactions to other sidechains, so each part of the world can have its own local blockchain network.

However, the entire network would still be connected through these relay peers, as shown in the following map:

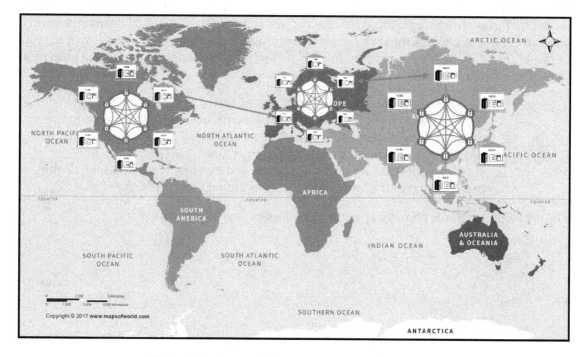

World map showing three separate blockchain networks connected to each using relay peers

 When designing your blockchain application and the underlying platform, the number of active nodes is an important question that an architect needs to answer.

For a permissioned blockchain, it is not necessary for every user to be a peer, but you need to have a minimum number of peers to run a stable network and eventually to be able to reach consensus. Also, the number of nodes has a direct impact on how the decentralized data is stored and how trust is maintained.

 When designing the platform, an architect needs to incorporate in their calculation the fact that nodes can disconnect from and connect to the network, so they always need to set up more nodes than are actually required. A network of nodes needs to consist of an uneven number so that the network can reach consensus on transaction; that is, 51% of all active nodes must agree on it.

My advice is to set up a minimum of seven validator nodes distributed among the various actors/partners within the network. This will allow a tolerance of two nodes to be offline or even be malicious at any one time. Depending on the network's parameters, the transaction is either verified instantly or transcribed into a secured record and placed in a queue of pending transactions. In this case, nodes—the participating computers or servers in the network—determine whether the transactions are valid based on a set of rules to which the network has agreed.

Combining TXs in a block structure

After a transaction is distributed and verified by the peers, over a certain time period, these transactions are combined into a block by the data layer until the maximum block size is reached (1 or more megabytes). The block size and structure can be different across networks depending on its parameters. The block structure used by Hyperledger Fabric, for example, is similar to the following structure:

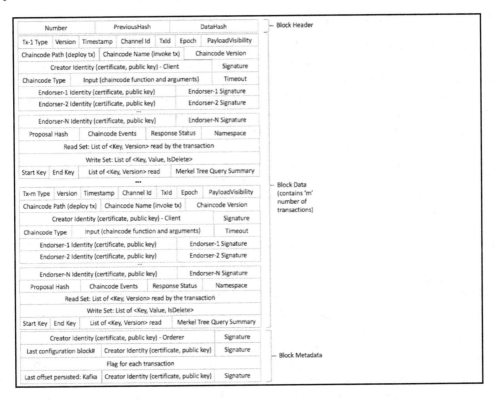

Technical structure of a block in Hyperledger Fabric

As shown in the preceding diagram, the block structure contains a header, data fields (for each transaction), and occasionally some extra metadata. The first set of fields identifies the header, which always includes a reference (hash) of the previous block in the chain. The previous hash is used as a parameter when generating the new hash. The linked sequence of these hashes goes all the way back to the first block, which creates a secure, independent, and indestructible chain. In some cases, the header also includes the solution to the mathematical puzzle (nonce) so that validators can easily verify the block.

The second set of data fields is different for most blockchain software frameworks out there. The data fields contain a variety of types of information, so that the peers in the network can verify and execute the transactions in the correct way using the software. For each transaction, these fields are repeated.

The third set of data fields holds extra metadata and is used to identify the peer that created the block.

Validating and verifying a block

After a peer combines a set of transactions into a block, which, depending on the network parameter, it can choose itself, for example, based on the incentive it receives, the block first needs to be validated by the majority of the network in order to be added to the blockchain. This is done by the consensus layer of the architecture. There are many forms of validation, or consensus methods. As I explained in `Chapter 4`, *Blockchain 101 - Blocks, Chains, and Consensus*, these consensus methods each work differently and can have different values for matching parameters. For example, the number of nodes available to reach consensus can be as little as 51%, but with some methods, such as the **Practical Byzantine Fault Tolerance** (**PBFT**), even two-thirds, or 67% of the nodes need to agree before a block is validated. Public blockchains typically use much more difficult and secure consensus methods than private or permissioned blockchains.

Public blockchains use consensus methods such as **Proof of Work** (**PoW**) or (Delegated) **Proof of Stake** (**PoS**). These methods propose a reward, which is part of the incentive layer, to peers to engage in the validation process of blocks. The PoW method, for example, gives the peer that mines the block a certain amount of assets (for example, Bitcoin) in return, plus additional transaction fees (that is, an amount of cryptocurrency) given by the participants who submit the transactions in order to get them validated much faster. Other methods, such as PoS, only work with transaction fees. As I explained previously, the amount of reward/transaction fees, and from whom these fees need to be transferred, will become part of the block's data. Private and permissioned blockchains use much lighter, quicker, and cost-efficient consensus methods, and, in contrast to public blockchains, they do not provide an incentive to participating nodes.

When a block is validated by a peer, it is broadcast to all peers in the network and the block is verified by checking the validity of the block or the given solution to the mathematical problem. If the block is accepted by the peer, it is added to the longest chain of which it is currently aware. In most cases, this is the chain on which the majority reached consensus. If a malicious peer submits (broadcasts) an altered block to the rest of the network, the other nodes can easily detect the changes and reject the block from the majority chain, preventing corruption of the data. If your transaction is included in a validated block and added to the majority chain, depending on the consensus method used, you still have to wait a few blocks until you can be really sure that your transaction is processed. The majority can still reject the block. Based on the block generation time of the network (up to 10 minutes), you can calculate the time it takes before you can be sure that your transaction is accepted. Networks using consensus methods that don't work with an incentive mechanism usually don't have this drawback, and you can be assured that the transaction is verified after it is added to the chain.

Summary

In this chapter, I combined the things you learned during the last three chapters, and, in a brief recap, reviewed the basic flow of data and transactions on a blockchain. I also described how the data is processed in a step-by-step approach. Besides the flow of data, I explained the layers that are part of the architecture used by a blockchain. In the sections that followed, I went into each step of the data and transaction flow and explained them in more detail. The goal of this chapter was to map certain terms learned in previous chapters to the basic flow and the layer architecture of the blockchain.

I continued by answering the question of how a transaction can be initiated using different kinds of channels using the available APIs and native client SDKs, which are part of the application layer of the architecture. I explained that when implementing a new blockchain application, it is best to start with the data model and always design it through the eyes of the participant/end user.

I reviewed the process of how submitted transactions are broadcast to other peers in the network through the use of the peer-to-peer protocol of the network layer and how each peer verifies the submitted transaction on its own. Depending on the network's parameters, a transaction can either be verified immediately or put into a secure queue of pending transactions. When a transaction is received by a peer, it determines whether the transaction is valid based on a set of rules, which can be checked by a smart contract.

Finally, I answered the question of how and when single transactions are combined into a block. I explained that the structure of a block includes a set of transactions, a reference to the previous block, and some extra metadata to verify whether the created block is valid and not maliciously altered. I looked back at the different consensus methods available, and explained that public blockchains generally use different, more secure, but costly methods that include incentives for solving a mathematical puzzle required for making a block valid, whereas private or permissioned blockchains use much lighter, quicker, and cost-efficient methods without an incentive model. After a block is created, it is broadcast, just like a transaction, to all peers in the network to be verified. Verified blocks are added to the majority (longest) chain of the blockchain.

In the next chapter, I will explain in more detail the differences between public, private, and permissioned blockchains. We will explore some of the current providers on the market for each of these types of blockchains and what their added value can be for your blockchain applications.

7
Public Versus Permissioned Blockchains and their Providers

In chapter 3 through chapter 5, I explained the core concepts and terminology of a blockchain. In the previous chapter, I combined everything we had learned up to that point into a brief summary. Then, taking a step-by-step approach, I mapped certain terminology to the actual steps of the data processing flow in a blockchain and the layered architecture behind it. I described how transactions can be submitted, the differences between structured and unstructured data, how single transactions are combined into a block and a block's structure, and explained how the process of broadcasting and verifying blocks throughout the whole network works.

Back in Chapter 5, *Blockchain 101 - Security, Privacy, and Smart Contracts*, I began explaining the main differences between public and private blockchain networks. In this chapter, I will delve deeper into describing the differences between public and private (or permissioned) blockchains. I will take you on a journey through the current blockchain providers on the market. This chapter explains their differences at the network level, the advantages and disadvantages of each type, how you can start a blockchain network yourself, and what providers are currently available for each type of blockchain.

In this chapter, you will learn about the following topics:

- What types of blockchain currently exist?
- How to choose the right type of blockchain based on the differences between the blockchain types, the advantages and disadvantages of each type, and the challenges of working with particular blockchains?
- Which public and private providers are currently on the market and what is their mission?

What types of blockchain currently exist?

Over the years, many blockchains have evolved, and the terminology used to describe them is often misinterpreted. In general, there are three types of blockchain: a **public blockchain**, a **consortium**, and a **private blockchain**. It is easy to confuse them due to the many similarities between the blockchain types. As explained in the previous chapter, all blockchain types follow the same data flow, use the same layered architecture, and follow similar rules when executing and validating transactions. All blockchains are decentralized peer-to-peer networks, which distribute submitted transactions to each participant. Each participant has a replica of the shared ledger, in which digitally-signed transactions are appended. Blockchains keep replicas in sync through the network's consensus protocol, which provides certain guarantees of the immutability of the ledger, even when some of the participants are offline or are behaving in a malicious manner.

Back in `Chapter 5`, *Blockchain 101 - Security, Privacy, and Smart Contracts*, I explained the differences between public and private blockchains on a security level, and that a consortium blockchain is partially private. In this chapter, I will recap the three types of blockchains and discuss them in greater detail. For each type of blockchain, I will review its advantages, disadvantages, and the challenges that working with it presents.

Public blockchains

When using a public blockchain, virtually anyone in the world can access and read transactions. Furthermore, anyone in the world can send transactions and see them once they are valid and included in the blockchain. Finally, anyone can choose to participate in the consensus (validation) process to assist in authenticating transactions to determine which get added to the blockchain and to verify the current form and status of the blockchain. Using third-party blockchain explorers, the origins of a single asset can be tracked all the way back to its creation.

Advantages

Some of the major advantages of a public blockchain are as follows:

- **Everybody can join**: You can become a member of the blockchain network as easily as by downloading and installing the required software on your computer device. Software can be downloaded from the website of the blockchain platform provider and, in most cases, in multiple formats (full or light client). Clients can usually be installed on Windows, macOS, and Linux-based desktops/laptops, but some offer clients for different devices, such as mobile phones and USB-based hardware wallets. Since everybody can join the network, a public blockchain is designed to cut out centralized monopolies or "middlemen," and they reduce costs, for example, by providing a huge network out-of-the-box). This not only increases competition in the market, but by making it easy to join, it puts pressure on all participants to become more efficient.

- **Trustless**: A public blockchain is generally considered decentralized, and one of its main advantages is that it is *permissionless* or *trustless*. Without knowing the geographic location of a user, public blockchains have shared equality and power to help reach a consensus before any data is stored. There is no requirement for trust, since the consensus protocol serves this purpose. By distributing to many nodes and using the consensus protocol to synchronize them, it allows participants who do not know each other to believe that the transaction between them is performed and that it is real. Since a public blockchain can have an infinite number of nodes, or "peers," it is close to impossible to undo transactions, which makes them fairly immutable.

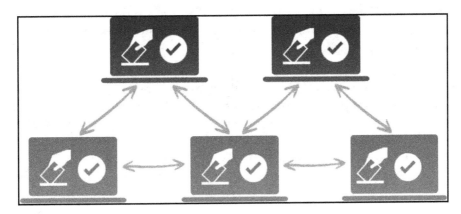

Reaching a consensus about transactions serves as trust in a trustless system

- **Privacy:** By design, a public blockchain attempts to protect your identity. Every participant is identified by a wallet, as explained in `Chapter 5`, *Blockchain 101 - Security, Privacy, and Smart Contracts*, which can be created anonymously without connecting it to a physical identity. Thus, participants can conduct transactions with each other without knowing each other's real identity.

- **Influence:** Most public blockchains are secured by **cryptoeconomics**, a combination of economic incentives (for example, financial reward or transaction fees) and cryptographic verification. A public blockchain is guided by a general principal, in which a participant's degree of influence in the consensus process is proportional to the quantity of economic resources they bring to the table (that is, hashing power) or share (such as, wealth in the network). Thus, users are willing to invest in the network to gain more influence.

Also consider the benefits of the following application features of a public blockchain:

- **Crowdfunding**: For example, an **Initial Coin Offering** (**ICO**) to fund your yet-to-be-built blockchain application. With an ICO, you can raise money and use the currency in your final application as a way of payment.

- **Decentralized cloud storage**: On a platform such as *WeTransfer*, for example, you can upload files that are stored on participating nodes in small fragments. When somebody wants to download a file, the fragments are combined to regenerate the original file.

- **Buy and sell goods**: On a platform like *TicketSwap*, you can buy and sell tickets to events. TicketSwap can run its own cryptocurrency, without the need for real-world money.

- **Loyalty program**: With a frequent flyer program of a supermarket savings program, saved points can easily be used in other financial ecosystems.

Challenges

Here are some of the challenges, or disadvantages, of using a public blockchain:

- **Wasteful and limited scalability**: In order to maintain a consensus across a public blockchain, every (full) node needs to run the entire blockchain. Each node in the network repeats the same task (for example, executing a smart contract) to reach a consensus, which eats up a lot of time and electricity along the way. This process makes the execution of tasks (that is, computations) extremely slow and more expensive than on a traditional centralized computer or shared database. The time required to process a block of transactions can take anywhere from seconds to minutes, and during peak periods, it can even take longer. Compare that with the almost instantaneous transaction confirmations of traditional systems. While a decentralized consensus mechanism offers the core benefits of a blockchain, it comes at the cost of scalability since, by design, decentralization limits the number of transactions that a blockchain can process. Thus, the two practical limitations here are low throughput and slow transaction times. We saw the direct impact of these constraint on the Ethereum network. In late 2017, a game called CryptoKitties, where you could breed your own crypto cat, accounted for 10% of all network traffic on the main net of Ethereum. Due to the game's popularity, the use of the network grew exponentially and slowed down other transactions.

List of cryptokitties that were available to buy at the peak of the game's success on Ethereum network

- **Storage constraints**: Another drawback of a public blockchain is that the data stored on it expands more rapidly when you run your blockchain application on your own network. For nodes to profit from economic incentives, they need to run the entire blockchain, and as the size of the blockchain grows, the requirements for computer power, storage, and bandwidth also increase. At some point, this becomes cumbersome and only feasible for the few nodes that can afford the resources to process blocks. On large implementations of a public blockchain, this leads to the use of smaller ledgers and the risk of centralization. Since not every node can carry a full copy of the blockchain, using a smaller version can potentially affect its immutability and consensus. Due to the higher barrier to operating as a full node, it leads to a larger amount of centralization, in which bigger players are able to seize greater control over the network. Both scenarios are undesirable for an enterprise blockchain application, and will likely affect the use cases of blockchain variants.

- **Network speed and cost**: The economic incentives provided by a public blockchain can have a negative impact on network speed and cost. As traffic increases, transactions become more expensive to execute quickly. When the number of submitted transactions is larger than the network can handle, nodes will seek higher rewards for completing transactions in a supply and demand fashion. This leads to slower transactions and higher costs, since nodes prioritize transactions that offer higher rewards, building up a backlog of transactions. In this case, if your blockchain application is running on such a network, you or your users will need to pay higher transaction fees to complete a transaction more quickly.

- **Tight to speculative markets**: Public blockchains generally run on cryptoeconomics and use token/currency models to fund the development of blockchain applications (ICOs) or to manage the economics of nodes. For example, on the Ethereum network, the Ether (ETH) currency is used to pay for computation power (also called Gas). The value of these cryptocurrencies is highly volatile. While the value of currencies like EUR and USD (also called Fiat currencies-reference: https://en.wikipedia.org/wiki/Fiat_money) are linked to their respective economies, which are regulated and generally stable, cryptocurrencies like BTC and ETH are not. Cryptocurrency markets are lightly regulated, highly speculative, and thus are prone to rapid fluctuations and manipulations, leading to spiking values. For example, a cryptocurrency can be valued at $100 USD one day and $90 USD the next—a fluctuation of 10%. As seen recently with Bitcoin, an established cryptocurrency can fluctuate thousands of dollars over a period of days. Negative fluctuations present a high degree of uncertainty for projects developed on a blockchain.

- **Immutable smart contracts**: As explained earlier, one of the advantages of a public blockchain is its immutability. Besides the effect that immutability has on transactions and blocks, it also has the same effect on smart contracts. Once added to the blockchain, it cannot be changed or manipulated. A drawback of this effect is that if there are any flaws in the code that results in your application not working as intended, or in such a way that hackers might even exploit it, these flaws are there forever. This is not a concern if your smart contract is not being used, but flaws in the smart contract code can lead to a large loss in value/assets. As the public blockchain is immutable, these transactions are difficult to undo. When designing a smart contract on a public blockchain, test it first in a sandbox environment. Also, always build in a kill switch and include a version number in the name because, in a public blockchain, the name of a smart contract cannot be reused. One example of a smart contract gone wrong is the story of the DAO (reference: `https://www.multichain.com/blog/2016/06/smart-contracts-the-dao-implosion/`), where bugs in the code lost a lot of money for a lot of people, which could not be solved because of immutable code.

- **Privacy may be more limited**: It is a given that transactions on a public blockchain are not directly tied to your real-world identity and appear to be more private. On the one hand, this is certainly true since transactions are recorded and stored in a public shared ledger, but they are only linked to your pseudonym, which is an endpoint (or account) address. Without a real-world identity attached to it, it appears that the originator of the transactions is impossible to track. However, this is a false sense of security. Your privacy is preserved as long as your pseudonym (wallet) is not linked back to you. Once anyone makes the connection to your real-world identity, you are no longer anonymous. For example, when running your application on a public blockchain, exposing its functionality through your website, web trackers and cookies can easily track and leak information about a transaction. When leaked onto the web, anyone, including a malicious user/hacker, government agency, or law enforcement organization, can make use of that information. With platforms such as Ethereum, this allow users to interact with smart contracts, which can have a much greater impact. All of the details, including transaction data, its metadata (sender and recipients), and the executed code and state are stored publicly.

 WARNING: A public blockchain shouldn't be used for critical business data, where unauthorized parties (including competitors and hackers) can view the information.

- **Software updates**: The last drawback to address when running your application on a public blockchain is software updates. When nodes perform software updates, this can potentially lead to a "fork" in the chain when the blockchain community is divided over the changes it brings. Nodes that are running newer software will accept different transactions than nodes running an older version of the software. When the community is divided, the fork will create a new blockchain with the same history, but it will continue separately for participants who are running the newer versus the older software. This means that your application (smart contract) will also run on multiple networks.

Now consider the following items to be avoided for applications on a public blockchain:

- **Sharing identity (verification) data**: Avoid sharing information such as social security numbers, which should not be stored publicly in any event. Also, since the data on a public blockchain is immutable, you will have a big challenge when, following the **GDPR (General Data Protection Regulation)** ruling (an EU law on data protection, giving people the right to be forgotten-reference: `https://en.wikipedia.org/wiki/General_Data_Protection_Regulation`), you are asked to remove the data you have collected.
- **Financial and legal documents**: Avoid revealing such documents, which can be publicly-associated with real-world identities or addresses that can be easily traced.
- **Electronic medical records**: These personal records contain extremely private and sensitive information. Making this information public jeopardizes patient confidentially.

Consortium blockchain

When using this type of blockchain, the consensus process is controlled by a (pre) selected set of nodes. You can say that a consortium blockchain is partially private. For example, imagine a consortium of seven entities, consisting of four ministries (or departments), a regulator node, and two validator nodes, in which five nodes need to verify (sign) every block in order to be valid. Consortium blockchains fall into the category of permissioned blockchains. They differ solely based on the built-in presence of an access controller layer in the node software. Permissions to read may be public or restricted to any of the participants, and together with API restrictions, it is possible to limit the number of queries that participants can make. Furthermore, it allows the network to appoint a group of participants who are given write permissions on given asset types and transactions, or the authority to validate blocks of transactions. Finally, participants can only see transactions in which they participate or have been granted permission to see.

Advantages

Some of the major advantages of a consortium blockchain are as follows:

- **Known validators and well-connected nodes**: The main distinguishing factor of a consortium blockchain is that the validators are (pre) selected nodes and are known to every participant in the network. Think of these nodes as trusted elders within a council that decides who has read and/or write access to the blockchain ledger. Thus, any risk of malicious entities colluding and performing a 51% attack does not apply to this network, since it is easily detectable and can involve legal action. Trusted entities can also be considered well-connected nodes. Owing to the mutual agreements in place and their stake in the network, these trusted entities tend to keep the node running 24/7 on highly-available and fast internet connections. A node can always go offline and this would not result in any disruptions, since the network would be large enough to handle this. This type of blockchain is beneficial for an organization that wants to collaborate within a single country's borders, or with other trusted entities outside of them.

- **Better performance**: There is little doubt that consortium (or "permissioned") blockchain networks offer better performance than public blockchains in general. Both types require full nodes that perform all computations redundantly, but since a consortium blockchain has a preselected number of nodes to validate a transaction, the time needed to reach a consensus is much less. Another reason a consortium blockchain offers better performance than a public blockchain is that it runs a limited number of applications—usually just one. Compare this with running a full node on a public blockchain, where a node has to deal with all computations for all applications on the network—not just the application that you offer or use on it. On some consortium blockchains, like Hyperledger Fabric, it is even possible to make one-to-one or one-to-many channels, over which participants can communicate, where each channel has its own shared ledger. This way, it is possible to run different applications on each channel.

- **More cost-efficient**: The consensus method employed by a consortium blockchain generally differs from the methods used by public blockchains. The methods used on a consortium blockchain are much lighter because of the existing trust between the participating entities. Heavy-duty consensus methods such as PoW and PoS do not apply here. This makes combining transactions into a block and validating such blocks by other peers a lot less time-consuming. Compared to a PoW consensus, solving a mathematical puzzle is not required, which costs less energy (that is, lower CPU/GPU computations) and higher block-generation times. Compared to a PoS consensus, no transaction fees are required when submitting your transaction or for your transaction to be processed by incentive-driven nodes.

- **Better governance**: Enterprises that are thinking of placing their business processes into consortiums, or who already have such a business model and are seeking ways to use blockchain technology, need a network that can change direction. By comparison, public blockchains are run and controlled by every participant, so it is challenging to perform governance when it comes to ensuring network evolution and updates to its rulebook and interaction models. Since the majority of the network needs to agree on these changes, innovation is slow. Using a consortium (or permissioned) blockchain network, however, allows for transparent governance within the group of participating entities only. In this sense, it is certainly easier to ensure innovation and network evolution. At times, it still can be challenging, though, since some participants don't have the financial budget to support such changes, or will not back these changes. Nevertheless, it is less challenging to convince one participant than it is to persuade half of the world. As a consortium, you can iteratively choose to address very specific business problems and optimize the network, for example, making changes to the consensus method, access control, or the application itself (such as, smart contracts). In the end, with a consortium blockchain, it is much easier to govern changes and the impact that they have on the business processes running on the network.

- **Access control**: One of the main properties of a consortium blockchain is that it is permissioned. This is secured by the access control layer, which is baked into the node software. Using access control, the network administrator can grant permission to nodes to participate in the consensus process, grant read and write access on assets to nodes or fine-grained application/user roles, allow deploy and execute permissions on smart contracts, and grant privileges to other participants to become a network administrator. Generally, this is accomplished through an identity service that manages and authenticates all participants on the network in combination with access control lists that provide an additional layer of authorization on specific network operations. Because this access control layer is baked into every node, nodes can perform a lot of local validation. When a transaction is submitted by a participant, the receiving node can locally validate if the participant has the required permissions. If not, the node can reject the transaction immediately without broadcasting it to the rest of the network.

- **Better privacy**: Such a permissions model directly improves privacy on the network. For example, participants can only see and interact with data for which they have permission. This can be personally-submitted transactions or transactions in which they are involved. So, although participants know each other, they do not know what each other is doing. Of course, the shared ledger contains all of the data, but it is only accessible to validator nodes and possibly network administrators. For groups of entities that require private or confidential transactions, some consortium blockchains offer the concept of channels. These channels are separate messaging paths that are restricted to a subset of participants on the network who want to improve their privacy even more. All data on a channel is saved in its own shared ledger, coexisting on the same network, and only visible and accessible to participants explicitly granted access to the channel. You can say that this data is on a need-to-know basis.

- **Interoperability**: A consortium blockchain can host multiple applications, just like a mobile app store. However, unlike mobile apps, blockchain applications running on the same network are interoperable, which means that they can talk to each other and share data as long as they have the respective permissions to do so. As a developer, this enables you to reuse smart contracts (code) and build them into your own, more complex application. For example, a loan provider can reuse a credit check module from the **Internal Revenue Service (IRS)** application running on the same network.

Consider the benefits of the following features of a consortium blockchain:

- **Digital identity**: A consortium blockchain is a platform that allows individuals to own and control their (digital) identity. Individuals can decide what data they want to disclose to counter-parties. The consortium does not have to hold sensitive data to verify transactions—it only needs to verify the permissions on the data.

- **Automated mortgage contracts**: Imagine a consortium of mortgage brokers, mortgage holders, insurers, and the IRS. When an individual wants to buy a house and needs a loan, without working through a bank (as a trusted middleman), the parties are automatically connected, providing a less error-prone process. Using smart contract payments that can be processed automatically, property liens can be released when the loan is paid, and required insurance payments can be settled (for example, due to the untimely death of the borrower). All of the data of the smart contract would be visible to all participating entities in that contract.

- **Supply chain**: A consortium blockchain is a platform that can provide real-time visibility for every step in the chain. Imagine a consortium of factories, warehouses, and stores that use IoT-connected devices to record each step as a product moves from a factory floor to the shelves in a store. Such a platform would offer enhanced tracking and verification, reducing the risk of theft and fraud.

- **Vehicle insurance**: Think about a consortium of drivers, insurers, emergency services, and vehicle repair shops. Together, they operate a blockchain running an application that can record insurance policies, driver reports, and driving records. This consortium allows an IoT-equipped vehicle to execute a claim automatically when it is involved in an accident. The application supports automated claim processing, verification, fraud detection, and payment, eliminating duplicate reports and sharing all data in a transparent manner so that repair shops don't have to contact the insurance company first before repairing the car, because they already know that the claim is approved and payment will be made.

Challenges

Now consider the following potential obstacles when using a consortium blockchain:

- **Bringing the consortium together**: When setting up a consortium blockchain, the first challenge is bringing all participating entities together, and just as with any IT integration project, reaching a consensus about the architecture of the network, the data model, smart contracts, network governance, regulations, and so on. Every entity may have their own opinion, and how long the initial setup of the consortium takes is dependent on the size of the consortium at the start. By way of comparison, when deploying an application on a public blockchain, the network and governance of the nodes is already in place. Try to keep the initial consortium simple, and expand it in stages. Start with only the key players and a single application.

- **Power over permissions**: Another challenge when forming a consortium is deciding who has the power to grant permissions to participating entities and end users. As a consortium, you will have to decide which nodes can participate in the consensus, which entities can invite other nodes to join the consensus process, and who can grant read, write, execute, and deploy permissions. It is also important to appoint someone who has the jurisdiction to intervene when it comes to reversing transactions due to legal reasons. A good approach is to have a regulator entity who performs the initial blockchain setup, authorizes would-be consortium members to join the network, grants permissions to all or some of the members to join the consensus process, and assigns a network administrator for each (key) entity so that they can grant the rest of the permissions.
Network administrators are responsible for the governance of the network, authorizing end users, setting up channels, deploying applications, and keeping the network running. End users or applications that integrate with the blockchain don't necessarily have to hold any power over network permissions.

- **Too many chains**: There is a great risk to all of the consortium blockchains in development that the private space is becoming fragmented. Many projects are simultaneously in development, and companies are forming islands of consortia, each developing a specific blockchain implementation. For example, at the time of writing, there are four blockchain technologies in use by different consortia of banks, namely Ripple, R3, Quorum, and Hyperledger. Having multiple blockchains serve the same purpose is undesirable due to the fragmentation of users across networks and the fragmentation of (interoperable) applications. Before investing in the development of your own blockchain, always check to be sure there isn't already one available that meets your needs. If you do blockchain and fragment the space within a specific business domain (such as banking), then the benefits of blockchain may be severely restricted.

- **Fragmentation of users**: Since each blockchain generally uses a different protocol and implementation, it automatically leads to interoperability problems between consortium networks, which results in different storage models, privacy and confidentiality regimes, and permission controls. The benefit each member receives by participating in one of the consortiums is directly in proportion to the number of members in its network. For example, what if there are 1,000 financial institutions evenly distributed across each of the four consortia. If so, each member can only interact with 250 members at most. Challenges arise when a member needs to interact with someone outside the consortium. These challenges include the following:

1. Will both networks maintain the records?
2. Can someone be part of both consortia using the same credentials?
3. Can you trust the information from the other side?
4. How long does payment settlement take due to this factor?

These challenges are very similar to the ones that we face today, even without using a blockchain.

- **Fragmentation of applications**: As discussed previously, a consortium blockchain can host many applications. The challenge for developers in the fragmented landscape of available consortium blockchains is that the available apps may also be fragmented across these networks. For example, if you a want to take out loan and go to a finance company, they need to perform a credit check and get employment information from each different blockchain application. What if these are scattered across multiple blockchains and the loan company is unable to access one of the required records. In that case, the finance company may choose not to lend you the money, or do so on less favorable terms. Currently, fragmentation of data may make consortium blockchains a less-than-ideal option.

- **Integration concerns**: The last challenge to address is an extension of the previous one. It occurs when attempting to integrate a blockchain with existing IT systems and (cloud) applications. Currently, there are no standard protocols for integrating such systems with the various available blockchains. Most consortium blockchains offer RESTful APIs (web services) and native **Software Development Kits** (**SDKs**), but they all work differently (for example, different message structures and operations). The challenge is to try to decouple the blockchain APIs through an integration layer so that the existing applications can easily interact with the blockchain using tailored contracts. Some third-party tooling may be available, however. For example, Hyperledger Composer offers customized RESTful APIs based on the deployed application that is running on the Hyperledger network.

Finally, think about the following, which should be avoided for applications on a consortium blockchain:

- **Streaming data**: For applications that deal with millions of transactions, such as a streaming service like Spotify, no single blockchain can scale to that level at present. Spotify has over 30 million songs in its catalog, and serves billions of streams a day (source: `https://spotifycharts.com/`). The same goes for mid-scale IoT applications that regenerate a lot of raw data. Don't put those transactions on a blockchain.

- **Document sharing**: Document management systems that store physical copies of documents can clog up the available space in the block and might not even fit due to the file size of the documents stored. Always store physical files separately from the blockchain—documents just record the link to the file.

Private blockchains

This type of blockchain works in virtually the same way as a consortium blockchain, however, the network control and write permissions are maintained by one organization or entity (centralized) and so they are fully private. Furthermore, authorization for read permissions may be public or restricted to an arbitrary extent. Finally, private blockchains also fall into the category of permissioned blockchains and thus provide the same benefits, such as setting permissions on individual entities or end users. Types of applications that would likely run on a private blockchain include auditing, database replication, and internal usage for a single company. In many cases, the data doesn't have to be readable publicly, but in other cases, such as permit requests, it is possible to configure a public user so that data can be audited by the public through a (central) website. If a private blockchain application is used correctly, it can be very effective in documenting the actions of each individual entity or end user for accountability purposes.

Advantages

Some of the major advantages of a private blockchain are as follows:

- **Distributed database**: Imagine a database that needs to be highly available, meaning that there are one or more backup copies, or "slaves" of the primary database, or "master." The primary database runs on high-end hardware and is closely monitored for problems, with transactions being replicated to backup copies. If the master database goes down (for example, due to a power outage or hardware failure), one of the slave databases at a different physical location will take over and become the new primary, or master, database location. With a standard database, the data is replicated between the master and the slave databases, usually in near real-time. To make standard databases highly available, however, you need to employ a combination of expensive infrastructure and data recovery procedures. There are many techniques available for replication, but normally at runtime only one of the databases is active while the others are in a passive state.

The advantage of using a private blockchain is that the data is replicated through the distribution of transactions to every location represented by a node in the network using the peer-to-peer network. All nodes are active and should have the same data available at runtime. They can be accessed individually, so there are, in essence, only "active databases." In addition, extra copies (nodes) can be added to or removed from the network without a lot of preparation and configuration. For example, instead of having three physical locations running the same high-end hardware, where two of the databases are idle most of the time, which is very expensive and notoriously difficult to maintain, you can have 10 blockchain nodes running on commodity hardware, on different sides of the world, that are all accessible simultaneously. So, whereas a central database generally uses master-slave type replication, a private blockchain is distributed, similar to multi-master replication (https://en.wikipedia.org/wiki/Multi-master_replication).

- **Ensuring consistency**: As with every other type of blockchain, transactions and data are distributed to all nodes (or "databases") in a private network. Even if a central database is perfectly trusted, a private blockchain can be seen as a new method of ensuring consistency. The blockchain technology prevents double spending, meaning two concurrent transactions cannot change the same data. This is theoretically similar to how a relational database uses **multiversion concurrency control** (**MVCC**) (https://en.wikipedia.org/wiki/Multiversion_ concurrency_control) or **optimistic concurrency control** (**OCC**)(https://en. wikipedia.org/wiki/Optimistic_concurrency_control) to prevent two transactions from modifying the same row in a database. This is done by implementing a confirmation mechanism to prevent the same record from being modified simultaneously using a chronologically-ordered and time-stamped transaction log. For example, Hyperledger Fabric uses an Apache Kafka-based order to control concurrency.
- **Ensuring performance**: As there are multiple copies of the database available at different physical locations, the end user can choose to query data from the location nearest to them. So, in locations where the internet is not always stable or connections speeds are slow (for example, in foreign countries), they can still access the data on the blockchain fairly quickly.

- **Disintermediation**: A private blockchain lets you share a database across boundaries of trust without requiring a central administrator. The advantage here is that transactions contain their own validity and authorization checks, and because of the consensus mechanism, those transactions can be verified and processed by each node independently, ensuring that all nodes stay in sync. This disintermediation has added value over a shared relational or NoSQL/document database, because even though a database consists of just bits and bytes that store the contents in memory and on disk on a particular server, anybody with sufficient access to that server can corrupt the data and destroy the database from within. This is much harder to do with a private blockchain, since every node in the network has a copy of the data, and a malicious user would need to perform the same attack to 51% of all of the network's nodes in order to succeed. Furthermore, when entrusting data to a single, shared, centralized database, every user becomes dependent on the people or organization that administers the database. In most organizations, this is not a problem, because users have earned this trust. However, the organization needs to have a bunch of people and processes in place in order to prevent such an attack. Hiring people and designing processes take both time and money. As with many technologies that came before it, a private blockchain can replace part of this human organization with a distributed database, enclosed by smart permissions and cryptography of the data. Moreover, once smart contracts are written and well debugged, using a a private blockchain tends to be a lot cheaper.

Some of the major advantages of a private blockchain are as follows:

- **Inter-departmental auditing**: A private blockchain application designed for the police force, for example, could track accountability for each individual entity or end user working for the police force. When data on a subject or a restricted web service is queried, it's logged in the blockchain instead of in a central system that is under the administrative control of a specific department. All departments have access to the data, making it difficult to erase occurrences of unauthorized access. It also allows departments to find patterns between unauthorized access across multiple systems.
- **Distributed databases**: Consider any system of records that is replicated over multiple passive (or even active) instances. Instead of replicating it, the data in a private blockchain is distributed in a manner similar to hard drives functioning in a **RAID (Redundant Array of Independent Disks)** (`https://en.wikipedia.org/wiki/RAID`).

Challenges

Now consider the following potential barriers to using a private blockchain:

- **Confidentiality**: As explained earlier, nodes that are participating in the consensus process can independently verify and process every transaction. This is possible because these nodes have full visibility of the current state of the database, all modifications (requested by transactions), and the digital signature that proves the origin of a transaction. This full transparency for each node can be a deal breaker for certain applications (for example, financial applications). Like private blockchains, standard databases restrict the queries that a user can perform, but these restrictions are only imposed at one central location, and the full database only needs to be visible at that location, rather than having full visibility on every node. Requests to read and write data go through the central human organization that administers the database, which can choose to accept or reject those requests. Hiding information on a private blockchain requires cryptography of the data and the related computational power of the nodes in the network. So, if confidentiality is your only goal, and trusting of database administrators is not, then a private blockchain has no clear advantages over a centralized database.

- **Performance**: While private blockchains can ideally be used for a system of records or a transaction platform, they will always be considered slower than centralized databases. This is not just because blockchain technology is still new and likely unoptimized, but it is also due to the nature of the technology, which causes some sacrifices in speed. While the nodes in the network work independently, they do not share processing power. Each node does the same work simultaneously, and then they compare their results with the rest of the network until a consensus is reached about the submitted transactions. Performance is also influenced by the signature verification process of each transaction, because they must be signed using a public-private key cryptography scheme, such as **ECDSA (Elliptic Curve Digital Signature)** (https://en.wikipedia.org/wiki/Elliptic_Curve_Digital_Signature_Algorithm), so the source of the transaction can be proven. The generation and verification of such signatures is complex and requires numerous computations. By comparison, once a connection to a centralized database has been established, each individual transaction or request does not need to be verified. In conclusion, a private blockchain can do all of the same things as a regular database, but it carries with it these three additional burdens:

- **High performance**: When transactions must respond or be committed in a millisecond, a (private) blockchain will be too slow.
- **No complex business logic**: When you have no need for smart contracts or any business logic, but just need a database for simple data storage, a private blockchain is overkill.
- **No need to keep things private**: When your data doesn't have to be private and, moreover, is publicly available, the cryptography and consensus of a private blockchain will just slow your application down.

Public blockchain providers

Now that we know the difference between the types of blockchain, let's go on a tour of the various blockchain providers, starting with the most widely-used and including anticipated platforms available for decentralized applications. In the public space, we will explore four platforms: *Ethereum*, *Neo*, *IPFS*, and *Blockstack*, but the number of platforms is growing fast.

Collection of public blockchain platforms

Ethereum

Ethereum is one of the longest-existing public blockchains. It is an open platform that lets you build, run, and use decentralized applications using blockchain technology. It is an open source project created by Vitalik Buterin. It is maintained by developers all over the world, so no individual truly owns Ethereum (https://ethereum.org/), rather it is maintained by the community. This decentralized platform runs applications in the form of smart contracts—applications that run exactly as programmed without censorship, fraud, or interference by a third party. Because of the decentralized nature of the platform, there is no possibility of downtime.

The network is fueled by a type of crypto token, called **Ether** (**ETH**), and it is used to pay miners (validator nodes) for the work they do to validate transactions and create blocks. Ether is also used by end users and application developers to pay for transaction fees and services that run on the network. Besides transaction fees, the network requires another type of fuel to execute transactions on smart contract code itself, which is called Gas. The reason the Ethereum network does not use Ether for this as well is because Ether is a cryptocurrency, and the value of this asset is volatile, therefore it uses the other internal measuring unit, Gas, which represents a fixed conversion rate that can calculate the amount of Ether at the time a transaction is submitted. The minimum amount needed to execute each transaction or smart contract invocation is precalculated based on the computation power required and how long the transaction takes to run. In the end, you will still pay with Ether, but the fee is calculated based on the amount of Gas needed to perform computations.

For example, when sending ETH from one account to another, the default Gas price of one unit will be 0.02 microether, or 0.00000002 ETH. If ETH has a value of $1,000 and 25,000 in Gas is needed for your transaction to be accepted, the transaction will cost you 0.00000002 * 1000 * 25000 = 0.5 dollars, or 50 cents.

Applications running on Ethereum are built as smart contracts, which is actually computer code that can facilitate the exchange of anything of value, such as money, content, property, or shares. These contracts are written in a programming language called Solidity, which was influenced by existing languages such as C++, Python, and JavaScript. It was specifically designed to target the Ethereum network. Solidity is a statically-typed language, which means that the programmer must specify the type of each variable. It supports inheritance, libraries, and complex user-defined types. The main advantage of Solidity is that the compiler can check on code validity and memory usage, therefore catches bugs at a very early stage.

Smart contracts run on the **Ethereum Virtual Machine** (**EVM**), which is Turing complete software (https://simple.wikipedia.org/wiki/Turing_complete) that allows code to be verified and executed on the blockchain. Regardless of the programming language in which it is written, as long it is compiled into EVM byte code, Solidity will run the same way on everyone's machine, given enough time and memory.

There will be more coverage of Ethereum in Chapter 8, *Ethereum Versus Hyperledger*.

NEO

This public blockchain is similar to Ethereum, and is often called the "Ethereum of China." However, it has a different mission and offers some interesting features. The main goal of NEO is to offer a platform that, based upon the information on their website (https://neo.org/), utilizes blockchain technology in combination with a digital identity to digitize assets and automate the management of those digital assets using smart contracts in order to achieve a "smart economy" using a distributed network. Where, Ethereum is (pseudo) anonymous, NEO uses digital identities.

NEO describes digital assets as anything that exists in a binary format with someone having the right to use them. There are two types of digital assets that can be used on the NEO platform: global and contract assets. Global assets are accessible by the entire system and can be used by all smart contracts and clients. Contract assets are only accessible by their specific contracts and cannot be used by others.

The NEO platform utilizes the widely accepted X.509 digital identity standard, which is a digital certificate issuance model based on public key infrastructure (https://en.wikipedia.org/wiki/X.509). It supports the web of trust point-to-point certificate issuance model as well (https://en.wikipedia.org/wiki/Web_of_trust). Identity verification is done using multifactor methods, such as the use of facial recognition, fingerprints, voice, SMS, and so forth.

NEO has its own independent smart contract system, called NeoContract, and it integrates seamlessly into your existing developer ecosystem. As a developer, you don't need to learn a new programming language, such as Solidity. You can use C#, Java, and Python in one of your familiar IDE's, including Visual Studio, Netbeans, Eclipse, and so on, when programming smart contracts and in debugging and compilation. These smart contracts run on a virtual machine, called NeoVM, and NEO claims to have the advantages of high availability, concurrency, and scalability. NEO is similar to Ethereum in that it also uses a crypto token to fuel the network.

Where NEO claims to beat Ethereum is that its transactions are cheaper—less fuel is needed to perform computations, and NEO executes these more quickly. NEO uses a different, more scalable consensus method, called Delegated Byzantine Fault Tolerance, whereas Ethereum uses a combination of PoW and PoS, and smart contract development under NEO is more native to the developer's current ecosystem. Where NEO is also different than Ethereum is in the type of application it targets to run on the network. NEO's focus is solely on smart financial and economic applications.

More in-depth information about NEO can be found at https://neo.org/.

IPFS

The third public blockchain platform on our tour is the **InterPlanetary File System**, or **IPFS** (`https://ipfs.io/`). IPFS is a peer-to-peer distributed filesystem that seeks to replace HTTP and build the web of tomorrow for everybody. In some ways, IPFS is similar to the web, but you could also compare it to a BitTorrent network exchanging objects within a single Git repository. IPFS provides a content-addressed block storage model with high throughput and content-addressed hyperlinks.

When you download a file with HTTP, the pieces come from a single computer at a time, rather than multiple computers simultaneously. IPFS claims that it can save 60% in bandwidth costs by distributing high volumes of data with high efficiency and zero duplication. Another issue that IPFS addresses is that on the current web, the average lifespan of a web page is 100 days. After that, it is deleted from history. Most big events currently happening in the world are not written into history books anymore, but only find their way onto the internet, which makes our primary medium very fragile. IPFS provides historical versioning, similar to Git, and it makes it simple to mirror data and to set up resilient networks. Because of these resilient networks, IPFS facilitates persistent availability, with or without connectivity to the internet backbone. Thus, in the case of a governmental outage, natural disasters, and intermittent connections, the content is still available somewhere else in the world.

IPFS works as follows:

- When you add a file, it is given a unique fingerprint (cryptographic hash).
- IPFS removes duplicate files across the network and tracks version history.
- Each node in the network can choose to store the content in which it is interested. Nodes can also store indexing information about who is storing what.
- When you search for a file, you're actually asking the network to find the content behind the unique hash.
- Every file can be located by a human-readable filename by using **InterPlanetary Naming Service** (**IPNS**), which is a decentralized naming system.

IPFS has some interesting use cases, as follows:

1. If you are an archivist or researcher and want to store information in a way that anyone can remember how to find it, or if you want to analyze large, distributed datasets with fast performance and decentralized archiving.

2. If you are a service provider that delivers large amounts of data and wish to save a lot of bandwidth through peer-to-peer content delivery.

3. If you are a content creator that wants the freedom of an independent web at a low cost so that everyone around the world can enjoy your content without censorship.

More information on IPFS can be found at `https://ipfs.io/`.

Blockstack

Blockstack is a platform that is aiming to be the new internet of decentralized apps, where users own their data and maintain their own privacy, security, and freedom, instead of these being held by the application provider. Note that IPFS is one of the many storage systems that Blockstack supports. IPFS/IPS can be seen as a successor to Amazon S3, whereas Blockstack views itself as a successor to the web. In addition to its blockchain platform, Blockstack also offers its own browser, which you can use to access the available apps. It uses the existing lower level of the public internet, but applications are serverless and decentralized. Blockstack also provides a decentralized **domain name system** (**DNS**), decentralized public key distribution system, and a registry for apps and user identities.

For developers, Blockstack provides the key tools and infrastructure to enable decentralized storage, authentication, and identity management. Building an application on Blockstack is as easy as building a single-page application in JavaScript, which plugs into an API that is run client-side, instead of frontend plugging into a centralized API. As a developer, you install a single library into your application without needing to run your own servers, maintain databases, or implement a user management system. Users can run the application through the Blockstack browser and give explicit permissions to read/write their data, which is encrypted and stored on the users' personal devices, or on their favorite storage provider (Dropbox, S3, or IPFS, for example). With Blockstack, you control your identity. When you log in to an app, by default, you are anonymous. You are authenticated by using an app-specific key, and you can reveal and prove your full identity at any time.

Blockstack solves the problem of having to deal with user passwords, hosting everyone's data, and running the necessary app-specific servers for your web applications. More information on Blockstack can be found at `https://blockstack.org/`.

Private/consortium blockchain providers

Next, I will take you on a tour through the various private, or permissioned, blockchain providers. In the private space, we will visit four platforms: Hyperledger Fabric, Oracle Blockchain Cloud Service, R3/Corda, and MultiChain. These blockchain platforms are highly suitable for enterprise applications.

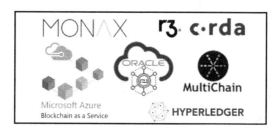

Collection of private/permissioned blockchain platforms

Hyperledger Fabric

Hyperledger Fabric is a blockchain framework implementation—a combination of **digital ledger technology** (**DLT**) and a Smart Contract Engine. It was first created by IBM and Digital Asset, and then open sourced in 2016 under the Hyperledger project, hosted by the Linux Foundation. It is a platform with a modular architecture for all kinds of distributed ledger solutions. It seeks to deliver a high degree of confidentiality, resiliency, flexibility, and scalability.

Hyperledger Fabric is a permissioned and private blockchain system, and network participants enroll through a **Membership Service Provider** (**MSP**). The pluggable options that Hyperledger Fabric offers include the storage of ledger data in multiple formats, switching the consensus mechanism, and different types of identity providers or MSPs. Beyond a permissioned blockchain, Hyperledger Fabric also lets you create secure, private channels, allowing a group of participants to create a separate shared ledger for their transactions. If two participants form a channel, then those participants—and no others—have copies of the ledger for that channel. Applications are written as smart contracts in chaincode, which can be programmed in Google's Go language, and can be invoked by an external application. The ledger itself is comprised of two components: the world state (a database holding the current state) and the transaction log (an update history of all transactions).

We'll talk more about Hyperledger Fabric in `Chapter 8`, *Ethereum Versus Hyperledger*. You can also visit their website at `https://hyperledger.org/projects/fabric`.

Oracle blockchain cloud service

At Open World in October 2017, Oracle presented their managed **Blockchain-as-a-Service** (**BaaS**) platform. The platform is built on top of the open source Hyperledger Fabric blockchain implementation, so it has similar features. However, it delivers a preassembled platform, which includes a web-based administration console to create, manage, and utilize your permissioned blockchain network for running smart contracts and maintaining a tamper-proof digital ledger. You can use the platform within your company or together with other entities in a consortium.

Oracle's **Blockchain Cloud Service** (**BCS**) comes with a complete set of infrastructure services and embedded resources: compute, containers, storage, identity management, and event streaming to help you quickly set up and run a production-ready blockchain. When you want to create a new network, you only have to specify a few parameters. After that, Oracle provisions the underlying infrastructure with the required Blockchain network components, REST proxy, and an administration console. You can provision the number of nodes that you need for all of the consortium partners. Furthermore, after sending them an invitation, they can create a service instance themselves and simply log in to complete the certificate exchange and join the existing blockchain network. Consortium partners can even run a node on a totally different IaaS platform such as Amazon AWS, and still join the BCS network. Because it runs on the cloud, you can scale the network so that it continually runs smoothly for all participants, effectively handling the transaction volumes on the network. It uses Hyperledger Fabric as the backbone, a permissioned blockchain, with secure access protected by Oracle's Identity Cloud Service. With Hyperledger Fabric, you can set up confidentiality domains using secure channels to conduct private transactions.

We will talk more about Oracle's Blockchain Cloud Service in subsequent chapters, as it's the main platform used throughout the rest of the book.

R3/Corda

As I mentioned earlier, there are consortium blockchains that focus on specific markets. Corda, from R3, is a distributed shared ledger platform specifically designed for recording and processing financial and legal agreements from regulated financial institutions. The platform supports smart contracts, which in this case are agreements whose execution can both be automated through computer code guided by human input and control, and whose rights and obligations, as expressed in legal prose, are legally enforceable. Corda links the business logic and data of smart contracts to the associated legal prose in order to ensure that the financial agreement(s) follow the law and can be enforced.

Corda itself is not a traditional blockchain but is heavily influenced by them, though it is lacking some of the traditional blockchain design choices. Some of the principal features that the Corda platform offers are:

- Recording and managing financial agreements and shared data between multiple parties that can be identified in a way that follows existing legal constructs and that is compatible with existing and upcoming regulations
- Instead of having a global consensus, it supports consensus between firms at the level of individual deals, and it offers regulatory and supervisory nodes to observe deals
- Corda can record precise links between written legal documents and smart contract code
- Corda is a permissioned system that restricts access to the data within an agreement only to those entities that are entitled to have such access and to those that have logical privileges

More information on Corda can be found at `https://corda.net/`.

MultiChain

MultiChain is a platform that enables everyone to create and deploy a blockchain in minutes, which can then be used within or between organizations. MultiChain seeks to overcome the key obstacle of deploying of blockchain technology in your organization. MultiChain is a fork of the original Bitcoin core code, but with some optimizations. MultiChain lets you configure the blockchain in a way that you would like it to behave. For starters, anyone can install MultiChain on their computer since it supports Windows, Linux, and Mac servers and desktops. It provides a simple API and command-line interface that makes it easy to maintain and deploy a blockchain network.

MultiChain lets you configure everything on the network, such as the block size, what type of transactions are permitted, transaction and mining parameters, and consensus requirements. It also includes a fine-grained permission layer to configure who can do what (for example, who can connect, send/receive transactions, administer the network, and who can create assets, streams, and blocks). Nonetheless, you can make it as open or closed as you need. On the blockchain that you create with MultiChain, you can issue unlimited assets, exchange multi-assets, and perform multi-party transactions. MultiChain does not support smart contracts, but it features data streams, which makes it possible to create multiple key-value, time series, or identity databases, which makes it a system of record applications.

More information on MultiChain can be found at `https://multichain.com`.

Summary

In this chapter, you learned that there are three types of blockchain: public, consortium, and private. I described each blockchain—what makes them different, the advantages and disadvantages of each, and what challenges they pose.

Public blockchains run on community-driven networks that are incentivized by cryptocurrencies. Virtually anyone can access, read and send transactions, and choose to participate in the consensus process. The advantage of a public blockchain is that it is open for anyone to join. Furthermore, it is anonymous, so no one needs to know a participant's location and real identity. Moreover, a public blockchain is a trustless (permissionless) system because of the consensus mechanism, where a participant can influence the network by owning a bigger stake in the blockchain due to the economic resources they bring to the table. A public blockchain also presents challenges, such as limited scalability, storage constraints, network speed and costs, immutable smart contracts, and the installation of software updates that can lead to disagreements between participants.

Consortium blockchains run on private and permissioned networks where the consensus process is controlled by a set of nodes. Read permissions may be public or restricted, and write permissions can be given to participants on asset types and transactions. The advantages of a consortium blockchain are that the validator nodes are known and trusted, it has better performance because a limited number of nodes participate in the consensus simultaneously, and it runs a limited amount of applications—in fact, usually just one. It is also more cost-efficient than public blockchains, because there is no need to solve a mathematical puzzle, such as a mine of blocks, it uses less energy and has faster block generation times. Consortium blockchains are permissioned, so they give you fine-grained access control and better privacy. The challenges of working with such a blockchain is in bringing the consortium together—who has the power to set permissions and how do you control the fragmentation of users and applications?

The last type of blockchain covered was the private blockchain. It functions virtually in the same way as a consortium blockchain, but it is controlled by a single organization. Read permissions may be public or restricted and write permissions remain centralized. The advantage of a private blockchain is that it can replace the replication of regular databases by distributing the data instead. All nodes are active and can be queried by different end users concurrently. A private blockchain also ensures that the data stays consistent in all of the nodes and prevents two transactions from modifying the same data simultaneously. A private blockchain is more secure than a standard database, because a centralized database can be corrupted and destroyed by anyone with sufficient access to the database server. In a blockchain with multiple nodes, the same attack needs to be carried out on at least 51% of the nodes simultaneously in order to be successful.

The challenge of using a private blockchain is that is considered slower than a centralized database, because all nodes need to verify the data before it becomes available. Each node in a private blockchain does the same work simultaneously. Also, once connected to a centralized database, individual requests do not need to be verified every time the connection is used, as opposed to a private blockchain. Even if a private blockchain is permissioned, the validator nodes have full visibility of all transactions. This might be a deal breaker for financial organizations.

The chapter concluded by taking you on a tour of some of the public and private blockchains currently available. Public providers include Ethereum, NEO, IPFS, and Blockstack. The Private providers include Hyperledger Fabric, Oracle Blockchain Cloud Service, R3/Corda, and MultiChain.

In the next part of the book, *Implementing a permissioned blockchain*, we will set up and build our own permissioned blockchain. The first chapter in that part introduces two of the blockchain providers in more detail. It compares Ethereum (the largest public blockchain for decentralized/distributed applications) with Hyperledger Fabric (the permissioned blockchain used by Oracle).

Part III

Implementing a Permissioned Blockchain

8

Ethereum Versus Hyperledger

The previous chapter concluded Part II of this book, *Blockchain Core Concepts and Terminology*, which reflected a greater technical focus than Part I, *Implications of the Blockchain*. This chapter begins Part III, *Implementing a Permissioned Blockchain*, which employs a hands-on approach so that you can start to build your own decentralized application. In this part, we will take a look at the differences between two platform giants, Ethereum and Hyperledger, the transition that awaits you when going from traditional middleware applications to the blockchain, and how to implement your own permissioned blockchain and decentralized application running on the **Oracle Autonomous Blockchain Cloud Service (OABCS)**.

Before you get your hands dirty setting up and running your own permissioned blockchain, let's take a look at the two platform giants. In this chapter, I provide an extensive analysis of the most notable differences between Ethereum and Hyperledger (Fabric), two DLTs. This comparison covers areas such as the mode of operation, the users and participating nodes, the consensus protocol(s) used, the development and execution of smart contracts, the existence of built-in currency and incentives, and topics such as the security, privacy, and debugging of decentralized applications.

In this chapter, you will learn about the following topics:

- How do Ethereum's capabilities compare to that of Hyperledger Fabric?
- Who is responsible for the governance of each platform?
- How do users join, participate in, and use each platform?
- How do these platforms compare in maturity, ease of use, and development?
- How can I start developing my own applications on both platforms?

Two leading platform frameworks

Over the past several years, **Distributed Ledger Technologies** (**DLTs**) have gained a lot of interest and enthusiasm across many different industries, such as banking and healthcare. Enterprises operating in these industries are seeking to use a DLT to process, validate, and authenticate transactions, for example, exchanges of data, in a more scalable and secure way. In previous chapters, I introduced several of the open source platforms available that use this technology. However, two of the leading platform frameworks are Ethereum and Hyperledger (specifically the Hyperledger Fabric framework). When you compare both frameworks, based on their whitepaper and documentation, it is obvious that Hyperledger Fabric (`http://hyperledger-fabric.readthedocs.io/en/latest/`) and Ethereum (`https://github.com/ethereum/wiki/wiki/White-Paper`) are very different in both their product vision and field of application.

The first thing to observe is that the development of each platform is driven by a different perspective. Hyperledger Fabric is driven by concrete use cases, and it provides a modular and extendable architecture with a lot of pluggable components that you can mix and match. It is a platform that is tailored to enterprise solutions, and it can be employed in various industries, such as banking, healthcare, insurance, and supply chain management. In contrast, Ethereum presents itself as independent of any specific field op applications, and it can be employed by everyone without extensive knowledge of its inner workings. It is not driven by modularity, but instead Ethereum provides a generic platform for all kinds of transactions and applications. The following table summarizes the two frameworks:

Characteristic	Ethereum	Hyperledger Fabric
Launched date	July 2015	July 2017
Governance of platform	Ethereum developers and Enterprise Ethereum Alliance	Linux Foundation, IBM, Digital Asset, Oracle, and others
Kind of platform	Generic platform	Modular/pluggable platform
Mode of operation	Permissionless, both public and private (own testnet)	Permissioned, both private (on-premises) and consortium (cloud)
Consensus algorithm	Reached by mining: Proof of Work (soon to be Proof of Stake in Casper release)	Pluggable consensus algorithm, such as Practical Byzantine Fault Tolerance (PBFT)
Build-in cryptocurrency	Powered by Ether. Can create custom tokens via Coin API	No built-in currency, but can create custom tokens (chaincode)
Smart contracts	Applications are smart contracts, usually written in Solidity	Transactions execute chaincode, usually written in Golang, Java, or JavaScript
Transaction fees	A fee needs to be paid for each transaction in the form of Gas	A transaction does not have to be paid. There are no fees.
Security and privacy	(Pseudo) Identity using ERC20 wallet	Trusted identity through membership

Before comparing these two frameworks on specific areas of blockchain technology, let's talk about the differences in vision, concept, governance, and field of application.

Ethereum

Ethereum was first proposed in a whitepaper published by Vitalik Buterin, a 20-year old cryptocurrency researcher and developer, in late 2013. It is an open source, decentralized platform that enables developers to build and deploy decentralized applications running on a blockchain through the use of smart contracts. Officially launched on June 30, 2015 as a public and permissionless blockchain platform, it has gained traction and has become the platform of choice for many different applications as well as for creating and launching **ICOs (Initial Coin Offerings/crowdfunding)**. Ethereum's long-term vision is to be a generic platform that solves both the scalability and governance problems of blockchain applications, ensuring that the eventual system is well maintained and stays in check.

The platform is under the governance of two groups: the core developers and the Enterprise Ethereum Alliance, launched in early 2017. At the time of writing, there are around 40 contributors to the open source projects maintained by the Ethereum Foundation, which include the official Golang, Python, and Java implementations of the Ethereum protocol. Development is not limited to the core developers—any developer around the world can submit an **Ethereum Improvement Proposal** (**EIP**), for example. Besides the core developers, the Enterprise Ethereum Alliance connects enterprises, startups, academics, and technology vendors, and together they define enterprise-grade software proposals capable of handling complex, highly-demanding applications on the Ethereum platform. Members include Consensys, Intel, Microsoft, BP, JPMorgan, and ING.

Applications that run on the Ethereum platform are based on the execution of smart contracts. A smart contract defines rules and penalties around an agreement, and it enforces those obligations. In Ethereum, smart contracts can be interpreted as autonomous scripts or decentralized applications and are stored in the Ethereum blockchain for later use or timed execution. Smart contracts can be implemented in various programming languages, such as **Solidity** (a closed language developed for Ethereum: `https://github.com/ethereum/solidity`), or the new experimental language **Viper** (a strongly-typed Python-derived decidable language: `https://github.com/ethereum/vyper`). For the execution of the embedded instruction of a smart contract, the user pays for it in ether (technically paid as "Gas," an internal measuring scale).

Its public nature and built-in currency make Ethereum a great fit for every developer who builds applications for decentralized organizations. You can find a list of Ethereum DApps here: https://www.stateofthedapps.com/.

Hyperledger fabric

Hyperledger Fabric started as IBM Fabric, and it was the original a result of a hackathon by a company called Digital Asset. It was rebranded when it joined the Hyperledger project at beginning of 2016. Hyperledger itself doesn't refer to a specific technology, but it is a banner project of the Linux foundation, which hosts multiple blockchain and DLT technologies and supports the collaborative effort to create blockchain-based distributed ledgers. Besides Hyperledger Fabric, the project includes other technologies and frameworks, such as Sawtooth (from Intel), Iroha, Indy, and Burrow, as well as tools such as Composer and Explorer. You can find a list of business-oriented blockchain frameworks hosted by Hyperledger Fabric here: https://www.hyperledger.org.

Hyperledger Fabric has been under continuous development, and version 1.0 was officially launched on July 11, 2017. Fabric is a permissioned blockchain platform supporting both private and consortium infrastructures. It provides a modular and pluggable architecture and delimitation of roles between nodes, the deployment and execution of smart contracts, a configurable consensus algorithm, a pluggable data source, and membership services. Hyperledger Fabric is also open source, and has gained a lot of attention from major technology and software vendors that began to contribute to the project. Hyperledger Fabric has become the leading blockchain technology framework for business applications, and its long-term vision is to provide better integration with other applications, encryption libraries for sensitive data, and improvements in performance and scalability. With one minor release per quarter and the adoption of a **long-term support** (**LTS**) strategy, Hyperledger Fabric aims to be the platform for mission-critical applications.

The platform is under governance of the Linux foundation and members of the Hyperledger project, such as IBM, SAP, Hitachi, GE, Digital Asset, Oracle, and many more. In total, 159 engineers from 27 organizations contributed to the release of version 1.0, and this number is increasing. Compared to Ethereum, these contributors maintain a single GitHub repository that includes all of the code, tools, examples, tests, and proposals. As a developer, if you want to contribute you can join by reading the instructions on how to do so here: http://hyperledger-fabric.readthedocs.io/en/latest/CONTRIBUTING.html.

Hyperledger Fabric is a private or permissioned blockchain platform framework, and as compared to Ethereum, it does not have a public infrastructure that you can use. This means that to run an application on Hyperledger Fabric, you need to set up your own network. A Hyperledger Fabric network is comprised of trusted nodes (or "peers"), which independently interface with applications, execute smart contracts, give access to data in the ledger, and endorse transactions. The framework supports the execution of smart contracts (which is call "chaincode" in Hyperledger Fabric) and can be implemented in various open programming languages, such as Golang, Java, and JavaScript. In contrast to Ethereum's closed smart contract language, this potentially makes it more flexible and maintainable. Users can interact with smart contracts by using application services in the form of an SDK for Node.js, Java, and Golang. Fabric itself doesn't offer an administration console or any other user-facing services.

Hyperledger Fabric's private or permissioned nature and extensive framework make it a great fit for mission-critical applications that need out-of-the-box security and privacy. Some companies that are developing application platforms based on Hyperledger Fabric are ABN Amro (banking), NAD Grid (energy), and MedicalChain (healthcare/electronic health records).

Mode of operation and participation

As I explained previously, with a traditional database the data is stored at a central location, and only a single entity, usually the owner, keeps a copy of the database, grants access to other users, and controls what data is contributed. With the arrival of blockchain and other DLTs, this approach to data storage and operations has changed radically. Instead, blockchain favors a distributed data storage model where each participating entity holds a copy of the database. All participating entities take part in a peer-to-peer network of nodes that distribute the data among themselves. Because of the difficulty of keeping all nodes in sync, the nodes need to be sure that they agree on the correctness of the ledger; that is, the common truth. Arriving at this common truth is called *consensus*, which is described in a later section. Let's compare the mode of operation and participation of both platform frameworks.

Ethereum

The mode of operation of Ethereum falls into the *permissionless* category. This means that everyone can join the network without needing explicit access. To join the network, you need an Ethereum wallet, which acts as a gateway to decentralized applications on the Ethereum blockchain. It allows you to hold and secure the built-in cryptocurrency Ether and other crypto-assets built on Ethereum, as well as the capability to write, deploy, and use smart contracts. No real identity is attached to the wallet; instead, it is just a network address value called where every participant is pseudo-anonymous. You can download the desktop version, mobile version, or use an online wallet, paper wallet, or hardware wallet. The differences between each wallet are explained in Chapter 5, *Blockchain 101 - Security, Privacy, and Smart Contracts.*

With respect to the mode of participation, the Ethereum network consists of various participants who all depend on each other in different ways. Ethereum is a network of different actors and different pieces of software. By definition, a public or permissionless mode of operation is one where all actors and software applications need to agree on the protocol in order for the network to work. Because of this, no one can take sole ownership of making protocol decisions (not even the founder, Vitalik Buterin). The Ethereum ecosystem recognizes the following actors: developers, users, miners/forgers, node operators, and improvement proposals. These are explained in the following list:

- **Developers**: Ethereum developers build the software used to interact with the ledger of the blockchain. Some examples of this software are Geth (Go implementation of the protocol, https://github.com/ethereum/go-ethereum), Parity (node software powering the network, https://www.parity.io/#intro), Metamask (browser extension to run Ethereum dApps, https://metamask.io/), and Status.im (mobile Ethereum OS, https://status.im/). Developers can build their own software that follows the protocol, and they are incentivized as their software is used.
- **Users**: Ethereum users take advantage of the Ethereum blockchain and its ledger to send and receive assets, and they are free to use any software that follows the protocol. Users can use any decentralized application running on the network with their Ethereum wallet.

- **Miners**: Ethereum miners build and/or use software to create new blocks in which transactions from network users are hashed and ordered. A well-known example of mining software is ethminer (miner with OpenCL, CUDA, and stratum support, `https://github.com/ethereum-mining/ethminer`). Miners are incentivized with Ether (Ethereum's cryptocurrency) to mine new blocks of transactions. However, mining is going to be discontinued in the future when the network switches its consensus algorithm from **Proof of Work** (PoW) to **Proof of Stake** (PoS). The miners will transition to minters, who do the proofing of transactions based on their stake in the network, as they mint new coins.

- **Node operators**: Ethereum node operators run "full nodes" that validate blocks created by miners and process the transactions submitted by users in those blocks. The advantage of running a node is that your business can directly connect to the blockchain and its ledger, else you would need to connect to one of the available nodes.

- **Ethereum Improvements Proposals (EIPs)**: EIPs define the protocol and how developers, miners, and node operators are to interpret a specific EIP. EIPs are similar to traditional RFCs (internet standards) and JEPs (JDK/Java Enhancement Proposals). Anyone can submit an EIP and follow what is being proposed. Once consensus is reached on the proposal by the developers of the Ethereum foundation, it is included as part of the official protocol.

More information how to participate and interact with Ethereum can be found at: `http://www.ethdocs.org/en/latest/ethereum-clients/index.html`.

Hyperledger fabric

The mode of operation of Ethereum falls into the *permissioned* category. This means that anybody who wants to join the network needs permission to do so. To join the network, you need a membership. For example, you need first to receive an invitation by one of the network maintainers. To enable this mode of operation, Hyperledger Fabric provides a membership identity service that manages user IDs and authenticates participants on the network. Additionally, it offers authorization of specific network operations through the use of access control lists. For example, one specific user ID can query data in the ledger, but it is blocked when invoking a smart contract. In a Hyperledger Fabric network, members know each other by their identity, but they do not know what each other is doing because of the network's privacy and confidentiality rules.

With respect to the mode of participation, a Hyperledger Fabric network also consists of various participants who depend on each other to run a successful business network. By definition, with a private or permissioned mode of operation, all actors need to be identified and authenticated by a **Membership Service Provider** (**MSP**). An MSP offers an abstraction layer for user authentication and all cryptographic protocols and mechanisms that are behind issuing and validating certificates. An MSP is allowed to define its own choice of identity, the rules by which they are governed (that is, identity validation), and the rules by which they are authenticated (namely, signature generation and validation). The Hyperledger Fabric ecosystem recognizes the following actors: developers, users, and nodes (clients, peers, endorsers, and orderers).

- **Developers**: Contributors to the project build the software that make up the framework in which businesses can install and run on-premises and/or in the cloud to create their blockchain network and decentralized applications. Developers can use the available APIs and SDK to interact with the blockchain and its ledger and develop their own decentralized applications.
- **Users**: Businesspeople use the application(s) running on their private or consortium Hyperledger Fabric blockchain and interact with its ledger by invoking transactions.
- **Nodes**: Hyperledger Fabric nodes are the communications entities of the blockchain. Multiple nodes of different types can run on the same physical server, so in a sense a "node" only acts as a logical function. Best practice here is to group nodes in "trust domains" and associate logical entities that control them. The following actors depict the different types of nodes:
  - **Clients**: A client represents an entity that acts on behalf of an end user. In order to communicate with the blockchain, it must connect to a peer. A client node may choose to connect to any peer node. Clients create and then submit a transaction to the endorser (peer) nodes and then broadcasts transactions to the ordering service proposals that it agrees upon with these nodes.
  - **Peers**: A peer receives ordered state updates in the form of blocks from the ordering service and maintains the state and ledger. Additionally, it can take up the role of an endorsing peer.
  - **Endorsers**: A special peers node whose main function takes place with respect to a particular smart contract and consists of endorsing a transaction before it is committed. Every smart contract (chaincode) may specify an endorsement policy that refers to a set of specific endorsing peers, so an endorser is only responsible for the transactions that trigger the chaincode to which it is assigned.

- **Orderers**: These nodes form the ordering service: a communication fabric that guarantees the delivery of transactions. A business network may implement the ordering service in different ways than a centralized service (one node, used during development and testing) to distribute protocols (multiple nodes that target different network and node fault models). The ordering service provides a shared communication channel between clients and peers, and it offers a broadcast service for transactions (that is, messages) submitted by connected clients that are then delivered to all peers. It delivers the same messages in the same logical order to all connected peers.

More information how nodes participate and interact with each other can be found here: `http://hyperledger-fabric.readthedocs.io/en/release/arch-deep-dive.html`.

Consensus algorithm

With respect to participating in consensus, the two platforms under discussion are at opposite ends of the spectrum. Ethereum is a public and permissionless blockchain, whereas Hyperledger Fabric is a private and permissioned blockchain. This means that the consensus algorithm used for these platforms differs in complexity (namely, cryptographic difficulty) and execution. Because trustless operations can be performed on the Ethereum network, it requires certain PoW (for example, cryptographic hashing) by miners to keep the data in the ledger consistent. In contrast, Hyperledger Fabric's interpretation of consensus is more refined due to its operating in permissioned mode, which provides more fine-grained access control to records and thus enhances privacy. Furthermore, since only the endorser (peer) nodes take part in reaching consensus, there is a gain in performance.

Ethereum

Since Ethereum is a public platform, all participants have to reach consensus over the order of all submitted transactions, regardless of whether they participate in a particular transaction or not. The order of transactions on the platform is crucial to keep the state of the ledger consistent. If the order cannot be established or has been compromised, there is a chance that someone can double-spend, meaning that they have submitted two parallel transactions that transfer the same asset to different recipients, virtually creating a copy out of thin air.

As participants are pseudo-anonymous, a consensus mechanism needs to be employed to protect the ledger against fraudulent transactions or malicious participants. At the time of writing, Ethereum uses a PoW algorithm (*ethash*) to reach consensus, but it will be moving to a hybrid PoW/PoS algorithm (*casper*) sometime in 2018.

The current implementation of Ethereum uses nearly the same mining process as Bitcoin based on the PoW scheme. As explained in `Chapter 4`, *Blockchain 101 - Blocks, Chains, and Consensus*, miners use computing power (CPU/GPU) on each block of transactions in order to solve a mathematical puzzle. They employ this power to guess the answer repeatedly until the correct one is found. Every block has a target hash that miners need to match. Based on the transactions' content, miners need to guess an arbitrary value, or nonce, in order to match the target hash by hashing the content and nonce together. The miner is awarded for this work by an amount of the built-in cryptocurrency Ether. Other nodes can easily validate the block by solving the puzzle yet again using the content and the used nonce. It takes approximately 12-15 seconds for a miner to mine a new block, and if a miner works more slowly or more quickly, the algorithm automatically readjusts itself; that is, modifying the difficulty of the problem so that miners again only need 12 seconds to mine a new block. Thus, Ethereum depends on luck and the amount of computing power available. Nevertheless, as mentioned earlier, Ethereum might not need miners much longer.

With the transition to the Casper hybrid PoW/PoS scheme expected sometime in 2018, the profit motive for miners is going to decrease and eventually end. The first version will only use a PoS consensus to validate every 100th block, called **checkpoints**. There is no way that miners can proceed working on a chain without the validated block, even if 99% of the miners support a chain that does not include this block. This removes a lot of the decision-making power that miners currently have, but in return it will help with the network's scaling issues by enabling new blocks to be created more quickly and efficiently through **sharding**, a method of partitioning large databases into smaller and more manageable parts, or shards. Furthermore, it uses less energy to run the network, reduces centralization of nodes, and makes it much more difficult to perform a 51% attack. To reduce the profitability for miners, Ethereum intends to decrease the block rewards to every 100th block, and increase the mining difficulty exponentially over time until the chain becomes impossible to mine, leading to an event that is called the "Ethereum Ice Age".

Hyperledger fabric

In contrast to Ethereum, Hyperledger Fabric's understanding of consensus is much broader and allows for multiple approaches. Consensus is not only reached on the ledger/block level like Ethereum, but differentiates itself on the entire transaction, starting from a client proposing a transaction and endorsement by the network to ordering, validating, and committing the data to the ledger. As I explained previously, in Hyperledger Fabric's mode of participation, there are various types of nodes with each playing different roles and performing different tasks in the process of reaching consensus. With Ethereum, the roles and tasks of participating nodes are identical.

The current implementation of Hyperledger Fabric uses a "pluggable" consensus algorithm, meaning that the network starter can choose between various algorithms that suits their application-specific requirements. For example, one can choose between variants of the **Practical Byzantine Fault Tolerance** (**PBFT**) algorithm or use no-op (no consensus). Using PBFT, consensus is ultimately achieved when the order and outcomes of a block's transactions have met the policy criteria checks explicitly set out by the network and the executed smart contracts. These checks take place during the lifecycle of a transaction. For example, the platform can use endorsement policies to dictate which specific members must endorse a certain class of transactions, as well as system contracts (called chaincodes) to ensure that these policies are enforced and maintained. Before a transaction is committed, designated peers will use these system chaincodes to make sure that an adequate number of endorsements are present. Before the transactions are appended to the ledger, a versioning check will take place during which time the current state of the ledger is agreed to or upon which there is consent. This provides protection against double-spend operations and other threats that might compromise the integrity of the data. In addition to these checks, during the lifecycle of a transaction there are ongoing identity verifications happening in the background. Hyperledger Fabric also implements **access control lists** (**ACLs**) on all layers of the network that permit or block certain interactions within the blockchain and repeatedly authenticate, sign, and verify message payloads as a transaction passes the different layers and components. More information about the lifecycle can be found here: `https://hyperledger-fabric.readthedocs.io/en/latest/txflow.html`.

Hyperledger Fabric also has support for channels, a private ledger of communications between two or more specific members, for example, to conduct private and confidential transactions. Each channel has its own ledger and chaincode application(s), and it is accessible to members of the network that have been granted explicit access. A channel also includes peers that sign, validate, and verify the data in the ledger. For each channel, a leading peer can be elected by its members, or assigned by an algorithm, which communicates with the ordering service on behalf of the members.

The consensus algorithm orders transactions, adds them to a block, and delivers the block to each leading peer, which distributes the block across the channel. Due to the partition of message flow when using a channel, clients see transactions and the included payload of the channels of which they are a part, but are unaware of other channels.

In contrast to Ethereum, Hyperledger Fabric allows fine-grained control over the type of consensus and the level of restricting access to transactions, which results in the improved scalability of the network and better privacy. The consequence of this way of operating, though, is that consensus is reached at transaction level, whereas consensus with Ethereum is reached at the ledger level.

Built-in cryptocurrency

One noteworthy difference between Ethereum and Hyperledger Fabric, which admittedly is a little one-sided, is the use of a built-in cryptocurrency. This relates to the mode of operation, consensus algorithm, and rules for distributing incentives set by the network.

Ethereum

Of the two platforms, only Ethereum features a built-in cryptocurrency, called *Ether*. The main reason for this is that it is a public platform and in order to maintain its scale, decentralization, and usage, it needs to incentivize participants, such as miners, for their work. Moreover, it also requires users to pay transaction fees for the infrastructure of the network. Ether (ETH) is the currency that fuels the Ethereum blockchain, and it can be used to program many different use-cases, such as enabling smart contracts, building **decentralized applications** (**DApps**), generating your own digital tokens, and for making standard P2P transactions. This means that if you want to do anything on the Ethereum platform, you will need to pay for it.

Payments or transaction fees (TX fees) are calculated in ETH using two intermediary measuring values called **gasprice** and **gaslimit**. The equation for calculating the needed transaction fee is as follows:

$$Ether = TXfees = gaslimit \times gasprice$$

This formula means that the final TX fee is derived by multiplying the gas limit by the gas price. To understand the two measuring values, let's take a look at the following example.

Suppose your car consumes five gallons of gasoline that costs $16.50 USD. If you drive for 100 miles and get 25 miles per gallon of gasoline, that trip will cost you $13.20 USD. If your total trip is actually 300 miles, you will need to put in 12 gallons of gasoline to reach your destination and you will spend $39.60 USD. Similarly, to perform an operation on Ethereum, or run a line of code, as with your car, you need to burn fuel. There is a minimum gas limit where each unit of gas comes at a price. Compared to a car, where we paid $3.30 (gas price) per gallon (gas limit), in Ethereum, instead you pay 0.021 micro-ether or 21 Gwei (gas price) per gas (gas limit). You can calculate the needed transaction fee easily using the website ETH Gas Station at `https://ethgasstation.info/calculatorTxV.php`, as shown in the following screenshot. I will discuss the gas price further in this section:

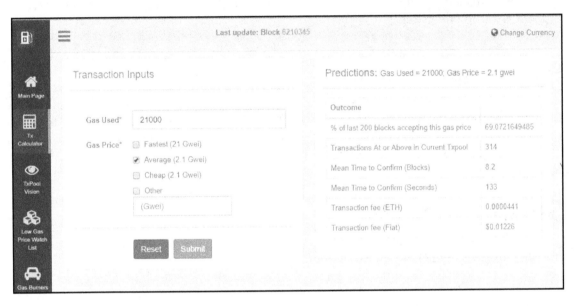

ETH Gas Station transaction fees calculator, including the time it takes to confirm your transaction

With Ethereum, **gas** is the *unit of cost* used to pay for performing an action. The requestor pays this cost to the miner, who mines and validates the transaction. For example, if you want to execute 100 lines of code, it requires 5 gas units. **Gas limits** are already determined based on the number of lines of code needed to execute the particular operation on the blockchain. If you pay less gas than is needed to run the particular operation, it will fail and result in an "Out of Gas" error. Thus, you should always avoid this situation by always paying for the minimum amount of required gas. The gas limit needed to execute your transaction can be tricky, and it depends on the complexity of the transaction, so always check the gas limit using an Ethereum block explorer, such as `https://etherscan.io`. In the real world, a normal P2P transactions costs 21,000 gas. To lower the final cost of your transaction in terms of the gas price, you can play around with the other variable.

Gas prices are determined by the market (supply and demand) and range between 2 and 9 Gwei. Gwei is the internal unit for the gas price, and when exchanged for Ether, then 1 Gwei = 0.00000001 ether. So, if you pay a lower gas price, your transaction will take longer to be validated—when your price is too low, it may never get picked up. On average, you need to pay 4 Gwei per unit of gas. That said, a normal transaction will cost you *21000 gas * 4 Gwei = 84000 Gwei = 0.00084 ether* ($0.49 USD). On the other hand, some smart contracts use a 200,000 gas limit.

Furthermore, on Ethereum you can create your own digital token for custom use-cases by deploying a smart contract that conforms to the pre-defined ERC20 token standard. Companies create these digital tokens to kick-start their decentralized application projects or to crowdfund other causes.

Hyperledger Fabric

Because of the private/permissioned nature of the platform, Hyperledger Fabric does not require a built-in cryptocurrency, as the available consensus algorithm does not use mining to reach consensus. However, it is possible to develop a native currency or digital token by programming a specific smart contract with chaincode.

Smart contracts

In the context of blockchains and cryptocurrencies, a smart contract governs interactions with the digital ledger. They allow agreements between network participants to be executed automatically and can act as a complement, or substitute, for legal agreements. A smart contract is prewritten logic (computer program code) stored and distributed on the blockchain that directly controls certain aspects of transactions under certain conditions. A smart contract not only defines the terms and conditions (rules and penalties) around an agreement, but is also capable of automatically facilitating, executing, and enforcing the negotiation or performance of an agreement. A smart contract does this by taking the input, putting that input through the rules set out in the smart contract, and executing the required actions defined by those contractual clauses. Both platforms, Ethereum and Hyperledger Fabric, feature smart contracts in the sense of smart code that can be written in various programming languages.

Ethereum

On the Ethereum blockchain, smart contracts are account-holding objects that contain code functions and can interact with other contracts, make independent decisions, store data, and send Ether to other participants. You can define contracts yourself, but their execution, and the other services such as the distribution and consensus of transactions, or calling external Oracles (trusted data providers via REST APIs), is provided by the Ethereum network. These contracts are permanently part of the network, and by default will be executable as long as the network exists. Contracts will only disappear if they are programmed to self-destruct.

Hyperledger Fabric

Fabric's interpretation of a smart contract is called chaincode, which is programmable code that can be deployed on any Hyperledger Fabric network. It is executed on the network and validated during the consensus process by validator nodes. You can use chaincodes to develop business contracts, asset definitions, and decentralized applications that can be managed by the whole consortium. Smart contracts are executed when they are associated in a transaction by the endorsing peers of the network. These can be submitted by clients using the available peer APIs. In contrast to Ethereum, Hyperledger Fabric supports uninstalling and upgrading chaincodes (to a newer version). In a future release, a chaincode will be able to be stopped and started without having to uninstall it.

How to develop a smart contract

Developing smart contracts works very differently on each of the two platforms discussed in this chapter, both in terms of the programming language used and in its development. In this and the following sections, we will explore how to develop and run smart contracts on these platforms.

The example I'm going to use for both platforms represents a contract that can create a voting ballot to decide the name of an upcoming conference. To form a ballot, the creator provides a list of proposed items. Then the creator of the contract instance, acting in a role similar to a chairman, gives others the right to vote. Everybody with rights can vote for one of the proposals.

Ethereum

Smart contracts that can run on Ethereum are primarily written in **Solidity** (http://solidity.readthedocs.io/en/latest/), a program language influence by JavaScript, C++, Python, and PowerShell. It is one of four languages designed to target the EVM, the runtime engine of Ethereum, which you will learn about later in this chapter. Others include Serpent and LLL, but these are deprecated by the community, and Viper is still in an experimental phase. Solidity is a statically-typed programming language, meaning that the program is guaranteed to satisfy some set of type safety properties for all possible inputs. A compiler is needed to prove that your program is well-typed. That being the case, it results in a compiled binary that is smaller and allows the EVM to run the program faster. More information about static type checking can be found here: https://en.wikipedia.org/wiki/Type_system#Static_typing.

The following code shows how to program the example mentioned above in Solidity, and is available on GitHub at https://github.com/packtpublishing/blockchain-across-oracle. The code is self-explanatory, but I will go into some more detail in a moment:

```solidity
pragma solidity ^0.4.16;

/// @title Voting for event proposals
contract Ballot {
  // This declares a new complex type which will be used
  // for variables later. It will represent a single voter.
  struct Voter {
   uint weight; // weight is accumulated by delegation
     bool voted; // if true, that person already voted
     uint vote; // index of the voted proposal
   }

  // This is a type for a single proposal.
  struct Proposal {
     bytes32 name; // short name (up to 32 bytes)
     uint voteCount; // number of accumulated votes
   }
  address public chairperson;

  // This declares a state variable that
  // stores a `Voter` struct for each possible address.
  mapping(address => Voter) public voters;

  // A dynamically-sized array of `Proposal` structs.
  Proposal[] public proposals;

  /// Create a new ballot to choose one of `proposalNames`.
  function Ballot(bytes32[] proposalNames) public {
```

```
      chairperson = msg.sender;
      voters[chairperson].weight = 1;

      // For each of the provided proposal names, create a new
      // proposal object and add it to the end of the array.
      for (uint i = 0; i < proposalNames.length; i++) {
        // `Proposal({...})` creates a temporary Proposal object
        // and proposals.push`appends it to the end of proposals
        proposals.push(Proposal({
          name: proposalNames[i],
          voteCount: 0
        }));
      }
    }

    // Give `voter` the right to vote on this ballot.
    // May only be called by `chairperson`.
    function giveRightToVote(address voter) public {
      // If the argument of `require` evaluates to `false`,
      // it terminates and reverts all changes to the state and to
      // Ether balances. It is often a good idea to use this if
      // functions are called incorrectly.
      require(
        (msg.sender == chairperson) &&
        !voters[voter].voted &&
        (voters[voter].weight == 0)
      );
      voters[voter].weight = 1;
    }

    /// Give your vote to proposal `proposals[proposal].name`.
    function vote(uint proposal) public {
      Voter storage sender = voters[msg.sender];
      require(!sender.voted);
      sender.voted = true;
      sender.vote = proposal;
      // If `proposal` is out of the range of the array, this will
      // throw automatically and revert all changes.
      proposals[proposal].voteCount += sender.weight;
    }
  }
```

All source files should (but are not required to) be annotated with a version `pragma`. An instruction to the compiler is to reject the program if the code is compiled with a newer version that might introduce incompatibilities. The version `pragma` is as follows:

```
pragma solidity ^0.4.16;
```

With this `pragma` version, the code will only compile on compilers that support 0.4.x—it will not compile on older or newer versions (for example, 0.5.x). This is done by using the ^ sign. There are also more complex rules for controlling the version using the semantic versioning method (`https://docs.npmjs.com/misc/semver`). The other parts of the code are already described through comments, but let's look at the keywords used that are part of the programming language (in order of occurrence in the code):

Keyword	Usage
`/// @title`	Documents the code, for example, title of contract or function
`//`	Generic comments not part of documentation
`contract`	Lets the compiler know where the contract code is starting
`struct`	Declares a complex type that contains multiple fields (or variables)
`{structName}[]`	Declares a dynamically-sized array based on a declared `struct`
`uint`	Declares an unsigned integer
`bool`	Declares a Boolean
`bytes32`	Declares a character byte string up to 32 bytes
`address`	Declares an Ethereum wallet address (a pseudo identity)
`mapping`	Declares a mapping (that is, a hash table), which consists of key and value type pairs
`function`	Declares a executable function and define its input parameters
`for`	Creates a for each loop to process an array of items, for example
`require`	Checks if the inner statement result is true, otherwise changes are reverted

There are many more keywords used in the programming language that are not included in this example (such as `event`, `enum`, and `modifier`). For a full list, take a look here: `http://solidity.readthedocs.io/en/develop/structure-of-a-contract.html`.

Hyperledger fabric

Smart contracts (called chaincode) that can run on Hyperledger Fabric are primarily written in Go, originally developed by Google. It is a programming language influenced by C and Oberon. Besides Go, more languages will be supported in the next release(s), such as Java and JavaScript. Each chaincode is an isolated program, and when implemented it maintains its own private state of the ledger. However, you can program a chaincode to allow other chaincodes to query its private state. Essentially, you can write arbitrary code, but your chaincodes (smart contracts) have to conform to a common interface that peers use to control them.

Each chaincode you write needs to implement an Init and an Invoke method. The Init method is used for setup, whereas the Invoke method is used to execute the logic of the chaincode and perform the necessary work. Both methods accept one parameter, which implements ChaincodeStubInterface. It carries a client for interacting with the distributed ledger and allows for querying other chaincodes. It also holds a list of arguments that the caller passes to the chaincode. This allows the code to implement different behaviors and enables the execution of different scenarios. Besides these two methods, a single chaincode can implement multiple functions, and based on the input arguments, the Invoke method can select a specific function to be called.

The following code shows how to program the above-mentioned voting ballot example in Go. The code is self-explanatory, but I will go into some more detail in a moment:

```go
package main

// imports needed for chaincode
import (
  "encoding/json"
  "fmt"
  "github.com/hyperledger/fabric/core/chaincode/shim"
  pb "github.com/hyperledger/fabric/protos/peer"
)

// Ballot implements a voting chaincode to manage event proposals
type Ballot struct {}

// Voter declares a new complex type which will be used
// for variables later. It will represent a single voter.
type Voter struct {
  VID     string `json:"vid`      // registration id of a voter
  Weight uint    `json:"weight"`  // weight is accumulated
  Voted  bool    `json:"voted"`   // if true, person voted
  Vote   string `json:"vote"`     // name of the voted proposal
}

// Proposal is a type for a single proposal.
type Proposal struct {
  Name       string `json:"proposalName"` //short name
  VoteCount uint    `json:"voteCount"`     //number of votes
}

// Main function starts chaincode, required by the Go language
func main() {
  err := shim.Start(new(Ballot))
  if err != nil {
    fmt.Printf("Error starting Ballot chaincode: %s", err)
```

```
    }
  }

  // Init initializes chaincode
  func (t *Ballot) Init(stub shim.ChaincodeStubInterface) pb.Response {
    // Get the args from the transaction proposal
    // In our case it is the registration id of the chairman
    args := stub.GetStringArgs()
    if len(args) != 1 {
      return shim.Error("Incorrect arguments.
             Expecting registration id of chairman")
    }

    // Set up any variables by calling stub.PutState()
    // We store the chairman value on the ledger as a byte array
    err := stub.PutState("chairman", []byte(args[0]))
    if err != nil {
      return shim.Error(fmt.Sprintf("Failed to assign chairman:
                        %s", args[0]))
    }

    return shim.Success(nil)
  }

  // Invoke - Our entry point for Invocations
  func (t *Ballot) Invoke(stub shim.ChaincodeStubInterface) pb.Response {
    function, args := stub.GetFunctionAndParameters()
    fmt.Println("invoke is running " + function)
    // Handle different functions
    if function == "initProposals" {
      return t.initProposals(stub, args)
    }
    else if function == "giveRightToVote" {
      return t.giveRightToVote(stub, args)
    } else if function == "vote" { //receive vote from individual
      return t.vote(stub, args)
    }

    // Return error when unknown function is received
    fmt.Println("invoke did not find func: " + function)
    return shim.Error("Received unknown function invocation")
  }

  // createProposals - create for each proposal a new entry in state
  func (t *Ballot) initProposals(stub shim.ChaincodeStubInterface, args
  []string) peer.Response {
    chairmanAsBytes, err := stub.GetState("chairman")
    if chairmanAsBytes != nil {
```

```
    chairman := string(chairmanAsBytes[:])
    if chairman != args[0] {
      return shim.Error("Invoker is not the chairman")
    }
  } else {
    return shim.Error("No chairman found: " + err.Error())
  }

  for i := 1; i < len(args); i++ {
    // Create proposal object and marshal to JSON
    var proposalName = args[i]
    proposal := &Proposal{proposalName, 0}
    proposalJSONasBytes, err := json.Marshal(proposal)
    if err != nil { return shim.Error(err.Error()) }

    // Check if proposal doesn't exists
    proposalAsBytes, err := stub.GetState(proposalName)
    if proposalAsBytes == nil {
      // Save proposal to state
      err = stub.PutState(proposalName, proposalJSONasBytes)
      if err != nil { return shim.Error(err.Error()) }
    }
  }

  // Proposals saved
  fmt.Println("- end init proposals")
  return shim.Success(nil)
}

// giveRightToVote - give the right to vote to a specific id
func (t *Ballot) giveRightToVote(stub shim.ChaincodeStubInterface, args
[]string) peer.Response {
  // Same code as above to only allow chairman to invoke - skipped
  // Retrieve voter from state to check if not yet voted - skipped
  // Create voter based on arguments
  // Args only include registration id from individual
  vid := args[0]
  voter := &Voter{vid, 1, false, ""}
  voterJSONasBytes, err := json.Marshal(voter)
  if err != nil {
      return shim.Error(err.Error())
  }

  // Save voter to state
  err = stub.PutState(vid, voterJSONasBytes)
  if err != nil {
    return shim.Error(err.Error())
  }
```

```
    return shim.Success(nil)
}

// vote - receive and store vote from individual
func (t *Ballot) vote(stub shim.ChaincodeStubInterface, args []string)
peer.Response {
  // Check if voter exists based on arguments
  // Args include reg id, and the name of proposal voted for
  vid := args[0]
  voteProposal := args[1]
  voterAsBytes, err := stub.GetState(vid)
  if err != nil {
    return shim.Error("Failed to get voter:" + err.Error())
  } else if voterAsBytes == nil {
    return shim.Error("Voter does not exist")
  }

  // Retrieve the proposal
  proposalAsBytes, err := stub.GetState(voteProposal)
  if err != nil {
    return shim.Error("Failed to get proposal:" + err.Error())
  } else if proposalAsBytes == nil {
    return shim.Error("Proposal does not exist")
  }

  // Placeholder for stored proposal object
  proposalObj := Proposal{}
  err = json.Unmarshal(proposalAsBytes, &proposalObj) //unmarshal
  if err != nil {
    return shim.Error(err.Error())
  }

  // Placeholder for stored proposal object
  voterObj := Voter{}
  err = json.Unmarshal(voterAsBytes, &voterObj) //unmarshal it
  if err != nil {
    return shim.Error(err.Error())
  }

  proposalObj.VoteCount += voterObj.Weight // Update vote count
  voterObj.Voted = true // Update voter voted status

  // Store updated proposal object
  proposalAsBytes, err = json.Marshal(proposalObj)
  err = stub.PutState(voteProposal, proposalAsBytes) //rewrite
  if err != nil {
    return shim.Error(err.Error())
  }
```

```
    // Store updated voter object -- skipped
    return shim.Success(nil)
}
```

Comparing the above code with the Ethereum example, you might have noticed that to achieve the same functionality, you need a few more lines of code. One of the reasons why this is so is the way that the programming language works. It is also due to a stricter compiler (you cannot initiate a variable that you do not use), and the way the Hyperledger Fabric interface forces you to interact with the ledger and catch every occurrence where an error can be thrown.

The other major difference is the need for a package name and dependency imports. In terms of the package name, you can organize your code in smaller pieces, but in most cases chaincode is written under `package main`. The reason for the dependency imports is that the Go language is not specifically written for Hyperledger Fabric, so it needs extra libraries to build and run the program.

Because Go is a more difficult language, it might take you some time to become familiar with it. From my experience, I would say that the learning curve is much steeper than that of Solidity. Just as we did for Solidity, let's look at the keywords used and other important functionality that is part of the programming language:

Keyword/Action	Usage
`//`	Generic comments not part of documentation
`package`	A package's name provides context for its contents
`import`	A list of dependencies that your code refers to or uses
`type ... struct`	Declares a complex type that contains multiple fields (or variables)
`string`	Declares a string
`uint`	Declares an unsigned integer
`bool`	Declares a Boolean
`func`	Declares an executable function and defines its input parameters
`for`	Creates a for each loop to process an array of items, for example
`shim.Start`	Notifies the Hyperledger Fabric container to start the chaincode
`shim.Error`	Creates an error object that can be returned
`shim.Success`	Lets the client know that the transaction proposal was successful
`fmt.Printf`	Formats a string for output to the console
`fmt.Println`	Writes a string as output to the console
`stub.GetStringArgs`	Retrieves string arguments passed by the client to the chaincode

Keyword/Action	Usage
`stub.GetFunction AndParameters`	Retrieves invoked functions and string arguments passed by the client to the chaincode
`stub.PutState`	Writes data objects to the ledger
`stub.GetState`	Retrieves data objects from the ledger
`json.Marshal`	Creates a byte array from a type for better storage in the ledger
`json.Unmarshal`	Creates an instance of a type based on the byte array from the ledger

Table of important Go and Fabric keywords

Once again, the example only discusses a small portion of the keywords used in the programming language and by the Hyperledger Fabric interface. I also didn't discuss how you can query data from the ledger to check the voting results. We will examine a more complete example when we implement our application using the Blockchain Cloud Service from Oracle in Chapter 12, *Designing and Developing Your First Smart Contract*. For the full specification of the Hyperledger Fabric interface, see here: `https://godoc.org/github.com/hyperledger/fabric/core/chaincode/shim`.

Where do your smart contracts run?

Not only is developing smart contracts very different on Ethereum vs. Hyperledger Fabric, but the way that individuals interact with smart contracts varies significantly between these platforms. While I will not review the steps for building and deploying the example contracts on these platforms, I will indeed compare the runtime environment of both platforms.

Ethereum

The runtime environment for smart contracts on the Ethereum platform is known as the Ethereum Virtual Machine. Code running on the EVM is not only sandboxed, but it is completely isolated, meaning that your code does not have access to network, filesystem, or other processes. Every full Ethereum node in the network runs its own EVM implementation which is capable of running the same instructions (contract bytecode) independently from other nodes.

The EVM can execute code of arbitrary algorithmic complexity, which in computer science terms means that Ethereum is "Turing complete" and maintains the consensus across the blockchain. In the case of the EVM, all smart contracts run on one instance, which has an impact on its efficiency since available computing resources are shared for all executed contracts. More complex contracts take up more resources than simple asset transfers.

Technically, the EVM is a stack-based virtual machine containing a memory byte array and key-value storage. All elements on the stack are 32-byte words, and all keys and values are stored in 32 bytes. The EVM currently understands over 100 instructions or opcodes, divided into 9 categories, including contract-specific instructions. When compiling the Solidity code, it generates a binary file with the corresponding instructions.

The EVM architecture is shown in the following diagram, showing that the code and storage is non-volatile (permanent) and is maintained as part of the system state, where as the call data and the memory is volatile (not permanent).:

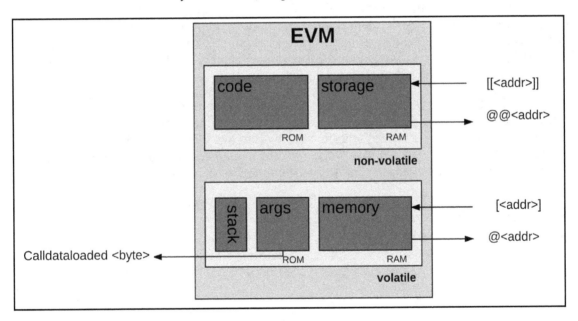

Architectural overview of the Ethereum Virtual Machine, or EVM

If you want to know more about the inner workings of the runtime environment of Ethereum, I recommend that you look at the following guide by CoinCulture: `https://github.com/CoinCulture/evm-tools/blob/master/analysis/guide.md`.

Hyperledger Fabric

All transactions taking place on Hyperledger Fabric are executed and processed through chaincode. Each chaincode runs in a secured Docker container that is isolated from the endorser peer process; however, it is orchestrated by the peer node. The state created by the chaincode contract is exclusively accessible to that chaincode, and it can't be accessed directly by other chaincode. However, within the same network and granted the right permissions, a chaincode is allowed to invoke another chaincode to access its state. Each peer is responsible for managing the chaincode container's lifecycle and networking. To interact with the chaincode deployed on these containers, the peer acts as a proxy and offers chaincode APIs (CLI, REST, or SDK) that a client can use.

Besides containers that run external-user chaincode, there are also system chaincodes that run as part of the peer process instead of in a separate container. The chaincodes are used to implement low-level ledger features such as the endorser system, query system, and validation system, and they are available to all other chaincode containers. Because of the fundamental nature of these system chaincodes, they are deployed when the peers start, whereas user chaincodes can be dynamically added later. External chaincode is actually published and stored in the ledger, and network participants need to reach consensus on the chaincode before the container is deployed.

I believe that Hyperledger Fabric is more scalable than Ethereum when it comes to running smart contracts, since each chaincode runs in its own container. This allows for parallel execution of different chaincodes without sharing the same virtual machine and system/node resources. Since it uses Docker for the containers, it would even be possible for Hyperledger Fabric to support multiple containers for one chaincode.

If you are interested in the full life cycle of chaincode on Hyperledger Fabric, you can see their Chaincode for Operators guide at: `https://hyperledger-fabric.readthedocs.io/en/latest/chaincode4noah.html`.

Summary

In this chapter, we examined the differences between Ethereum and Hyperledger Fabric. The most fundamental difference is in the way that they are designed, operate, and target different audiences. Ethereum is a publicly-available blockchain network. At its heart is the Ethereum Virtual Machine, or EVM. It offers a built-in cryptocurrency, Ether, with its associated transaction fees and smart contracts. Ethereum is a generic platform that can be used by everyone in an universal way. Hyperledger Fabric, on the other hand, has a modular architecture with pluggable components, such as its consensus mechanism and storage, which provides flexibility in terms of which components you want to use or not use, as if you were dining a la carte.

Ethereum's public mode of participation allows anyone to join the network. Because of its permissionless mode of operation, Ethereum offers total transparency, meaning that it is not possible to have restricted transaction visibility, since everyone can view all of the transactions on the blockchain and deploy and execute smart contracts. However, this comes at a cost of performance, scalability, and privacy. The performance is negatively impacted since participating nodes receive all transactions submitted to the network, which they then need to process individually. Because of the huge numbers of transactions, it is harder to scale the network since nodes may not be able to handle the size of the blockchain and the resources needed to participate in the consensus. The public nature of this blockchain is mostly targeted towards decentralized organizations and applications.

Hyperledger Fabric solves these issues by operating in a permissioned mode using a simpler consensus algorithm, PBFT, and fine-grained access control. You can join the network through a specific invitation or by exchanging security certificates. You will only be able to view transactions of which you are part. The number of validating peers needed to reach consensus on transactions occurs in a fraction of the time. Further, the modular architecture allows you to customize Hyperledger Fabric to target a multitude of applications.

A characteristic that you will only see in Ethereum is a built-in cryptocurrency called Ether. Ethereum is a natural fit for applications that require this capability to pay for services received or used. However, in many B2B transactions, this could also be a disadvantage as there are several use-cases where cryptocurrency is not really needed.

Both platforms provide smart contracts, or programmable code that acts as a substitute for legal and financial contracts or even business logic normally found in back-office applications. Ethereum uses a proprietary language, Solidity, that was created especially to run on the EVM. Solidity is very compact and easy to learn. In contrast, Hyperledger Fabric uses the more generic Go language, which is more complex and requires more code to perform the same actions. On the other hand, the types of applications that you can write in Go are much more powerful. Whereas smart contracts targeted for Ethereum are easier to write, the single EVM runtime per node is less scalable than the separate Docker container approach that Hyperledger Fabric uses.

As you have learned in this chapter, these two platforms have their positives and negatives depending on the use-case you are implementing, so choose wisely when implementing your specific ones.

In the next chapter, we will continue using Hyperledger Fabric as a part of the OBCS. First, we will look at how Blockchain is going to disrupt traditional Oracle B2B and Middleware solutions.

9
Building a Next-Generation Oracle B2B Platform

Before we take a deep dive into the **Oracle Blockchain Cloud Service** (**OBCS**) solution and learn how to set up a permissioned, consortium blockchain, and how you can build and run your own decentralized blockchain application, we need to take a step back and look at the B2B and middleware solutions that Oracle currently offers.

In this chapter, I will present a real-world business case that involves multiple **B2B** (**business-to-business**) and **B2C** (**business-to-consumer**) partners participating in a business network involving vehicle accidents and insurance policies, who conduct transactions between each other. These partners are all connected to each other through a **trusted third party** (**TTP**) using traditional B2B broker software. They use the Fusion Middleware stack to process data to and from their own back-office systems. I will review the common architecture, how connectivity between organizations is handled, explain the basic implementation for processing messages, and address the issues that usually occur during production.

Then, we will look at how blockchain will disrupt traditional B2B and middleware solutions, and how it solves most of the issues that you will encounter with these kinds of cross-organizational applications. Using the example presented, we will redefine the architecture, connectivity, security, and the way that data is shared and processed across each participating organization.

In this chapter, you will learn about the following topics:

- What are the solutions that Oracle currently offers for B2B and B2C transactions?
- How are traditional cross-organizational applications commonly implemented?
- What are the common issues involved with such implementations during production?

- How will blockchain disrupt the way you distribute and process shared data?
- How will blockchain disrupt and improve your daily work as a developer/architect?

Introducing the business case

Let's begin by visualizing the business case that we will use as a common thread throughout this chapter. The following diagram depicts a business network, portraying the different individuals and entities that interact when there is an automobile accident. The dotted lines show optional actions/relationships:

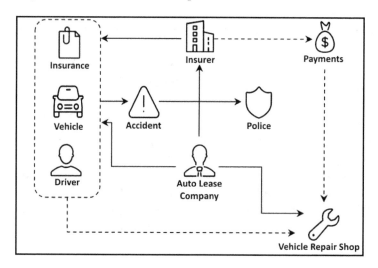

A business network showing the reporting of vehicle accidents, the handling of damages by the leasing company, damaged vehicle repair, and payments made by the insurer

Our business case is best described using the following scenario. Imagine that you are driving to work on a rainy day and some cars in front of you on the road slam on their brakes. The car behind you notices this too late, and it drives straight into your car with sufficient speed, causing your car's airbag to deploy. Your car includes an IoT-powered sensor that records the accident and automatically passes that information on to the emergency services. They call the phone number on record immediately, and luckily, because you don't have any serious injuries, you can answer the incoming call. The phone call is recorded, and you tell the emergency services representative what has happened and that it is important they send the police to help. Police officers are dispatched to the location and record both driver statements about what has occurred. Together, you fill in the accident report which is then sent to each of your insurers, who register the information in their back-office systems.

Because you lease your car, you also need to contact the leasing company to tell them what has happened. The leasing company registers this in their back-office system and requests that you send a copy of the accident report to them for their records. Since your car is damaged, the leasing company tells you that you need to have it fixed at a certain vehicle repair shop. Up until now, none of the parties involved have shared information with each other about the same accident report, though each has a copy of the accident report or the statement that you gave to the police. The same goes for the vehicle repair shop that you need to visit to have your car repaired. The first thing they tell you is that they need to contact your leasing company to check whether they are allowed to fix your car, as the leasing company ordered you to do. Finally, your leasing company communicates with both parties' insurers and eventually arranges for the vehicle repair shop to be paid.

Traditional cross-organizational applications

Now, let's take this business case and look more closely at how these traditional cross-organizational applications are normally implemented using the Oracle software stack. From my personal experience, these business applications generally use the following components:

- **Oracle B2B**: This is the software used to connect cross-organizational business processes by providing the secure and reliable exchange of documents between businesses, or in this case insurers, repair shops, and emergency services. Its architecture enables a unified document exchange platform, instance tracking, visibility, auditing, governance, and secure B2B transactions.
- **Oracle SOA Suite**: This software is Oracle's bona fide integration/middleware platform, and is used to create reusable service-based connectivity to existing enterprise applications, which allows you to transform complex application integration into tailored services. It provides a unified toolset for the development of services and composite applications that let you connect and orchestrate the flow of data between applications rapidly.
- **Oracle WebLogic**: This software is used to run both Oracle B2B and the SOA Suite, and it provides a scalable, enterprise-ready **Java Platform, Enterprise Edition (JEE)** application server. It supports the deployment of many types of distributed applications, including B2B, SOA, and others, such as ADF. Moreover, it also supports your own custom Java applications. System administrators can manage application connectivity, monitor and tune the performance of applications, and secure access to resources to prevent malicious attacks.

- **Oracle Database**: This software is used to collect, store, and retrieve related information for use by (database) applications. Oracle Database is a relational, table-based database that conforms to the relational model, and it is generally used by back-office systems so that business processes can interact with data.

For our business case, we will explore the Oracle B2B and SOA Suite in greater depth, since these are the components that are most affected by the blockchain.

Introducing Oracle B2B

Creating a bridge between organizations outside of their own boundaries can be a difficult task. You can choose to share documents (for example, Excel spreadsheets) and duplicate the data manually by sending them via email or uploading them to an FTP server. However, that isn't very cost or labor efficient, and some of the data might contain highly sensitive and/or confidential information, which you don't want to exchange in this manner. This is one of the reasons why, in the world of B2B and B2C, there are industry standard protocols that partners must use to exchange such business documents and transactions. Oracle B2B lets you quickly establish cross-organizational collaboration and automate business processes between partners. It supports industry standard protocols, including **RossettaNet**, **Electronic Data Interchange (EDI)**, **Applicability Statement 2 (AS2)**, and **UCCnet**, in order to provide a single integrated solution. In our implementation later in this chapter, we will use EDI in combination with the **ebMS (ebXML Messaging Service)** protocol.

Oracle B2B can be viewed as the entry point for cross-organizational enterprise applications, and it includes transport and exchange management, partner management, document management, and transaction reports and monitoring.

- **Transport and exchange management**: With business transactions, it is important that the communication is secure and that messaging between partners is reliable. Companies use Oracle B2B because it provides many secure transport protocols and different kinds of messaging services that allow users to define the protocol, transport parameters, exchange parameters, and security requirements separately for each communication channel. Oracle B2B supports message transports such as HTTP/s, FTP/s, sFTP, TCP/IP, and – less directly – JMS, Oracle AQ, SMTP, and IMAP.

- **Document management**: B2B documents and transactions can be defined in different formats based on industry standards. This means that the tool you use needs to provide the functionality to define, validate, and normalize, or translate, these documents. The document management capabilities of Oracle B2B provides this functionality, including the identification, correlation, batching, routing, and envelope generation of documents.

- **Partner management**: Furthermore, Oracle B2B enables the user to define partner profiles and agreements. **Partner profiles** are identities that can exchange information with each other. A profile includes partner identifications and their contacts, and it provides security and access to supported documents (defined under document management) and communication channels (defined under exchange management). **Partner agreements** define rules upon which both partners agree, such as the type of document, method of delivery, service level agreement (including such settings as Time to Acknowledge, Time to perform, and Retry Counts), and the level of identification required. Partner management also audits all interactions between partners for end-to-end monitoring.

- **Reports and monitoring**: To provide visibility into document activity, Oracle B2B provides **parameterized tracking reports**. These reports show activity based on a certain business, application, or conversation, and they let you drill down into errors. They also provide monitored metric, for example on the most active partners, most exchanged documents, and the number of messages processed or failed, including their average processing time. These reports are very useful in production because once something goes wrong during an exchange, it become visible immediately. For more system-level management, the Fusion Middleware console, which is part of the WebLogic Server, can be used to view end-to-end flow and statistics, and it allows the system administrator to view log files.

More information about Oracle B2B can be found at: `http://www.oracle.com/technetwork/middleware/b2b-integrations/overview/index.html`

Introducing Oracle SOA Suite

Once documents are exchanged and received by another partner, they usually need to be processed in their back-office system(s). In most cases, this is done in the middleware using an enterprise service bus or business process platform. Within the Oracle software stack, the go-to solution is Oracle SOA Suite.

Oracle SOA Suite falls under the same family of Fusion Middleware products as Oracle B2B and BPM, and it provides a toolset for developing (web) services and composite applications. It is a platform that simplifies integration between your business and IT environments, both on-premises and in cloud applications, such as Oracle B2B, Oracle ERP, Salesforce, and your databases. It can expose internal systems as services in order to make them consumable by modern web applications.

SOA Suite provides a standards-based integration platform that provides many capabilities, as can be seen from the following diagram:

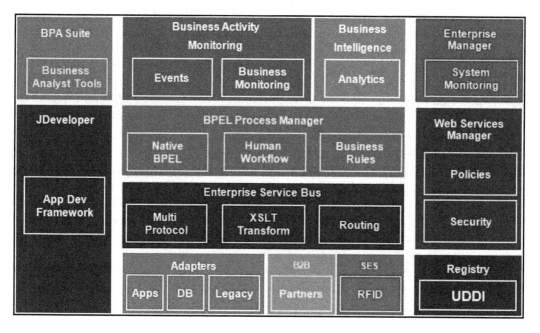

Diagram listing features of Oracle SOA Suite

Oracle SOA Suite can be seen as the integration and processing layer for connecting to enterprise applications, and it includes some of the key components used in our business case, namely **Oracle Service Bus** and **BPEL Process Manager**.

Oracle Service Bus: When implementing **service-oriented architecture** (**SOA**) principles, it is important that you build granular, loosely-coupled, and standards-based services to create business functions that can connect service consumers and back-end business services. **Oracle Service Bus** (**OSB**) is a component that offers a configuration-based, policy-driven enterprise service bus.

It provides a traditional message broker, service virtualization and management, adaptive messaging using adapters (JCA, JMS, REST, JDBC, FTP, EBS, SAP, and so on), and capabilities for service discovery and intermediation, service provisioning and deployment, and governance. OSB combines an intelligent message broker for the routing and transformation of messages, with the service management console for monitoring and administration (for example, SLA and Error Reports).

OSB leverages industry standards to connect with your existing applications and data sources, as shown in the following diagram:

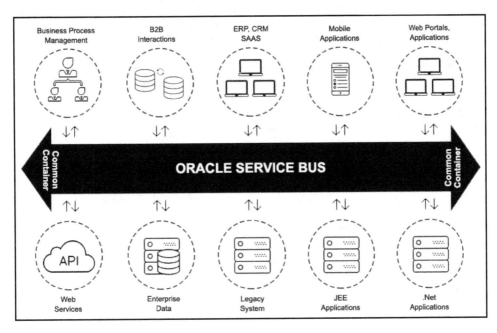

Oracle Service Bus is an enterprise-level service bus connecting business consumers with business applications

To learn more about the Oracle Service Bus, you can see the documentation here: `https://docs.oracle.com/middleware/12213/osb/index.html`

BPEL Process Manager: Another component commonly used in combination with Oracle Service Bus for more complex and transactional SOA composite services is Oracle **BPEL** (**Business Process Execution Language**) Process Manager.

It is a tool for designing and running business processes in a service-oriented architecture, and it provides a standards-based solution for creating, deploying, and managing cross-application business processes. It has native support for standards such as BPEL, XML, XSLT, XPATH, JMS, JCA, and Web Services. This makes it an ideal solution for creating integrated business processes.

Using the accompanying process designer, you can build a business process in a graphical and user-friendly way using BPEL as its native format. BPEL processes provide process orchestration and storage for either a synchronous or an asynchronous process. You design a business process that integrates a series of business activities and services into an end-to-end process flow. Such a process can implement different flows based on business rules and input data, as shown in the following screenshot:

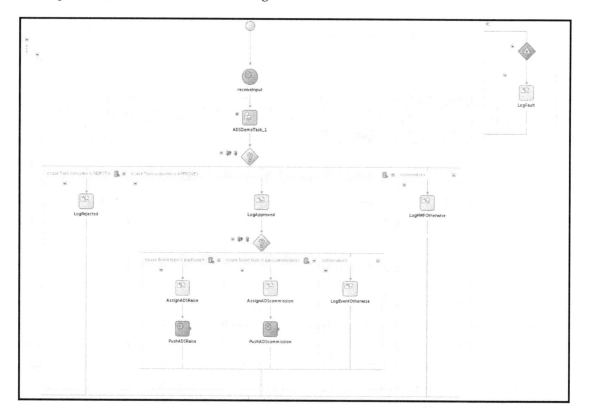

BPEL Process Manager lets you design an automated business process

To learn more about BPEL Process Manager, you can review the documentation at: https:/ /docs.oracle.com/middleware/12213/servicecomps/index.html

Implementing the business case on a B2B network

Now that you are familiar with the product solutions Oracle currently offers, let's look at how such a cross-organizational application can be optimized and implemented using these products. Let's review the business case proposed earlier in this chapter once again.

The parties in the proposed business case can exchange messages using Oracle B2B's message broker. Most exchanges would be peer-to-peer transactions between two of the Oracle B2B message brokers. In some cases, however, messages need to be routed to multiple parties. In our business case, for example, this is required when the cost of the insurance claim is estimated by the vehicle repair shop. The quote and detailed information about the repairs need to be sent to both the auto leasing company and the involved insurer(s). So, at minimum, that information needs to be sent to two other parties. As you can imagine, the larger the accident, the more parties are involved.

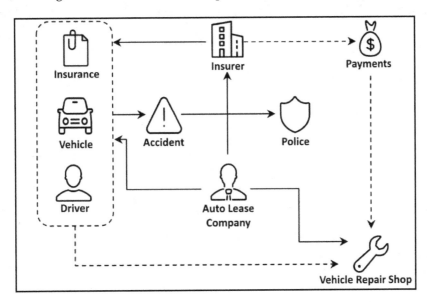

The proposed business case simulates the processing of a vehicle accident and its associated insurance claim

To address this issue, the parties involved exchange messages and documents through a TTP. This TTP offers IT services that allow B2B partners to connect to a central message hub instead of requiring all B2B partners to set up connections to each other. The TTP services include the configuration of partner profiles, and they provide transaction and exchange management in a uniform way.

After a B2B partner receives a message, it is up to them how they wish to process the exchanged information. In our business case, both the B2B partners and the TTP use Oracle Fusion Middleware products, such as SOA Suite and WebLogic Server, to process the data, execute business rules on that data, and store the data in an Oracle database. The type of business rules that the receiving parties need to implement redundantly on the middleware or back-end depends on the type of business transactions involved.

What is the common application architecture?

Before delving into the details of the implementation, let's examine the following application architecture, which connects the partners involved and the processes required to exchange business transactions:

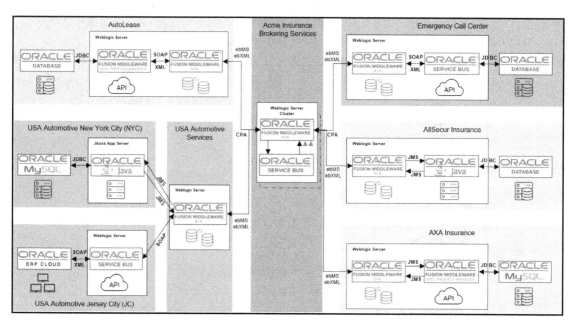

Application architecture showing how parties are connected with each other through the TTP

In the architecture shown in the preceding diagram, our business network connects a total of six partners through a TTP. On the right-hand side, three of the partners are listed: the Emergency Call Center and two insurance companies (AllSecur and AXA). On the left-hand side, the other three parties are listed: including the auto leasing company and two vehicle repair shops of the same franchise (USA Automotive, Jersey City and New York City), which are connected through a single B2B broker. The TTP in our case is Acme Insurance Brokering Services.

Acme Insurance Brokering Services provides a central message hub, and it is the original member of the business network. Its setup is not that complicated, and it consists of an Oracle WebLogic Server running in a two-node cluster with both Oracle B2B and Oracle Service Bus installed on top of it. Acme is responsible for the enrollment of each partner, the network connectivity setup using ebMS/ebXML infrastructure, and helping to define and implement **Collaboration Protocol Agreements** (**CPAs**) between partners. These capabilities are provided within Oracle B2B. They also route business transactions to multiple parties if required, which is built using Oracle Service Bus.

Communication between partners is established using ebMS, the messaging layer of the ebXML framework for exchanging B2B transactions. It specifies how messages are sent and received over an Internet or VPN connection, and it includes features for security, reliability, indisputability, and digital signatures. ebMS provides advanced privacy through the encryption of the messages and the authentication/verification of identities through the exchange of digital certificates.

The other parties, including AutoLease, AllSecur, and USA Automotive Services exchange business transactions through the use of Acme Insurance Brokering Services, with each having their own Oracle B2B broker running on-premises to send and receive messages. The communication between partners is established using ebMS, and the type of business transactions that can be exchanged are written down in a CPA, a collaborative agreement describing the messaging protocol between partners.

Trading partners need to specify this trading agreement (CPA) before they can exchange business documents/transactions. This is a combined XML document that describes the formal relationship between two parties and consists of each of the partner's abilities (**Collaboration Protocol Profile** or **CPP**).

Typically, a CPA document contains the following information:

- The unique identifier and roles of each partner within the relationship
- Required digital signatures and the type of algorithms they use
- The communication protocol used for exchanging documents
- The endpoint (URL, service, and action) to which to send messages
- Retry rules when messages are not received or cannot be delivered
- Acknowledgement and duplication rules for messages

Each of the partners can choose to implement their middleware and back-office system with different software tools—there are no limitations, other than the payload format of the messages. You can see the same action with the partners in our business case example.

AutoLease uses BPEL Process Manager, which runs BPEL processes to provide an integration layer between Oracle B2B and the Oracle database used by the back-office application. Using SOAP/XML, Oracle B2B calls a web service provided by one of the BPEL processes. BPEL messages are validated using the established business rules, which transform the information so that it can be sent to the database for storage.

The Emergency Call Center uses almost the same setup as AutoLease, but instead of using Oracle BPEL Process Manager, it uses Oracle Service Bus to provide the integration layer to connect Oracle B2B with their back-office database.

Oracle B2B supports multiple communication protocols, such as SOAP/XML, JMS, and File (via network sharing), which allows a middleware solution to connect and integrate with Oracle B2B. Where integration over SOAP/XML can be both asynchronous and synchronous, JMS, for example, is only asynchronous. In our case, it does not matter, since I will not go into that level of detail when reviewing the sample transactions. However, note that in our architecture, we see that AllSecur Insurance, AXA Insurance, and USA Automotive, New York City all use JMS to integrate with their middleware/back-end solution.

Some other noticeable differences between partners that you may have spotted are the use of a single B2B broker, a custom Java application, a different database vendor, and even a cloud/SaaS application for the back office. Partners such as AllSecure and USA Automotive, New York City have chosen Java as their integration solution so that their developers can easily check the necessary business rules in a programming language they understand. The New York and New Jersey branches of USA Automotive Services also use a single B2B broker so that these franchises do not have to deal with the administrative tasks surrounding the configuration of CPA agreements and the necessary infrastructure. The New Jersey Automotive Service does not use a traditional database for storage, but instead uses Oracle ERP Cloud to register and process business transactions. The service bus only performs the correct mapping of the data to and from the ERP Cloud APIs.

How do partners interact with each other?

Before partners can interact with each other, they all need to reach a consensus about the agreements and come up with a joint CPA that describes the interaction between them.

For our business case, this CPA contains these interactions (among others):

Action Id	Description	Can Send	Can Receive
BT01_BD01	Report new accident	Emergency Services	AutoLease
BT01_BD02	Accident acknowledgement receipt	AutoLease	Emergency Services
BT01_BD03	Accident error receipt	AutoLease	Emergency Services
BT02_BD04	Quote for repair	AutoLease	USA Auto., NYC USA Auto., JC
BT02_BD02	Quote acknowledgement receipt	USA Auto., NYC USA Auto., JC	AutoLease
BT02_BD03	Quote error receipt	USA Auto., NYC USA Auto., JC	AutoLease
BT03_BD05	Quote confirmation	USA Auto., NYC USA Auto., JC	AutoLease
BT03_BD02	Confirm acknowledgement receipt	AutoLease	USA Auto., NYC USA Auto., JC
BT03_BD03	Confirm error receipt	AutoLease	USA Auto., NYC USA Auto., JC
BT04_BD06	Insurance claim request	AutoLease	AllSecur Insurance AXA Insurance
BT04_BD02	Request acknowledgement receipt	AllSecur Insurance AXA Insurance	AutoLease
BT04_BD03	Request error receipt	AllSecur Insurance AXA Insurance	AutoLease
BT05_BD07	Insurance claim response	AllSecur Insurance AXA Insurance	AutoLease
BT05_BD02	Response acknowledgement receipt	AutoLease	AllSecur Insurance AXA Insurance
BT05_BD03	Response acknowledgement error	AutoLease	AllSecur Insurance AXA Insurance
BT06_BD08	Repair order request	AutoLease	AllSecur Insurance AXA Insurance USA Auto., NYC USA Auto., JC
BT06_BD02	Order acknowledgement receipt	USA Auto., NYC USA Auto., JC	AutoLease

Action Id	Description	Can Send	Can Receive
BT06_BD03	Order acknowledgement error	USA Auto., NYC USA Auto., JC	AutoLease
BT07_BD09	Payment request	USA Auto., NYC USA Auto., JC	AutoLease AllSecur Insurance AXA Insurance
BT07_BD02	Payment acknowledgement receipt	AllSecur Insurance AXA Insurance	AutoLease USA Auto., NYC USA Auto., JC
BT07_BD03	Payment acknowledgement error	AllSecur Insurance AXA Insurance	AutoLease USA Auto., NYC USA Auto., JC

Sample interactions between trading partners. The Action Id contains the business transaction number (BT) and business document number (BD).

In our case, due to the use of a TTP, the CPA needs to be configured between each partner and Acme Insurance Brokering Services redundantly instead of directly communicating with each other.

Aside from configuring the CPA and possible interactions, partners need to define the actual documents/messages that they send and receive per interaction. From my personal experience as an architect, these messages are usually defined in a functional document. This document describes the payload (XML document structure) in a human-readable form, and it spells out the business rules that need to be implemented by the receiving partner when processing the message. Examples of business rules include checking for duplicates, verifying whether all of the necessary fields are present, and reviewing other constraints regarding the combination of data.

In-depth look at interactions

Now that we have established the agreements between partners and their business transactions, let's examine the flow of three of these in more detail. Namely, a new accident report, an insurance claim request, and a repair order request.

New accident report

The new accident report transaction, identified by ID BT01_BD01, represents an accident report that is shared by the Emergency Call Center with the partner(s) that are involved in one way or another. In our case, this is the auto leasing company from whom you leased your car.

The receiving partner, AutoLease, needs to acknowledge the message (BT01_BD02) or send back an error (BT01_BD03) when one or more business rules are not met, for example, an unknown vehicle or driver/owner. The following diagram shows the complete interaction:

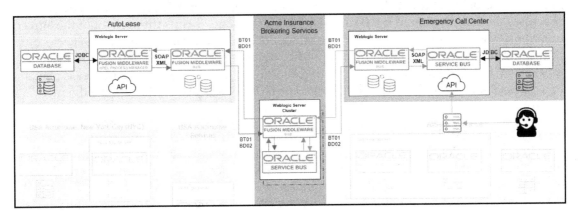

Interactions between the Emergency Call Center and AutoLease when a new accident is reported

This business transaction starts just after you call in the accident. The Emergency Call Center operator files the report using a front-office application and submits it at the end of your phone call. In the background, the application calls an API that is published by Oracle Service Bus and, based on the information provided, it transforms the data into an XML message that follows the structure on which both partners agreed. The API also persists the data into an Oracle database before sending the XML message over SOAP/XML to an API published by the Oracle B2B broker. Based on the metadata that the service bus transmits as part of the message sent to the API, Oracle B2B generates an ebXML envelope and delivers the message to the ebMS endpoint of the Oracle B2B broker run by Acme Insurance Brokering Services.

Once the message is received by the B2B broker of Acme Insurance Brokering Services, a simple acknowledgement message that is part of the ebMS protocol is sent back. The receiving B2B broker processes the ebXML envelope and routes it to an API running the service bus of Acme. This API decodes the received message and reads the content of the BT01_BD01 XML message. Based on the metadata in the message, it checks which partner(s) need to be routed the message. In this case, the message only needs to be routed to one partner, AutoLease. The service bus of Acme does not manipulate the business document itself, and it encodes the message back to a valid ebXML envelope. Then, through a second CPA between Acme and AutoLease, the message is exchanged with the B2B broker run by AutoLease.

The B2B broker of AutoLease receives the message, and when the ebXML message is deemed valid, it sends a simple acknowledgement message back to Acme. As with Acme, the B2B broker processes the ebXML message and routes it to an API, which this time is implemented using Oracle BPEL. The BPEL process decodes the received message and processes the information in the BT01_BD01 XML message. It runs through all of the agreed upon business rules described in the functional document, and after everything checks out, the information is persisted into the back-office database of AutoLease. To inform the Emergency Call Center that the information has been received correctly, AutoLease needs to send back a different business document, the BT01_BD02 (accident acknowledgement receipt).

This BD02 business document travels back as a reply to BD01 in the same manner, but this time in reverse order. The metadata used to send the message back is slightly different, where the sending and receiving partner IDs have switched places. The ebXML envelope travels from AutoLease via Acme to the Emergency Call Center, where the acknowledgement receipt relating to the accident report is logged by the service bus in the back office system.

Insurance claim request

The insurance claim request transaction, identified by id BT04_BD06, represents the creation of a new insurance claim and includes a copy of the accident report. The claim is initiated by the lease company, AutoLease, and sent to the insurance agencies involved, AllSecur and AXA. All receiving partners need to acknowledge the message (BT04_BD02), or send back an error (BT04_BD03) when one or more business rules are not met, for example, if it is a duplicate claim. The following figure shows the interactions:

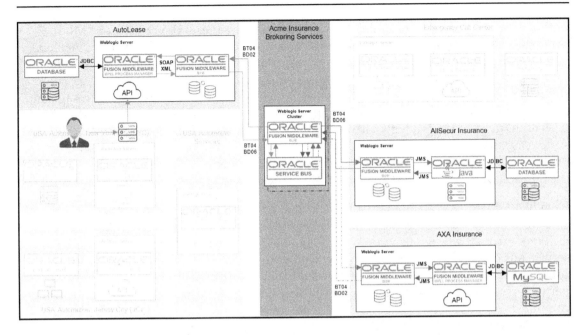

Interactions between AutoLease and the two insurance companies involved in the insurance claim

This business transaction starts just after a representative of the AutoLease company submits the insurance claim. In the background, the application calls an API that is published by Oracle BPEL Process Manager and, based on the information provided, it transforms the data into an XML message (BT04_BD06), upon which the partners have agreed. Just as in the previous interaction, the API persists the data into an Oracle database before sending the XML message over SOAP/XML to an API published by the Oracle B2B broker and it is routed to the ebMS endpoint of the Oracle B2B broker run by Acme Insurance Brokering Services.

Once the message is received by the B2B broker of Acme, it processes the ebXML envelope and routes it to an API provided by Acme's service bus. This API decodes the received message and reads the content of the BT04_BD06 XML message. Based on the metadata in the message, it figures out that it needs to route the message to two different partners (AllSecur and AXA insurance). The service bus of Acme does not manipulate the business document itself, but for each of the partners it encodes the message back to a valid ebXML envelope and sends two separate messages back to the B2B broker. Through separate CPAs between Acme/AllSecur and between Acme/AXA, the messages are exchanged with the B2B broker run by the partner.

Both B2B brokers of AllSecur and AXA receive their message, and when the ebXML message is deemed valid, they send a simple acknowledgement message back to Acme. As you can see in the preceding diagram, both insurance companies communicate over JMS (messaging queue) to their middleware / back-end application, and because of this, the processing of the message is handled asynchronously. AllSecur processes the message and business rules in their Java back-end and persists data into an Oracle database, while AXA uses BPEL in combination with a MySQL database to process the information. To inform AutoLease that the insurance claim is received correctly, both partners need to send back a different business document, BT04_BD02 (claim acknowledgement receipt). The contents of the message are similar to BT01_BD02 (accident acknowledgement receipt).

Each BD02 business document travels back as a reply to BD04 with yet another asynchronous call over JMS to the B2B broker, which routes the message to Acme. A big difference from the previous interaction is that before a response is sent to AutoLease, the service bus of Acme waits until it has received both responses back in order to make a combined response. The service bus knows this because it keeps track of how many partners received the original business transaction. Once all responses are received, a single combined response is encoded into an ebXML envelope which is sent through Acme's B2B broker back to AutoLease. AutoLease logs the claim acknowledgement receipt that relates to the insurance claim in their back office.

Repair order request

The repair order request transaction, identified by ID BT06_BD08, represents the request for the repair of a vehicle and it includes the part of the accident report that describes what should be repaired, plus the initial quote provided by the repair shop. The request for repair is initiated by the lease company (AutoLease) and sent to the repair shop involved (NY Automotive Services) and the insurance agency (AXA) of the responsible driver. This time, only USA Auto., NYC needs to acknowledge the message (BT06_BD02) or send back an error (BT06_BD03), for instance, if the referenced quote does not exist or has expired. The message to AXA is simply a notification that the repairs are being planned. The following diagram shows the full interactions:

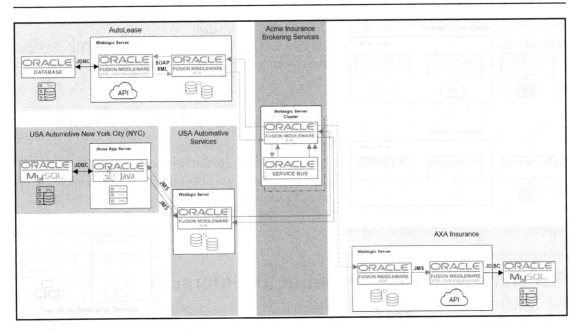

Interactions between AutoLease, the insurance company of the responsible driver, and the repair shop chosen to repair the vehicle

This case is not that much different than the previous scenario. The two things you should note are that AXA Insurance only has read rights (in a modern web application, this would result in a notification) and that the message to New York Automotive Service travels through the centralized B2B broker that every franchisee uses and is hosted by the holding company, USA Automotive Services.

The business transaction sent to AXA Insurance in this case is simply a notification that the request is made on behalf of AutoLease in order to allow for the car to be repaired. This interaction comes after both insurance companies have agreed upon the insurance claim. AXA registers the business transaction only as a progress event on the insurance claim resolution.

The business transaction sent to USA Automotive NYC is traveling through the central B2B broker of USA Automotive Services. A franchisee does not have to configure and manage a broker themselves, rather this is hosted by the franchisor (USA Automotive Services). This means that for both franchisees (New York City and Jersey City), the B2B broker has a separate CPA, allowing each to utilize a private communication channel. The broker just routes the business transaction to a remote endpoint running at the franchisee, in this case USA Auto., NYC. This partner does not use enterprise (Oracle) software, but has implemented its solution using a Java back-end running on JBoss and uses a MySQL database with stored procedures to process and store the data.

To inform AutoLease that the request for repair has been received correctly, USA Automotive NYC only needs to send back a repair acknowledgement receipt (BT06_BD02). The contents of the message are similar to the other two acknowledgement receipts.

Five implementation challenges and/or pitfalls

You probably have concluded that there are a number of problems with this way of interacting. Let's start with the fact that each interaction (business transaction) most often uses a different XML message (business document) with a different data structure and a different set of business rules when processing the data. Knowing this, I have developed the following list of five implementation challenges and/or pitfalls—there are surely many more.

Reaching a consensus about the interactions

Before even starting to configure the business network and implementing the business logic, all B2B partners need to reach a consensus on the interactions, business documents, and business rules. Usually, the information analysts from each partner involved would come together to define them, which eventually results in a functional document that can be handed over to the IT department. This can take a lot of time initially, depending on the number of stakeholders. For example, based on the technology used for implementing the business transactions, it can lead to business documents that need to be redesigned in a simpler form to support older (legacy) systems so that all partners can process the contents.

Configuring CPAs can be a redundant activity

In our business network example, the partners decide the contents of the business transactions, but the TTP is responsible for defining the CPAs between itself and each of the partners. Even though a TTP is used in our case, a new CPA needs to be created and configured on both sides. This is a redundant activity that requires manual labor for all B2B brokers involved. Nonetheless, the CPA itself is barely different; that is, in most cases only the organizational information is different, or a specific interaction is removed. Configuring and testing the connectivity needs to be done for each (new) partner in order to check that all interactions are working. This can become a painstaking task. Indeed, because it's a cumbersome activity, it also leads to a single B2B broker instance approach per partner for the production environment, which does not scale at all.

Partners need to implement the same business rules

After defining the interactions, business documents, and business rules, every partner needs to implement them in their own IT systems. This means that each partner needs to program the rules and logic to process the data into their back-office system. As shown in the architecture diagrams, most of the partners use (slightly) different IT software solutions to achieve this. As you can imagine, this can lead to differences in the implementation of the business transactions described in the functional document upon which all partners have agreed.

Are all rules implemented?

How do you know that each partner has implemented all of the rules in the same way and hasn't cut corners? There is no way of knowing that each partner has followed all of the defined rules, even though they are part of the same business network. In one instance of a project that I worked on, for example, a product owner instructed the development team to soften the rules or even not to implement them. This can lead to unexpected results when a business document is rejected by one partner but accepted by another due to this type of instruction.

Room for interpretation

Since the rules are written in a human-readable form, there is room for interpretation. It can occur that the individual who programs the business rules misinterprets what has been written. This too can lead to unforeseen results.

Use of different programming languages

Each partner can choose their own software platform and programming language to process the business transactions. When partners do not share a common codebase, they need to test their solutions individually. Code written in different languages can exhibit different behaviors and even unexpected bugs, which can't be resolved collaboratively when the code is not shared.

Different approaches to processing and storing data

Since each partner needs to implement the business logic themselves, they can choose to store only the data that is important to them. Also, they may add information only they know that is not part of the contents of the business document. Both actions have the effect that there is *no single point of truth* in the data.

Partners process and manipulate the data to fit within their own data store (database), because the B2B broker doesn't offer that functionality—it's just the ebMS. When issues arise, such as faulted or missed (lost) messages, the offline reconciliation of the data can become a painstaking task. This includes searching for the faulted instance/message in logs, removing or modifying the data in the data store, and retrying the message from the broker.

Offline reconciliation after uncompleted transactions

The biggest challenge is when a response to a partner (for example, AutoLease) requires that all receiving partners (AllSecur and AXA Insurance) respond with an acknowledgement or error receipt (message), but one partner fails to send one to the trusted third party (Acme Insurance Brokering Services). The TTP might wait indefinitely for a response, eventually failing to reply to the initiating partner (AutoLease).

Depending on the business rules of a particular business transaction, it is possible that, before the initiating partner can continue with the next business transaction, it needs to know whether the previous transaction was successful. This forces the initiating partner to build (program) a watchdog functionality that issues an alert when a response is not received after a certain amount of time. Nevertheless, the alert still leads to an offline reconciliation of the business transaction. In the worst case scenario, the initiating partner needs to contact all receiving partners to ascertain the status of the transaction. If, for some reason, both partners send back an acknowledgement, the problem may reside with the TTP (Acme), for example, missing or broken routing rules, timeouts, or bugs in the Service Bus processing.

This also raises the issue of the biggest pitfall (constraint)—end-to-end logging. Each partner only has visibility as to what occurred on their side. Each partner can review the activity log of the B2B broker to view the business transactions submitted and received, examine the service bus of BPEL instance data, inspect the data present or missing in the data store, or analyze the system error logs. What they can't see is each other's logs, so they need to work together to pinpoint exactly what went wrong.

Blockchain can solve these challenges

The proposed business case and its interactions are an ideal candidate for migrating to a blockchain-based system. Before we take a deep dive into the solution, let's start by once again visualizing the business case to see how we would use a blockchain, as shown in the following diagram:

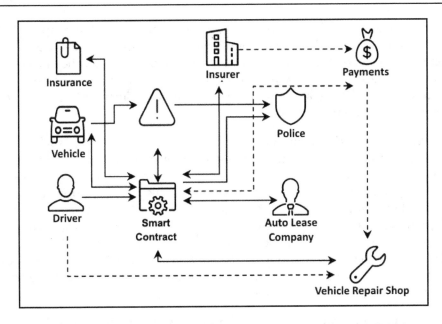

Our original business network, modified to show how the participants interact with the smart contract on the blockchain

As you can see in the preceding diagram, our business case now has a component called a **smart contract**. Here, it is portrayed as a central component, but it actually runs on all participating nodes (peers) in the blockchain business network. It holds the *single point of truth* for all interactions, business logic, and stored data.

Let's imagine the same rainy day as before, where cars that are driving in front of you suddenly slam on their brakes. The car behind you notices this too late and it drives right into your car at such speed that your car's airbag deploys. Instead of your car's IoT-powered sensor passing the recorded accident on to the endpoint of the IT system of the emergency services, the car submits a transaction to one of the available nodes in a blockchain network. Even if the IT system of the emergency services were down, the accident data would still be recorded. The transaction is distributed, and within seconds it is committed to the blockchain. An event is transmitted to the IT system of the emergency services, as well as every other system listening in on the event. You will still be called, but instead of the person on the other end of the line needing to ask you a set of questions about the accident (location, license number, and so on) they can view the data already present on the blockchain and focus on your injuries instead. The phone call is registered in a new *transaction* and added as an *asset* (including a transcript) relating to the accident in the blockchain. The previously-transmitted event is also received by the police, who are already on their way to the location that was registered when your IoT sensor recorded the accident.

The police arrive and, instead of recording your statement about what happened, they can read the transcript that was added to the blockchain (for example, by using a mobile application that calls an API exposed by the available nodes to query the blockchain) and verify the details of the transcript with you. They will also record the statement of the other driver and update the existing accident report by submitting another transaction on the blockchain (using the smart contract).

Together with the other driver, you fill in the rest of the accident report, such as the damage to both cars. This can be done with the existing accident statement form, which can be sent to each of your insurers, or it can be registered using a mobile application that can talk to APIs built on top of the blockchain's smart contract. In this particular use-case, the latter is used. The mobile application displays the registered accident and its details, since it already knows which drivers are involved. Using the app, the accident report can be updated and each of the drivers can sign the form before the transaction is submitted back to the blockchain. The transaction is distributed, and once a consensus is reached, it is committed and added to the blockchain. This commitment again results in an event being transmitted by the smart contract to the insurance companies involved.

Because you own a leased car, your leasing company is automatically notified since your insurance policy, which is stored in the blockchain, includes this data. Since your leasing company is recognized as a stakeholder, they receive the transmitted event. However, they can also query the blockchain to view the accident report. Now that the lease company is notified, they can also contact you directly about it. However, in our case, we call the leasing company ourselves.

The leasing company can easily find all of the information stored on the blockchain by querying the smart contract using your license plate number. The leasing company does not have to copy any data into their own system, and it can immediately act on the data.

Since your car needs to be fixed, the leasing company can inform the preferred repair shop that it is approved to repair your car. Thus, when you call the repair shop to make an appointment, it is automatically authorized to fix your car. Up until now, all of the entities involved have interacted directly with the data and business logic (smart contract) on the blockchain. Entities can still copy data to their back-office system, for example, reported damage, in order to create instructions for the mechanic. However, it's not used as the primary source of truth, as that is stored on the blockchain. When the garage finishes fixing the car, it can update the accident/insurance report, which then triggers an event to both of the insurers involved with the accident so that they can arrange for the garage to be paid.

How does it solve the traditional B2B challenges?

In the previous section, I explained five implementation challenges that I have personally experienced. These challenges were one of the main drivers for me to explore the technology behind blockchain. Let's take the same five challenges and examine how blockchain can help overcome them.

Taking out the middleman

With the B2B solution presented earlier, we had a TTP that connected partners to a central message hub that was responsible for sending business documents to multiple receiving partners. Using blockchain, we can solve some of the major challenges, such as message distribution to multiple partners, configuring redundant CPAs, and offline reconciliation.

Messages are distributed to partners in the blockchain

Since blockchain is a distributed peer-to-peer system, we do not have to use an enterprise service bus to route an incoming business document (message) to multiple receiving partners (peers). A business interaction (transaction) is directly executed against one of the blockchain peers, which distributes it and its message contents to all other active peers in the network. Depending on the blockchain type used (public or private), the message is sent to every peer, or only to the peers that are part of the private channel. The distribution of the messages is integrated into the technology.

Configuring redundant CPAs is a thing of the past

In that the blockchain is a platform framework where data and its business logic ("smart contracts") are shared with all active peers, some redundant tasks are a thing of the past. Depending on whether a public or private blockchain is used, the chances of this drawback happening is almost zero. When using a public blockchain, a partner can join the network on its own and only has to be authorized to use certain smart contracts to participate in a specific business network. When using a private ("permissioned") blockchain, a new partner can join an existing business network by sharing the public-key certificate and connection profile of their blockchain peer(s), which is generated when the peer software is installed. The owner or originator of the business network just has to import the profile and certificate and add the new partner to the accompanying channel(s). The new partner can then decide what peer(s) to join on the channel.

Solves offline reconciliation between partners

Considering that all transactions and their data are part of the blockchain and distributed to all peers, the chain can be used as the single point of truth of all business interactions. Transactions are only committed, depending on the endorsement policy, when enough peers have endorsed the transaction and its data, for example 51% of all peers, or a majority. Once committed, you can be sure that everything checks out. Since all transactions are appended to an immutable log, you immediately have a view of all interactions. Depending on the blockchain used (public or private) and the type of interaction (synchronous or asynchronous), peers get (immediate) feedback if a transaction fails, or they can listen in on rejection events.

The impact it has on the TTP

The business model of the trusted third party is indeed affected by the switch to a blockchain, but it also offers the TTP a new business model. In our business case, we want to use a permissioned blockchain as the transactions shouldn't be available publicly. The TTP could offer an industry-specific blockchain platform and provide IT services, such as a **Platform as a Service** (**PaaS**), managing partner adoption/registration, and smart contract consulting (for example, acting as a trusted verifier of the smart contract code).

Defining interactions is easier and more democratic

One of the most time-consuming parts of setting up an initial B2B business network is designing the interactions (transactions and events), business documents (assets), and business rules/logic (smart contracts) before implementation. Compared to a traditional B2B business network, a blockchain business network is not much different.

You still need to collaborate with the initial partners ("peers") to define the business network. The following questions need to be answered:

- What assets does the data model consist of (such as, entities, (required) fields, and so forth)?
- What are the available *transactions* and *events*, and who can execute which ones?
- What assets are necessary when submitting a transaction?
- What IF/THEN/ELSE rules need to be executed for each transaction?

The only difference when compared to a traditional B2B business network, is that with a blockchain business network, making changes is a more democratic and adjustable process.

With a traditional B2B network, a functional change (for example, a change in business transactions) first needs to be formalized with all of the partners consent, else you will get different results when implemented, as each partner needs to implement the changes in their own IT system. When one partner does not currently have the capacity to make a specific change, it might take that partner a long time to implement it.

When using a blockchain, however, change management depends on the endorsement policy in place. For example, the policy can state that the majority has to accept the change, rather than everyone having to accept it. Also, as the business rules/logic is part of the blockchain, it only has to be implemented once by updating the smart contract(s).

One smart contract to rule them all

With the B2B interactions discussed previously, all partners needed to implement the interactions, business documents, and business rules independently since no shared platform was used. For changes to be made, such as new interactions or updating business documents, every partner needs to program them redundantly on their own IT solution. You can imagine that this is a tedious process, and it can lead to different implementations since there is room for individual interpretation.

With blockchain, *transactions*, *events*, *assets*, business logic, business rules, and data queries are implemented using smart contracts. This can even be accomplished with a single smart contract per type of business network. The smart contract can be developed based on the functional document containing the business network components and shared with all partners for verification. After reaching a consensus on the contract code, all partners digitally sign the code and will run the same code, since it will become part of the blockchain. Compared to traditional B2B, with a blockchain network no custom implementation is required by the partners in order to interact with each other in a similar manner as with B2B, and it avoids room for interpretation and unforeseen bugs.

Using RESTful APIs or specific programming language SDKs (software development kits) provided by the blockchain framework software, the back-end applications, or even better, the front-end applications, can directly interact with the blockchain data by calling the transactions and queries defined in the smart contract.

Data is stored in the same way on each network peer

A direct result of using smart contracts is that the data is stored in an unambiguous structure on the blockchain. Using the smart contract, each peer in the network can store and query the data using the same approach.

Instead of the result of a transaction being distributed to all of the peers involved, the proposed transaction itself is distributed and executed redundantly on each peer. Data is only stored when the majority endorse the transaction. The data on the blockchain is the *single point of truth*. Rather than a back-end of the partner controlling the data, it just syncs the data for all of the partners.

Implementing the business case on a blockchain

What if the parties in the proposed business case switch to a permissioned blockchain, and instead of only exchanging messages (business documents) they use a common smart contract and data model (asset structure and relationships)? The smart contract can be written in a few programming languages, such as Java and JavaScript, but the main language is Go (developed by Google) and holds all of the transactions (functions), asset structure (types), attribute-based access control, and executable business logic.

A blockchain business network is set up between all of the parties so that they can communicate over a specific channel. In our business case example, the platform is offered as a service (PaaS) by our previous TTP, which has now rebranded itself as Acme Insurance Blockchain Services.

To set up the blockchain network, Acme and all of the other parties will install their own blockchain instance based on Hyperledger Fabric. All parties share their public-key certificates with Acme so that they can be added to access and join the channel. All parties and Acme install the agreed-upon smart contract, and Acme instantiates the smart contract on the channel.

To interact with the smart contract and the data on the blockchain, all parties use the RESTful APIs exposed by each of their peers. These APIs allow parties to execute the defined transactions. Each party (B2B partner) can build their own front-end or back-end solution on top of the blockchain, or they can sync the data with their previously-existing ERP solution.

B2B partners no longer have to implement all of the business rules since these are handled by the smart contract.

What is the blockchain platform architecture?

Before going into the details of the network implementation, let's look at the blockchain platform architecture that connects the participating partners and processes designed to exchange business transactions.

The following image shows the platform architecture using a blockchain that connects all of the partners together in a peer-to-peer network. Each partner has its own organization instance (peer) on the network. In this picture, Acme is the founder and facilitator of the network, and it generates ("mines") the genesis block, after which all other partners can join the network. The back-end applications of the partners connect either through a REST proxy or connect directly using the available SDKs.

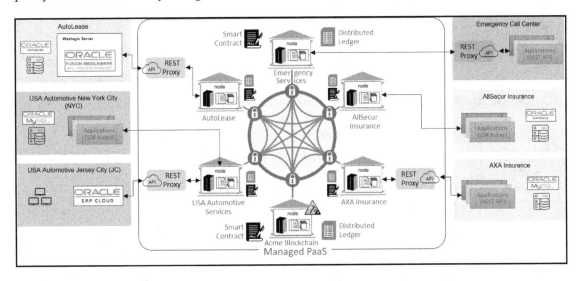

Application architecture demonstrating how parties are connected with each other using a permissioned blockchain

The preceding architecture diagram lists the same partners as earlier. However, it is somewhat simplified. On the left-hand side, you can see the existing (local) IT systems of AutoLease and USA Automotive, Jersey City and New York City. On the right-hand side, the IT systems of the Emergency Call Center and the insurers AXA and AllSecur are listed. In the center, the full blockchain network is displayed, which in our case runs on a managed PaaS that was founded by Acme Insurance Blockchain Services.

Each partner has its own blockchain peer, and thus has a copy of the distributed ledger and the smart contract. Both AllSecur Insurance and NY Automotive Services connect directly to their blockchain peer using the available application SDKs. The other partners, AutoLease, USA Automotive JC, and AXA Insurance, use an extra REST proxy to connect to the blockchain peer, which for them also runs in the cloud. The Emergency Call Center has chosen another option; that is, to run the REST proxy on-premises.

A partner has the option to build an application directly on the blockchain data and smart contracts, or to offload (synchronize) the data in their own back-office system. As you can see with our partners, they have chosen to use their old stack at minimum.

USA Automotive NYC, AllSecur, and AXA Insurance switch to a custom application, using Java or JavaScript, which connects to the blockchain APIs and offloads/enriches data in their existing databases. The Emergency Call Center, on the other hand, switched to a web application that directly interacts with the blockchain data and smart contract. Both AutoLease and USA Automotive Jersey City are still using their existing middleware and back-office systems, but modified the implementation so their integrations talk to the blockchain APIs instead of the B2B broker.

Smart contract interactions

Before partners can interact, they need to define a smart contract and reach a consensus about the smart contract code that represents the written interactions and business rules. The structure of the code is similar to the example code explained in the previous chapter. However, it will be explained in detail in `Chapter 12`, *Designing and Developing Your First Smart Contract*. In our business case, the smart contract contains the following interactions (*transactions* and *events*) among others.

Transaction	Description	Who can execute?	Who can read the data?
`ReportAccident`	Report new accident	Emergency Services AutoLease	Emergency Services AutoLease AllSecure Insurance AXA Insurance
`RequestQuote`	Request quote for repair	AutoLease	USA Auto., NYC USA Auto., JC
`OfferQuote`	Offer a repair quote	USA Auto., NYC USA Auto., JC	AutoLease USA Auto., NYC USA Auto., JC
`SendClaim`	Insurance claim request	AutoLease	AllSecur Insurance AXA Insurance AutoLease
`AcceptClaim`	Insurance claim response	AllSecur Insurance AXA Insurance	AutoLease AllSecur Insurance AXA Insurance
`RepairVehicle`	Repair order request	AutoLease	AllSecur Insurance AXA Insurance USA Auto., NYC USA Auto., JC AutoLease

Transaction	Description	Who can execute?	Who can read the data?
PaymentRequest	Request for payment	USA Auto., NYC USA Auto., JC	AutoLease AllSecur Insurance AXA Insurance USA Auto., NYC USA Auto., JC

List of transactions, who can execute them, and who can read the committed data

Event	Description	Transmitted after	Interested party
NewAccident	Notification of accident	ReportAccident	AutoLease AllSecur Insurance AXA Insurance
NewOffer	Notification of quote offer	OfferQuote	AutoLease
NewClaim	Notification of new claim	SendClaim	AllSecur Insurance AXA Insurance
RepairOrder	Notification of new order	RepairVehicle	USA Auto., NYC USA Auto., JC
PayOrder	Notification for payment	PaymentRequest	AutoLease AllSecur Insurance AXA Insurance USA Auto., NYC USA Auto., JC

List of events, when they are transmitted, and the interested party/parties

As you can see, our smart contract contains far fewer business transactions than a traditional CPA. This is because there is no need to receive a separate acknowledgement or error message, as the smart contract rules and endorsement policy will handle this before the data is ever committed.

Besides transactions and events, the smart contract also dictates the structure of the assets (business documents) and the business rules to be checked. Instead of assets being stored in an XML structure, the data is mostly stored and represented as a JSON document.

In-depth look into interactions

Now that we have established the interactions and developed the smart contract, let's look at same interactions discussed earlier in greater detail, namely the new accident report, insurance claim request, and repair order request.

New accident report

The `ReportAccident` transaction represents a new accident report that can be submitted by the application developed by the Emergency Call Center. The transaction is processed locally by the blockchain peer of the partner, and in our case, it is distributed and endorsed by everyone. Once the smart contract code that is executed by the transaction is complete, it transmits a `NewAccident` event. The application from AutoLease is listening to these kinds of events through websockets, and if the license plate number exists in their system, the data is queried and recorded in their back-end system. The insurance companies can also listen to the same kinds of events in order to understand that something happened to the vehicle. The following figure shows the full interaction:

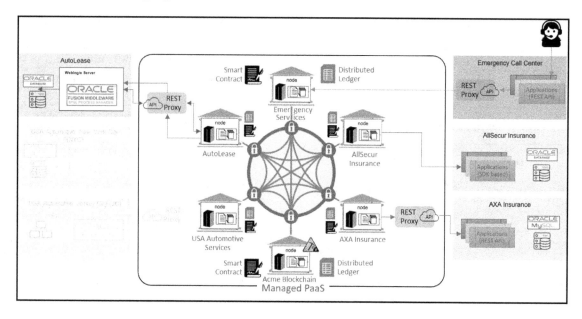

A transaction is submitted by the Emergency Call Center, which stores the data and transmits an event to AutoLease and the insurance companies.

As you can see, the transactions are much simplified and straightforward in the blockchain network. The initiator does not have to wait for a response, because it can rest assured that the other partner has access to the data stored in the blockchain and can act on it.

Insurance claim request

The `SendClaim` transaction represents the creation of a new insurance claim, and it includes a reference to the accident report. The claim is submitted by the leasing company, AutoLease, using their front-office system, which calls a web service exposed by BPEL Process Manager.

The associated BPEL process transforms the XML message into a REST API call that executes the correct smart contract code. The transaction is again processed locally by the blockchain peer, and it is once again distributed and endorsed by everyone. Once the smart contract is finished executing the code, it transmits a `NewClaim` event. The applications from AllSecur and AXA are listening to these kinds of events through web-sockets, and if the insurance policies involved exist in their systems, the data is queried and registered into their back-end system. The following diagram shows the full interaction:

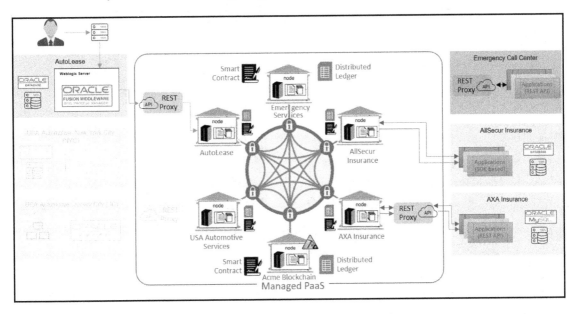

The transaction is submitted by AutoLease, which stores the data and transmits an event to the insurance companies. Both AllSecur and AXA query and store the data in their own systems.

Once the transaction is submitted, the smart contract code is responsible for checking all of the business rules. When the referenced accident report does not exist or some of the required data is missing, for example, the smart contract will throw an exception and the transaction will not be endorsed.

Repair order request

The `RepairVehicle` transaction represents the request for the repair of a vehicle, and it refers to the quote from the repair shop describing what is to be repaired and what it will cost. The request for repair is submitted by the leasing company, AutoLease, using their front-office system, which then calls a different web service exposed by BPEL Process Manager that transforms the XML message into a REST API call in order to execute the correct smart contract code.

If the transaction is endorsed and committed, a `RepairOrder` event is transmitted. The application from NY Automotive Services is listening in on these types of events through web-sockets, and upon receiving it they schedule an appointment in their back-office system to fix the car. The insurance companies involved also receive the transmitted event, but they do not act upon it.

The following diagram shows the full interaction:

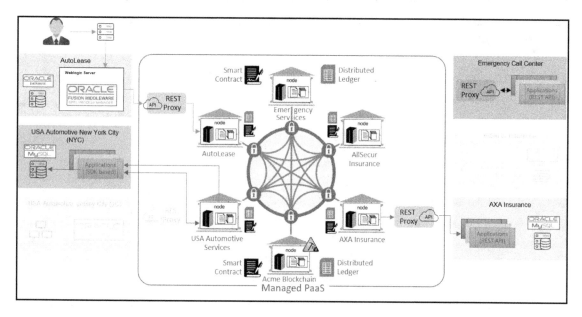

The transaction is submitted by AutoLease, which stores the data and transmits an event to the insurance companies. Both NY Automotive Services and AXA Insurance receive the event, but only NY Automotive Services acts on it and schedules an appointment.

So far, none of these interactions has communicated with the Acme blockchain peer, other than using the node for validation purposes. This means that the involvement of Acme is limited only to providing the platform and taking part as a trusted party in verifying transactions on the business network.

Blockchain – the next-generation B2B platform

As you can see from these three interactions, blockchain offers many advantages over traditional B2B transactions and it will certainly disrupt a lot of industries, including transportation, and energy supply chain.

Transactions are much faster and event-driven, and are evaluated by a single smart contract before the data is processed, committed, and stored everywhere in a consistent manner.

The blockchain network does not only disrupt the distribution of transactions without requiring the involvement of a TTP, but it also alters how existing IT systems are integrated.

Whereas in the past you needed to build expensive and complex web services and back-end applications in order to implement all of the business rules, with blockchain the logic is part of the smart contract and is available to every participating partner. Moreover, a smart contract can be programmed collectively instead of mandating that each partner program it redundantly.

With blockchain networks, developers can now focus on building applications directly on the *single point of truth* using the available APIs and know that the data in the blockchain will adhere to all of the business rules. The complexity is removed from the middleware and/or back-end systems, which makes the integrations far simpler and less error-prone.

And don't forget the totally different infrastructure and application architecture. Blockchain node software can run on commodity hardware and is built as open-source tooling, so it is very scalable without needing heavy-duty enterprise hardware and expensive licensed software, whereas traditional B2B, SOA, Weblogic Server implementations carry a very big footprint in this regard.

Not convinced yet? Stay tuned and experience this for yourself as I will use these interactions in `Chapter 12`, *Designing and Developing Your First Smart Contract*, to build this decentralized application for real.

Summary

In this chapter, I proposed a business use case for an accident registry and insurance network that connects six B2B partners who conduct business collaboratively. First, I explained the business case in which an accident leads to an insurance claim and a request for a vehicle repair. I used this business case to explain how such a cross-organization application was set up in a traditional sense and explained the software products Oracle currently offers (Oracle B2B and SOA Suite) that can be used to build such an application and the infrastructure required to support it. Furthermore, I implemented the business case and explained the common application architecture, how partners interact with each other, and how three of these interactions could be implemented.

Finally, I reviewed five commonly-experienced challenges when implementing and supporting such an application, including the painstaking task of offline reconciliation when something goes wrong during a transaction.

Then, I described how a blockchain network can solve these challenges, and I explained how it takes out the middleman, delivers a single point of truth using a shared ledger, and enforces all business rules using shared smart contracts.

Furthermore, I revisited the B2B business case and converted it into a blockchain platform architecture, went over the smart contract interactions (*transactions* and *events*), and showed how the same three interactions could be implemented in a blockchain network. Finally, I offered you my opinion that blockchain is the next-generation B2B platform.

In the next chapter, we will examine the managed PaaS that Oracle offers, which will allow us to implement the business case described in this chapter.

10
Introducing the Oracle Blockchain Cloud Service

Now that you have learned how a blockchain can disrupt traditional cross-organizational (B2B) applications, what a typical business case looks like, and how the proposed business case can be implemented using a permissioned blockchain, you can start working toward your own implementation.

During Oracle's Open World 2017 conference, the company introduced their **Blockchain Cloud Service** (**OBCS**) platform for managing and running a permissioned blockchain. (At the time of this writing in May 2018, this platform is not yet released.) The information supplied in this and the following chapters is based on the most recent beta release of this product.

In this chapter, we will explore and learn about the managed **Platform-as-a-Service** (**PaaS**) that Oracle offers for running your own permissioned blockchain. The chapter serves as an introduction to the product, and it explains Oracle's choice of using Hyperledger Fabric, covers both Fabric and OBCS architecture components and features—including the added value of using OBCS—and the deployment and integration models needed to make your network as much of a decentralized one as possible.

In this chapter, you will learn about the following topics:

- Why did Oracle pick Hyperledger Fabric?
- What component roles does Hyperledger Fabric fulfill?
- Why did Oracle build a managed PaaS?
- What component roles does OBCS fulfill?
- What are the added values of using OBCS over Hyperledger Fabric?

Why did Oracle pick Hyperledger Fabric?

When answering this question, you need to look at the kinds of industries and customers that Oracle actively serves. Oracle's largest customers can be found in supply chain management, transportation, healthcare, and government. These are all industries where different businesses work closely together and transact (confidential/private) information between each other (B2B). This, of course, needs to be handled with care and should not be leaked to the public.

With this in mind, the choice of Hyperledger Fabric is not very far-fetched. As already explained in Chapter 8, *Ethereum Versus Hyperledger*, Fabric is intended as a foundation for developing decentralized blockchain solutions in need of a distributed ledger, and it provides the required permissioned blockchain model and membership services.

We have seen that Fabric does not require/use cryptocurrency to keep the network running. The consensus model does not incentivize participating nodes for validating transactions, as the number of nodes is generally very stable due to the fact that they all transact with each other on the business network. No cryptocurrency means no transaction fees and better performance (that is, better validating speeds).

The open source platform offers a modular architecture allowing components, such as consensus and membership services, to be plug-and-play. This means that Oracle can alter the way in which their platform and active business networks behave in the future, as it enables pluggable data stores, consensus protocols, and the use of many different membership service providers.

The platform focuses on a scalable implementation using Docker containers. Each component runs in its own container, which can easily scale up and out, or scale down and back. New organizations can easily join an existing network or add extra peers to the network. Oracle leverages their **Infrastructure-as-a-Service** (**IaaS**) and the Application Container Cloud Service to provide the required scalability.

Fabric also enables end users to develop programmable smart contracts and host them on containers for the automation of business services. Instead of B2B partners implementing their own logic, they can leverage smart contracts to have the logic executed directly on the blockchain.

One of the important drivers of Oracle is confidentiality and privacy between transacting business partners, which is supported through use of Fabric's (private) channels. Network administrators can provision private channels wherein only a subset of all participating nodes are a part. In this way, the same blockchain network can be used by multiple decentralized applications.

What component roles does Fabric fulfil?

Before reviewing why Oracle built a managed PaaS on top of Fabric instead of just providing an Iaas, let's first examine the components of Fabric in more detail and what role each component fulfills.

The following diagram shows the components of a Fabric blockchain network:

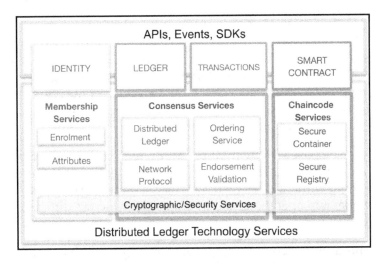

The software components of Hyperledger Fabric, including membership, consensus, and chaincode services

The architecture is divided into two layers: the **Digital Ledger Technology** (**DLT**) services and the APIs, Events, and SDKs. The DLT layer includes everything needed to run the blockchain, whereas the top layer lets the user interact with the blockchain.

The DLT includes the following three services:

- **Membership Services**: Pluggable identity services, which provide user enrolment (through **Membership Service Provider**, or **MSPs**), custom identity attributes (such as access lists), and authentication with the blockchain network. They also provide privacy and auditability of transactions.
- **Consensus Services**: Network services that provide the ordering and distribution of the ledger and its transactions and perform endorsement validation, cryptographic encryption, and consensus across nodes.
- **Chaincode services**: Secure container and registry services that provide the ability to deploy and run business logic against the blockchain (also called smart contracts).

The APIs, Events, and SDKs all provide ways to interact with the blockchain and the distributed ledger. You can build applications directly against REST and command-line APIs, or use language specific SDKs. Also, when listening to events, an application can be automatically triggered when something is executed on the blockchain that is of interest to that application.

Membership services

The Hyperledger Fabric framework uses pluggable membership service providers, also called MSPs. This component offers an abstraction layer of all membership-related operations. An MSP controls the enrolment of network members (organizations) and provides related cryptographic services. It abstracts away all of the cryptographic mechanisms for issuing and validating X.509 certificates for enrolment, transactions, communications (TLS), and user authentication.

A Fabric network can be governed by multiple MSPs, with each having a possible different implementation, as an MSP can define its own notion of identity and rules by which it governs (validates) and authenticates (verifies) those identities. This approach provides modularity of membership operations and interoperability across different security standards and architectures.

An MSP implements a **certificate authority** (**CA**) architecture with a root CA and intermediate CAs to identify and define the members (for example, an organization) of the trust network. It does this either by listing the identities of the members, or by identifying which CA is authorized to issue valid identities, or in most cases a combination of both.

For each of the different members (actors), including network peers, orderers, client applications, and admins, the MSP issues a digital identity encapsulated in an X.509 digital certificate. These identities determine the exact permissions over resources and access to information that actors have in a blockchain network. For membership enrolments, a MSP issues a so-called ECert. It can also issue TLS certificates for securing TLS communication among network nodes. The following screenshot shows an example of a human-readable version of an **enrolment certificate** (**ECert**):

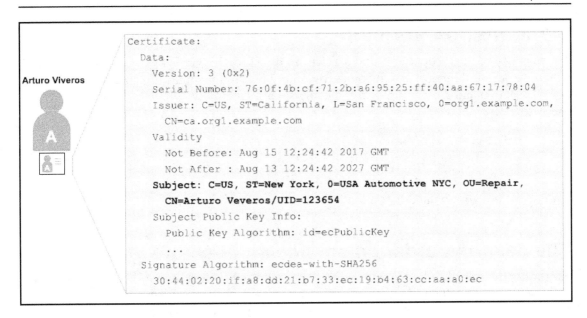

```
Certificate:
    Data:
        Version: 3 (0x2)
        Serial Number: 76:0f:4b:cf:71:2b:a6:95:25:ff:40:aa:67:17:78:04
        Issuer: C=US, ST=California, L=San Francisco, O=org1.example.com,
            CN=ca.org1.example.com
        Validity
            Not Before: Aug 15 12:24:42 2017 GMT
            Not After : Aug 13 12:24:42 2027 GMT
        Subject: C=US, ST=New York, O=USA Automotive NYC, OU=Repair,
            CN=Arturo Veveros/UID=123654
        Subject Public Key Info:
            Public Key Algorithm: id=ecPublicKey
        ...
    Signature Algorithm: ecdea-with-SHA256
        30:44:02:20:if:a8:dd:21:b7:33:ec:19:b4:63:cc:aa:a0:ec
```

Arturo Viveros

Enrolment certificate issued to Arturo Viveros (user ID #123654) of the organization New York Auto Services

The purpose of an MSP goes beyond simply identifying and listing members, as it can also identify specific identity roles (for example, admin) within the scope of the organization it represents. This also allows an MSP to define access privileges for members in the context of a network and on specific channels (such as channel admins, readers, and writers).

The association between these special roles and an identity is recorded through a principal. Principals can be compared with a user or group ID; however, they can include a wide range of properties, such as the actor's organization, organizational unit, role, or an even more specific identity.

For all interactions between the actors and the blockchain, the MSP provides client and node authentication through credential verification, cryptographic functions to provide signature generation and verification (using PKCS #7 – Cryptographic Message Syntax), and optional access control (based on **Attribute-Based Access Control (ABAC)**).

For more information about the membership services and identities within Fabric, examine the following reference documentation: http://hyperledger-fabric.readthedocs.io/en/release-1.1/identity/identity.html. When we set up our own network in the next chapter, we will take a closer look at these identity services.

Consensus services

The majority of the components and services in the Hyperledger Fabric framework relate to the consensus and integrity of the blockchain network and its data. The consensus services can be best explained by going over the components separately, which include the following:

- The peer and ordering service architecture
- The distributed ledger and world state
- Channels for limiting access and visibility
- Peer gossip data dissemination and consensus protocol

The peer and ordering service architecture

Naturally, the most fundamental building blocks of the Fabric framework are the network architecture and protocol. As you learned in `Chapter 8`, *Ethereum Versus Hyperledger*, the network architecture consists of peers and orderers (group forming the ordering service) and agreement on a protocol to query, endorse, and commit transactions.

Before exploring the details of the protocol, let's take a look at the following diagram. It shows a Fabric network architecture of four peers (two of which are also endorsers), the ordering service, two client applications, and the MSP:

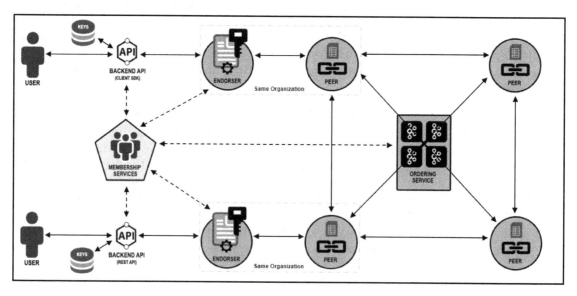

Basic Fabric peer and ordering service architecture including peer interactions (solid) and membership service interactions (dashed)

In the preceding diagram, there are a few different component roles that come into play:

- A **user** or client application proposes transactions to an endorser using the API or SDK. The client may choose to connect to any available peer.
- An **endorser**, or endorsing peer, endorses proposed transactions by the user/client application and executes the associated chaincode (smart contract). Not every endorser may participate in every chaincode execution, as every chaincode may specify an endorsement policy that refers to a set of endorsing peers.
- The **ordering service** (group of ordering peers) verifies that the endorsements meet the established (channel) policy, orders the transactions in batches and communicates these batches in the form of blocks with other peers.
- A **peer** receives ordered state updates (blocks) from the ordering service, and maintains the ledger and world state by committing transactions.
- The **membership services** constantly verifies whether the users and peers have the correct permissions to propose and execute (endorse and/or commit) transactions.

An endorser or endorsing peer does both the endorsement and commitment of transactions; they are displayed separately on the diagram, when actually upon runtime they are the same host.

The ordering service provides a shared communication channel and guarantees delivery of transactions by offering a broadcast service, meaning that all peers will see an identical series of delivered messages. A number of messages are grouped (batched) and output as blocks based on the configuration settings of the channel. During this process the ordering service imposes and conveys a deterministic ordering to support **multiversion concurrency control** (**MVCC**), as explained in Chapter 4, *Blockchain 101 - Blocks, Chains, and Consensus*, using a combination of timestamps and incrementing transaction IDs.

The ordering service can be implemented in different ways, ranging from a centralized service (for example, SOLO) for development and testing to distributed protocols (for instance, Kafka-based) that target different network models that support clustering. There are some interesting parallels between Kafka and a blockchain, as Kafka is a streaming platform that has the capability to publish and subscribe to streams of records, store streams of records in a fault-tolerant durable way, and process streams of records as they occur.

Depending on the ordering service, it may support multiple channels for parallelism similar to topics in publish/subscribe (pub/sub) messaging architecture. Channels are like a disk or database partition—clients can connect to one channel while being unaware of other channels that exist, but clients may choose to connect to multiple channels.

The distributed ledger and world state

The Hyperledger Fabric platform uses two types of data structures on its blockchain: a *world state* and a *distributed ledger*. The world state represents the latest state of the blockchain, and it is modeled as a versioned **key/value store** (**KVS**). It stores its keys as simple names or composites (that is, constructed keys) and values as arbitrary blobs, which often represent JSON documents. These entries can be manipulated by the chaincodes (smart contracts) running on the blockchain. A client application can execute these chaincodes through PUT and GET KVS-operations via the shim API. Keys in the KVS are partitioned and belong to a particular chaincode, which can easily be recognized from their names. This permits only transactions belonging to this chaincode to modify the keys. Any chaincode can read keys belonging to other chaincodes, as it can call another chaincode internally.

The world state persistently stores successful state changes in a pluggable database (by default LevelDB, but it can be any supported KVSes or even RDBMSes), and updates to the state are logged in a history and block index. Currently, this is just a pointer into the ledger in Fabric, but it is accessible via the getHistoryForKey() API. The world state is maintained only by peers, not by orderers and clients. Clients can call a chaincode to change the state, but they do not have a copy of the state.

The distributed ledger on the other hand is a file-based transaction log, and it provides a verifiable history of all state changes. The following diagram shows both data structures and their purposes:

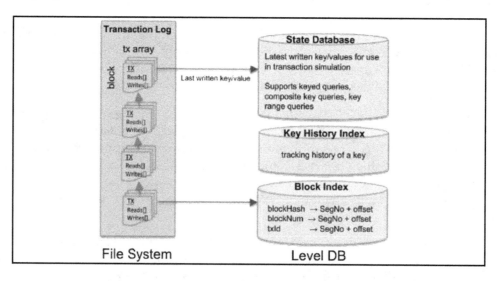

Both blockchain data structures and their content and storage location

The ledger is constructed in an ordered hashchain of blocks consisting of all successful state changes (valid transactions) and unsuccessful invocations to change the state (invalid transactions). The hashchain imposes the exact order of the blocks in the ledger, whereas a block contains an array of precisely ordered transactions. So, the state is the result of executing all successful transactions and can be rebuilt.

The ledger is kept at all peers, and optionally at some orderers. The ledger at a peer (PeerLedger) differs from the one an orderer keeps (OrdenerLedger), as peers also maintain a local bitmask that distinguishes valid transactions from invalid ones. Over time, the ledger grows and the peers may decide to prune (clean) their PeerLedger. The orderers maintain the OrdenerLedger for fault-tolerance and availability of the PeerLedger, as peers may decide to prune their PeerLedgers. The ledger allows (new) peers to replay the history of all transactions to get in sync with the rest by reconstructing the world state.

Channels for limiting access and visibility

One of the components of Hyperledger Fabric that makes it an interesting choice for business is the use of channels. Channels are a partitioning mechanism to limit access to and visibility of data (including transactions) only to authorized members.

A channel is created to represent a group of member organizations, called as a consortium, for the purpose of conducting private and confidential transactions. Each participating member assigns one or more of their peers who maintain a separate shared ledger specific for that channel—a "submit" of communication within a blockchain. Each transaction is executed on a channel where the ordering service treats transactions on different channels independently. The confidentiality on a channel is provided through restricted access and governed by joining and data access (read-only, read/write) policies, where each entity must be authenticated and authorized to transact on the channel.

An organization can join a single peer to multiple channels and maintain multiple ledgers or multiple peers to the same channel. An organization can also assign one of the peers to be an anchor peer on a channel. An anchor peer is a special peer per channel member, which allows other member's peers to discover all channel participants.

Is it required by Hyperledger to establish an anchor peer? No, you can also add a peer configuration manually, but a best practice is to assign an anchor peer (or multiple anchor peers) to prevent single point of failure.

The following diagram shows transactions flowing between clients that partially join the same channels that are governed by different endorsers. Each channel has its own ledger and world state (storage), so the orderers can treat transactions independently:

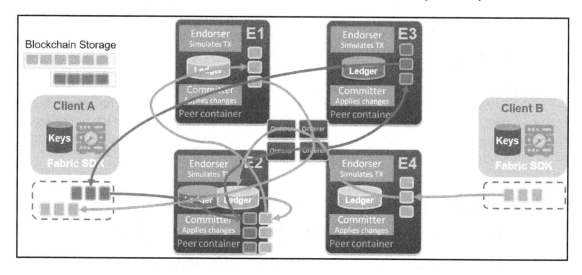

Two clients transacting on the blockchain using partially different channels

Peer gossip data dissemination protocol

In order for peers to communicate with each other, Hyperledger Fabric implements a gossip data dissemination protocol. This protocol provides performance, security, and scalability of data by dividing the workload across peers and ordering nodes.

Peers leverage the gossip protocol to broadcast ledger and channel data. The flow of messages is continuous, so each peer (that join a channel) constantly receives current and consistent ledger data from other peers. Each message that is broadcast (gossiped) is signed, thereby allowing peers to identify the sender of faked messages easily and prevent the distribution of messages to unwanted targets. It also allows for peers that were affected by delays, network partitions, or other causes resulting in missed blocks to sync up their current ledger state by contacting peers in possession of these missing blocks.

The gossip data dissemination protocol perform the following three functions:

- Manages peer discovery and channel membership by continually identifying which member peers are available. It can eventually detect peers that have gone offline, since all peers broadcast digitally signed "alive" messages.

- Broadcasts (disseminates) ledger data across all peers on a channel, allowing a peer whose data is out of sync with the rest of the channel to identify the missing blocks and sync itself by copying the correct data and reconciling its world state.
- Brings a newly connected peer up to speed by allowing other peers to send peer-to-peer state transfer updates of ledger data.

The protocol works in a way that peers receive messages from other peers on the channel and forward these to a number of randomly selected other peers on the channel. The number of random peers is a constant that can be configured.

For dissemination of blocks, the leader peer on a channel can pull data from an orderer and disseminate it to other peers on the channel. The leader peer can be defined (or elected) in two different ways:

- **Static**: Allows for a system administrator manually to define one or a set of available peers to be the leader within the organization. When defining multiple nodes to be the leader, it should be taken into account that creating too many peers to connect to the ordering service might lead to inefficient bandwidth utilization.
- **Dynamic**: Allows peers to execute a leader election procedure to select one peer in an organization to become leader, pull blocks from the ordering service, and disseminate blocks to the other peers in the organization. A leader is elected for each organization from the set of available peers and is responsible to send *heartbeat* messages to the rest of the peers as evidence of active participation. When no heartbeat message is received by one or more peers during a period of time, a new leader is elected.

Online peers constantly broadcast "alive" messages to indicate their availability, with each message containing the **public key infrastructure** (**PKI**) ID and the signature of the sender. If all other peers in the channel do not receive an alive message from a specific peer, this offline ("dead") peer is eventually purged from channel membership in order to maintain a properly working channel. Malicious peers can't imitate "alive" messages and impersonate other peers, as they are cryptographically signed with the private key of that peer, over which they do not have authorization.

Consensus protocol

The consensus protocol used by Hyperledger Fabric operates in a three-phase process: endorsement, ordering, and validation (commitment). Consensus is finally achieved when the order and results of a block's transactions have met all policy criteria checks that take place during the three-phase life cycle of a transaction, after which consensus peers can query the data.

During the life cycle, the use of endorsement policies dictates which specific members must endorse a certain class of transactions, and system chaincodes ensure that these policies are enforced and upheld. Before transactions are committed, these system chaincodes make sure that an adequate number of endorsements are present, and that they were derived from the appropriate organizations. Finally, a versioning check takes place to ensure that the current state of the ledger is agreed to or consented upon before appending the block of transactions to the ledger. Doing so provides protection against double-spend operations and other threats that may compromise data integrity.

Endorsement

This first phase of endorsement determines whether a transaction should be accepted or rejected. The endorsement process works as follows:

1. A client sends a signed proposal (transaction request) to the required peers.
2. The endorsing peers execute the requested chaincode (smart contract) function on a specified channel, accessing the channel's ledger and world state.
3. They capture the inputs and outputs and return them both as digitally signed **Read and Write** data, called **RW** sets, to the client. The execution itself is referred to as a "simulation," because the outputs are not persisted in the ledger until they are verified in the commitment phase.

The process also incorporates a transaction endorsement model. This model is designed to separate trust assumptions for smart contracts from trust assumptions for the ordering of blocks by ensuring that a required subset of entities with specific roles participates in the verification process.

The model enforces using the endorsement policies. A policy can be specified for each smart contract when it is first instantiated on a channel in such a length that each chaincode/channel combination can have a different endorsement policy. It specifies which peers and how many of them must validate the contents of the smart contracts. This can be a combination of M out of N organizations as well as specific organizations. The policy is enforced by peers every time they verify proposed transaction (batched in blocks).

Let's go over the endorsement model using a more visual approach. In the following flow diagram, you see a client application wanting to submit a transaction proposal for chaincode function **A**. On this specific chaincode, an endorsement policy is specified that the clients need to target the required endorsing peers, E_1, E_2, and E_3, when submitting a proposal. The other peers, P_4 and P_5, are not part of the endorsement policy:

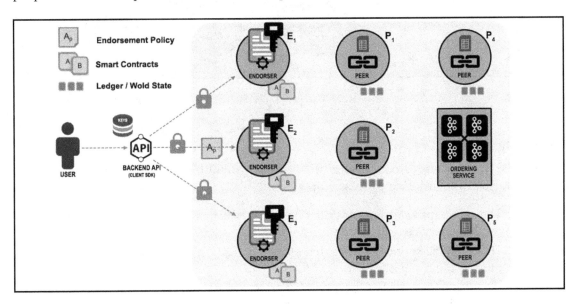

A user interacts with a client application to submit a transaction (proposal) to all three endorsers as required by the policy

After the endorsers **E1**, **E2**, and **E3** receive the proposal transaction, they each execute it. None of these executions will update the ledger, as they are "simulations" and will not be broadcast to peers **P4** and **P5**. Each execution will capture the RW sets. These sets are signed by each endorser and returned to the application:

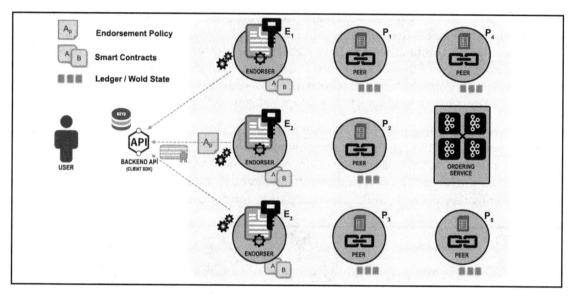

The smart contract is executed, and a signed RW set is returned by each endorser to the application

Ordering

The second phase of endorsement sorts all transactions that take place within a time period into a sequence. The ordering process works as follows:

1. The client application sends the received RW set as one transaction to the ordering service.
2. The ordering service verifies that all of the digital signatures of the RW set sent over by the client are valid.
3. The orderers sort all of the incoming transactions that take place within a certain time period into the correct sequence and batches them into a block. The block is sent to all peers on the channel.

Let's review the process in more detail once again using a visual approach. In the following flow diagram, you see a client application submitting the RW set as a transaction to the ordering service in order to be ordered. The ordering happens across the entire Fabric network in parallel with transactions being submitted by other applications:

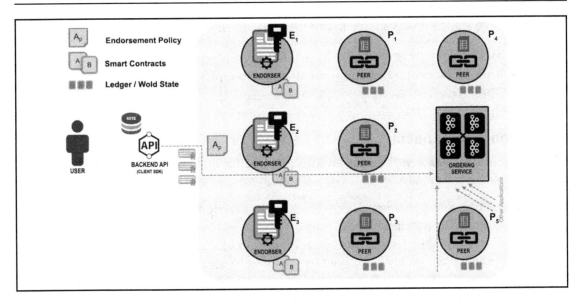

Client application submitting an RW set as a transaction to ordering service

The ordering service collect transactions into blocks for distribution to committing peers. Peers can deliver the blocks to other peers using the gossip protocol. The distribution is shown in the following flow diagram:

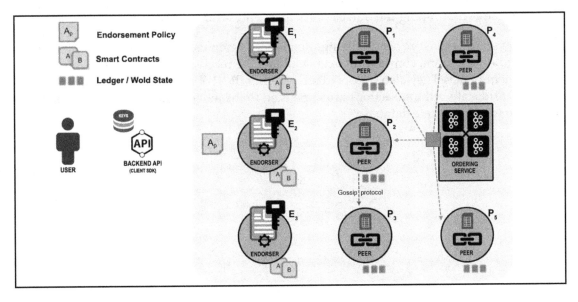

The ordering service distributes the blocks of ordered transactions to the committing peers. Peers can use the gossip protocol to redistribute blocks of transactions.

There are three algorithms available to order transactions:

- **SOLO**: A single ordering node, just for development
- **Kafka**: Blocks of transactions are mapped to topics
- **SBFT**: Tolerates faulty peers (future release 1.4)

Validation (commitment)

The third and final phase verifies the endorsement policy and checks to see whether the RW set is valid according to MVCC. The validation process works as follows:

1. All peers on a channel receive blocks of transactions from the ordering service or through the gossip protocol.
2. Each peer validates the transactions within a block and verifies that the endorsement policy is fulfilled by checking to see whether the required $N+$ endorsements have been received. It also verifies whether the version of the read set in the transaction matches the current version in the world state.
3. Each transaction within a block is tagged as being valid or invalid by updating its bitmap flag.
4. After verifying all of the transactions, the peer appends the block to the channel's chain, and for each valid transaction the write sets are committed to state database.
5. After committing the transactions, an event is transmitted to notify the client.

Finally, let's review the process in greater detail once again using a visual approach. In the following flow diagram, committing peers validate the received transactions against the endorsement policy. They also checks to see whether the RW sets are still valid against the current world state. All transactions are appended to the ledger, and valid transactions are written to the world state database:

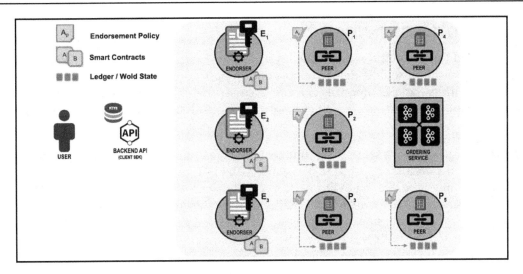

All peers validate received transactions against endorsement policy and commit them to the ledger/state

After the committing peers are done updating their ledger and world state, they notify the applications. Applications can register to be notified when transactions succeed or fail and when new blocks are added to the ledger. Applications will be notified by each peer to which they are connected, as shown in the following flow diagram. Thus, it is very important that applications be idempotent if they act on these notifications:

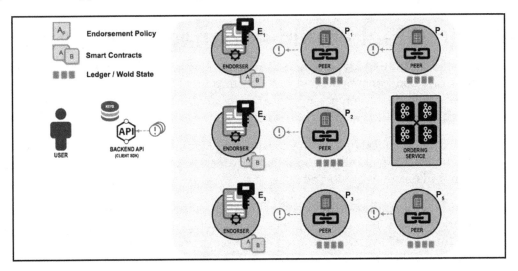

Peers emit notifications when transactions are committed and the ledger/state is updated

Chaincode services

As mentioned throughout this book, the Hyperledger Fabric framework uses smart contracts (application chaincodes) to enable other applications to interact with the blockchain and its data. Chaincodes execute business logic that is agreed upon by members of the network. The logic is based on business functions that can be executed by blockchain applications.

Chaincodes are actually a set of programs that run in a secured docker container that is isolated from the endorsing peer process. Since version 1, these programs could be built using the Go language. Starting with version 1.1, they can also be programmed in Java and JavaScript. Through chaincode, a blockchain application can submit transactions to initialize and manage the state of the ledger. A chaincode can perform GET and PUT operations on the KVS, but these requests are intercepted by the peer node, as the chaincode container does not have direct access to the ledger.

Once transactions are committed, the persisted data (key space) is available for client applications through query functions. The data accessible to the chaincode is restricted by its chaincode ID, meaning that each smart contract owns access to its data. Other smart contracts cannot access "foreign" data, except by invoking the other chaincode's query functions. A client application sends a signed message to one of the endorsing peers to run a query function. The peer executes the function and returns the signed results.

Why did Oracle build a managed platform?

Looking at the platform that Hyperledger Fabric offers, you could conclude that it contains all of the necessary components needed to run your own blockchain and applications. However, if you were to implement a production-ready blockchain, you will realize that is not that straightforward and is even little bit difficult.

When implementing a blockchain from scratch using Hyperledger Fabric, you will come across many challenges, including production readiness, operational difficulties, enterprise integration, and platform evolution hurdles:

- **Production readiness**: Blockchains depend on many complex technologies to work together. Implementing the Fabric blockchain requires you to install and set up the entire infrastructure and peer network yourself, keeping in mind things like scalability, resiliency, security, and recoverability.

- **Enterprise integration**: Integrating enterprise applications within the blockchain offered by Fabric is no mere out-of-the-box task. For each application, you need to build adapters (client applications) that utilize the Fabric SDK.
- **Operational challenges**: Member peers within a network are decentralized, since it spans many different organizations. Due to this situation, member on-boarding can be a long and slow process, and items such as supportability and life cycle management need to be aligned among member organizations.
- **Platform evolution**: The technology behind the blockchain is still a moving target. It is still rapidly changing. This means that when managing the network on your own, you need to stay involved in platform changes. A new version of Hyperledger Fabric is currently released every few months.

When you start to set up your first blockchain development environment, you immediately meet up with these challenges. To overcome them, Oracle's response is that wider adoption of the blockchain requires a managed platform, dubbed the OBCS.

The platform aims to promote flexibility and agility in order to explore different use cases without setting up a new infrastructure for each case. Oracle's strategy is to deliver a platform that simplifies provisioning and management of the necessary infrastructure across multiple data centers (including availability domains) in the cloud and/or on-premises, and is billed on usage-based consumption. The platform uses preintegrated technologies and preassembled infrastructure services to deliver a managed cloud service and simple integration APIs for new and existing applications.

Oracle's platform promises to implement common enterprise-grade requirements that can be reused, such as out-of-the-box resilience and **high availability (HA)**, scalability of peers across data centers, management of these peers (including autonomous recovery), and the on-boarding of new members. The platform focuses on faster consensus through parallelization and sharding, and it aims to provide greater privacy and confidentiality through security of identities, key management, and data-at-rest encryption.

Oracle's platform allows for common integrations with Open Banking APIs and existing ERP and **SaaS (Software as a service)** applications, such as NetSuite, by providing adapters in the Oracle Integration Cloud, for example. This means that your existing software can easily integrate with the blockchain without writing a lot of custom code. You can build blockchain applications using REST API-driven development or SDK-based development (Java, Node.js, and so forth) and deploy them on Oracle's other PaaS services, such as their Application Container Cloud Service or Java Cloud Service.

When used on its own, what is missing from Fabric is that it does not include any management and monitoring consoles. Everything is done using peer configuration files and APIs (REST or command-line). Monitoring environments can be done by looking into log files. On the other hand, Oracle's platform aims to provide easy-to-read dashboards that integrate monitoring and troubleshooting capabilities by implementing a common operations environment that lets you dynamically change the configuration.

Since the platform is managed by Oracle, you will get periodic updates on the underlying platform software. The updates can be managed and installed using the management console instead of having to install it all manually. The console controls the (necessary) upgrades, which then helps with the overall evolution of your platform.

What component roles does OBCS fulfill?

You have learned that OBCS is built as an implementation and extension of Hyperledger Fabric. The added value of OBCS lies in the extra components added in and around Fabric. Before going over the details of the new and modified components, let's look at the following model showing the reference architecture of an Oracle blockchain network:

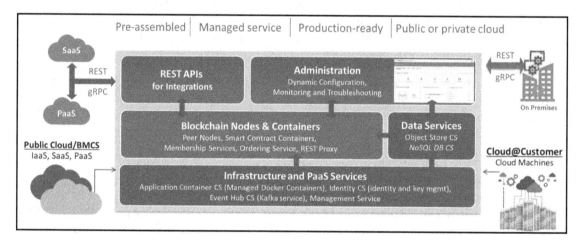

The blue components are (updated) Fabric components, and the red components are additions/changes made by Oracle

The OBCS architecture is divided into three layers: the infrastructure services, the blockchain and data services, and the management and integration services, each with its own components. The (partially) blue components are inherited from Hyperledger Fabric, whereas the (partially) red components are part of Oracle's blockchain platform.

The OBCS contains the following components:

- **Infrastructure and PaaS services**: OBCS comes as a preassembled, template-based provisioned platform on the Oracle Cloud or on-premises (through the use of Cloud@Customer machines). It incorporates underlying infrastructure dependencies (for example, managed containers, object storage, and Kafka) through existing Oracle Cloud Services.
- **Blockchain nodes and containers**: OBCS incorporates the Hyperledger Fabric framework for its peer nodes and ordering service, smart contracts containers, membership services, and basic APIs, and it configures and runs the blockchain software on the provisioned infrastructure.
- **Data services**: OBCS uses its own block and object store, instead of the default LevelDB/CouchDB. The key/value world state is stored using the NoSQL DB Cloud Service, whereas the ledger is stored using the Object Store Cloud Service.
- **Administration services**: OBCS offers a management/operations console that automates many administrative tasks, allows for dynamic configuration with (automatic) server restart, and makes it easy to monitor transactions.
- **REST Gateway/APIs**: OBCS offers a REST gateway that supports a subset of common Fabric APIs and enables synchronous invocation of these APIs. It simplifies integration and insulates applications from the underlying changes of the evolving platform.

Another perk when using the Oracle Blockchain Cloud Service is that it is going to be well integrated with other SaaS and PaaS services that Oracle offers. For example, there will be adapters in **Oracle Integration Cloud (OIC)** that directly connect to your business network.

Infrastructure and PaaS services

The first advantage of using the Oracle Blockchain Cloud Service instead of just vanilla Hyperledger Fabric is that your blockchain network comes as a preassembled platform, and it is provisioned based on a template. All of the necessary infrastructure dependencies to run the Fabric components are provisioned using new and existing IaaS and PaaS services that Oracle offers, before the peer nodes and ordering services are installed and configured.

The following diagram shows all of the Oracle Blockchain Cloud Service platform components with which you are mostly familiar already, as it is built on top of Hyperledger Fabric:

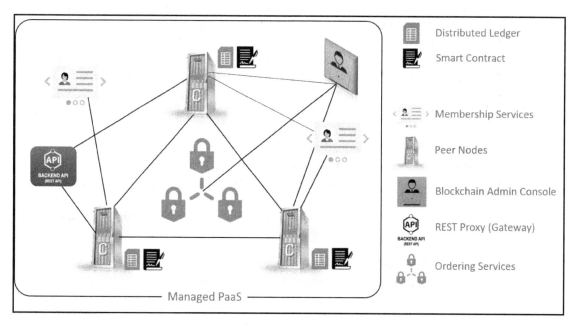

All components of the Oracle Blockchain Cloud Service

These components are all provisioned on new and existing Oracle Cloud services, such as Identity Management, Event Hub, and Application Container. In the following diagram, the IaaS and PaaS are represented as an overlay on the platform components:

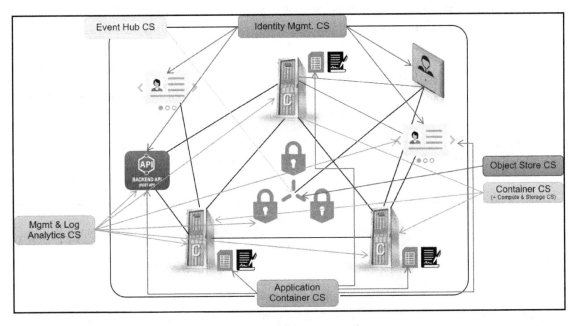

Overlay of a selection of IaaS and PaaS services used by OBCS

As you can see, the OBSC is heavily integrated with the Oracle Cloud infrastructure. Let's go over some of these cloud services in more detail and explore the role of each service:

- **Container Native CS**: In combination with the underlying **Compute and Storage CS**, this IaaS service hosts a managed VM with all of the peer and ordering nodes. New peers can be added to the pool using the BCS Admin console, which will be provisioned by this service on the necessary infrastructure.
- **Application Container CS** (**ACCS**): This PaaS service hosts the REST proxy container, a container for each executable chaincode, the container for the membership service and the BCS Admin console. ACCS provides elastic scaling, load balancing, autonomous health monitoring, and recovery.
- **Identity Management CS**: This PaaS service provides user/role management for the membership service and authentication for the BCS Admin console, REST proxy, and CA.

- **Event Hub CS**: This PaaS service is used by the ordering nodes to provide fault-tolerant cluster-based ordering of transactions. Event Hub is Oracle's managed Apache Kafka service.

- **Object Store CS**: This IaaS service is used to store and archive the ledger blocks and world state continuously. It provides continuous configuration backup and dynamic updates on the configuration used by the different Fabric components.

- **Mgmt. and Log Analytics CS**: This PaaS service provide integrated monitoring, management, analytics, and recovery services. With Log Analytics, for example, you can analyze all log data from your applications and infrastructure–enabling you to search, explore, and correlate this data to troubleshoot problems faster.

There might be a few other cloud services that are used in the background such as the **Oracle Cloud Infrastructure (OCI) Load-Balancer-as-a-Service (LBaaS)**. The following diagram shows the high-level service architecture when provisioning an OBCS instance:

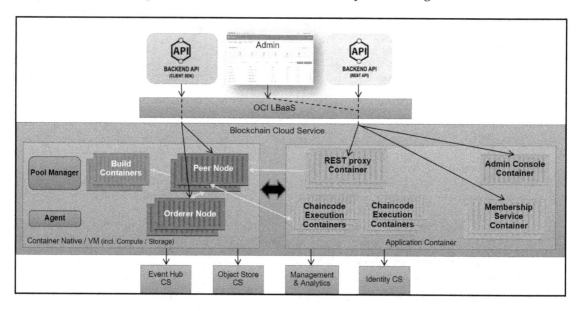

BCS high-level service architecture

Blockchain nodes and containers

As mentioned before, the BCS uses Hyperledger Fabric for the blockchain nodes. These nodes are deployed as Docker containers and run the necessary software. The peer and ordering nodes run as separate containers on a VM managed by Oracle's Container-Native platform and the chaincode (smart contract) containers, the Membership Service Container, REST proxy, and Admin console are hosted by ACCS. Oracle wouldn't be Oracle if they didn't enhance the standard Fabric container software. They have to if they want to integrate with their already existing cloud services. Let's go over the peer node and ordering services

OBCS peer node

The standard implementation of a Fabric peer maintains the ledger of successful and invalid transactions, a world state (key/value database), and a history/index database. The peers commit transactions (RW sets) per channel they joined, and some peers also, endorse transactions by executing chaincode (smart contracts) and producing RW sets based on the executed RW operations on key/value pairs.

The peer nodes used by OBCS have a few enhancements. An OBCS peer maintains a pool of GO build containers, which allow it to build new chaincode faster and store the binary after successful build in the object store for easy access by other peers belonging to that organization. When the chaincode is instantiated in a channel, the peers starts an execution container in ACCS, which loads the required binary from the object store.

It also provides data-at-rest encryption for the world state (Berkley K/V database) and the ledger so data is even harder to compromise from within.

OBCS orderer node

When provisioning an instance of OBCS, you can choose what kind of ordering (orderer) service you want to use. In version one of OBCS, you can choice between SOLO and Kafka. SOLO is mainly used for development and provides a single process, whereas Kafka performs the serialization of transactions and ensures high availability. When using vanilla Fabric 1.0, the Kafka cluster must set the retention period to infinity as it is the single source of truth and an essential part of keeping data integrity.

Oracle developed some enhancements for their orderer node. In OBCS, the orderer node uses the **Event Hub Cloud Service** (**EHCS**) as its managed Apache Kafka instance. It's maximum retention time is two weeks. So, instead of keeping all transactions on Kafka, the ledger is asynchronously backed up to the object storage. Recovery of nodes occurs from the object storage, and the remaining blocks of transactions are synced from EHCS. The orderer nodes also receive a new gRPC service in order to provide a list of channels that are accessible to the caller's organization. Thus we can assume that with vanilla Fabric, an organization needs to keep track the channels of which they have access.

OBCS MSP

The standard implementation of the Fabric MSP controls the enrolment of network members (organizations) and provides related cryptographic services. It implements a standardized CA architecture with the root CA and intermediate CAs. It provides certificate issuance, validation of digital signatures, and client and node authentication.

The version developed for OBCS integrates the Fabric membership service with **Identity Cloud Service** (**IDCS**). Any roles defined in IDCS are contained in the Fabric enrolment certificate as attributes, but only the ones that where available at enrolment time. Subsequent IDCS changes are not captured and require a new membership. These Fabric enrolment certificates are used for authentication and can be used for (roll-based) authorization.

All access control goes via Oracle Cloudgate and IDCS, including transport security via TLS, blockchain network messages are authenticates via digital signatures, admin access and REST API authentication, and protection of data-in-transit and at-rest encryption of transaction messages and stored world state and ledger blocks.

Data services

OBCS uses its own block and object store, instead of container native storage. The key/value world state is stored using the NoSQL DB Cloud Service, whereas the ledger is stored using the Object Store Cloud Service.

OBCS world state and history databases

Currently, Fabric supports both LevelDB and CouchDB for storing the key/value world state and history databases. At the time of writing, the beta version of OBCS only supports LevelDB as the storage option, but the potential OBCS enhancement is to use **Berkeley DB** (**BDB**), which is offered by the NoSQL DB Cloud Service.

OBCS is planning to use BDB instead of LevelDB, as Oracle says it faster in "virtually" all use cases, though I couldn't find any benchmarks just yet. The following research paper from 2012, however, points out the opposite result: `http://highscalability.com/blog/2012/11/29/performance-data-for-leveldb-berkley-db-and-bangdb-for-rando.html`. Nonetheless, a lot can change in over six years (`https://db-engines.com/en/system/LevelDB%3BOracle+NoSQL`). BDB also has a higher disk space usage than LevelDB.

When comparing LevelDB to CouchDB (available from Fabric 1.0), it provides CQL queries against the world state, including values, which is not possible with LevelDB. BDB also supports such query possibilities, but is significantly faster (or so Oracle promises) as CouchDB is a traditional client/server database, whereas BDB is embedded. The Berkeley K/V database supports JSON natively, so a client can query against JSON fields.

OBCS also is planning enhancements for the history database and anticipates using asynchronous replication on a traditional Oracle database, as it can better scale and handle very large histories.

OBCS – object store integration

Since Fabric uses Docker containers for the most vital components, it may bring the risk of data saved in the cloud container being lost. This is why OBCS integrates with the Oracle object store to persist data. So, what data is persisted in Object Store CS:

- **Orderer node**: The data persisted includes the ledger (that is, all block files from the orderer, including data for system channel and customer channels), a list of all channels, and the latest checkpoint (that is, to sync only newer blocks).
- **Peer node**: The data persisted includes the genesis block of the peer, a list of channels to which the peer is joined, and all of the source code of the deployed chaincodes.
- **Other files**: Besides orderer and peer data, OBCS also persists configuration files, node provisioning files, and (historic) log files.

As the data mentioned is persisted in the object storage, it can be used for recovery. When an orderer goes down and later returns, it will execute the following operations:

1. The orderer node retrieves the channel list from the object store
2. For each channel, it retrieves the latest checkpoint and downloads block files
3. For each block file, it recovers the block index database

When a peer node goes down and later returns, it recovers itself by executing the following operations:

1. The peer node retrieves the channels list from the object store
2. For each channel it belongs to it downloads the genesis block
3. For each channel it requests all the other blocks from the Orderer node
4. According to the block files sent by the Orderer it recovers the block index DB
5. Based on the block files and index DB it recovers its state and history DB

If you wanted to use the standard Fabric implementation, you would need to monitor your network very strictly in order to not lose the data. Using OBCS, you could, in theory, lose all the nodes in the network, without losing the data, and be able to restart from the last checkpoint.

Administration services

The biggest advance for management and operational activities of your blockchain network is the administration console, which runs on its own Docker container. It automates many common administrative tasks and replaces the Fabric CLI-based UI with an intuitive, JET-based web console for management, monitoring, and administration of your blockchain network. The UI simplifies the provisioning and monitoring of Fabric components and provides clear UI elements, such as drop-down lists, eliminating the need to guess or search for names of members, peers, channels, chaincodes, and so on.

The management console allows you to easily and dynamically provision new peers, channels, CAs and REST proxies, and join new member organization to the network. You can change settings on the fly and define policies when creating channels or deploying chaincode. The console lets you manage the life cycle of individual chaincodes, as well as the import/export of keys and certificates. Following is a list of admin tasks we can perform:

- Bringing the blockchain network up or down
- Controlling the nodes (peers, orderers, CA, gateway), including starting/stopping/restarting, adding nodes, and editing, configuration settings
- Adding and configuring channels and policies
- Deploying, instantiating, and upgrading chaincode (smart contracts)
- Joining other members by exporting/importing certificates, node information, and credentials

The UI makes it easy to monitor (and troubleshoot) network health, valid and invalid transactions, and committed ledger updates. The following is a list of monitoring and troubleshooting tasks we can perform:

- View the dashboard, including network topology, joined channels, and chaincodes
- Monitor status of peers, orderers, and other network components
- View the blocks appended to the ledger
- View the log files for troubleshooting nodes

Additionally, when making changes to the configuration, the management console performs automatic updates on the containers and restarts necessary servers. The following screenshot shows the peer management UI:

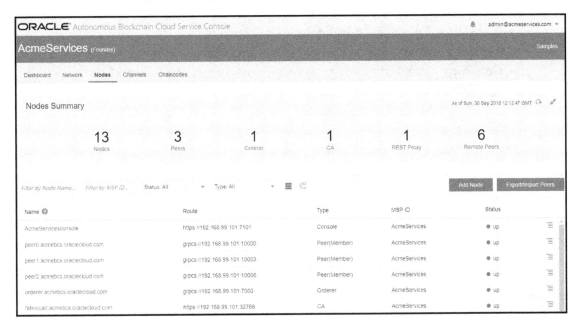

UI for managing nodes (peers, orderers, CA, and REST gateway)

We will explore the management UI in more detail in the next two chapters.

REST gateway (APIs)

To make it easy for your (decentralized) blockchain application to interact with the blockchain, the standard Fabric implementation offers language-specific SDKs.

The advantage of using OBCS is that it offers REST APIs via a gateway (proxy). T is an abstraction layer on top of the Fabric SDK and supports a subset of the most common Fabric APIs, such as Version, Query and Invoke.

The OBCS gateway provides synchronous invocation of these APIs, so there is no need to monitor for events or build support into your application for callbacks. This simplifies integration and insulates your application from the underlying changes of the evolving Fabric platform. Additionally, when invoking an API using the gateway, the IDCS users are mapped to the proxy configured credentials. So, the gateway easily detects unauthorized users (members).

The gateway supports the following REST APIs:

- **GetVersion**: Check the version of and connectivity to the gateway
- **Query**: Query assets persisted on the blockchain
- **Invocation**: Invoke an operation of a chaincode to perform a transaction
- **AsyncInvocation**: Perform an asynchronous invocation of an operation
- **GetStatus**: Get the status of an asynchronous invocation (transaction)
- **WaitStatus**: Get a list of (asynchronous) invoked transactions

Every instantiated chaincode can be exposed by the REST gateway, but you have to enable it manually in the gateway to call the chaincode, as shown in the following screenshot:

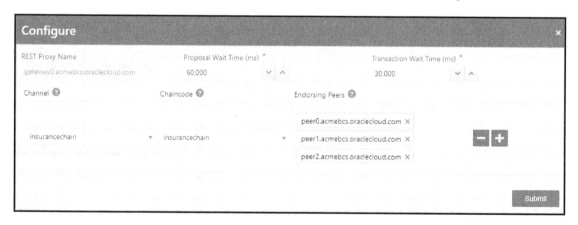

Allowing the gateway to expose the chaincode (smart contract) to external applications

Additionally, you are still able to use the Fabric SDKs to, for example, register new users, enroll and revoke certificates, create channels, install and instantiate chaincode on a channel, invoke transactions, query various components, and monitor events.

Summary

In this extensive chapter, we explored the platform and its components behind OBCS. You first learned the reasons why Oracle picked Hyperledger Fabric as their Blockchain framework, as it is a permissioned, scalable, and programmable blockchain.

Before going into why Oracle built their own managed PaaS, we explored the component roles that Fabric fulfills, and learned about the membership, consensus, and chaincode services. For each of the services, I explained the components that are part of it.

First, I explained that the membership services purpose lies in the enrolment, authentication and authorization of member organizations and that we can associate custom attributes for roll-based authentication.

Following, I then explained the consensus services that covered the peer and ordering service architecture, the world state and ledger, channels, peer gossip protocol, and finally the consensus protocol. I visually explained all the steps of the consensus protocol and how peers, orderers, and the client application communicate with each other.

Finally, I covered the chaincode services that are part of Fabric and explained that they allow us to program business logic on the blockchain.

Then I shifted focus toward OBCS and explained why Oracle built a managed PaaS service on top of Fabric and what component roles OBCS fulfills. You learned everything on the used infrastructure and platform service, Blockchain nodes, data services, administration services, and the REST gateway.

I covered the infrastructure and platform services that are used when you provision an instance of OBCS and explained what the role is of each cloud service. Following that, I covered the software that is running on the provisioned infrastructure, including the enhanced OBCS peer node, orderer node, and membership services, and compared the enhancements against Fabric's standard implementation.

We explored the biggest difference with using the vanilla Fabric framework, being the administration console for easily performing management and operational tasks, including monitoring and troubleshooting. Finally, I covered the integration of external application using the REST gateway provided by OBCS and discussed the available APIs.

In the next chapter, you will be setting up your own Blockchain network using the OBCS and starting to implement the case proposed in the previous chapter.

11
Setting Up Your Permissioned Blockchain

Now that you are familiar with blockchain terminology and concepts, and have learned about the differences between a public and a private blockchain, how blockchain will disrupt traditional cross-organizational applications, and everything that you need to know about Hyperledger Fabric and OBCS, you can use this newfound knowledge to set up your first permissioned blockchain network.

In this first implementation chapter, we will use OBCS to implement the business case proposed in Chapter 9, *Building a Next-Generation Oracle B2B Platform*. Your first steps will focus on creating a business network, setting up all of the environments, exploring the dashboards, adding all other member organizations to the network, and creating a private channel that allows all organizations to conduct transactions with each other.

 Disclaimer: In order for you to follow along in this chapter, you will need an Oracle Cloud subscription with sufficient universal credits. At the time of writing, the cloud service has just been made generally available, and you can get your instance at https://cloud.oracle.com/blockchain. Each Autonomous Blockchain Service instance will be charged on a transaction basis (500 transactions per unit of cost) at an hourly rate of $0.75 (pay as you go) or $0.50 (monthly subscription).

In this chapter, you will learn how to do the following:

- Provision your first blockchain network using OBCS
- Navigate through the available dashboards of the administration console
- Invite other member organizations to join your blockchain network
- Explore options for customizing and extending your network
- Create a new channel and add all organizations to the channel

Summarizing the problem

Every day, there are many traffic accidents. To address all of the issues relating to an accident, including casualties, vehicle damage, road repairs, and so on, many organizations need to work together. As already described in great detail in `Chapter 9`, *Building a Next-Generation Oracle B2B Platform*, in a traditional cross-organizational application, these organizations don't often use a centralized application; rather, each organization has its own back-office application.

These organizations exchange data about accidents, vehicle repair quotes, and insurance claims via EDI messages through a solid network of B2B brokers. However, they need to process the information in their own systems according to their agreed-upon business rules. The problem with these kinds of applications is that the participating organizations or partners tend to implement the business rules in different ways, leading to inconsistencies. This brings with it additional administrative costs for the organizations involved, which are passed on to their customers in order to compensate the organization. For detailed use cases, you can refer back to `Chapter 9`, *Building a Next-Generation Oracle B2B Platform*, as they are used in this and the next chapters.

Introducing the solution

A consortium of insurance companies, repair shops, lease companies, and emergency services has decided to implement blockchain technology in order to streamline accident reports and process insurance claims among its organizations. Some of the members have chosen to use OBCS while others will run an on-premises Hyperledger Fabric network, but they all join the same network.

You are hired by Acme Insurance Brokering Services to set up the consortium blockchain. Your network will run an actual decentralized application (smart contract), but this will be covered in the next chapter. This chapter focuses only on the infrastructure.

The consortium business network will include six different member organizations:

- **Acme Insurance Blockchain Services**: Founder of the network, running OBCS
- **Emergency Services**: Organization joining the founder network, running OBCS

- **AutoLease**: Organization joining the founder network, running OBCS
- **AllSecur Insurance**: Organization joining the founder network, running OBCS
- **AXA Insurance**: Organization joining the founder network, running OBCS
- **USA Automotive Services**: Organization joining the founder network, running an on-premises Hyperledger Fabric network

The following diagram shows the blockchain network that we want to implement:

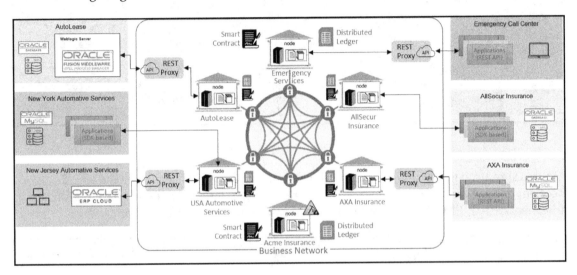

The business network to be implemented (partially)

Provisioning the environments

To set up our consortium blockchain and start our business network, first we need to provision the required environments. When provisioning an instance of OBCS, we first need to have an account set up for each of the member organizations. If you already have an Oracle Cloud account, you don't need to perform these steps again.

If you don't have an Oracle Cloud account, you can request a free one by visiting `https://cloud.oracle.com/tryit` and clicking on the **Create a Free Account** button, as shown in the following screenshot:

Welcome page to sign up for a new Oracle Cloud account

On this sign up page, you will need to fill in some account details, such as the cloud account name, which becomes part of the organization's URL, the default data region (for instance, APAC, EMEA, LAD, or NA), and company/personal information:

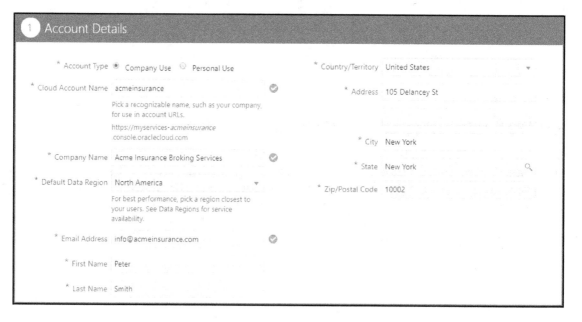

Account Details section of the sign-up page to request a new Oracle Cloud account

In addition to the account details, you need to verify that you are not a robot by requesting a verification code via a cell phone and adding your credit card details, as reflected in the following screenshots. Every new account is issued credit to run a trial version for a maximum of 30 days, or until you reach a total of 3,500 hours. Thus, you will not be billed straight away, but only after you upgrade your account:

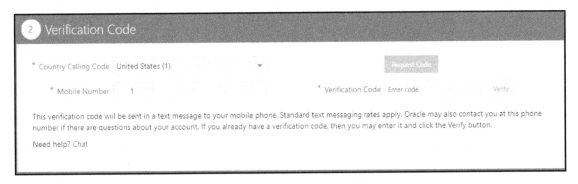

Verification Code section requesting you to verify that you are not a robot

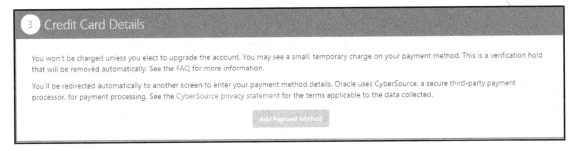

Credit Card Details section requesting that you supply a payment method

Once you have registered and confirmed your account, you are able to provision the required cloud environments. At the time of writing, OBCS has just been made generally available, so the following steps might look slightly different in the future.

Once you are logged into your *myservices* account, click on the **Create Instance** button at the top left. This will show a dialog window, as shown in the following screenshot, which lists all of the cloud services available to you. To find the *Autonomous Blockchain Cloud Service* easily, click on the **All Services** tab and search for the term `blockchain`.

Click on the **Create** button on the right-hand side of the entry to create a new instance:

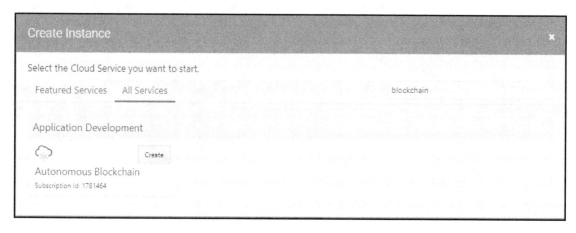

Create Instance dialog window for generating new instances of any of the available services, for example, Autonomous Blockchain

There are two ways to provision your environment. One way is to provision an environment using the **QuickStarts** option, which creates a founder instance with two peer nodes by only entering the name of the instance. The second option is more advanced. It allows you to configure the service region and options. The following screenshot shows the two options you can choose:

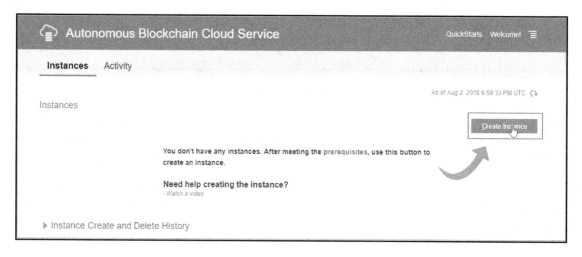

The Autonomous Blockchain Cloud Service instance creation page

We will use the second option by clicking on **Create Instance**.

The following screenshot shows how provisioning using the creation wizard currently appears in the generally-available version of OBCS. This may change in the future, however. You need to supply some service details, select the region in which to run the instance, and choose your service options:

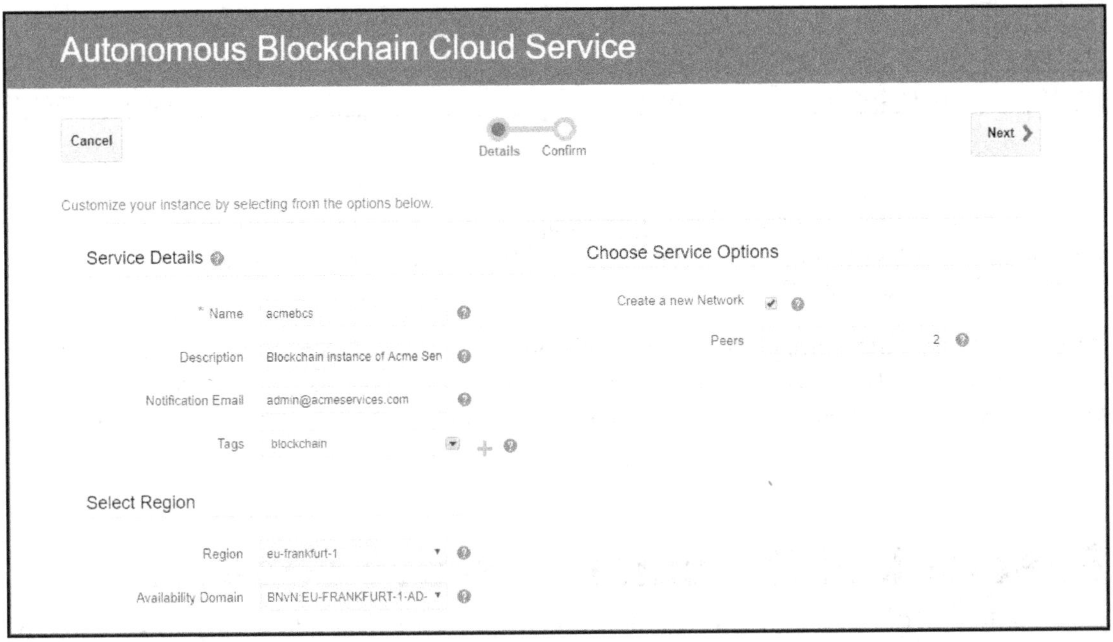

Creation wizard of an OBCS instance

You choose a name for your instance, enter an optional description, and designate where a notification email should be sent. You also need to select one of the OCI regions, for example, `eu-frankfurt`, and one of the availability domains in that region. Finally, configure the number of peers that the organization wishes to manage and whether you want to create a new network or join an existing one. The number of peers determines the stability, availability, and recoverability of a blockchain instance. You can compare it with a clustered environment. The option to create a new network can be unchecked when an organization wants to join an existing business network. The result is that fewer components are provisioned, such as an ordering service (orderer), as they already exist. This saves computing resources and storage. In most cases, only the founder of the business network keeps this option checked.

For our network, I have provisioned the following instances of OBCS with the following configurations:

Name	Description	Number of Peers	Create New Network
acmebcs	Instance for Acme Insurance Services	3 (for resiliency)	Yes (network founder)
ersbcs	Instance for Emergency Services	2 (for scalability)	No (network member)
alebcs	Instance for AutoLease	2 (for scalability)	No (network member)
ascbcs	Instance for Allsecur Insurance	1	No (network member)
axabcs	Instance for AXA Insurance	1	No (network member)

Configuration of the provisioned OBCS instances

USA Automotive Services runs their Hyperledger Fabric network on-premises instead of on a hosted OBCS environment. They will later join the network that is set up by Acme Insurance Blockchain Services.

After you submit the form, Oracle will provision the necessary components. Once this is done, you will likely receive an email including information on how to access the environment. You can also check the status under the **my services** console of your cloud account.

First look at the administrative console

After setting up the environment and receiving the information on how to access it, we can start to configure our business network. Let's first start by logging into the administrative console of the founder of the network (Acme). The URL may look similar to this one: `https://acmebcs-acmeinsurance.blockchain.ocp.oraclecloud.com`.

Once you are logged into the console, you are welcomed by the **Dashboard** page.

Using the menu shown in the following screenshot, you can easily explore the remaining capabilities that the administrative console offers, including some samples that you can try out prior to coding a smart contract yourself:

Main menu of the Autonomous Blockchain Cloud Service

Keep in mind that the UI will evolve over time, so you can always go to the official Oracle documentation at `https://docs.oracle.com/en/cloud/paas/blockchain-cloud/index.html` if it looks different.

Using the main menu, you can navigate to the following pages of the console:

- **Dashboard**: Provides a summary of your blockchain setup and system status.
- **Network**: Lets you manage the network that you created and the members participating in it. You can also access a network in which you participate in. Additionally, you can view a graphical representation of your network topology.
- **Nodes**: This option allows you to manage (configure, provision, or decommission) the network peers of your organization, view detailed information about a peer's performance, and monitor its logs. Additionally, you can view a graphical representation of your organization's channel topology.
- **Channels**: This option lets you manage the channels to which your organization belongs. Channels provide a means of executing transactions that are only visible to select network participants. Additionally, you can view the ledger details associated with each channel that your peers are members of.
- **Chaincodes**: This option allows you to manage the chaincodes (smart contracts/business logic) that govern updates to your ledger. It enables you to deploy, upgrade, and install (instantiate) chaincode across your channels and member peers.

In the next few sections, we will take a quick look at each of these pages. Not very far down the road, we will take a more detailed look at these pages when we go through the steps of setting up our business network.

Blockchain Dashboard

From within the menu, we can explore the setup and status of our blockchain by navigating to the **Dashboard** page. Additionally, after selecting the checkbox on the welcome page, this page will become the default landing page.

The **Dashboard** page, as shown in the following screenshot, presents a summary of your blockchain network setup and status:

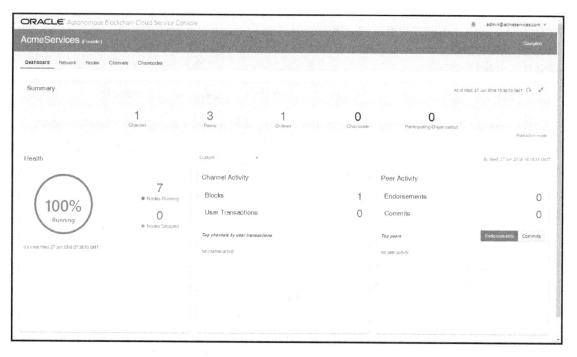

Dashboard page displaying the network setup, health, channel, and peer activity

The page is divided into a few sections. There is a section that provides a summary of the organizations that are part of your network, the number of peers and orderers recognized by your network, the number of channels of which your organization is a part, and the number of deployed chaincodes on your network.

The other sections show a graph displaying the health (running nodes in percentage) of the blockchain, followed by your **Channel Activity** and **Peer Activity** summaries. The **Channel Activity** section shows the total number of blocks created, the total number of user transactions executed, and a list of the most active channels. The **Peer Activity** section, on the other hand, shows the number of endorsed and committed transactions and a list of the most active peers.

Both activity sections show data based on a specified time range (for example, the last hour). You can change the time range by selecting between the last hour, last day, last week, last month, or a custom range. When selecting a custom range, you need to specify the start and end date, both of which can be in the past. All of the options and the date/time picker are shown in the following screenshot:

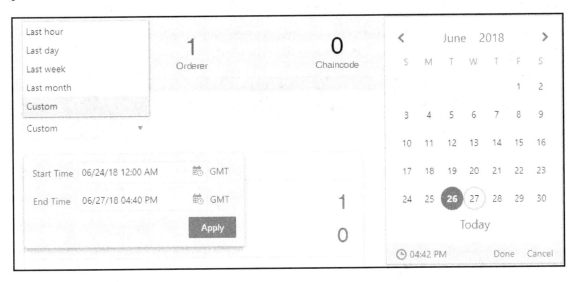

Specify a custom time range to view all executed transactions in a specific time frame

We will revisit this dashboard a few times in this and the next chapter to show the effects of executed transactions.

Blockchain Network

The second menu item navigates us to the **Network** page. We can use this page to manage the participating organizations in our network. The page includes a summary of our network, showing the number of participating organizations and a list of members in it. The list specifies each member, its **Organization ID**, **Role** (*founder* or *participant*), and **MSP ID** (member service provider ID). You can also filter the list on the ID of an organization or its role.

The **Network** page allows you to add member organizations by uploading certificates for members that you want to add to the network and configure the blockchain **Ordering Service Settings** (for instance, Kafka). Additionally, for each organization, you can perform different tasks, such as exporting certificates, credentials, and orderer settings.

The following screenshot shows the main network page. We do not yet have participating organizations, but Acme Services is listed as the **Founder**:

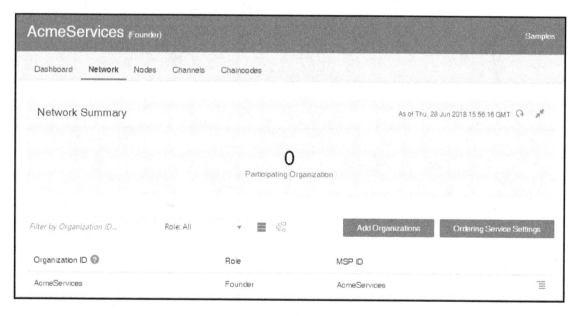

Network page for managing and extending your blockchain network

Additionally, you can switch between a list and a topology view by clicking on the second icon, which represents a flow chart. The topology view shows a diagram of our current network's structure and the relationships between organizations and nodes. We will revisit this page and its capabilities when we add our member organizations to the network.

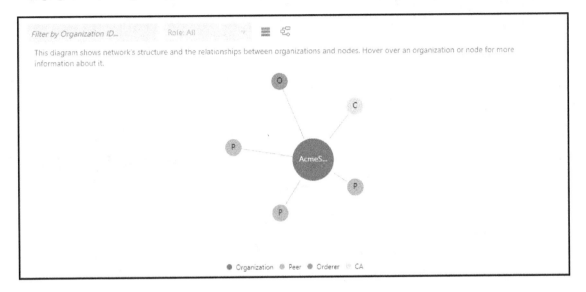

Topology view of our initial business network, including one organization, three peers, one orderer, and one CA

Blockchain Nodes

To manage the network peers of our organization, we can navigate to the **Nodes** page. The **Nodes** page, as shown in the following screenshot, can be used to configure, provision, and decommission network peers.

It allows you to stop/start individual peers after making changes to their configurations:

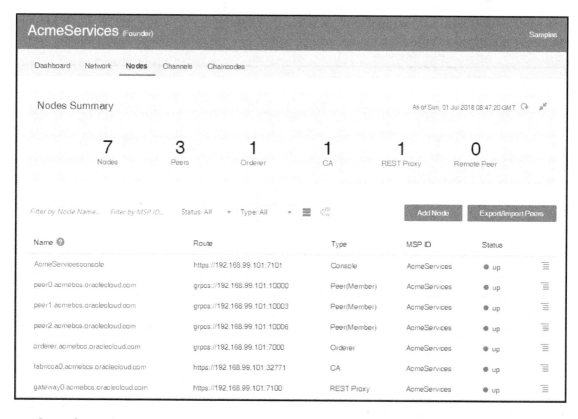

Summary of our network nodes, including the number of (remote) Peers, Orderers, CAs, and REST Proxies. A list of identified nodes within our network is shown.

Once again, the top of the page includes a summary, this time displaying the total number of identified nodes in our network and the amount of each node type (that is, **Peer**, **Orderer**, **CA**, **REST Proxy**, and **Remote Peer**).

The bottom part of the page includes a detailed list of all of the nodes identified in our network. The list specifies the name of each node (usually a domain name), the route (endpoint) to access the node (through http/s or grpc/s, including host IP and port), the node's type, to which MSP ID the node belongs, and the status of the node (for example, **up/down/restarting**).

You can filter the list by **Node Name**, **MSP ID**, **Status**, and **Type**. If the GRPC protocol is new to you, then I recommend reading about it at `https://grpc.io`. Furthermore, the **Nodes** page allows you to provision/add new nodes (for example, peers and REST proxies) to extend your members' network, using a configuration wizard, and to export or import (remote) peers. Additionally, you control each node's lifecycle (**Stop/Restart/Remove**) and can perform different tasks depending on its type, such as editing its configuration, joining a new channel, or cloning the node. This is all done using the options menu on the right-hand side of each entry in the list.

The following screenshot shows the options for a **Peer**, **Orderer**, **CA**, and **REST Proxy**:

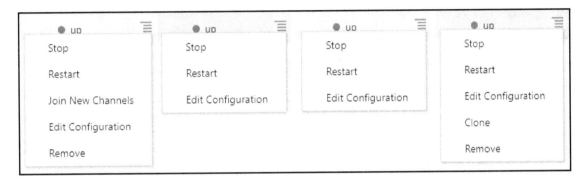

Options for managing differing types of nodes

As on the **Network** page, you can also switch between a list or a topology view by clicking on the second (flowchart) icon. This time, the topology view shows a diagram of the relationships between our peers and channels. A founding member already has a default channel created, so the diagram shows all three peers being part of that channel; that is, *acmeservicesorderer*:

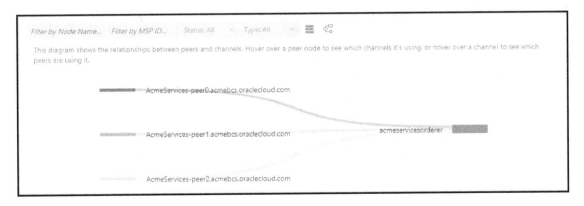

Topology view of our initial peer network showing the relationship between the three peer nodes and the default channel

Back in the list view, you can also view detailed information about a node's performance, monitor its logs and, depending on the node type, perform specific actions such as joining an existing channel. You can view this detailed information by clicking on the name of the peer, which navigates to the corresponding subpage for that node. The following screenshot shows the detailed information of peer #0, for example:

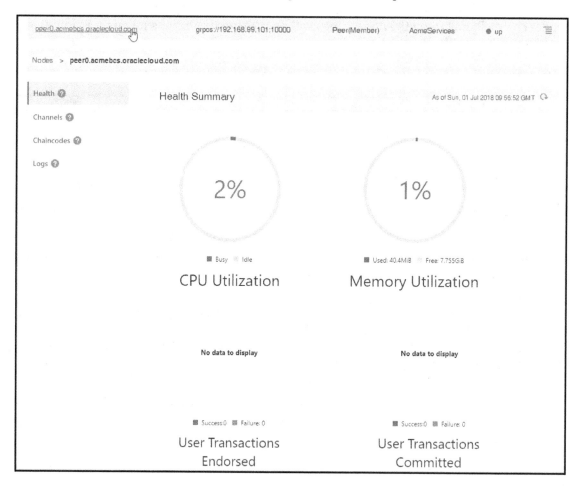

Health and performance summary of peer #0

We will revisit the **Nodes** page and detailed subpages when we import remote peers from other members in order to get a full picture of our peer network, and when we add peers of other member organizations to the same existing channel.

Blockchain Channels

To manage our organization's channels, we can navigate to the **Channels** page. This page can be used to create new channels and perform actions on existing channels to which our organizations belongs. Channels provide a means to execute transactions that are only visible to select network participants.

The page includes a summary displaying the number of channels to which your organization belongs and a list of those channels. The list specifies each channel's name, the number of instantiated (meaning running) chaincodes (smart contracts), the number of your peers that joined the channel, and which organization originally created the channel. You can also filter the list on the channel name or its creator. The following screenshot shows the main **Channels** page, which by default lists the channel created by the founder organization, *acmeservicesorderer*:

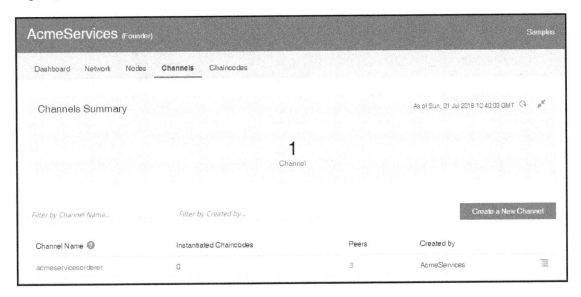

Channels page for managing the channels to which your organization belongs

The **Channels** page allows you to create a new channel between specified network members, which we will explore later in this chapter. It also provides the ability to propose changes to an existing channel, such as adding new member organizations, or updating the ordering service settings. You can also join peers from your organization to a channel to which you belong. The actions can again be performed using the options menu on the right-hand side of each entry in the list.

The following screenshot shows the options for a channel that you created:

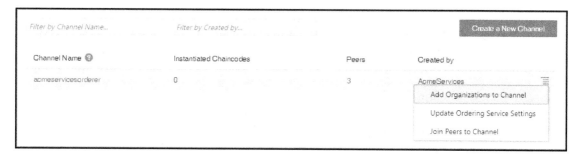

Options for managing channels that you created and/or to which you belong

Additionally, you can view the details associated with each channel of which your peers are members, such as the status of the ledger, the instantiated chaincodes (smart contracts), your organization's peers that joined the channel, and a list of member organizations that are part of, or allowed to join, the channel. You can view the channel's details by clicking on the name of the channel, which navigates to the corresponding subpage. The following screenshot shows the ledger activity of the *acmeservicesorderer* channel, which was created by default. Because no transactions have taken place yet, it does not show any data:

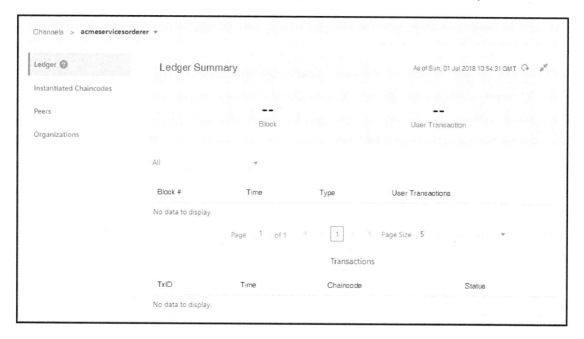

Ledger summary of the selected channel, acmeservicesorderer

We will revisit the **Channels** page and detailed subpages when we create our own channel between our member organizations.

Blockchain Chaincodes

The final major capability in the administrative console is the **Chaincodes** page. With this page, we can manage the chaincodes (smart contracts/business logic) that govern updates to our ledger(s). It enables us to deploy, upgrade, and install (instantiate) chaincode across our channels and member peers.

The top of the page shows a summary displaying the total number of installed chaincodes, and the bottom of the page includes a detailed list of installed or even just instantiated chaincodes. The list specifies each chaincode's ID, the available versions, the path to the installed chaincode, the number of peers on which the chaincode is installed, and the number of channels on which it is instantiated. You can filter the list by chaincode ID.

The following screenshot shows the main chaincodes page. At present, we do not yet have any chaincodes installed, but in a later chapter this page will be one of our main focal points:

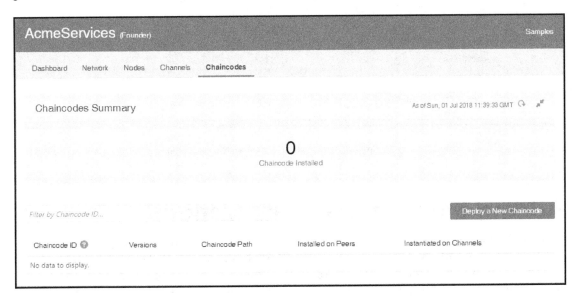

Chaincodes page for managing the smart contracts used by your business network

The **Chaincodes** page allows us to deploy a new chaincode, directly instantiate it on a channel, and expose it to external applications via one of our REST proxies using a deployment wizard. It also provides the ability to manage deployed chaincodes (for example, to instantiate them on multiple channels). Additionally, we can view the details of each installed chaincode version.

We will discuss these capabilities in the next chapter, as we will develop, deploy, and run our own chaincode on the business network that we will configure in this chapter.

If you can't wait and want to try out basic chaincode functionality, you can always take a look at the chaincode samples provided. You can access the samples by clicking on the **Samples** link at the top-right corner of the page. One of the samples is the Marbles chaincode, as shown in the following screenshot:

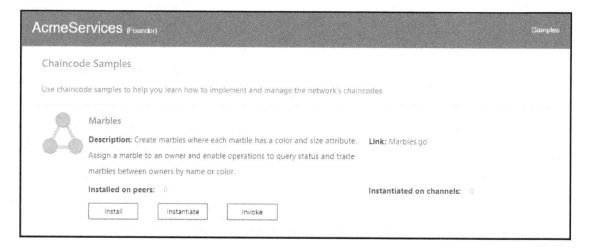

Chaincode Samples page showing the Marbles chaincode

Adding the member organizations

Now that you are familiar with the capabilities of the administrative console, let's configure our business network by adding all of the member organizations. In order for organizations to transact with each other, we need to join our member organizations and make them part of the network of the founder organization. To achieve this, we need to execute the following tasks for each member organization:

1. Export member organization's certificates
2. Export member organization's peer nodes

3. Import certificates of member organizations at founder
4. Import peer nodes of member organizations at founder
5. Export orderer settings from the founder (only once)
6. Import orderer settings from the founder at member organization

Export member organization's certificates

To be able to add a member organization to an existing blockchain network, we need to export the client certification for each of the member organizations. Let's start with the emergency and rescue services by logging into their administration console. In our case, the URL to use is similar to: `https://ersbcs-emergencyservices.blockchain.ocp.oraclecloud.com`.

We are again welcomed by the **Dashboard** page. However, instead of showing the health of the organization's network and channel and ledger activity, we are faced with the steps required to join an existing OBCS network.

The following screenshot shows the dashboard displayed when we login to the member organization's console for the first time. The dashboard states that we need to export the organization's certificates and import the corresponding orderer settings. Also notice that the **Dashboard** page shows fewer summary details, as a member organization does not include an orderer node:

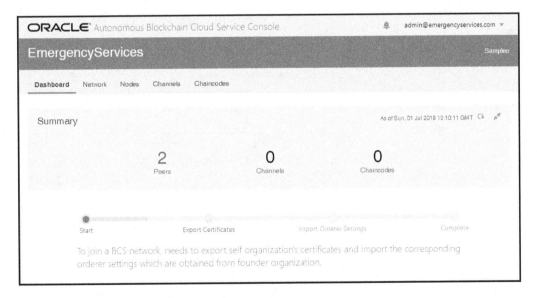

Dashboard of the administrative console of a member organization at first login

To export the organization's certificates, we need to navigate to the **Network** page. The **Network** page of Emergency Services lists only one participating organization—itself—but it has a different role than Acme Services, namely **Participant**, whereas Acme has the role of **Founder**. Using the options menu on the right side of the listed organization, as shown in the following screenshot, we can export its certificates:

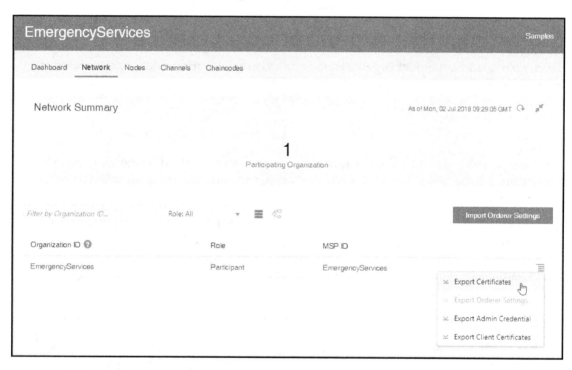

Exporting the certificates of a member organization

Performing this action will download a JSON file called `{membername}_certificates.json`. Thus, in our case, it downloads the `EmergencyServices_certificates.json` file. You can open this human-readable file with any text editor, and it will contain the MSP ID of the organization and three certificates, namely its `admincert`, `cacert`, and `tlscacert`. The following snippet shows the contents of the downloaded JSON file:

```
{
  "mspid": "EmergencyServices",
  "certs": {
    "admincerts": "-----BEGIN CERTIFICATE-----
\nMIICLDCCAdKgAwIBAgIRALLXmKiY4NS15JEmtm+fMcwwCgYIKoZIzj0EAwIwfzEL\nMAkGA1U
EBhMCVVMxEzARBgNVBAgTCkNhbGlmb3JuaWExFjAUBgNVBAcTDVNhbiBG\ncmFuY2lzY28xHzAd
```

BgNVBAoTFmVyc2Jjcy5vcmFjbGVjbG91ZC5jb20xIjAgBgNV\nBAMTGWNhLmVyc2Jjcy5vcmFjb
GVjbG91ZC5jb20wHhcNMTgwNjI3MTUxOTU1WhcN\nMjgwNjI0MTUxOTU1WjBhMQswCQYDVQQGEw
JVUzETMBEGA1UECBMKQ2FsaWZvcm5p\nYTEWMBQGA1UEBxMNU2FuIEZyYW5jaXNjbzElMCMGA1U
EAwwcQWRtaW5AZXJzYmNz\nLm9yYWNsZWNsb3VkLmNvbTBZMBMGByqGSM49AgEGCCqGSM49AwEH
A0IABDXX7Wst\nJK68+C47eaz4KvMdCryK4GiMLssJ3YAq2XYQXFEreQKJCi48Dw2WXyoh9+C8y
UTE\n+PMfQk6binKWOdejTTBLMA4GA1UdDwEB/wQEAwIHgDAMBgNVHRMBAf8EAjAAMCsG\nA1Ud
IwQkMCKAIJZYq7ZAtSjtcHtPF3X46etkrrNN0QifIe2z721pLUqqMAoGCCqG\nSM49BAMCA0gAM
EUCIQDNXkuDBYeaXpWjKzDWmRy3piw6KPm7itLIRBhUM4Bn4AIg\nZ13WGIDt4imJLBGE4dy5yz
ekYelDSK0sXeXLsfk5EDw=\n-----END CERTIFICATE-----\n",
     "cacerts": "-----BEGIN CERTIFICATE-----
\nMIICWjCCAgGgAwIBAgIQczEGojCQozthy70JMcXZXTAKBggqhkjOPQQDAjB/MQsw\nCQYDVQQ
GEwJVUzETMBEGA1UECBMKQ2FsaWZvcm5pYTEWMBQGA1UEBxMNU2FuIEZy\nYW5jaXNjbzEfMB0G
A1UEChMWZXJzYmNzLm9yYWNsZWNsb3VkLmNvbTEiMCAGA1UE\nAxMZY2EuZXJzYmNzLm9yYWNsZ
WNsb3VkLmNvbTAeFw0xODA2MjcxNTE5NTVaFw0y\nODA2MjQxNTE5NTVaMH8xCzAJBgNVBAYTAl
VTMRMwEQYDVQQIEwpDYWxpZm9ybmlh\nMRYwFAYDVQQHEw1TYW4gRnJhbmNpc2NvMR8wHQYDVQQ
KExZlcnNiY3Mub3JhY2xl\nY2xvdWQuY29tMSIwIAYDVQQDExlYS5lcnNiY3Mub3JhY2xlY2xv
dWQuY29tMFkw\nEwYHKoZIzj0CAQYIKoZIzj0DAQcDQgAE6tYi29rf7wL3GA4mtDpnVCMDxk0Yh
gzN\nuXYj/eY84xJgXKmuBlFNVWk581eTb86VbpMuymCczqx0tuszxRguYKNfMF0wDgYD\nVR0P
AQH/BAQDAgGmMA8GA1UdJQQIMAYGBFUdJQAwDwYDVR0TAQH/BAUwAwEB/zAp\nBgNVHQ4EIgQgl
lirtkC1KO1we08Xdfjp62Sus03RCJ8h7bPvbWktSqowCgYIKoZI\nzj0EAwIDRwAwRAIgTbjM/d
D0hw3ACMM9Xz8eCeWxehFu314WWmnyLNddVvwCIGKh\nEN5+0lKc3AZMiNiWmMN9jivVi7oX5Dc
mQJx+VEK4\n-----END CERTIFICATE-----\n",
     "tlscacerts": "-----BEGIN CERTIFICATE-----
\nMIICYjCCAgmgAwIBAgIQEL7VIPGDRKuxF1FetjEVizAKBggqhkjOPQQDAjCBgjEL\nMAkGA1U
EBhMCVVMxEzARBgNVBAgTCkNhbGlmb3JuaWExFjAUBgNVBAcTDVNhbiBG\ncmFuY2lzY28xHzAd
BgNVBAoTFmVyc2Jjcy5vcmFjbGVjbG91ZC5jb20xJTAjBgNV\nBAMTHHRsc2NhLmVyc2Jjcy5vc
mFjbGVjbG91ZC5jb20wHhcNMTgwNjI3MTUxOTU1\nWhcNMjgwNjI0MTUxOTU1WjCBgjELMAkGA1
UEBhMCVVMxEzARBgNVBAgTCkNhbGlm\nb3JuaWExFjAUBgNVBAcTDVNhbiBGcmFuY2lzY28xHzA
dBgNVBAoTFmVyc2Jjcy5v\ncmFjbGVjbG91ZC5jb20xJTAjBgNVBAMTHHRsc2NhLmVyc2Jjcy5v
cmFjbGVjbG91\nZC5jb20wWTATBgcqhkjOPQIBBggqhkjOPQMBBwNCAAQwK1f2oKa+hUGi6dmGP
lUm\nRQIjqCLWcTMrfVdoagTFzUhd7UhcR2KOLAFz30PZj7z9++wn5o21iKMfrQqv6SP4\no18w
XTAOBgNVHQ8BAf8EBAMCAaYwDwYDVR0lBAgwBgYEVR0lADAPBgNVHRMBAf8E\nBTADAQH/MCkGA
1UdDgQiBCDkSepbu9VSHGstY2ZBcNUAS/tYKiFoz/xahLdgmDIB\nAjAKBggqhkjOPQQDAgNHAD
BEAiAiMZReX2iuBP847icOu9yYU3oI1dLGUtKalw2W\nuWe2JwIgZbldsX/Yat9WzDC+8RFrLsc
dckkELO+TZdUM4T5aVv8=\n-----END CERTIFICATE-----\n"
     }
}

To be able to set up our business network completely, we also need to perform these steps for the other member organizations that use OBCS (that is, AutoLease, Allsecur Insurance, and AXA Insurance).

Once we have done this for each organization, we should have a total of four JSON files.

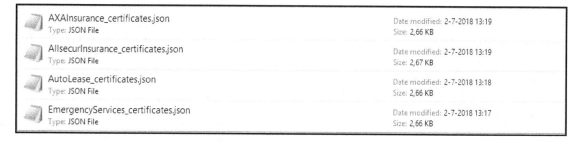

AXAInsurance_certificates.json Type: JSON File	Date modified: 2-7-2018 13:19 Size: 2,66 KB
AllsecurInsurance_certificates.json Type: JSON File	Date modified: 2-7-2018 13:19 Size: 2,67 KB
AutoLease_certificates.json Type: JSON File	Date modified: 2-7-2018 13:18 Size: 2,66 KB
EmergencyServices_certificates.json Type: JSON File	Date modified: 2-7-2018 13:17 Size: 2,66 KB

List of all member organizations' certificate files

Export member organization's peer nodes

The next step is to export the peer nodes of the participating member organizations. This is not necessary for the organizations to communicate with each other, but it enables us to get a complete picture of all of the peers identified in the business network. Let's explore this step using the environment of AutoLease by logging into their console. In our case, the URL to use is similar to:

`https://alebcs-emergencyservices.blockchain.ocp.oraclecloud.com`.

The peer nodes configuration can be exported by navigating to the **Nodes** page. The AutoLease organization consists of five nodes, including two peer nodes, one CA, one REST proxy, and an administrative console. In order to have a stable network, we need many peer nodes to be part of it. To achieve this, we export the configuration of both peers. This can be done by clicking on the **Export/Import Peers** button and selecting **Export**.

Export/import the configuration of peer nodes

After selecting the **Export** option, a dialog box will pop-up, as shown in the following screenshot. In the dialog box, we can select the peers that we want to export. The **Peer List** field allows us to select the peers that we want to export:

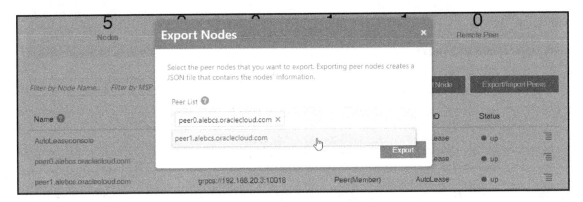

Pop-up dialog box for selecting the peers that we want to export

In our case, we select both peers (peer0 and peer1). Click on the **Export** button to download the configuration file with the exported peer nodes. The downloaded configuration file also uses the JSON format and it is called `{membername}-exportNodesToRemote.json`. Thus, in our case, it downloads the `AutoLease-exportNodesToRemote.json` file. If we open the file in a text editor, we see that it contains the technical details of each exported peer and the public TLS certificate of the CA. The following snippet shows the content of the downloaded JSON file:

```
{ "peers": [
    {
        "nodeName": "peer0.alebcs.oraclecloud.com",
        "address": "grpcs://peer0.alebcs.oraclecloud.com:7051",
        "eventAddress": "grpcs://peer0.alebcs.oraclecloud.com:7053",
        "type": "Peer",
        "typeDisp": "Peer",
        "mspId": "AutoLease",
        "joinedChannels": [],
        "installedChaincodes": [],
        "externalPort": "10015",
        "externalAddr": "192.168.20.3"
    }, {
        "nodeName": "peer1.alebcs.oraclecloud.com",
        "address": "grpcs://peer1.alebcs.oraclecloud.com:7051",
        "eventAddress": "grpcs://peer1.alebcs.oraclecloud.com:7053",
        "type": "Peer",
        "typeDisp": "Peer",
        "mspId": "AutoLease",
```

```
        "joinedChannels": [],
        "installedChaincodes": [],
        "externalPort": "10018",
        "externalAddr": "192.168.20.3"
      }
    ],
    "tls_ca_certs": "-----BEGIN CERTIFICATE-----
\nMIICZDCCAgqgAwIBAgIRAJcNk5MOb0L8iBkeRk1Uu7QwCgYIKoZIzj0EAwIwgYIx\nCzAJBgN
VBAYTAlVTMRMwEQYDVQQIEwpDYWxpZm9ybmlhMRYwFAYDVQQHEw1TYW4g\nRnJhbmNpc2NvMR8w
HQYDVQQKExZhbGViY3Mub3JhY2xlY2xvdWQuY29tMSUwIwYD\nVQQDExx0bHNjYS5hbGViY3Mub
3JhY2xlY2xvdWQuY29tMB4XDTE4MDYyNzE1MjA0\nMFoXDTI4MDYyNDE1MjA0MFowgYIxCzAJBg
NVBAYTAlVTMRMwEQYDVQQIEwpDYWxp\nZm9ybmlhMRYwFAYDVQQHEw1TYW4gRnJhbmNpc2NvMR8
wHQYDVQQKExZhbGViY3Mu\nb3JhY2xlY2xvdWQuY29tMSUwIwYDVQQDExx0bHNjYS5hbGViY3Mu
b3JhY2xlY2xv\ndWQuY29tMFkwEwYHKoZIzj0CAQYIKoZIzj0DAQcDQgAEQOywAV57Hr74JHUSZ
kDm\nEiF/NMKU3Y+GKjkyDBO93I99CWVs/h6l+hP9WbXls/UMeUaZ1n5rGhQO0Cp7+0MF\n/qNf
MF0wDgYDVR0PAQH/BAQDAgGmMA8GA1UdJQQIMAYGBFUdJQAwDwYDVR0TAQH/\nBAUwAwEB/zApB
gNVHQ4EIgQgLPDNrpl/WjfO5j4hOQ1iko04mV8/RmA9Qh/vlLzH\nnvrkwCgYIKoZIzj0EAwIDSA
AwRQIhAO9fGpSQ/lyeWX/IqkL27G2bGOOzXld25snQ\nnOXmbksoSAiB9N8+fQrdz4zaDkjxjQIK
0qfiE552cPVJeyWyCU3S6hg==\n-----END CERTIFICATE-----\n"
    }
```

To be able to identify all of the peers in our business network, we need to perform these steps for the other member organizations that use OBCS. Not all organizations have the same number of peer nodes, for example, Allsecur and AXA Insurance only have one peer, but for each organization we will export all provisioned peers. Once we do this for each organization, we should have a total of four JSON files:

List of exported member organizations' peer configuration files

Import certificates of member organizations

In the last two tasks, we exported both the certificates and the peer node configurations of each of our member organizations. The next task in adding our member organizations to our existing business network is to import the downloaded files in the OBCS instance of the founder, that is, Acme Services.

To do this, we need to log back into the administrative console of Acme and navigate to the **Network** page. Then, we can add the member organizations by clicking on the **Add Organizations** button, as shown here:

Add member organizations to your existing business network

A dialog box will pop-up in which we can find and upload the certificates for the members that we want to add to the network. We can upload multiple certificates at the same time. In our case, we can upload the certificate files we exported/downloaded from our member organizations in one step. In the dialog box shown in the following screenshot, you can click on the **Upload Organization Certificates** link and select the file that you want to upload. Click on the plus (+) icon to add each of the certificates files:

Upload each of the member organization's certificates file, and press the plus (+) icon to add multiple organizations.

Notice that when you upload a certificates file, the MSP ID of the organization is immediately recognized in the user interface. This means that you uploaded a valid certificates file. Once all organization certificates are uploaded, we can persist them by clicking on the **Add** button at the bottom-right corner of the dialog box. In the background, the organizations are added to the list. To close the dialog box, click on **Finish**. Alternatively, you can directly export the orderer settings from the dialog, but we will do that in one of the upcoming steps. Our list now counts five organizations (one founder and four participating members):

Network page of the founder showing the four new participating member organizations

We will add the last organization, USA Automotive Services, in `Chapter 14`, *Configuring, Extending, and Monitoring Your Network*, when we extend our network by connecting an existing Hyperledger Fabric network to the network hosted by the founder running OBCS.

Once we have added our member organizations, we immediately have a better understanding of our network as we have now enabled most of the capabilities of OBCS. If we look at the topology view of our network, we see an updated diagram that shows our network's structure and the relationships between organizations:

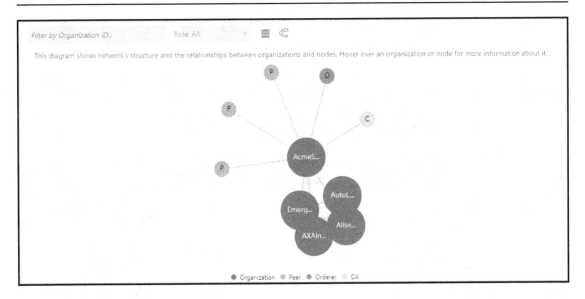

Topology view of our network after adding member organizations that use OBCS

Import peer nodes of member organizations

Notice in the previous diagram that we can see the individual organizations, but we still don't have the full picture as no peer nodes have been identified for these member organizations. Wouldn't it be nice to have that picture? The following step is not essential to run your network and to allow organizations to transact with each other, but it can be useful in understanding how decentralized your network is in reality.

When logged into the administrative console of the founder, Acme, navigate to the **Nodes** page. From this page, we can import the configuration of the exported remote peers from all member organizations. Click on the **Export/Import Peers** button, and select the **Import** option.

Import remote peers for other member organizations

A dialog box appears that allows us to import remote nodes from other organizations. Using the dialog box, we can find and upload the JSON files containing the nodes' information (`*-exportNodesToRemote.json`). In our case, we can upload the files created when we exported the peers' configuration from the other member organizations. Within the dialog, you can click on the **Upload remote nodes configuration** link and select the file you want to upload, as shown in the following screenshot. Click on the plus (+) icon to add each of the configuration files or import them separately:

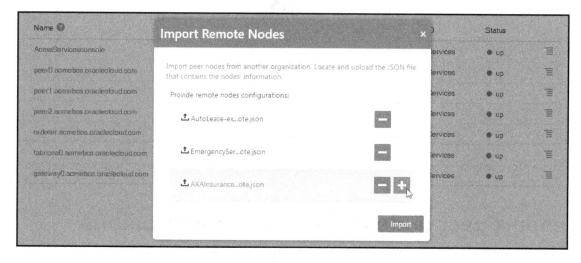

Import each of the remote peers' configuration file of the member organizations

Finally, click on **Import** at the bottom-right corner of the dialog box to persist the information and add the remote peers to the list of identified peers. If the configuration files are correct, the dialog box will briefly show a green confirmation message before it automatically closes. The remote peers are now visible in the list of identified nodes, and they are added to the total number of nodes in the **Nodes Summary** section.

The following image shows that, from the perspective of the founder, we have a total of 13 identified nodes, including the 6 imported remote peers. The list only shows the remote peers when a filter on this type is active. The status is **N/A** because it is not managed by this instance, and there is currently no remote health-check functionality:

Nodes page showing the identified nodes from the founder's perspective

Notice in the preceding screenshot that for each remote peer, the MSP ID to which it belongs is automatically recognized by OBCS. The result of importing remote peers is visible in the topology view of the network.

Navigate to the **Nodes** page and click on the flowchart icon to see the result, as shown in the following diagram:

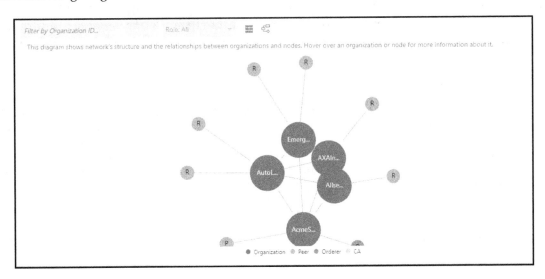

Topology of our network after importing the peer configuration of each member organization

Export orderer settings from founder

In order for participating organizations to connect to the existing network of the founder, they need to know the configuration settings of the ordering service. These settings can be exported via the founding organization.

As the founder (Acme), navigate to the **Network** page. From this page, we can export the ordering service configuration by clicking on the options menu on the right-hand side of the **AcmeServices** entry in the list of organizations and selecting **Export Orderer Settings**:

Exporting the Ordering Service settings managed by the founder organization, Acme Services

Performing this action will download a JSON file called `{foundername}_orderer_settings.json`. In our case, it downloads the file `AcmeServices_orderer_settings.json`. If you open this file with a text editor, you will see that it contains the MSP ID of the founder organization, the TLS certificate of the corresponding CA, and information on how to connect to the ordering service (IP address, port, and so on). The following snippet shows the contents of the downloaded JSON file:

```
{
  "mspid": "AcmeServices",
  "tlscacerts": "-----BEGIN CERTIFICATE-----
\nMIICZjCCAg2gAwIBAgIQYaE18EUOf7aftpx94MmnVTAKBggqhkjOPQQDAjCBhDEL\nMAkGA1U
EBhMCVVMxEzARBgNVBAgTCkNhbGlmb3JuaWExFjAUBgNVBAcTDVNhbiBG\ncmFuY2lzY28xIDAe
BgNVBAoTF2FjbWViY3Mub3JhY2xlY2xvdWQuY29tMSYwJAYD\nVQQDEx10bHNjYS5hY21lYmNzL
m9yYWNsZWNsb3VkLmNvbTAeFw0xODA2MjcxNTE5\nMTNaFw0yODA2MjQxNTE5MTNaMIGEMQswCQ
YDVQQGEwJVUzETMBEGA1UECBMKQ2Fs\naWZvcm5pYTEWMBQGA1UEBxMNU2FuIEZyYW5jaXNjbzE
gMB4GA1UEChMXYWNtZWJj.........\n-----END CERTIFICATE-----\n",
  "ordererSeviceInfo": [
    {
      "address": "192.168.99.101",
      "port": 7000,
      "native": true,
      "restport": 8080
    }
  ]
}
```

Import orderer settings at member organizations

The final step that we need to perform to connect our member organizations to the existing network is to import the settings of the Ordering Service. This step needs to be done for each of the member organizations. Let's illustrate this step with the Allsecur Insurance organization by logging into their administrative console. In our case, the URL to use is similar
to: `https://ascbcs-allsecurinsurance.blockchain.ocp.oraclecloud.com`.

In order to import the settings, simply navigate to the **Network** page and click on the **Import Orderer Settings** button on the right-hand side of the filter options:

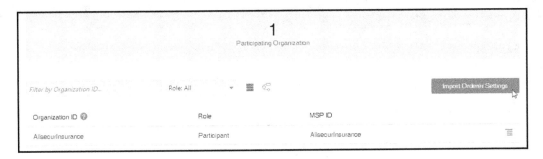

Import the ordering settings of the founder organization

A dialog box will appear that asks you to provide an Orderer settings JSON file that contains the MSP ID, orderer address, and TLS CA certificate of an OBCS organization. Click the **Upload Orderer Settings** link to upload the exported settings file from the founder organization. Select the `AcmeServices_orderer_settings.json` file, and see the new **Orderer Address**, which is part of the settings file, appear in the dialog box.

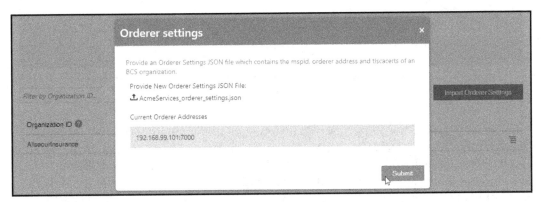

Upload orderer settings of the founder organization

To check whether the OBCS instance of the member organization is connected to the network of the founder, you can navigate to the **Dashboard** page. You should see the summary displaying the number of peers, channels, and chaincodes managed by the organization, as well as information about the organization's health, channel, and peer activity.

The following screenshot shows the **Dashboard** page of Allsecur Insurance after configuring the ordering service settings. It looks a bit simpler than the dashboard of the founder, Acme, since a member organization does not have an orderer and other participating organizations:

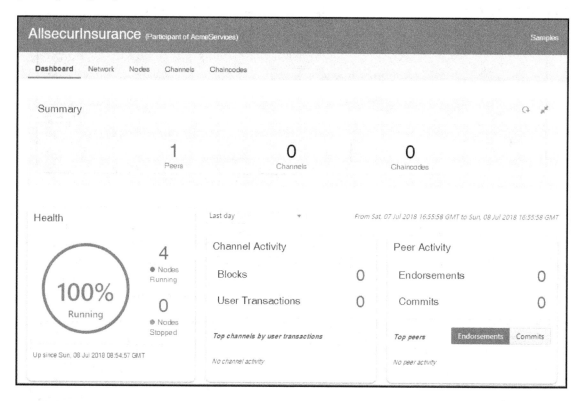

Dashboard of Allsecur Insurance after joining the existing business network

After performing all of the steps described, almost all of the member organizations have joined our business network. One organization, USA Automotive Services, is the odd one out as it already uses Hyperledger Fabric within its IT landscape and needs to be connected in a different way to the network. I will explain the steps to join an external/non-OBCS organization in Chapter 14, *Configuring, Extending, and Monitoring Your Network*.

Setting up a private channel

Now that we have joined the member organizations to the existing business network, we can set up a new communication channel between those organizations. A channel is generally created by the founder organization, which permits member organizations to join the channel. To achieve this, we need to execute the following tasks:

1. Create a new channel as the founder
2. Join each of the member organization's peers to the channel

Create a new channel as the founder

In order for the organizations of our network to transact with each other, we first need to create a new channel (or edit the default channel) and configure which organizations can join the channel. In our case, we are going to create a new channel. We will create the channel as the founder organization and will name it *insurancechain*.

While logged into the administrative console of the founder, Acme, navigate to the **Channels** page. This page already lists one channel, called *acmeservicesorderer*, which is the default channel created when provisioning the founder instance of OBCS. We will ignore this channel and create our own. To do so, click on the **Create a New Channel** button, as shown in the following screenshot:

Creating a new channel in which member organizations can transact with each other

A dialog box is shown, in which we need to specify the name of the new channel and which organizations' peers can join the channel.

Use the following information when creating the new channel:

Field Name	Field Value	Description
Channel Name	Enter `insurancechain`	Only lowercase ASCII alphanumerics. The name must start with a letter, and it can't be longer than 15 characters.
MSP ID	Select `all organizations`	Select the organizations that you want to allow to join the channel. You can also create more private channels that include a subset.
ACL	Select `ReaderOnly` for AcmeServices; Select `ReaderWriter` for other organizations	Choose `ReaderOnly` if you want the organization only to allow reading of channel information and blocks on the channel and to invoke chaincode.
Peers to Join Channel	Select all available peers (0, 1, and 2) from Acme Services	Selects zero, one, or more peers to join the channel. Selecting zero peers still results in channel creation.

Information required to create a new channel

The following screenshot shows the **Create a New Channel** dialog box with the information specified in the preceding table:

Dialog box for creating a new channel among member organizations

Click the **Submit** button, in the bottom-right corner, to create the new channel. When you specify peers to join the channel, they will also be joined in the process. The dialog box closes automatically, and the channel is shown in the list of available channels.

If you need to add organizations to the channel later, update the ordering service settings or add peers to the channel. To do this, you can use the options menu on the right-hand side of each entry:

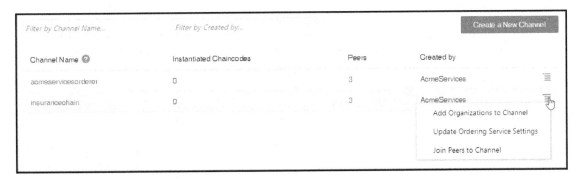

After the channel is created, these options allow you to add organizations to the channel, for example

At any time, you can check which organizations are allowed to join the network by viewing the channel's details. Click on the name of the channel (for instance, insurancechain) to view its details and navigate to the **Organizations** section to view the list of participating organizations and the **ACL** (**Access Control List**) policy set for each organization.

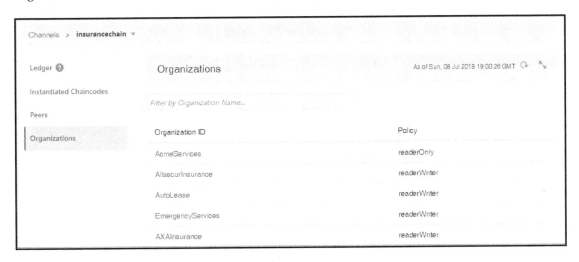

Channel details, including organizations that are allowed to join and set ACL policies

Adding member peers to the channel

Now that the member organizations have joined the business network and the channel has been created, we can finally join the peers of the participating organizations. This step needs to be performed for each organization. Let's illustrate this step with the AXA Insurance organization by logging into their administrative console. In our case, the URL to use is similar to:

`https://axabcs-allsecurinsurance.blockchain.ocp.oraclecloud.com.`

While logged into the administrative console of AXA insurance, navigate to the **Nodes** page. From this page, we can add specific peers to the channel. AXA and Allsecur only have one peer, but AutoLease and Emergency Services have two peers each. The following steps need to be performed for each of the peers that you want to add to an existing channel. To add a peer to a channel, click on the name of the peer. In our case, we will join `peer0.axabcs.oraclecloud.com` to the *insurancechain* channel:

Select the peer that you want to join to an existing channel

On the details page of the peer, navigate to the **Channels** tab. This tab, as shown in the following screenshot, displays a list of channels that the peer node uses to communicate with other nodes. You can use this tab to add the peer node to channels. To add a peer, click on **Join New Channels**:

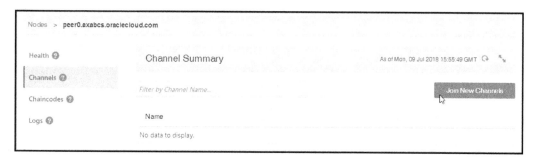

Use the Channels tab to join the peer node to channels

This action will display the following dialog box, asking you to specify the channel name that you want the peer to join. Enter the exact name of the channel, for example, *insurancechain* (names are case-sensitive), and click **Join**:

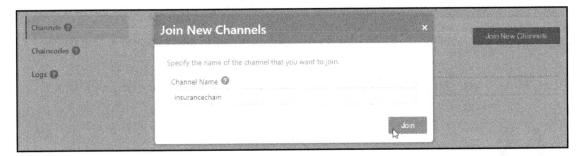

Enter the exact name of the channel you want the peer to join

If the peer of the organization is allowed to join the channel, you will briefly see a message such as the one shown in the following screenshot, stating **Channel joined successfully!** If the channel does not exist, or if the organization is not allowed to join it, an error message similar to the following is shown:

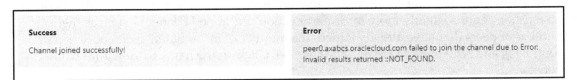

Possible success and error messages displayed when joining a channel

Joining a valid channel is nearly instantaneous, and it results in the automatic closure of the dialog box, returning you to the channel list of the peer node. The list now shows the channel that we just joined, as shown in the following screenshot:

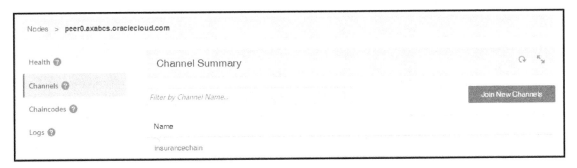

Peer0 of AXA Insurance successfully joined the *insurancechain* channel

We need to perform the following steps for all participating organizations' peers. In our case, we still have to join the following peers:

- `peer0.ascbcs.oraclecloud.com` of *Allsecur Insurance*
- `peer0` and `peer1.ersbcs.oraclecloud.com` of *Emergency Services*
- `peer0.alebcs.oraclecloud.com` and `peer1.alebcs.oraclecloud.com` of *AutoLease*

> You can easily join peers to a channel via the Nodes page using the menu options on the right side of the peer node entry:

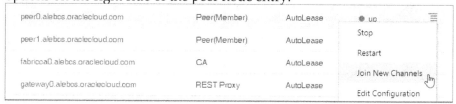

To see the details of the channel, you can click on its name in the list of channels that a peer has joined, or you can navigate to the **Channels** page and find a list of all of the channels over which the organization communicates. The list on this page, as shown in the following screenshot, reports slightly more information about the joined channels, such as the number of peers that have already joined, the number of instantiated chaincodes (smart contracts), and who initially created the channel. Click on the name to view the channel's details:

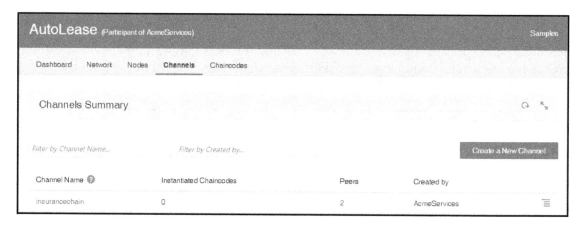

List of channels that the AutoLease organization has joined with one or more peer nodes

You can, for example, view the peers that have joined the channel. The following screenshot shows that both peer nodes of AutoLease have successfully joined the *insurancechain* channel. Notice that the option to set one or more anchor peers on the channel is checked.

As explained in `Chapter 10`, *Introducing the Oracle Blockchain Cloud Service*, for better discovery of the network, organizations using the channel are advised to designate at least one anchor peer (or multiple anchor peers to prevent a single point of failure). This allows for peers belonging to different members to discover other peers on the channel.

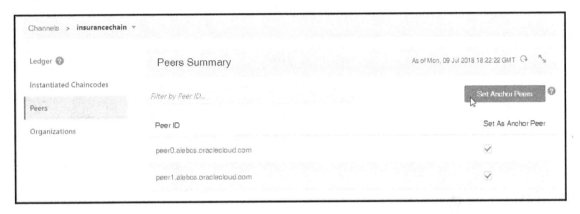

List of peers that joined the channel for the AutoLease organization. Both peers are set as anchor peers.

For each organization in our network, including the founder, we need to set at least one anchor peer. For organizations that joined two or more peers to the channel(such as AutoLease, Emergency Services, and Acme Services), you set a minimum of two anchor peers.

After performing this last task, our business network is set up and able to run a smart contract (chaincode) between our organizations.

When we look at the ledger details of our newly-created channel, as shown in the following screenshot, we see that each **Set Anchor Peers** action created a new block on the chain of type **config**, meaning that no asset data was persisted.

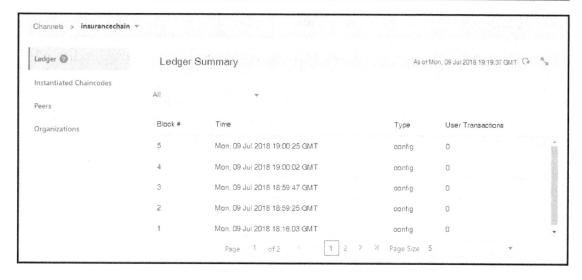

List of config transactions (blocks) persisted to the ledger of our insurancechain channel

Summary

In this first implementation chapter, we set out to set up our own permissioned blockchain using the OBCS. The chapter started by summarizing problems with traditional cross-organizational applications, and it introduced a solution using OBCS. Next, I explained how you can provision your own OBCS environments for all member organizations of your business network.

After provisioning the environments, we explored the administrative console and its main capabilities, namely the health dashboard, blockchain network, nodes, channels, and chaincodes. For each capability, we went over the UI, its layout, and the tasks we can perform.

After glancing over the administrative console, we started joining the member organizations to the same business network. We began by exporting the client certificates and peer nodes of each of the member organizations. Once we had exported the required certificates and peer configuration files, we imported them into the environment of the founder and added the member organizations to the business network.

For member organizations to be able to communicate with the rest of the network, we exported the ordering service settings and imported the settings for each of the members or participating organizations. Finally, we created a new channel and joined all of the peer nodes of each organization to that channel so that they could communicate and transact with each other.

In Chapter 12, *Designing and Developing Your First Smart Contract*, we will design and program our own smart contract (chaincode), including the setup of our development environment.

Designing and Developing Your First Smart Contract

12

In the previous chapter, we created an OBCS environment for each of our participating members, set up the permissioned blockchain, and joined all of the organizations to the same private channel. Now that we have this up and running, we can design and develop our first decentralized blockchain application.

In this chapter, we will first design our business network and define its data model (that is, its assets and participants), transactions, and events. I will explain each of these concepts in relation to what we are going to develop. Next, we will use the defined model to develop our decentralized application (that is, a smart contract) in the **Go** programming language. To actually program a smart contract we need to install the required software tools and set up our **integrated development environment** (**IDE**). The tools required include **cURL**, **Docker**, the Go language binaries, and some platform-specific binaries for Fabric. The IDE we are going to use will be **Visual Studio Code**, as this is an open-source/free tool with plugins for writing and debugging Go applications and thus our chaincode, but you can use any source code editor that supports the Go language.

After installing the software, we will program our chaincode in a step-by-step approach so you can easily follow and program the chaincode yourself. In this chapter, we will not program the complete chaincode, as that would be very time consuming. In this chapter, we will develop the first transaction for reporting accidents and all required data objects and functions. The complete chaincode is available at `http://bit.ly/insurancechain`.

In this chapter, you will learn how to do the following:

- Design your first smart contract from scratch
- Set up your development environment for creating smart contracts
- Develop your first smart contract (chaincode) following our design

The proposed application

Before developing our decentralized application (smart contract), let's recap the use cases that we want to program into the smart contract and from there design our data model, transactions, and events. As explained in Chapter 9, *Building a Next-Generation Oracle B2B Platform*, the goal is to create an application that allows for a unified way of working and sharing data about accidents, insurance policies and claims, and vehicle repairs among involved organizations. All organizations will use the same smart contract, deployed on the blockchain, as the single source of truth for querying data and executing transactions, whereas with traditional cross-organizational applications, every organization has its own back-office system.

To re-familiarize yourself with the use case, look at the following diagram, which shows the smart contract interactions among the participating organizations:

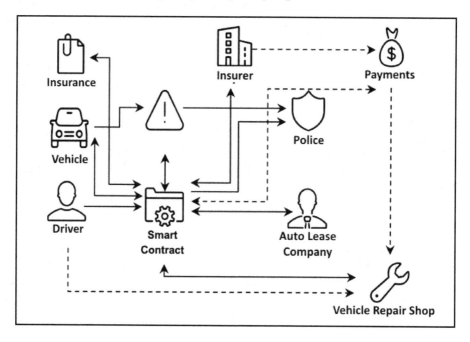

Organizations interact with each other on the blockchain through an identical smart contract

The smart contract that we are going to develop can be used to do the following:

- Register required participants and assets (for example, emergency services, drivers, insurers, insurance policies, vehicles, and repair shops)
- Automate the registration of accidents when they happen (for example, via IoT sensors)
- Allow accidents to be dispatched to/administered by any emergency service
- Enable the lease company to act as mediator between insurers and repair shops
- Allow the lease company to request a quote for repairs on a vehicle
- Permit individual repair shops to prepare a quote and submit an offer
- Allow an insurer to send a claim to another insurer related to an accident report

The transactions that we are going to implement are a subset of the transactions discussed in Chapter 9, *Building a Next-Generation Oracle B2B Platform*, and they include the most important transactions required to develop our **minimum viable product** (**MVP**). The following table lists the transactions examined in Chapter 9, *Building a Next-Generation Oracle B2B Platform*, indicating which transactions are to be implemented in this chapter:

Transaction	Description	Part of MVP
ReportAccident	Report a new accident (automatic or manual)	Yes
UpdateReport	Dispatch an ERS to location and update details	Yes
RequestQuote	Request a quote for the cost of vehicle repairs	Yes
OfferQuote	Offer a quote (estimate) of the cost of the repairs	Yes
IssuePolicy	Issue a new insurance policy to the registrant	Yes
SendClaim	Send an insurance claim to the insurer of the party of fault	Yes
AcceptClaim	Accept the insurance claim (and blame)	No
RepairVehicle	Request to repair vehicle based on the offered quote	No
PaymentRequest	Request for payment for vehicle repairs	No

List of all proposed transactions in the use case indicating the transactions that are part of the MVP

Besides the transactions, our smart contract will also transmit events. Events are very convenient when you want to notify a front-end application asynchronously instead of having it wait on an answer. The following table lists the events discussed in `Chapter 9`, *Building a Next-Generation Oracle B2B Platform*, indicating which transactions are to be implemented in this chapter:

Event	Description	Part of MVP
NewAccident	Notification of when a new accident is reported	Yes
ReportUpdated	Notification of when details of a report are updated	Yes
RequestForQuote	Notification of when a quote for repairs is requested	Yes
NewQuoteOffer	Notification of when a quote estimate is submitted	Yes
NewClaim	Notification of when a new insurance claim is filed	Yes
RepairOrder	Notification of when the order to repair is placed	No
PayOrder	Notification of when a payment request is submitted	No

List of all proposed events in the use case indicating the events that are part of the MVP

Now that we have decided on the five transactions and the five events that are part of our MVP, we can sit down and start designing our data model.

Model-first design approach

As with most modern (micro)services or APIs, it is best to start by designing the specification first and defining what operations are exposed to the outside. The same goes for smart contracts on the blockchain. It's best to start every new contract using a model-first design approach. What I mean by this is to define the data objects (*participants, assets* (including its attributes), *complex types*, and *enumerations*) and the request and response objects for our transactions and events. You can start out on paper, use tools to create **entity relationship diagram (ERD)** models (for instance, `https://draw.io`), or design your business model using **Hyperledger Composer**, a declarative modeling language and development toolset for smart contracts that is deployable on Hyperledger Fabric.

For this chapter, we are going to design the models as a custom ERD diagram, since explaining a toolset such as Hyperledger Composer is a bit on the heavy side, apart from the fact that it is not yet officially supported by Oracle. Nonetheless, it is still interesting to examine Composer (`https://hyperledger.github.io/composer/latest/`), as much of its terminology is used to design and explain the ERD diagrams that follow.

When you design a smart contract, it is good to treat it as something that runs separately on top of your blockchain infrastructure and peer network. For instance, your smart contract can facilitate users other than the ones who are managing the network. These users are commonly addressed as **participants**, and they can be compared to role-based data or entity objects; for example, insurer, car owner, insurance policy holder, and so forth.

As you continue designing the required transactions (that is, interactions) of your smart contract, the first step is to decide what information it is that you want to store on the blockchain, in what format (such as objects and their attributes) and size (for example, the data structure and number of attributes for each object). These data objects containing your application information are commonly known as **assets**, and they can be transacted or modified by members of your business network. Keeping the size of an asset low allows for better reuse and sharing of that information.

Another practice to follow when designing your smart contract is to take the reuse of data structures a step further, and instead of designing multiple assets with the same address attributes, model them in their own data type. These data types don't exist as information on the blockchain itself; rather, they form the structure of an asset and are commonly known as **concept** types.

Finally, the last practice about which you should be aware is the possibility of modeling certain constraints on accepted values for an attribute; for example, a list or enumeration of potential values. Such lists are commonly known as **enum** types.

Besides the data model, a contract consists of *transactions* and *events*. **Transactions** are functions of your smart contract that can be executed from an external application, whereas **events** are notifications that can be sent by the smart contract to external applications that are listening to these events. Both transactions and events will have a data object that they either expect to receive or send. When modeling a transaction or event, you can reference existing assets on the blockchain or define its attributes. Just know that the payload (that is, the data object) that you send in a transaction or event does not have to resemble an asset on the blockchain. The logic of the smart contract can query the asset from the blockchain; for example, before modifying its information.

In the next couple of sections, I will go over the design of the smart contract and its data model. I have chosen to separate the data objects, transactions, and events in four different groups (commonly known as *namespaces* or packages).

The four different model groups are as follows:

- **Base**: All participants, non-domain specific assets, and types
- **Accident**: All assets, transactions, events, and types relating to accidents
- **Vehicle repair**: All assets, transactions, events, and types relating to repairs
- **Insurance**: All assets, transactions, events, and types relating to insurance

Designing the participants and base assets

Let's start by identifying our participants (a special type of asset), who reflect users within the application. Besides participants, we need to identify the assets that can be used as base assets by multiple additional data domains.

In our case, we can identify the following participants:

- **Registrants** (legal entities) that own vehicles or hold insurance policies. A registrant can be an individual, corporation, or a lease company.
- **Emergency services** that respond to accidents and administer the report.
- **Insurers** that issue insurance policies to registrants, request repair quotes, and process (send, accept, or decline) insurance claims.
- **Repair shops** that respond to repair quotes with estimates and repair vehicles.

You might wonder why we don't identify vehicle owners, insurance policy holders, and lease companies as separate participants. The reason is that a user of the application can represent one or more of these types of entities. As you will see in a moment, these entities share the same data fields. Do you really want to register duplicate information?

 When designing a data model, avoid duplication of similar participant types, as it makes reuse easier, keeps data in sync, and allows for greater fine-grained access control and business rules. It is better to use an enumeration to define the type of participant; in our case, a type that defines the different legal entities.

Besides participants, there can be assets that are used by multiple data domains. For example, in our case, we only have `Vehicle` as a base asset. This asset is used in accident reports, insurance policies, insurance claims, and repair quotes.

When designing a data model, the idea is to place non-domain-specific assets together so that they can be reused and won't result in similar copies in other data domains.

Now that we have established the participants and the base asset(s), we can model the information that we want to store in the blockchain for these data objects. One practice to follow here is that assets on the blockchain always need a unique identification so that they can easily be referenced, transacted, modified, or queried. This is similar to database tables, Java classes, or other entity objects that persist relational data. Before I review the details of the data objects, look at the following diagram, which shows the modeled participants and base asset as well as the relationships among them:

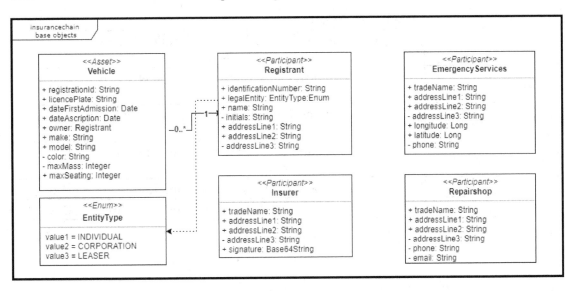

ERD diagram of base objects, including the different participants and Vehicle asset

The `Registrant` participant has the following data fields:

Data field	Data type	Purpose	Optional
identicationNumber	String	Unique identification (for example, `accountName`)	No
legalEntity	Enum	Legal entity (type constraint), either `INDIVIDUAL`, `LEASOR`, or `CORPORATION`	No
name	String	Last name or trade name	No
initials	String	Initials of individual	Yes

Data field	Data type	Purpose	Optional
addressLine1	String	First address line (for instance, street and house number)	No
addressLine2	String	Second address line (such as postal code and city)	No
addressLine3	String	Third address line (for example, state and country)	Yes

Data structure of the Registrant object

The Emergency Services participant has the following data fields:

Data field	Data type	Purpose	Optional
tradeName	String	Unique identification (for example, chamber of commerce (COC) trade name)	No
addressLine1	String	First address line (for instance, street and house number)	No
addressLine2	String	Second address line (such as postal code and city)	No
addressLine3	String	Third address line (for example, state and country)	Yes
longitude	Long	East-west position of responding location	No
latitude	Long	North-south position of responding location	No
phone	String	Direct phone number	Yes

Data structure of the Emergency Services object

The Insurer participant has the following data fields:

Data field	Data type	Purpose	Optional
tradeName	String	Unique identification (for instance, COC trade name)	No
addressLine1	String	First address line (for example, street and house number)	No
addressLine2	String	Second address line (such as postal code and city)	No
addressLine3	String	Third address line (for instance, state and country)	Yes

Data field	Data type	Purpose	Optional
signature	String	Base64 of real signature	No

Data structure of the Insurer object

The Repair Shop participant has the following data fields:

Data field	Data type	Purpose	Optional
tradeName	String	Unique identification (for example, COC trade name)	No
addressLine1	String	First address line (for instance, street and house number)	No
addressLine2	String	Second address line (such as postal code and city)	No
addressLine3	String	Third address line (for example, state and country)	Yes
phone	String	Contact phone number	Yes
email	String	Contact email address	Yes

Data structure of the Repair Shop object

Finally, the asset Vehicle has the following data fields:

Data field	Data type	Purpose	Optional
registrationId	String	Unique identification (for example, VIN/vehicle ID)	No
licensePlate	String	License plate	No
dateFirstAdmission	Date	Date of first admission	No
dateAscription	Date	Date of owner registration	No
owner	Registrant	Reference to existing registrant ID	No
make	String	Make of vehicle	No
model	String	Model of vehicle	No
color	String	Color of vehicle	Yes
maxMass	Integer	Maximum mass (weight) of car	Yes
maxSeating	Integer	Maximum number of seats	No

Data structure of the Vehicle object

You will also find `EntityType` on the diagram. This is the enumeration used by the `Registrant` object, and it is useful for programming specific business rules or access control.

Designing the accident assets and transactions

The next set of assets, and the first transactions and events that we are going to define, all fall into the accident domain. This domain contains transactions and assets needed to report and store new accidents and make it possible for emergency services to respond to and update these reports.

In our case, we can identify the following assets, transactions, and events:

- `AccidentReport`: An asset that stores the details of an accident
- `ReportAccident`: A transaction to report a new accident at a specific location
- `UpdateReport`: A transaction to update the accident report
- `NewAccidentEvent`: An event transmitted after a new accident is reported
- `ReportUpdateEvent`: An event transmitted after an accident report is updated

The following diagram shows the modeled assets, transactions, and events of the accident domain and the relationships among them. The diagram includes three kinds of relationships:

- The use of concept objects, better known as inner classes/structs in many programming languages. They can't be stored on their own on the blockchain.
- Relationships among assets and participants (defined as data fields).
- References to existing assets and participants through their unique ID.

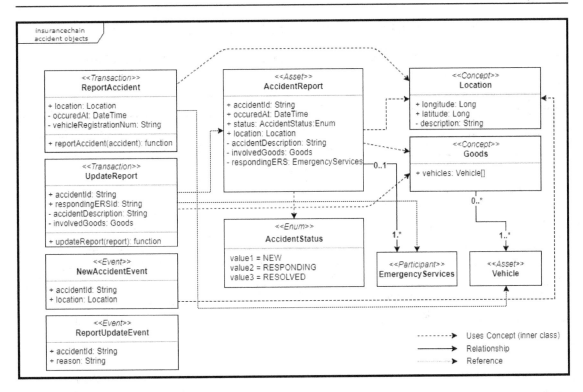

ERD diagram of accidents objects, including the different assets, transactions, and their relationships

When designing your assets, always think about how you can reuse data structures in the best way. Designing physical relationships or concept objects makes your application (including the smart contract) more scalable and dynamic.

When an accident is reported, `location` (including longitude, latitude, and description) is sent (as a data object) to the transaction exposed by the smart contract. The same structure is part of the `AccidentReport` asset and part of `NewAccidentEvent`. So, instead of defining the fields separately it's better to define a concept/struct object and include it in the asset, transaction, or event that wants to use the same structure. The same goes for the `goods` concept object. This is an extensible object where you could add other physical objects that are involved, such as casualties or road damages, in future.

When designing relationship among assets or participants, you can reference them either by their unique ID, or by a pointer to the stored object. It is up to the programmer of the smart contract on how to implement the relationships, which mostly depends on the programming language in use.

As in the previous section, let's go over the defined objects part of this domain.

The `AccidentReport` asset stores all of the details of an accident, and it contains the following data fields:

Data field	Data type	Purpose	Optional
accidentId	String	Unique identification (generated by contact)	No
occurredAt	DateTime	Moment when accident occurred	No
status	Enum	Accident status (enum/type constraint), either NEW, RESPONDING, or RESOLVED	No
location	Location	The location of the accident	No
accidentDescription	String	Description of what happened at accident	Yes
involvedGoods	Goods	The involved goods (for example, vehicles involved)	Yes
respondingERS	Emergency Services	Relationship to a responding ERS participant	Yes

Data structure of the AccidentReport object

The `AccidentReport` object uses two concept objects: `Location` and `Goods`. With these kinds of objects, you can create more complex assets instead of defining and programming them directly as part of the asset. The `Goods` concept (or struct) currently only contains an array of relationships to `Vehicle` assets involved, whereas the `Location` concept contains the following data fields:

Data field	Data type	Purpose	Optional
longitude	Long	East-west position of responding location	No
latitude	Long	North-south position of responding location	No
description	String	Description to identify the location easily	Yes

Data structure of the Location object

On the diagram, you will also see a reference to the `AccidentStatus` object. This is an enumeration used by the accident report object, and it is useful for programming specific business rules or access control. For example, you can block an update to a report if the report is already resolved.

The other objects defined in the ERD are the two transactions, `ReportAccident` and `UpdateReport`, and the two events, `NewAccidentEvent` and `ReportUpdateEvent`. These events are a reaction to the successful execution of the corresponding transactions.

The `ReportAccident` transaction creates a new `AccidentReport` object and stores it on the blockchain. It has no business rules other than checking to see whether the required fields have been submitted. The transaction defines the following data input fields:

Data field	Data type	Purpose	Optional
location	Location	The location of the accident	No
occuredAt	DateTime	Moment when the accident occurred. When empty, the current date/time should be stored.	Yes
vehicleRegistrationNum	String	Unique ID referencing the vehicle asset that is reporting the accident	Yes

Data structure of the ReportAccident transaction

Once the asset is successfully stored in the blockchain, an event called `NewAccidentReport` is transmitted. This event contains the unique ID of the accident, generated by the smart contract code, and the location of the accident so that `Emergency Services` knows where the accident occurred and can respond if it is in their jurisdiction.

The `UpdateReport` transaction updates the accident report and can be executed/called at two different times. First, it can be called when an accident is new, and `Emergency Services` can assign itself as the responding ERS. Second, it can be called to update the report with details about the accident. Only the responding ERS can update the report details. The transaction defines the following data input fields:

Data field	Data type	Purpose	Optional
accidentId	String	Unique ID referencing the accident report	No
respondingERSId	String	Unique ID referencing an Emergency Service	No
accidentDescription	String	Description of what occurred at the accident scene	Yes
involvedGoods	Goods	The involved goods (for example, vehicles involved)	Yes

Data structure of the UpdateReport transaction

Once the asset is successfully updated in the blockchain, the `ReportUpdateEvent` event is transmitted. This event contains the unique ID of the accident and the reason for the update (for instance, responder en route).

Designing the repair assets and transactions

The third set of assets, transactions, and events that we are going to define fall into the vehicle repair domain. This domain contains the transactions and assets needed to request for a quote to repair a damaged vehicle and generate quote with repair estimates. We can identify the following assets, transactions, and events, as shown in the following diagram:

- `QuoteRequest`: An asset that stores a request for vehicle repairs
- `RepairQuote`: An asset that stores a repair quote based upon a specific request
- `RequestQuote`: A transaction to request a new quote to repair vehicle damages
- `OfferQuote`: A transaction to offer an estimate for a specific request
- `RequestforQuoteEvent`: An event transmitted after a new request is submitted
- `NewQuoteOfferEvent`: An event transmitted after a new quote is offered

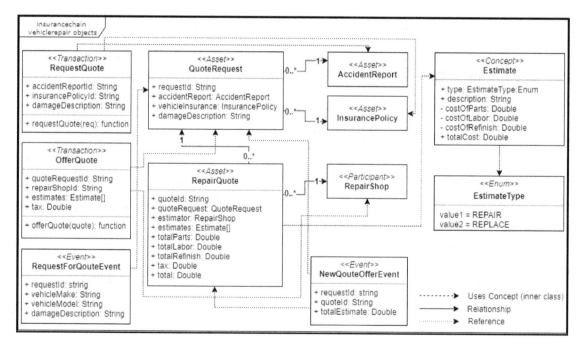

ERD diagram of vehicle repair objects, including the different assets, transactions, and their relationships

The vehicle repair domain contains the most assets, transactions, and inter-relationships when compared with other domains. The assets in this domain relate to other assets and participants that are stored on the blockchain, such as the accident reports, repair shops, and insurance policies (part of the insurance domain). Once again, let's go over the defined objects part of this domain. The `QuoteRequest` asset stores all of the details of a request to repair vehicle damages, and it contains the following data fields:

Data field	Data type	Purpose	Optional
requestId	String	Unique identification (generated by contact)	No
accidentReport	Accident Report	Relationship to an existing accident report	No
vehicleInsurance	Insurance Policy	Relationship to the insurance policy of the owner of the vehicle	No
damageDescription	String	A description of the vehicle damages to be fixed	No

Data structure of the QuoteRequest object

The `QuoteRequest` object is related to an existing accident report and the insurance policy of the owner of the car. Storing these relationships allows for a repair shop to gain access to the information stored in these assets.

The `RepairQuote` asset stores all of the details of a quote submitted by a repair shop, and it includes the following data fields:

Data field	Data type	Purpose	Optional
quoteId	String	Unique identification (generated by contact)	No
quoteRequest	Quote Request	Relationship to an existing quote request	No
estimator	Repair Shop	Relationship to the shop submitting the quote	No
estimates	Estimate[]	One or more estimates (array of objects)	No
totalParts	Double	Total cost of estimated parts	No
totalLabor	Double	Total cost of estimated labor	No
totalRefinish	Double	Total cost of estimated refinishes	No
tax	Double	Tax that needs to be paid on the total amount	No
total	Double	Total cost of repairs, including taxes	No

Data structure of the RepairQuote object

The `RepairQuote` object is related to the original quote request and the repair shop that submitted the quote. The asset also uses the `Estimate` concept object (in array form), which includes information on each of the estimated repairs. The `Estimate` concept (or struct) contains the following data fields:

Data field	Data type	Purpose	Optional
`type`	Enum	Estimate type (enum/type constraint), either `REPAIR` or `REPLACE`	No
`description`	String	Description of repairs	No
`costOfParts`	Double	Estimated cost of parts	Yes
`costOfLabor`	Double	Estimated cost of labor	Yes
`costOfRefinish`	Double	Estimated cost of refinishes	Yes
`totalCost`	Double	Calculated total of estimated costs	No

Data structure of the Estimate object

You also see a reference to the `EstimateType` object on the preceding diagram. This is an enumeration used by the `Estimate` object to indicate the type of repairs.

The other objects defined in the ERD diagram are the two transactions, `RequestQuote` and `OfferQuote`, and the two events, `RequestForQuoteEvents` and `NewQuoteOffer`. The events are a reaction to the successful execution of the corresponding transaction.

The `RequestQuote` transaction creates a new request for a quote estimating the vehicle damages and stores it on the blockchain. The transaction executes some business rules; for example, it checks to see whether the given insurance policy is part of the accident report. The transaction defines the following data input fields:

Data field	Data type	Purpose	Optional
`accidentReportId`	String	Unique ID referencing an accident report	No
`insurancePolicyId`	String	Unique ID referencing the insurance policy of the requestor	No
`damageDescription`	String	A description of the vehicle damages to be fixed	No

Data structure of the RequestQuote transaction

Once the asset is successfully stored in the blockchain, an event is transmitted called `RequestForQuoteEvent`. This event contains a generated ID of the request, the vehicle make and model listed in the insurance policy, and the description of the damages. Repair shops can review these events and, based on the information, submit a quote.

The `OfferQuote` transaction submits a new repair quote with the cost estimate related to the vehicle damages listed in the quote request. The transaction executes some business rules; for example, it checks to see whether the request exists and performs internal calculations for the total cost before storing it on the blockchain. The transaction defines the following data input fields:

Data field	Data type	Purpose	Optional
requestID	String	Unique ID referencing a quote request	No
repairShopId	String	Unique ID referencing the repair shop	No
estimates	Estimate[]	One or more estimates (array of objects)	No
tax	Double	Taxes that needs to be paid on the estimates	No

Data structure of the OfferQuote transaction

Once the asset is successfully stored in the blockchain, the `NewQuoteOffer` event is transmitted. The original requestor (that is, the insurance policy holder) can review these events and decide which repair offers the best deal.

Designing the insurance assets and transactions

The last set of assets, transactions, and events that we are going to define fall into the insurance domain. This domain contains transactions and assets for issuing insurance policies sending insurance claims from one insurer to another.

In our case, we can identify the following assets, transactions, and events:

- `InsurancePolicy`: An asset that stores a newly issued insurance policy
- `InsuraceClaim`: An asset that stores an insurance claim between insurers
- `IssuePolicy`: A transaction to issue a new insurance policy
- `SendClaim`: A transaction to offer a quote for a specific request
- `NewClaimEvent`: An event transmitted after a new claim is submitted

The following diagram shows the modeled assets, transactions, and events of the insurance domain and the relationships between them. The insurance domain contains the assets with the most relationships to other assets and participants, as it combines all of the available information. For example, an insurance policy is related to a participating registrant (policy holder), a participating insurer, and a vehicle. The same goes for an insurance claim, which is related to an accident report, insurance policies of both parties, and a repair quote:

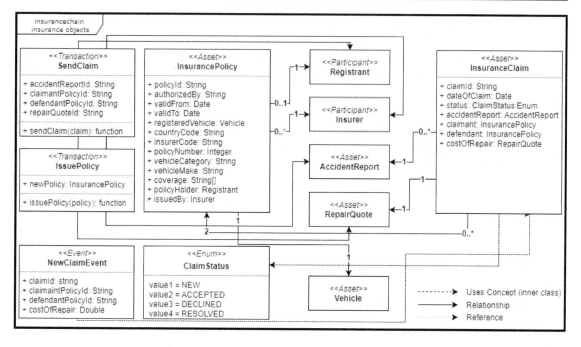

ERD diagram of insurance objects, including the different assets, transactions, and their relationships

For the final time, let's go over the defined objects that are part of this domain. The first asset is `InsurancePolicy`. It stores information about an issued insurance policy covering vehicle damages, and it contains the following data fields:

Data field	Data type	Purpose	Optional
policyId	String	Identification made up of `countryCode`, `insurerCode`, and `policyNumber`	No
authorizedBy	String	Bureau that authorized the issued policy	No
validFrom	Date	Date when policy is valid from	No
validTo	Date	Date when policy is valid to	No
registeredVehicle	Vehicle	Relationship to an existing vehicle asset	No
countryCode	String	Country code in which policy is issued	No
insurerCode	String	Insurer code of company that issues the policy	No
policyNumber	Integer	Unique number of the issued policy	No
vehicleCategory	String	Category of insured vehicle	No
vehicleMake	String	The make of the vehicle, which should be same as the registered vehicle	No

Data field	Data type	Purpose	Optional
Coverage	String[]	List of countries in which the vehicle is insured	No
policyholder	Registrant	Relationship to a participating registrant	No
issuedBy	Insurer	Relationship to a participating insurer	No

Data structure of the InsurancePolicy object

Storing the relationship to the registered vehicle, policy holder, and insurer makes it possible for other transactions defined by the smart contract (for example, request quote) simply to check whether the registered vehicle was involved in the related accident. If not, it can easily cancel the transaction.

The `InsuranceClaim` asset stores a claim for vehicle damages to be paid by the party at fault, and it includes the following data fields:

Data field	Data type	Purpose	Optional
claimId	String	Unique identification (generated by contact)	No
dateOfClaim	Date	Date when claim was submitted	No
status	Enum	Claim status (enum/constraint), either NEW, ACCEPTED, DECLINED, or RESOLVED	No
accidentReport	Accident Report	Relationship to the relevant accident	No
claimant	Insurance Policy	Relationship to the insurance policy of the claimant	No
defendant	Insurance Policy	Relationship to the insurance policy of the party at fault	No
costOfRepair	Repair Quote	Relationship to the relevant repair quote	No

Data structure of the InsuranceClaim object

Besides the previously mentioned relationships, this asset also references the `ClaimStatus` object. This is an enumeration to indicate the status of the claim. Our MVP does not process claims, so the value will stay `NEW`.

The other objects defined in the ERD diagram are the two transactions, `IssuePolicy` and `SendClaim`, and one event, `NewClaimEvent`. There is no event planned after issuing a new policy, as it is an administrative task for the insurer itself.

The transaction `IssuePolicy` issues a new insurance policy to a registrant and stores it on the blockchain. The transaction executes some business rules, as it should check to see whether the referenced participants exist and whether the registrant does not already have a valid policy on the same vehicle. The transaction defines the following data input fields:

Data field	Data type	Purpose	Optional
newPolicy	Insurance Policy	A full insurance policy object with all required fields	No

Data structure of the IssuePolicy transaction

The second `SendClaim` transaction sends a claim to pay for vehicle damages from the claiming insurer to the insurer of the at-fault party. The transaction again executes some business rules to check to see whether all of the referenced information and assets are valid in order to make the claim. If claim is valid, an `InsuranceClaim` asset is stored on the blockchain. The transaction defines the following data input fields:

Data field	Data type	Purpose	Optional
accidentReportId	String	Unique ID referencing relevant accident	No
claimantPolicyId	String	Unique ID referencing policy of the claimant	No
defendantPolicyId	String	Unique ID referencing the policy of the at-fault party	No
repairQuoteId	String	Unique ID referencing the selected repair quote	No

Data structure of the SendClaim transaction

Once the asset is successfully stored in the blockchain, the `NewClaim` event is transmitted to notify the insurer of the at-fault party.

This concludes the design portion of our decentralized application. In the steps that follow, we are going to set up our development tools and code the actual smart contract in the Go language.

Setting up the necessary development tools

Before we can develop/code our smart contract, we need to download and install all prerequisites. At the time of writing, the **Oracle Autonomous Blockchain Cloud Service** uses version 1.1 of Hyperledger Fabric as its foundation. When downloading the required software, remember that it should be compatible with that version of Fabric.

When following along in this part of the chapter, you can choose to develop your contract on a Linux or Windows system. The following sections explain the installation steps required to use a Linux system, specifically Ubuntu 18.04 LTS. You can follow the Linux tutorial (`https://linuxhint.com/install_ubuntu_18-04_virtualbox/`) on how to install a clean VirtualBox image with Ubuntu 18.04 LTS. If you prefer to develop in Windows, you can follow the steps described in the Hyperledger Fabric documentation (`https://hyperledger-fabric.readthedocs.io/en/release-1.0/getting_started.html`).

Installing cURL

Currently, there is no (visual) installer available for installing Hyperledger Fabric. Instead, it uses cURL to download the necessary platform-specific binaries. cURL is an open-source, command-line tool and library, and it is used to transfer data with URLs, hence the name. You can download the latest version of the tool from the cURL website (`https://curl.haxx.se`), or you can use `apt-get` (advance package tool), a package-management utility, available on Ubuntu and other Debian-based Linux distributions.

To install cURL, open a Terminal shell and execute the following command:

```
$> sudo apt-get update && sudo apt-get install curl -y
```

This should result in the following output:

```
[sudo] password for hyperledger:
...
The following NEW packages will be installed:
  curl libcurl4
...
Setting up curl (7.58.0-2ubuntu3.2) ...
```

Installing Docker and Docker Compose

To test your smart contract, sometimes no development environment may be available, as is the case with the Oracle cloud, for example. To test the validity of your chaincode and test the deployment, however, you can always run a development environment locally.

To be able to do so, you need to install the docker-ce (version 17.03+) and docker-compose utilities, as Hyperledger Fabric runs on several Docker images. If you are installing docker setup on a new host machine you need to set up the Docker repository first. The instructions can be found here: `https://docs.docker.com/install/linux/docker-ce/ubuntu/#set-up-the-repository`. During the set up cURL is used for the first time.

To install Docker, enter the following command in the Terminal shell:

```
$> sudo apt-get install docker-ce -y
```

This should result in the following output:

```
The following NEW packages will be installed:
  aufs-tools cgroupfs-mount docker-ce git git-man liberror-perl
...
Setting up docker-ce (18.06.0~ce~3-0~ubuntu) ...
```

The easiest way possible to install **Docker Compose** is through **Python pip**, a package manager for managing and installing software written in Python, which fortunately is the case for Docker Compose. To install pip, execute the following command in the Terminal shell:

```
$> sudo apt-get install python-pip -y
```

This should result in the following output:

```
Setting up python-pip-whl (9.0.1-2.3~ubuntu1) ...
Setting up python2.7 (2.7.15~rc1-1) ...
```

Execute the following command in the Terminal shell to install Docker Compose using `pip`:

```
$> sudo pip install docker-compose
```

The output to the preceding command should be similar to this:

```
Successfully installed PyYAML-3.13 backports.ssl-match-hostname-3.5.0.1
cached-property-1.4.3 certifi-2018.4.16 docker-compose-1.22.0 chardet-3.0.4
docker-3.4.1 ...
```

After the installation of both the docker-ce and docker-compose utilities, you can check the installed version by executing the following command in the Terminal shell:

```
$> docker --version && docker-compose --version
```

This should result in an output similar to the following:

```
Docker version 18.06.0-ce, build 0ffa825
docker-compose version 1.22.0, build f46880f
```

In some cases, as with Ubuntu, for example, you need to add your local user to the Docker system group of your **operating system (OS)** and reboot.

Enter and execute the following commands:

```
$> sudo usermod -a -G docker $USER
$> sudo reboot
```

Installing the Go programming language

As stated at the beginning of this section, OBCS uses Hyperledger Fabric (1.1) as its foundation. This version of Fabric employs the Go programming language (1.7+) for writing smart contracts. Once OBCS upgrades its version of Hyperledger Fabric, you will need to install a newer version of the Go language, so always check the prerequisites page of the Fabric release (`https://hyperledger-fabric.readthedocs.io/en/latest/prereqs.html`).

Step 1 – Installing Go

As we are going to program our smart contract (or chaincode) in Go, we need to download the source code, install the compiler, and set up some environment paths. Execute the following command in a Terminal shell to download Go 1.10.3:

```
$> sudo curl -O https://dl.google.com/go/go1.10.3.linux-amd64.tar.gz
```

This should result in an output similar to the following:

```
  % Total    % Received % Xferd Average Dload
100 126M  100 126M     0      0 26.6M
```

Next, use `tar` to unpack the downloaded file. The following command will use the Tar tool to open and expand the contents of the file and create a folder called `go`. The second command moves the folder to the preferred `/usr/local` location:

```
$> sudo tar -xvf go1.10.3.linux-amd64.tar.gz
$> sudo mv go /usr/local
```

The Go package is now in `/usr/local`, which also ensures that Go is in your `$PATH` for Linux. It is possible to install Go to an alternative location, but the `$PATH` information will change. The location that you pick to house your Go folder will be referenced later in this chapter, so remember where you put it if the location is different than `/usr/local`.

Step 2 – Setting environment paths

The next step is to set some of the environment paths that Go needs. As our Go installation location is /usr/local, all of the steps provided are relative to that path.

First, you need to edit your .bashrc profile to tell Go where to look for its files:

```
$> sudo nano ~/.bashrc
```

Add the following lines at the end of the file:

```
export GOROOT=/usr/local/go
export PATH=$PATH:$GOROOT/bin
```

Save the file, and refresh your current session with the new $PATH value by running the following:

```
$> source ~/.bashrc
```

Now that you have installed Go and set the environment paths, you can test your installation to ensure that Go works properly simply by typing go version. It should yield the result go version go1.10.3 linux/amd64.

Step 3 – Setting up your Go workspace

To store your smart contract in a uniform location, create a workspace folder as follows:

```
$> mkdir -p $HOME/goapps/insurancechain
```

Edit the .bashrc file again, and add the following line at the end:

```
export GOPATH=$HOME/goapps
```

Once again, refresh your current session using source to set the new $GOPATH variable value.

Downloading platform-specific binaries

The most important prerequisites are now installed. Next, we will install the Hyperledger Fabric platform-specific binaries. Simply create a new directory in your home folder (for example, $HOME/fabric-tools) into which the binaries are extracted. Enter the directory, and execute the following command:

```
$> curl -sSL https://goo.gl/6wtTN5 | bash -s 1.1.0
```

This will download the corresponding Fabric binaries and Docker images:

```
===> List out hyperledger docker images
hyperledger/fabric-tools      x86_64-1.1.0   6a8993b718c8
hyperledger/fabric-couchdb    x86_64-1.1.0   9a58db2d2723
hyperledger/fabric-kafka      x86_64-1.1.0   b8c5172bb83c
hyperledger/fabric-zookeeper  x86_64-1.1.0   68945f4613fc
hyperledger/fabric-orderer    x86_64-1.1.0   368c78b6f03b
hyperledger/fabric-peer       x86_64-1.1.0   c2ab022f0bdb
hyperledger/fabric-javaenv    x86_64-1.1.0   50890cc3f0cd
hyperledger/fabric-ccenv      x86_64-1.1.0   33feadb8f7a6
hyperledger/fabric-ca         x86_64-1.1.0   002c9089e464
```

Upon conclusion of the Bash script, you may want to add the $HOME/fabric-tools/bin directory to the $PATH variable so that they can be picked up by the system without you needing to fully qualify the path when running any of these utilities. Edit your ~/.bashrc profile, and add the following line at the end:

```
export PATH=$PATH:$HOME/fabric-tools/bin
```

Save the file, and refresh your session again using the source command.

Installing Visual Studio Code (IDE)

The final application that we need to install will be an IDE, which allows us to code and compile our smart contract. For this purpose, I prefer to use Visual Studio Code, or **VSCode** for short, as it has a clean design, plugin system, and integrated Bash shell. You can download the latest version of VSCode manually from https://code.visualstudio.com/Download and select the version for Ubuntu, for example, or you can execute the following curl command from your ~/Downloads folder (for version 1.25):

```
$> sudo curl -O
https://az764295.vo.msecnd.net/stable/1dfc5e557209371715f655691b1235b6b26a0
6be/code_1.25.1-1531323788_amd64.deb
```

After downloading the file, you can install it either via the Gdebi package manager or with the following command:

```
$> sudo dpkg -i ~/Downloads/code_*.deb; sudo apt -f install -y
```

This should result in the following output:

```
Setting up code (1.25.1-1531323788) ...
```

You can test to see whether the installation was successful by starting the IDE for the first time simply by typing `code` in a Terminal shell. This will start the graphical interface, as shown in the following screenshot:

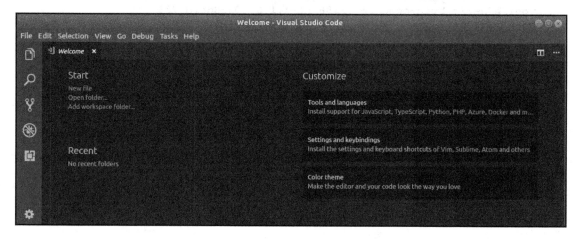

VSCode Welcome page

Finally, you need to install the VSCode extension for the Go language. On the left, you will find a vertical menu of icons. Select the fifth icon (a square box), and enter `"Go language"` in the search field. Click on the item found to view its details, and click on the **Install** button to get the Go extension:

Finding and installing the Go extension within Visual Studio Code

After the installation is complete, you are asked to reload the application. Click on **Reload** to do so. After reloading the application, you are done with the setup of your development environment.

Programming the smart contract

Up until this point in the chapter, we have designed the data model for our assets, transactions, and events, and have installed the development tools necessary to write our smart contract. The next step is to program the actual smart contract (called chaincode from this point forward) in the Go language. In the following sections, we will do the following:

- Set up a workspace in VSCode for our chaincode project(s)
- Install and initialize some missing Go packages/commands
- Program the actual chaincode, including the data objects, transactions, and events

Setting up a workspace in VSCode

Back in VSCode, either select the menu item **File** | **Add Folder to Workspace**, or if you see the **Add Folder** button, click on that. A window will open where you can select the folder to add to your workspace. Select goapps under your user's home folder, and click the **Add** button in the lower-right corner of the window:

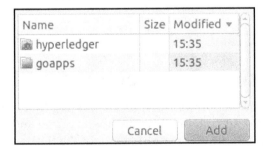

Select the goapps folder to add to your VSCode workspace

This will add the goapps folder, including its children, to your new workspace. You can save your workspace by selecting the menu item **File | Save Workspace As**, entering a name of the workspace (for example, blockchain), and clicking on **Save**. This will create a file called blockchain.code-workspace. We will do nothing with this file in this chapter, but by using workspaces in VSCode, you can easily switch between different projects or customers.

Now that we have set up our workspace, we can create the Go file in which we will program our chaincode. In VSCode, first select the insurancechain folder and then, when hovering over the name of your workspace with your cursor, select the first icon to create a new file called insurancechain.go, as shown in the following screenshot:

Creating a new file called insurancechain.go under the goapps/insurancechain folder

Installing missing Go packages and commands

VSCode may notify you that certain commands are missing that the Go extension prefers for better development of your code, such as the go-outline and gopkgs commands. These notifications pop-up in the lower-right corner of the IDE. Click on the **Install All** button to accept this recommendation and download all of the missing commands. The following screenshot shows the pop-up that I received after creating the insurancechain.go file:

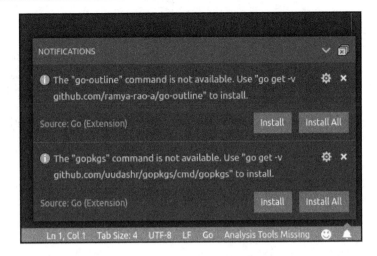

Notification indicating that some Go commands are missing, asking you to install them

The IDE will switch to a different view, and it shows you an internal Terminal window that starts executing the installation of the missing Go packages and commands.

You will see a result similar to the following:

```
Installing 10 tools at /home/hyperledger/goapps/bin
  gocode
  gopkgs
  go-outline
  . . .
  go-lint

. . .
All tools successfully installed. You're ready to Go :).
```

After a successful installation of the missing packages, the `insurancechain.go` file is immediately validated, and because it is empty, the compiler will issue an error message that it is expecting the `package` keyword. This means that we are ready to start programming.

Programming the actual chaincode

In this section, we are going to code part of our chaincode using a step-by-step approach so that you can easily follow along yourself. The part that we are going to implement is the definition of the base and accident assets and objects and the registration of a new accident. The chaincode will take shape after finishing each step, so don't worry if the compiler raises exceptions during development. Look at the error, and debug the program if there is something that you may have missed.

You can program applications in Go, separating data objects called structs in different files. Hyperledger Fabric expects all of the data objects and transactions in one chaincode file with the same name as the parent directory in which it is created.

The steps that this section describes include the following:

- Program the initial chaincode skeleton
- Add the data model objects (for example, types, participants, assets, and events)
- Program the `ReportAccident` transaction as a new function
- Make it possible for the outside world to call the function

Programming the initial chaincode skeleton

The first step is to create the skeleton of the chaincode. In order for the validator in VSCode not to mess up your progress, it is best to program the skeleton in one step before saving the file. Add the following code to your file:

```
package main

import (
  "fmt"

  "github.com/hyperledger/fabric/core/chaincode/shim"
  pb "github.com/hyperledger/fabric/protos/peer"
)

// InsuranceChaincode smart contract implementation
type InsuranceChaincode struct {
}
```

Each chaincode starts with the package declaration. In our case, it is called `main`. Following this line of code, we need to add a few essential imports, such as `"fmt"` to print log messages to the console, and most essential, the `shim` interface and the peer implementation of Fabric so that we can program the interactions with the blockchain and its ledger. If you are interested in what the `shim` interface has to offer, check out its documentation at `https://godoc.org/github.com/hyperledger/fabric/core/chaincode/shim`. After the imports, the name of the chaincode is defined as a simple type with an empty structure. This object will be used in the rest of the chaincode to bind functions to.

Next, add the `main` function at the end of your file as follows:

```
// Main
func main() {
    err := shim.Start(new(InsuranceChaincode))
    if err != nil {
        fmt.Printf("Error starting chaincode - %s", err)
    }
}
```

Each Go application needs to have a `main` function. The `main` function starts a standalone instance of the chaincode. If for some reason, the chaincode cannot be started, an error is added to the error logs/console.

Add the `Init` function to the end of your file as follows:

```
// Init - Initialize the chaincode
func (t *InsuranceChaincode) Init(stub shim.ChaincodeStubInterface) pb.Response {
    return shim.Success(nil)
}
```

The `Init` function is called during the instantiation of the chaincode in order to initialize any data. In our case, we do not have to initialize any data, as this is done by calling a setup transaction when it is deployed for the first time. The function just returns `shim.Success`.

Add the `Invoke` function to the end of your file as follows:

```
// Invoke - Our entry point for Invocations
func (t *InsuranceChaincode) Invoke(stub shim.ChaincodeStubInterface) pb.Response {
    return shim.Error("Received unknown invoke function name")
}
```

The `Invoke` function can be called during runtime, and it can be an API or SDK call from an external application. Later in this chapter, we will add some functionality to this function in order to expose the `AccidentReport` transaction to external applications. At this moment, the function will always return `shim.Error` when an unknown function is called.

The current chaincode skeleton can now be saved in VSCode. While saving, the code is validated by the compiler and any errors will show up in problems and the output palettes of the IDE. For example, in the following screenshot, I made a typo in the smart contract name:

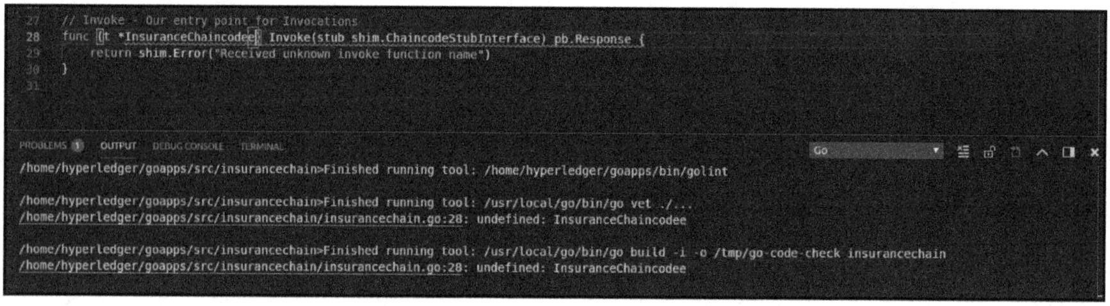

Compilation errors displayed when saving chaincode with a typo in the name of the chaincode

Adding the data model objects

Now that we have a skeleton of our chaincode ready, we can start adding our data objects. In the Go language, we define data objects as *structured types* as they always start with the `type {name} struct` expression.

Let's start by adding the code for the concept types following the declaration of `type InsuranceChaincode struct {}`:

```
// Concept Definitions - Concept struct types
// =============================================

// AddressConcept - address type
type AddressConcept struct {
  Class        string `json:"$class"`      //base.Address
  AddressLine1 string `json:"addressLine1"`
  AddressLine2 string `json:"addressLine2"`
  AddressLine3 string `json:"addressLine3,omitempty"`
}
```

```
// LocationConcept - location type
type LocationConcept struct {
   Class         string  `json:"$class"`        // accident.Location
   Longitude     float64 `json:"longitude"`
   Latitude      float64 `json:"latitude"`
   Description   string  `json:"description,omitempty"`
}

// GoodsConcept - goods type
type GoodsConcept struct {
   Class      string   `json:"$class"`      // accident.Goods
   Vehicles   []string `json:"vehicles"`    // class name + # +registrationid
}
```

The structure of a type can have zero or more fields. Each field is declared first by its name, starting with a capital, its data type (primitive or other type), and the representation when output in a JSON document for use both as the storage format on the ledger and as the format for communication with external applications. For example, take the LocationConcept struct. The first field is called Class, and it is an indication (for instance, a namespace) for an external application to be able to recognize the type of object easily. When present in a JSON document, its fieldname is $class. The second and third field are the Longitude and Latitude, and they have the datatype float64. They are represented in a JSON document by their lowercase names. The last field is Description. Notice that it has an extra attribute defined in the `json:""` declaration. With the omitempty attribute, you can indicate that the field is optional. Thus, when the value is empty, it does not have to be returned to the external application. You can also define a data object array by placing the bracket characters ([]) before the data type declaration. A list of all of the available types in the Go language can be found in the documentation at https://golang.org/ref/spec#Types.

Next, let's add the following code after the previous set, which includes the abstract type Company used by some of our participants (for example, Emergency Services, Insurer, and Repairshop).

```
// Abstract Definitions - Abstract struct types
// ===============================================

// CompanyAbstract - company type
type CompanyAbstract struct {
   TradeName string          `json:"tradeName"`
   Address   AddressConcept  `json:"address"`
}
```

The `CompanyAbstract` type uses the `AddressConcept` type for its address information, and it is presented in the JSON documents as the address field, which will include the `addressLine` fields as children.

We have only two sets of objects left: our participants and assets used for creating an accident report. Let's start by defining the four types of participants. Add the following code after the `CompanyAbstract` type:

```
// Participants Definitions - Participants the ledger will store
// ================================================================
// Registrant - participating policy holder, vehicle owner
type Registrant struct {
  Class                string        `json:"$class"` // base.Registrant
  IdentificationNumber string        `json:"identificationNumber"`
  LegalEntity          string        `json:"legalEntity"`
  Name                 string        `json:"name"`
  Initials             string        `json:"initials,omitempty"`
  Address              AddressConcept `json:"address"`
}

// Insurer - participating insurer
type Insurer struct {
  Class     string `json:"$class"` // base.Insurer
  CompanyAbstract
  Signature string `json:"signature"`
}

// EmergencyServices - participatin ERS
type EmergencyServices struct {
  Class     string           `json:"$class"` // base.EmergencyServices
  CompanyAbstract
  Location LocationConcept `json:"location"`
}

// RepairShop - participating repair shop
type RepairShop struct {
  Class string `json:"$class"` // base.RepairShop
  CompanyAbstract
  Phone string `json:"phone,omitempty"`
  Email string `json:"email,omitempty"`
}
```

Three of these participants types extend the already-defined `CompanyAbstract` type. By not defining a name or a `` `json:""` `` declaration, the fields defined in the `CompanyAbstract` type will become part of the `Insurer`, `EmergencyServices`, and `RepairShop` object structure. The field can be accessed in future code, as it is its own field. The `LegalEntity` field of the `Registrant` type is declared as a string instead of an enumeration, as it is hard to program such types in Go. To address this, you can validate permitted values when programming the implementation of a transaction.

Next, let's add our definitions for the `Vehicle` and `AccidentReport` assets. Add the following code following the `RepairShop` type:

```
// Asset Definitions - Assets the ledger will store
// ================================================

// Vehicle = asset type of vehicle
type Vehicle struct {
    Class               string     `json:"$class"` // base.Vehicle
    RegistrationNumber  string     `json:"registrationNumber"`
    LicensePlate        string     `json:"licensePlate"`
    DateFirstAdmission  time.Time  `json:"dateFirstAdmission"`
    DateAscription      time.Time  `json:"dateAscription"`
    Owner               string     `json:"owner"`
    Make                string     `json:"make"`
    Model               string     `json:"model"`
    Color               string     `json:"color,omitempty"`
    MaxMass             string     `json:"maxMass,omitempty"`
    MaxSeating          string     `json:"maxSeating"`
}

// AccidentReport - asset type of accident report
type AccidentReport struct {
    Class         string           `json:"$class"`
    AccidentID    string           `json:"accidentId"`
    OccuredAt     time.Time        `json:"occuredAt"`
    Status        string           `json:"status"`
    Location      LocationConcept  `json:"location"`
    Description   string           `json:"accidentDescription,omitempty"`
    InvolvedGoods GoodsConcept     `json:"involvedGoods,omitempty"`
    RespondingERS string           `json:"respondingERS,omitempty"`
}
```

These two types are our main assets, and they will be used in the code that implements the `ReportAccident` transaction. A few things that we need to address here are the relations to other types, such as our participants. The `Owner` field declared in the `Vehicle` struct is a string. The value of this has a specific format; that is, [Registrant class name]#[IdentificationNumber] – for example, `base.Registrant#192876345`.

The same goes for the `RespondingERS` field of the `AccidentReport` type, and it has a similar value; for example, `base.EmergencyService#21JumpStreet`.

Now that we have defined our base objects and the accident objects used in the first transaction, there is one special type remaining that we need to define. Remember, we want to transmit an event when a new accident is reported. When you program these events in your chaincode, you publish either a string value or a complex data structure in JSON format. For our smart contract, we'll select the second option. For this, we need to define a new type called `NewAccidentEvent`. Add the following code after the `AccidentReport` struct:

```
// Event Definitions - Events the ledger will emit
// ==================================================

// NewAccidentEvent - new accident event type
type NewAccidentEvent struct {
  AccidentID string `json:"accidentId"`
  Location   string `json:"location"`   //Longitude, Latitude
}
```

Now that all objects are added to our chaincode, we can save our progress and continue programming the function that will implement the `ReportAccident` transaction.

Programming the ReportAccident transaction

Finally, we arrive at the most interesting, but most complex, part of the chaincode development: implementing the code of the `ReportAccident` transaction and the publication of the `NewAccident` event. Let's start by adding the following empty function to the end of the file:

```
// reportAccident - Create a new accident report, store into state
func (t *InsuranceChaincode) reportAccident(stub
shim.ChaincodeStubInterface, args []string) pb.Response {
  var err error

  // simple data model arguments
  // 0=longitude 1=latitude 2=occured at 3=involved vehicle
  // 52.0920511 5.06641270 2018-08-03T10:20:20.325Z base.Vehicle#1012
```

```
    fmt.Println("- Accident Report created")
    return shim.Success(nil)
}
```

This function will contain our full implementation at the end of this chapter, but what it receives is the `shim` interface as the `stub` variable and an array of strings as the `args` variable. When the end of the function is reached, it will print a message to the logs/console and return a `shim.Success` object/message. It also holds some information on how an external application would need to call this function.

Let's continue by programming some sanity checks in order to see whether all of the required input arguments are sent to the function. The following piece of code checks to see whether a minimum of two arguments are included in the call to the function and that the values are not empty. Add this piece of code before the `fmt.Println` instruction:

```
// === Check input variables ===
if len(args) != 2 {
  return shim.Error("Incorrect number of arguments. Expecting minimum of
2")
}
if len(args[0]) <= 0 {
  return shim.Error("1st argument must be a non-empty string")
}
if len(args[1]) <= 0 {
  return shim.Error("2nd argument must be a non-empty string")
}
```

If the value of the first or second argument is an empty string, it will return a `shim.Error` object with a well-described error message. Next, we are going to initialize the arguments into variables and check to see whether we have a third argument, which is optional, telling us when the accident occurred. Add the following code after the previous block:

```
longitude, err := strconv.ParseFloat(args[0], 64)
latitude, err := strconv.ParseFloat(args[1], 64)
occuredAt := time.Now()

// === Parse occuredAt dateTime format ===
if len(args[2]) > 0 {
  occuredAt, err = time.Parse(time.RFC3339, args[2])
  if err != nil {
    return shim.Error("3rd argument must be a RFC3339 dateTime string")
  }
}
```

The preceding code converts the first two string arguments into a 64-bit float for both the longitude and the latitude variables. We also initialize the `occuredAt` variable with the current date/time for when we do not receive a third argument, as this field is required when storing the `AccidentReport` asset. If there is a third argument given to the function, the string value is parsed using the time.RFC3339 format. This is the same as the standard ISO 8601 date/time format; that is, `2018-08-01T14:20:50.52Z`. When the third argument is not in the correct format, a `shim.Error` message is returned.

There is also a possibility that a reference to a vehicle involved in an accident is reported in the function call. When this happens, we first want to check whether the vehicle exists in the system in order to prevent any malicious reports. Add the following code after the previous block:

```
// === Check if optional vehicle exists ===
if len(args[3]) > 0 {
  vehicleRef := args[3]
  if len(vehicleRef) > 0 && !strings.Contains(vehicleRef, "#") {
    return shim.Error("4th argument must be a valid vehicle reference")
  }

  vehicleAsBytes, err := stub.GetState(vehicleRef)
  if err != nil {
    return shim.Error("Failed to get vehicle: " + err.Error())
  } else if vehicleAsBytes == nil {
    return shim.Error("This vehicle doesn't exists: " + vehicleRef)
  }
}
```

This piece of code first checks to see whether a fourth argument is given and whether it is in the expected format; that is, `[Vehicle class name]#[RegistrationNumber]`. Next, the code does a call to the `stub` function `GetState`. Using this function, you can retrieve data from the ledger previously stored on the blockchain. Using the reference string, the function checks to see whether there is data available, and when no vehicle is found, an error is returned.

We are almost at the end of our function. Next, we need to create the `AccidentReport` object that we want to persist to the ledger. Add the following code after the previously-added block:

```
// === Create report object and marshal to JSON ===
accidentObjClass := "accident.AccidentReport"
accidentID := time.Now().Unix()
location := LocationConcept{"accident.Location", longitude, latitude, ""}
accidentReport := &AccidentReport{Class: accidentObjClass, OccuredAt:
occuredAt, Status: "NEW", Location: location}
```

```
accidentJSONasBytes, err := json.Marshal(accidentReport)
if err != nil {
  return shim.Error(err.Error())
}
```

The preceding code generates an `accidentID` instance based on the Unix timestamp in order to identify it as a unique object. When an ID is the same, it will override/update the data on the ledger. The code eventually creates an `AccidentReport` object based on the information received. To store the data on the blockchain, the object needs to be marshaled as a JSON byte array. The line `accidentJSONasBytes, err := json.Marshal(accidentReport)` is responsible for doing this.

Finally, we can store the new accident by adding the following piece of code:

```
// === Save vehicle to state ===
accidentRef := fmt.Sprintf("%s#%d", accidentObjClass, accidentID)
err = stub.PutState(accidentRef, accidentJSONasBytes)
if err != nil {
  return shim.Error(err.Error())
}
```

The second line in the preceding code generates a unique identification or reference ID. The value is a concatenated string, consisting of the object class name of the accident report asset and the generated accident ID. Using the `shim.PutState` function, we can put the accident object in the chaincode state. After consensus is reached by the network peers, the data will be appended to the ledger.

The last thing missing in our code is the transmission of the event to external applications that are interested in reported accidents. Add this final block just after the previous piece of code. The code creates the event payload based on the `NewAccidentEvent` type:

```
// === Create event payload ===
locationStr := fmt.Sprintf("%f, %f", longitude, latitude)
newAccident := &NewAccidentEvent{strconv.FormatInt(accidentID, 10),
locationStr}
eventJSONasBytes, err := json.Marshal(newAccident)
if err != nil {
  return shim.Error(err.Error())
}

// Emit event
stub.SetEvent("NewAccidentEvent", eventJSONasBytes)
```

The initialized object is then marshaled to a byte array so that it can be sent using the `stub.SetEvent` function to external applications that are listening for these types of events.

Up until this point, we have programmed around 35-40% of the final smart contract for our MVP. To keep this chapter from becoming a book on its own, the final contract is available in this book's resources, or it can be downloaded at `http://bit.ly/insurancechain`. We will work with the completed version in the next chapter.

Summary

In this chapter, we designed and partially developed our first smart contract, or chaincode, following the use case described in `Chapter 9`, *Building a Next-Generation Oracle B2B Platform*. To begin, I explained why it is best to start designing your smart contract with a model-first approach. It is important to get to know your participants and design your data objects, transactions, and events before coding the contract. Also in this chapter, we designed our model and separated the data objects, transactions, and events into four different domains (commonly known as namespaces), namely basic, accident, vehicle repair, and insurance. For each of the domains, I reviewed the contents of the data objects, its purpose and relationships, and I described the transactions and events that we want to expose to external applications.

After designing the smart contract, I explained how to set up your development environment, including tools such as cURL, Docker and Docker Compose, the Go programming language, Hyperledger Fabric binaries, and finally VSCode, which is used to program the smart contract (chaincode).

Once we had set up our development environment, we started programming the chaincode. First, we programmed the initial skeleton of the chaincode with the required imports, object types, and functions. Every chaincode imports the `shim` interface used to communicate with the Fabric blockchain and the peer library to communicate with its member peers. The `shim` interface requires you to implement the `main`, `Init`, and `Invoke` functions.

After programming the skeleton, which can be reused for other chaincodes, we added the data model object as structured types. Types were classified as concepts, abstracts, assets, and event types.

Finally, we programmed the `ReportAccident` transactions using the structured types that we added to the chaincode and let it automatically compile to be sure that the code was valid.

The data objects and transactions that we did not program in this chapter are part of the complete chaincode example, which you can download from my GitHub account at `http:/` `/bit.ly/insurancechain`. This version of the chaincode will be used in the next chapter, as we are going to deploy and test the chaincode on the consortium blockchain network that was set up in the previous chapter.

13
Deploying and Testing Your First Smart Contract

In the last two chapters, we set up our blockchain network and designed our smart contract. It is based on the use case described in Chapter 9, *Building a Next-Generation Oracle B2B Platform*, which uses a Model-First design approach. After defining all of our assets, transactions, events, and their data structures, we implemented the smart contract by developing the chaincode. Now that this complex task is complete, we can deploy and test our smart contract.

In this chapter, we will return to our blockchain network and deploy the chaincode to all member organizations. I will explain the steps to deploy the chaincode successfully using the OBCS management console. Further, I will describe how a deployed chaincode can be installed on one or more channels. I will also show you that chaincodes are versioned so that you can make changes to the code without affecting the installed version.

After installing and deploying the chaincode, I will explain how you can expose it to external applications using the REST proxy. In the final part of this chapter, we will test some of the transactions available using a REST API tool called Postman. Finally, we will monitor these transactions using OBCS dashboards and inspect the data.

In this chapter, you will learn how to do the following:

- Deploy and install a smart contract on your blockchain network's channel
- Expose the smart contract as a RESTful API using the REST proxy
- Test and monitor transactions using the management console of OBCS

Deploying your smart contract

Before we can deploy our smart contract, we need to put the latest version of the chaincode into a .zip file. The content of the .zip file is a directory with the same name as the Go source file, and of course the Go source file itself is placed in that directory. You can download the latest version of this file from https://git.io/fAH3Q.

Follow these steps to create a valid deployment artifact:

- Create a directory called insurancechain on your filesystem
- Put the downloaded file (insurancechain.go) into this directory
- Create a .zip archive of the insurancechain directory

The artifact should look like the following screenshot:

The insurancechain .zip archive, including the insurancechain directory and Go source file

After creating the .zip artifact mentioned in the preceding steps, we can start deploying and installing it on our business network. Let's start by first logging into the administration console of the founder of the network (Acme). The URL may look similar to this one: https://acmebcs-acmeinsurance.console.oraclecloud.com/.

Installing chaincode on the founder's peers

Once you are logged into the console, you are welcomed again on the **Dashboard** page. From the menu, navigate to the **Chaincodes** page. We already visited this page very briefly in `Chapter 11`, *Setting Up Your Permissioned Blockchain*. In that chapter, I explained that it can be used to deploy and install new chaincodes or new versions of an existing chaincode. The following screenshot shows the main **Chaincodes** page (currently none are installed).

To deploy our chaincode, we can click on **Deploy a New Chaincode** just below the summary on the right-hand side of the page.

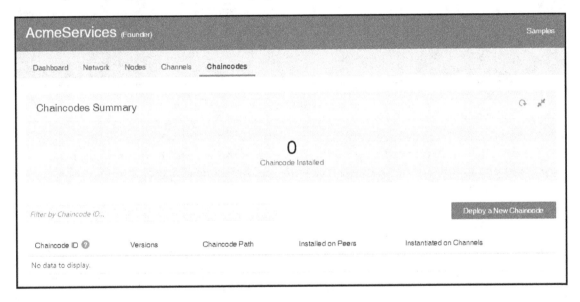

Chaincodes page, used for managing the smart contracts in use by your business network

After clicking on **Deploy a New Chaincode**, a dialog box pops up. It gives you two options for how you want to deploy your chaincode. In the dialog box, as shown in the following screenshot, you can choose between **Quick Deployment** and **Advanced**. Both options will install and start (instantiate) the chaincode, and enable the chaincode in the REST proxy.

The **Quick Deployment** option offers one-step deployment with default options, while the **Advanced** option offers step-by-step deployment for full flexibility.

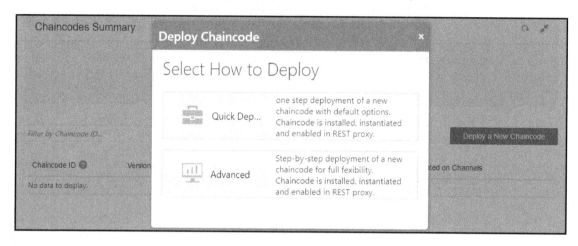

Choose how you want to deploy your chaincode using the Quick or Advanced options

Let's take a look at the **Advanced** option and carry out a step-by-step deployment of our chaincode. Click on **Advanced** to go to the first step of the wizard. In this first of three steps, we need to upload the .zip archive with the chaincode file and specify its name, version, and the target peers on which we want to install it. Use the following details:

Field	Value	Description
Chaincode name	Enter: insurancechain	The name needs to be between 1 and 64 characters long. It may include alphanumerics, "_", and "-".
Version	Enter: v1 (default)	The name needs to be between 1 and 64 characters long. It may include alphanumerics, ".", "_", and "-".
Target peers	Select: peer0, peer1 and peer2.acmebcs.oraclecloud.com	Choose the member peers on which you want to install the chaincode.
Chaincode source	Pick: Insurancechain.zip	Specify the location of the .zip file.

Data to be entered in the first step of the deployment wizard

After entering the data, a dialog box will appear, as shown in the following screenshot:

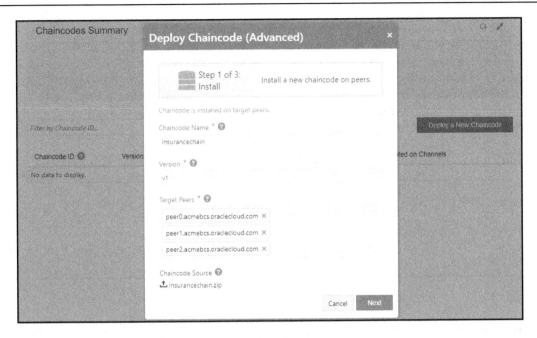

Step 1 of 3: Install a new chaincode on peers

If your chaincode is valid, it will show a **SUCCESS!** message, as shown in the following screenshot. When choosing the **Advanced** option, you can skip step, two and three of the wizard. We could complete the other two steps, but to give you a better understanding of what is happening when executing each step, we will perform steps two and three manually. Notice that our new chaincode is listed in the background, and it also indicates that it is available to start on any of our channels.

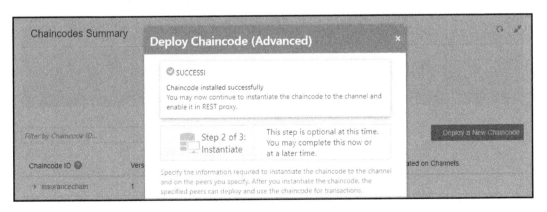

Step 2 of 3: Instantiate (start) the chaincode on a channel. This step can be skipped.

Close the wizard to skip steps two and three and return to the **Chaincodes** page. From that page, we can view the details of a chaincode or a specific version of a chaincode. To view all installed versions of a chaincode, click on the arrow in front of the name to expand the entry. Click either on the name of the chaincode or on the specific version to see its details. From the **Chaincodes** page, you can also directly instantiate the chaincode on one of your channels by selecting **Instantiate** from the options menu on the right-hand side of each entry.

List of installed chaincodes, including ours (insurancechain), and the option to instantiate the chaincode

In our case, we are navigating to the details of the version that we just deployed. Let's click on the specific version **v1** link. This navigates us to a new subpage listing the peers on which this version is currently installed. You can't install on other/new peers from this page, as you need to follow the same steps as before, but you can navigate to the **Instantiated on Channels** section to instantiate a chaincode on one of your channels.

The following screenshot shows that our chaincode is installed on all three of the peers managed by Acme Services. From the menu on the left, you can view the channels on which the chaincode is instantiated (activated).

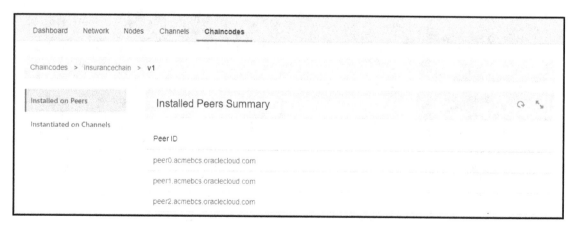

Chaincode details of the installed peers

Activating the chaincode on a channel

We also need to install the chaincode on the OBCS instances of the other members, since for members to endorse transactions produced by the chaincode invocation of other members, they need to execute the transaction redundantly on their own nodes. But before we do that, let's activate the chaincode on the channel and give permission to other members to configure the REST proxy and execute the transactions exposed by the chaincode.

Let's pick up where we left off a moment ago. Click on the **Instantiated on Channels** menu item on the left to navigate to that section. The page now shows a list of channels on which the chaincode is active. Of course, this list is currently empty, as we haven't yet activated our chaincode. Let's do so by clicking on **Instantiate on a New Channel**:

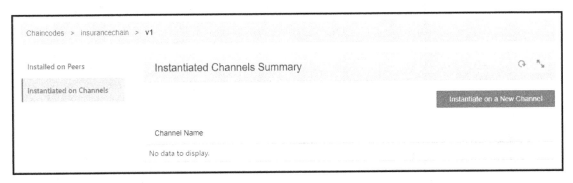

Channel details of the instantiated channels

This will again reveal a dialog popup similar to the second step of the deployment wizard. This form contains some more options than the deployment step, which will cause a different result in the way that transactions are endorsed when used. Use the following information to activate our chaincode to the `insurancechain` channel we created earlier:

Field	Value	Description
Channel	Select: `insurancechain`	Select a channel on which to activate the chaincode.
Peers	Select: `peer0`, `peer1`, *and* `peer2.acmebcs.oraclecloud.com`	Choose the peers that you want to be able to use the chaincode. The chaincode needs to be installed on these peers.

Field	Value	Description
Initial Parameters	Leave empty	Optional parameters when instantiating the chaincode. We are not using this functionality.
Endorsement Policy	Add an *identity* for all participating organizations of the network with the role "Member".	The peers that need to endorse a transaction.
Expression Mode	Select: `Basic`	Choose between **Basic** and **Advanced** expression mode (that is, it uses Fabric's endorsement policy expression syntax (`https://hyperledger-fabric.readthedocs.io/en/latest/endorsement-policies.html#endorsement-policy-syntax`), for example, `{"2-of":[{"signed-by":1},{"signed-by":2}]}]}`.
Signed By	Enter: `3`	Number of organizations needed to endorse submitted transactions.
Transient Map	Leave empty	Provide static information to the chaincode.

Data to enter when activating (instantiating) a chaincode on the insurancechain channel

The most important part of this form is the **Endorsement Policy**. If you leave this empty, only one member needs to endorse the transaction before it is offered to the other peers via the ordering service. In our case, we are adding all five organizations to the identity list. Out of the five organizations, the majority, need to endorse the transaction. The following screenshot shows the endorsement policy configuration as described in the table:

Endorsement policy configuration when activating the insurancechain chaincode

After filling in the information required by the form, click on **Instantiate** in the bottom-right corner to activate the chaincode on the `insurancechain` channel. This might take a few minutes depending on the number of organizations that need to be notified and the number of peers assigned as endorsers. When the activation process is finished, a quick success message is visible before the dialog box is automatically closed. After refreshing the page, the **Instantiated Channels Summary** will appear showing that the chaincode is activated on the channel, as shown in the following screenshot:

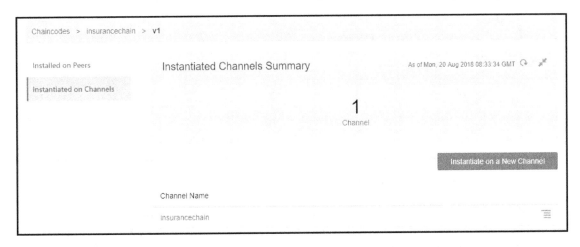

Activated chaincode is listed in the summary and channel table

The reason why the activation process can take a few minutes is because it spins up a **Docker Container** for each endorsing peer node of that specific organization, containing the executable binary of our chaincode application.

If you can **Secure Shell (SSH)** in to the **Virtual Machine (VM)** provisioned on Oracle Cloud, you can use the following command to get the list of images:

```
docker ps --filter "name=insurancechain-v1" --format "{{.Image}}"
```

This command will list all Docker Images that contain `insurancechain-v1` in their name, which in my case resulted in the following list for Acme Services:

```
acmebcs.oraclecloud.com-peer0.acmebcs.oraclecloud.com-insurancechain-
v1-101d060f9770dbc1ae5605120c08d7c6f62b8d011cd423bc57d7f1926ed5e800

acmebcs.oraclecloud.com-peer2.acmebcs.oraclecloud.com-insurancechain-
v1-6955c2b3111d115eef4276309e2248aeb6b57cb17c29213430355c1d8c7f330c

acmebcs.oraclecloud.com-peer1.acmebcs.oraclecloud.com-insurancechain-
v1-979c71fc7212e8f6daf955596063decd17272dd459a998c11b080ac7c40fba55
```

From the chaincode channel page, we can view the transaction that was added to the ledger as a result of our action by clicking on the name of the channel. This will navigate us to the channel details, including the summary of transactions added to the ledger. This summary, as shown in the following screenshot, lists the activation of the chaincode as a data (**sys**) transaction, as it does not include user transactions:

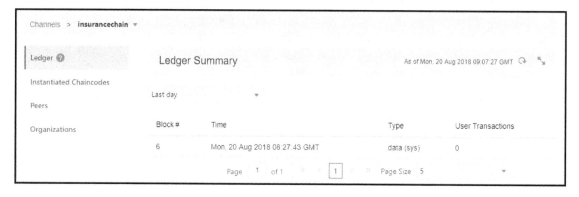

Ledger summary of the insurancechain channel, filtered by last day, listing the activation transaction of the chaincode

To see the data that was sent in a transaction, you click on the block that contains the transaction and, as a result, the list of transactions at the bottom of the page is refreshed. This block only contains one transaction. The following screenshot shows the list of transactions in the selected block, **6**:

Transactions			
TxID	Time	Chaincode	Status
▸ 3baf6dbed1dbd5cb43b867a914cfaf6f2e4d84ede3ea46480a646454dbd829ba	Mon, 20 Aug 2018 08:27:43 GMT	Iscc	Success

The transaction responsible for the activation of the chaincode on the channel

For each transaction, the transaction (Tx) ID, time, called chaincode, and Tx status is listed.

To see the details of the transaction and the data sent in the transaction, you can expand the entry by clicking on the arrow to the left of the entry. This will show, for example, the function that was invoked on the chaincode, the arguments used to invoke the function, whether the validation result was valid, and who the initiator and the endorsers of the transaction were.

The following screenshot shows the details of the `deploy` function invoked by the transaction. This function is part of the `iscc` system chaincode.

◢ 3baf6dbed1dbd5cb43b867a914cfaf6f2e4d84ede3ea46480a646454dbd829ba	Mon, 20 Aug 2018 08:27:43 GMT	Iscc	Success

Function name:	deploy
Arguments:	["insurancechain",{"chaincode_spec":{"type":"GOLANG","chaincode_id": {"path":"","name":"insurancechain","version":"v1"},"input":{"args": ["init"]},"timeout":0},"exec_env":"DOCKER","effective_date":""},{"version":0,"policy":{"Type":"n_out_of","n_out_of": {"N":3,"policies":[{"Type":"signed_by","signed_by":0},{"Type":"signed_by","signed_by":1},{"Type":"signed_by","signed_by":2}, {"Type":"signed_by","signed_by":3},{"Type":"signed_by","signed_by":4}]}},"identities": [{"principal_classification":0,"msp_identifier":"AcmeServices","Role":"MEMBER"}, {"principal_classification":0,"msp_identifier":"AutoLease","Role":"MEMBER"}, {"principal_classification":0,"msp_identifier":"EmergencyServices","Role":"MEMBER"}, {"principal_classification":0,"msp_identifier":"AllsecurInsurance","Role":"MEMBER"}, {"principal_classification":0,"msp_identifier":"AXAInsurance","Role":"MEMBER"}]}]
Validation Results:	VALID
Response:	200
Initiator:	AcmeServices: Admin@acmebcs.oraclecloud.com
Endorsor:	AcmeServices: peer0.acmebcs.oraclecloud.com AcmeServices: peer1.acmebcs.oraclecloud.com AcmeServices: peer2.acmeb...

Transaction details showing the deployment of the chaincode to the insurancechain channel

Installing a new version of our chaincode

Before installing the chaincode on the other member nodes, let's talk about upgrading an existing chaincode deployed on a channel. As you probably noticed when deploying the chaincode, you need to give it a version—even if it's the default version.

This means that you can upgrade your existing chaincode to a new version. I will now address this possibility, as this version number is going to be used in the rest of the chapter, for example, in the REST API calls.

Navigate back to the **Chaincodes** page. Now that the chaincode is activated on our channel, it is possible to upgrade the chaincode using the options menu on the right-hand side of the chaincode entry. From the menu, select the **Upgrade** option:

Option to upgrade an active chaincode

This will launch a popup dialog box, as partially shown in the following screenshot. From this dialog box, you can select or install a new version of the chaincode. In our case, we are going to install a new version, so select that option for the version source. This time, enter version v2, and select all three of the peers of Acme Services. Upload the same chaincode artifact as before, that is, `insurancechain.zip`, and click on **Next** to install the new version:

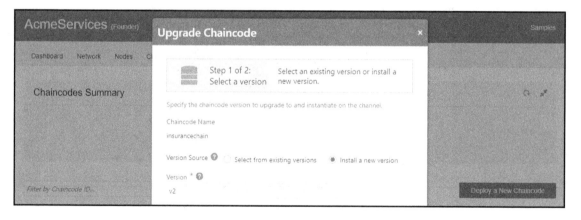

Dialog box for upgrading an existing chaincode

In the second step of the upgrade wizard, we need to select the peers on which we want to activate this version and specify a new endorsement policy for this version. So you can have different versions installed on different peers. You can also downgrade to an older version when running into bugs.

Reuse the same information as before to activate the chaincode on the `insurancechain` channel. Confirm the channel, select all three founder peers, and add all five identities as members in the endorsement policy (remember, a minimum of three organizations need to sign the transaction). Click on **Next** to upgrade the chaincode on the channel.

Again, this might take a few minutes, so just be patient. If the upgrade successful, the dialog box will show a chaincode upgraded successfully message and a large green check mark. You can close this dialog box manually.

The following screenshot shows the two installed versions of the `insurancechain` chaincode application. Notice that the new version is added to the list of chaincode versions of the `insurancechain` entry, and that version **v1** is no longer active (instantiated) on a channel.

There can be only one version of a chaincode active at a time:

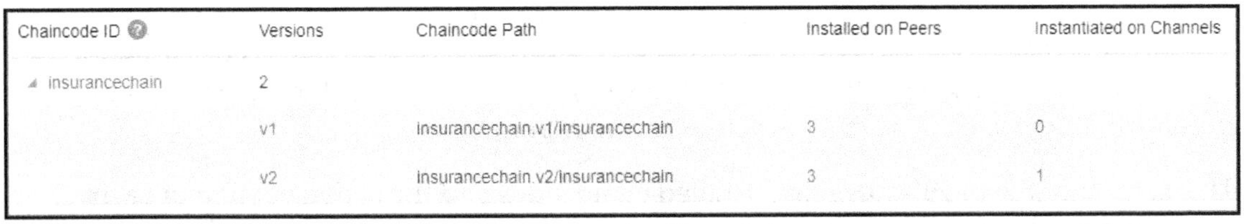

Chaincode ID ❓	Versions	Chaincode Path	Installed on Peers	Instantiated on Channels
◢ insurancechain	2			
	v1	insurancechain.v1/insurancechain	3	0
	v2	insurancechain.v2/insurancechain	3	1

There are two versions of the chaincode installed, but only version v2 is active on the channel

If you navigate to the channel and look at the ledger summary, another block is appended to the ledger. It again includes one transaction, but instead of the `deploy` function of the `iscc` chaincode being invoked by the transaction, the `upgrade` function is invoked. The following screenshot shows the details of the transactions after successfully executing the upgrade of the chaincode:

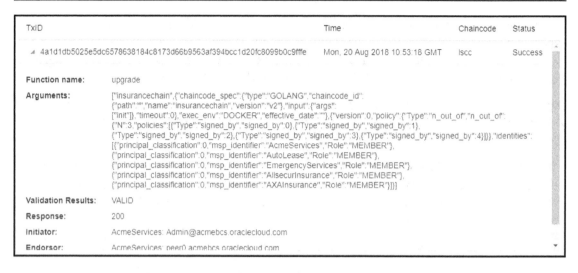

TxID	Time	Chaincode	Status
◢ 4a1d1db5025e5dc6578638184c8173d66b9563af394bcc1d20fc8099b0c9fffe	Mon, 20 Aug 2018 10:53:18 GMT	lscc	Success

Function name:	upgrade
Arguments:	["insurancechain",{"chaincode_spec":{"type":"GOLANG","chaincode_id": {"path":"","name":"insurancechain","version":"v2"},"input":{"args": ["init"]},"timeout":0},"exec_env":"DOCKER","effective_date":""},{"version":0,"policy":{"Type":"n_out_of","n_out_of": {"N":3,"policies":[{"Type":"signed_by","signed_by":0},{"Type":"signed_by","signed_by":1}, {"Type":"signed_by","signed_by":2},{"Type":"signed_by","signed_by":3},{"Type":"signed_by","signed_by":4}]}},"identities": [{"principal_classification":0,"msp_identifier":"AcmeServices","Role":"MEMBER"}, {"principal_classification":0,"msp_identifier":"AutoLease","Role":"MEMBER"}, {"principal_classification":0,"msp_identifier":"EmergencyServices","Role":"MEMBER"}, {"principal_classification":0,"msp_identifier":"AllsecurInsurance","Role":"MEMBER"}, {"principal_classification":0,"msp_identifier":"AXAInsurance","Role":"MEMBER"}]}]
Validation Results:	VALID
Response:	200
Initiator:	AcmeServices: Admin@acmebcs.oraclecloud.com
Endorsor:	AcmeServices: peer0.acmebcs.oraclecloud.com

Transaction details showing the upgrade of the chaincode on the insurance channel

You can always navigate to the **Instantiated Chaincodes** section of the channel detail page to confirm that a specific version is active on the channel.

This section of the page shows the installed chaincodes and the active version of each chaincode, as shown in the following screenshot:

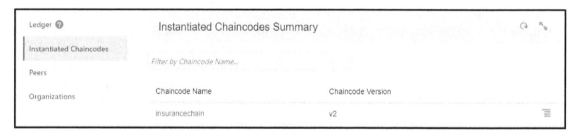

As expected, version v2 of the insurance chaincode is active on the channel

Installing chaincode on member organizations

Now that the chaincode is installed on the founder and activated on the `insurancechain` channel, we can deploy the chaincode on the environment of each of the member organizations. The following steps need to be performed for each environment, but I will demonstrate them on the environment of emergency services.

After logging into their environment, you are welcomed by the **Dashboard** page. From there, navigate to the **Chaincodes** page and follow the same process as with the founder, but this time, you only have to complete the first step.

Deploy a new chaincode using the advanced method, and enter the following values:

- Chaincode name: `insurancechain`
- Version: `v2`
- Target peers: `select all available peers`
- Chaincode source: `upload insurancechain.zip artefact`

Click **Next** to install the chaincode on the peers and close the dialog box. You won't be able to instantiate it on a channel (for example, `insurancechain`) on which the chaincode is already activated. As the founder already activated the chaincode on the channel, it is automatically instantiated in the member organization's environment, as shown in the following screenshot.

If we had installed the chaincode under version v1, this would not have happened automatically:

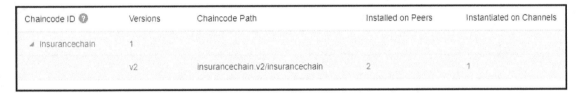

Chaincode ID ❓	Versions	Chaincode Path	Installed on Peers	Instantiated on Channels
◢ Insurancechain	1			
	v2	insurancechain.v2/insurancechain	2	1

Previous instantiated chaincode is automatically activated on the member's channel after deployment

Exposing smart contracts using the REST proxy

Any active smart contract, or chaincode, can be exposed to external applications using the REST proxy that is part of OBCS. The only thing that you need to do is to enable the chaincode that you want to expose in the REST proxy configuration. This can be done using two methods: the **Quick** method or the **Advanced** method.

Exposing chaincode using the Advanced method

I'm going to demonstrate the Advanced method using the founder organization, Acme Services. Let's log in to their environment and navigate to the **Nodes** page. This page lists all of the nodes that are part of the founder's network and includes the REST proxy. You can find the REST proxy listed under the entry with the name starting with `gateway`. In our case, we have a REST proxy with the name `gateway0.acmebcs.oraclecloud.com`, as shown in the following screenshot, but this may be different in a newer version of the service. It is also possible to have multiple REST proxies, but they are easily recognized by their type:

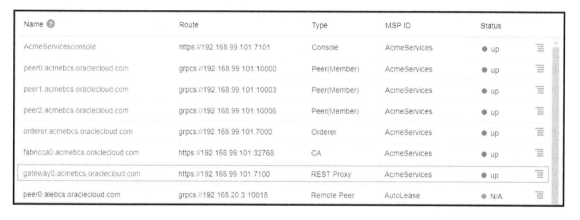

Name	Route	Type	MSP ID	Status	
AcmeServicesconsole	https://192.168.99.101:7101	Console	AcmeServices	● up	≡
peer0.acmebcs.oraclecloud.com	grpcs://192.168.99.101:10000	Peer(Member)	AcmeServices	● up	≡
peer1.acmebcs.oraclecloud.com	grpcs://192.168.99.101:10003	Peer(Member)	AcmeServices	● up	≡
peer2.acmebcs.oraclecloud.com	grpcs://192.168.99.101:10006	Peer(Member)	AcmeServices	● up	≡
orderer.acmebcs.oraclecloud.com	grpcs://192.168.99.101:7000	Orderer	AcmeServices	● up	≡
fabricca0.acmebcs.oraclecloud.com	https://192.168.99.101:32768	CA	AcmeServices	● up	≡
gateway0.acmebcs.oraclecloud.com	https://192.168.99.101:7100	REST Proxy	AcmeServices	● up	≡
peer0.alebcs.oraclecloud.com	grpcs://192.168.20.3:10015	Remote Peer	AutoLease	● N/A	≡

Nodes overview listing the REST proxy as gateway0.acmebcs.oraclecloud.com

To edit the configuration of the REST proxy and expose our chaincode, we can click on the options menu on the right-hand side of the entry and select the **Edit Configuration**. This will reveal a popup dialog box in which you can add the chaincode that you want to expose to external applications. In this dialog box, you can normally add multiple entries, however, in our case, we only have one to add for the `insurancechain` chaincode:

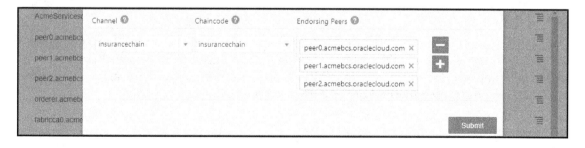

Exposing the insurancechain chaincode through the REST proxy

In the dialog box, as shown in the following screenshot, select the channel (`insurancechain`) on which the chaincode needs to be invoked. Next, select one of the activated chaincodes (`insurancechain`) on that channel. Then, select one or more peers that endorse the selected chaincode. As we want to have a reliable connection to the network, select at least two peers when available. In the case of Acme Services, select all three endorsing peers.

Finally, click on **Submit** to reconfigure the REST proxy. The node is automatically restarted so that the chaincode is immediately available to external applications, which takes a second. Best practice here is to have multiple REST proxies so that one is always online.

By using the REST proxy's **Edit Configuration** dialog box, you have greater control over the chaincodes exposed via REST. You can easily add or remove multiple chaincodes in one step. The dialog box also allows you to configure the default proposal and transaction wait times to limit the wait times for receiving enough endorsements and the request timeout:

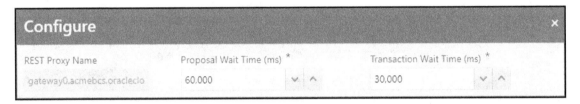

The edit configuration dialog box allows you to configure proposal and transaction wait times

Exposing chaincode using the Quick method

The second method works much more quickly if you want to expose your chaincode through the REST proxy, but you will lose some flexibility and control. Let's expose our chaincode on the other member organizations using this method. I will demonstrate the quick method using one of the participating organizations, that is, AutoLease.

After logging into their environment, navigate to the **Chaincodes** page once again. For AutoLease, we can see that we only have version **v2** installed, as shown in the following screenshot. To expose the chaincode through the REST proxy, click on the options menu for the main entry and select **Enable in REST Proxy**:

Quickly enabling a chaincode in the REST proxy

After selecting option, a dialog box will popup, in which you need to select the channel on which the chaincode should be invoked. Select the REST proxy through which the chaincode is enabled and choose which peers should endorse the chaincode. Click on **Submit** to accept your choices and expose it to external applications. The following screenshot shows this dialog and the choices made for the AutoLease organization:

Enabling the chaincode in the REST proxy for the AutoLease organization on both peers

If everything goes well, a short **Set attributes successful!** message is shown before the dialog box is automatically closed. If you want to be sure that the chaincode is exposed by the REST proxy, you can always check that the REST proxy configuration is the same as when we enabled it using the advanced method.

Testing a smart contract using a REST client

Up until this point, we have designed and developed our smart contract, deployed and installed it on all member peers, activated it on our channel, and exposed it to external applications by enabling the chaincode in the REST proxies of all members. Currently, we have five access points to the smart contract, one for each of the organizations in the network.

The two repair shops are still missing as entry points, as these existing, on-premises Hyperledger Fabric member organizations have not joined our business network yet. Either way, they would not have their own REST proxy as this is part of the OBCS offering.

These two organizations will need to use the SDK provided by Fabric to invoke the functions of the chaincode, but more on this in the next chapter.

In this section of the chapter, we will do the following:

- Install a REST client to call the API and chaincode functions
- Test some of the functions in depth and examine the results of others
- Monitor the results of the transaction in the management console

Installing a client to call the REST proxy's API

Before we can call the API and the functions of the chaincode, we need to install a tool. You can use any tool that you prefer (for example, Insomnia, Advanced REST client, or online tools such as API Fortress), but for this book I will use one of my favorite desktop clients, **Postman**. This tool is available for Windows, macOS, and many Linux distributions, such as Ubuntu.

Postman is a free tool with which you can create simple HTTP REST requests or collections of REST requests. You can use Postman to create API documentation, mock servers, schedule automated tests, and check the performance of APIs as well. You can download it at https://www.getpostman.com/apps. If you plan to use the same virtual environment as when we developed the smart contract, you need to download the x64 version of Postman for Linux.

Importing and testing chaincode API requests

After downloading and installing Postman, you can start the application by double-clicking the Postman executable. For your convenience, I have created a Postman collection project that can be imported. Start by downloading this collection project from the official Packt GitHub repository of this book at `https://git.io/fAH3N`. The collection includes all of the API calls to the chaincode functions. We will look at some of them in great detail, while you can try out others yourself in your own environment. You can import the collection file by starting the Postman application and clicking on the **Import** button in the top-left corner, just to the right of the **New** button. In the dialog window, click on **Choose Files** and select the Postman collection file that you just downloaded, `Insurancechain.postman_collection.json`. The following screenshot shows the **IMPORT** dialog window:

Importing the existing Postman collection file

This will import the collection project containing multiple HTTP requests. In the following sections, I will go over each of these HTTP requests. The Postman collection uses environment variables in the HTTP requests. If you want to follow the upcoming sections in your own environment, you should change the values of the variables so that they point to one of your REST proxy endpoints. The project has an environment configured called `insurancechain`. You can edit the values of the variables by clicking on the *eye* icon next to the drop-down list listing the available environments, then selecting the environment, and clicking on the edit link to change the values, as shown in the following screenshot:

Edit the environment variables to represent your Oracle Cloud instances

The second thing that you need to change is the **Basic Auth** settings of the collection. This setting makes it easy if you are testing this contract on only one environment, as it can be set at the collection level for each of the HTTP requests, so you don't have to specify it separately for each HTTP request. You can edit the settings of a collection by hovering over the name of the collection in the collections tree and clicking on the three dots on the right-hand side to expand the options menu. To open the configuration, select the **Edit** option. This will show a dialog window in which you can change the authorization. Enter a username and password that has access to the Blockchain Cloud Service environment(s). The following screenshot shows a portion of this dialog window:

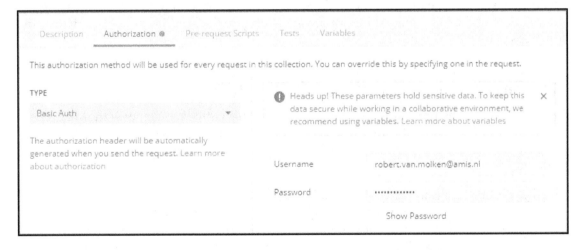

Edit the configuration of the collection, and enter the username and password for the cloud environment correctly

Even if you have set this at the collection level, each HTTP request can overwrite it by configuring the authorization at the request level.

Available REST proxy APIs

The HTTP request in the collection uses the available REST APIs of the REST proxy. In Chapter 10, *Introducing the Oracle Blockchain Cloud Service*, I reviewed the available REST APIs, but let's briefly go over them again.

The REST proxy currently in production at Oracle exposes these four resources (`https://docs.oracle.com/en/cloud/paas/blockchain-cloud/rest-api/rest-endpoints.html`):

Task	Method	Path
Invoke a method (Sync)	POST	`/bcsgw/rest/v1/transaction/invocation`
Invoke a query	POST	`/bcsgw/rest/v1/transaction/query`
View the status of a specific transaction	GET	`/bcsgw/rest/v1/transaction`
View version	GET	`/bcsgw/rest/version`

The REST proxy APIs

The tasks that use the POST method require a JSON body with a certain message structure, while the tasks that use the GET method require HTTP query parameters to retrieve the information. In the following API request, we mainly use the invocation resource to execute functions of our smart contract.

Getting the version of the OBCS API

As you can see in the preceding list of available resource paths, we can view the version of the REST API. The returned information is not of interest for our use case, but with this resource we can check whether the REST proxy is online and can process our HTTP requests.

The first HTTP request in the Postman collection calls the `{{AcmeProxyHost}}/bcsgw/rest/version` endpoint. Notice that it uses the `AcmeProxyHost` environment variable. Under the hood, this is replaced with the actual value when sending the HTTP request. As you can see in the following screenshot, the request includes an HTTP header for the authorization.

When sending the request with the endpoint available and the correct authorization included in the request, the server will respond with the result message `{ "version": "v1.0" }`:

Overview of chaincode interactions

Before we test the other functions of the smart contract, let's go over all of the interactions using the following sequence diagrams. The calls in the sequence diagrams are in the same order as in the sections that detailed the interactions.

The following sequence diagram shows the first six interactions: setting up of demo assets, reporting a new accident, retrieving the accident report, updating the accident report (twice), and issuing a new insurance policy:

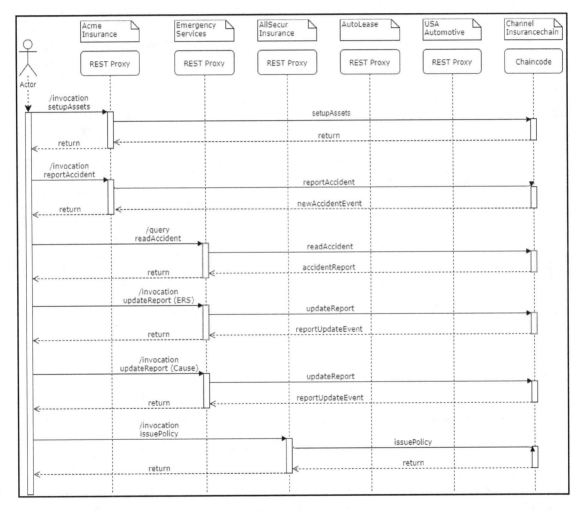

Sequence diagram of the first six interactions

The next sequence diagram shows the other main interactions that are executed after issuing a new insurance policy. They include requesting a quote estimation, retrieving the quote request, offering a quote estimation, retrieving the quote offer, and sending an insurance claim:

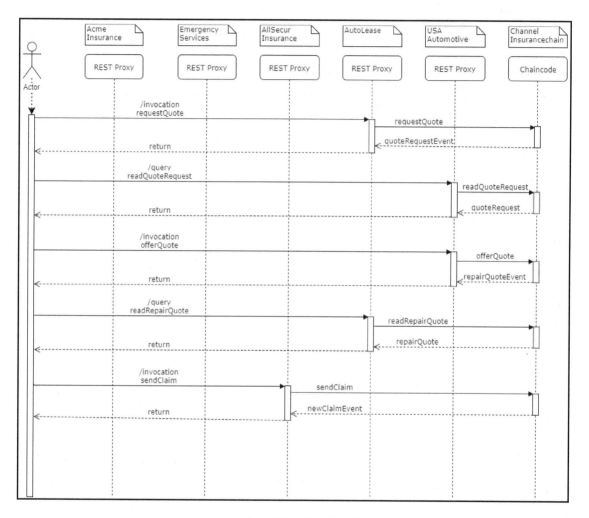

Sequence diagram of the second set of interactions

In the following section, we will test the interaction described in the sequence diagrams. You can also check them when you want to know where you are in the flow. In some interactions, you have optional read queries to validate the assets that are created, and for that reason they are not listed in the sequence diagrams.

Setting up all of the required demo assets

The first function that we are going to execute on the transaction is the `setupAssets` function. This function creates the demo assets used in the upcoming transactions. The chaincode function creates the following demo assets, which we are going to use:

Type	Identification	Description
Registrant	9081237645	Participant: AutoLease
Registrant	170632064	Participant: J. Smith
Emergency Services	NYPD 34th Precinct	Participant: New York Police
Insurer	AllSecur Insurance	Participant: AllSecur Insurance
Insurer	AXA Insurance	Participant: AXA Insurance
RepairShop	USA Automotive NYC	Participant: USA Automotive, New York
RepairShop	USA Automotive JC	Participant: USA Automotive, Jersey City
Vehicle	JN6ND01S3GX194659	Asset: BMW X5
Vehicle	1HTZR0007JH586991	Asset: Toyota Prius
Insurance Policy	USA-AS204-1042919	Asset: Policy for Toyota Prius

Demo assets types, identifications, and descriptions

The HTTP request calls `{{AcmeProxyHost}}/bcsgw/rest/v1/transaction/ invocation` using the `POST` method. Because it is a `POST` request, we need to define a JSON payload in the body of the request. The following code snippet contains the JSON message to invoke the `setupAssets` transaction/function of the chaincode:

```
{
    "channel":  "insurancechain",
    "chaincode":  "insurancechain",
    "method":  "setupAssets",
    "chaincodeVer":  "v2",
    "args":  [],
    "proposalWaitTime": 50000,
    "transactionWaitTime": 60000
}
```

The preceding JSON message is the generic message for invoking transactions. It is defined by the Oracle REST proxy and contains the following fields:

Field	Description
Channel	Name of the channel on which the chaincode should be invoked.
Chaincode	Name of the chaincode that should be invoked.

Field	Description
Method	The transactions/method to execute the chaincode.
ChaincodeVer	The version of the chaincode (not used in the current version, as only one version can be active).
Args	An array of arguments passed to the specific method.
ProposalWaitTime	Specifies the time in milliseconds in which the proposal process must complete. If the proposal does not finish in the specified time, the returnCode is "Failure" and the transaction is not submitted.
TransactionWaitTime	Specifies the time in milliseconds in which the transaction process must complete. If the transaction does not finish in the specified time, the returnCode is "InProgress".

The JSON fields of a request message

The request does not require any arguments, so we can leave the array empty. The result of calling this function is that the demo assets are created and stored on the blockchain. The response message that the chaincode function returns contains the following payload:

```
{
    "returnCode": "Success",
    "result": {
        "payload":
"[{\"$class\":\"base.Registrant\",\"assetId\":\"908123764\"},{\"$class\":\"
base.Registrant\",\"assetId\":\"170632064\"},{\"$class\":\"base.EmergencySe
rvices\",\"assetId\":\"NYPD 34th Precinct\"}, ...,
{\"$class\":\"insurance.InsurancePolicy\",\"assetId\":\"USA-
AS204-1042919\"}]",
        "encode": "UTF-8"
    },
    "txid":   "bf26c3cc2e7575c1f1c833850e1eeed868b430c367c9a16c90c27..."
}
```

The preceding JSON message is the generic response, and it always contains a returnCode, an optional payload, and the transaction's Id (txid). In our case, the payload contains an escaped JSON message that includes an array of created assets with their type and identification. The following screenshot shows the HTTP request and HTTP response for this transaction:

HTTP request for invoking the setupAssets transaction/function of the chaincode

You can monitor the transaction in the management console of the OBCS instance. To do this, navigate to the channel's ledger details and select the last created block. It contains the transaction that invoked the `setupAssets` function, as shown in the following screenshot:

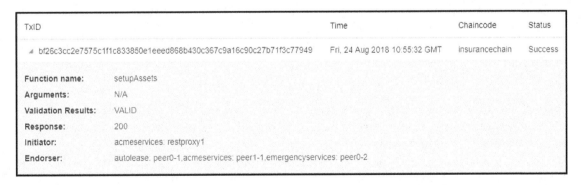

Transaction invoking the setupAssets function appended to the ledger of the insurancechain channel

To give you an example of the code responsible for creating and storing assets on the blockchain, let's examine the following code snippet:

```
// === Create insurance policy USA-AS204-1042919
dateValidFrom, err := time.Parse(time.RFC3339, "2018-05-01T00:00:00Z")
dateValidTo, err := time.Parse(time.RFC3339, "2020-04-30T00:00:00Z")

insurancePolicy := &InsurancePolicy{policyObjClass, "USA-AS204-1042919",
"State of New Jersey", dateValidFrom, dateValidTo,
"base.Vehicle#1HTZR0007JH586991", "USA", "AS204", 1042919, "AF", "Toyota",
[]string{"US", "CA"}, "base.Registrant#170632064", "base.Insurer#AXA
Insurance"}

// Marshal object to bytes
pOneJSONasBytes, err := json.Marshal(insurancePolicy)
if err != nil {
  return shim.Error(err.Error())
}

// Store Insurance Policy - USA-AS204-1042919
stateRef = fmt.Sprintf("%s#%s", policyObjClass, insurancePolicy.PolicyID)
err = stub.PutState(stateRef, pOneJSONasBytes)
if err != nil {
  return shim.Error(err.Error())
}
```

First, the `InsurancePolicy` object is created with some static values and the object is marshaled to a bytes string. Next, the object is stored in the chaincode state by persisting the bytes string under an easily searchable reference.

Reading asset data to check the current values

To be sure that all demo assets have been created, or to check what the data object of a certain asset contains, we can execute the second HTTP request in the collection. This HTTP request invokes the `readAssetData` transaction (chaincode function). In our case, the HTTP request retrieves (reads) the data from one of the `Vehicle` assets (registration number: `JN6ND01S3GX194659`).

Instead of calling the same REST proxy of Acme Services, we call the REST proxy of one of the other member organizations, such as emergency services, in order to demonstrate that the data is distributed to the other member organizations. The request will call the `{{ErsProxyHost}}/bcsgw/rest/v1/transaction/invocation` endpoint. The `ErsProxyHost` variable is configured in the environment settings to have the correct node endpoint.

The JSON payload used in the request is as follows:

```
{
    "channel":  "insurancechain",
    "chaincode":  "insurancechain",
    "method":  "readAssetData",
    "chaincodeVer":  "v2",
    "args":  ["base.Vehicle", "JN6ND01S3GX194659"],
    "proposalWaitTime": 5000,
    "transactionWaitTime": 10000
}
```

If the vehicle is found in the chaincode state, the JSON object representation of the `Vehicle` asset is returned. After sending the preceding request, the result contains the same generic message as before, but the payload contains the `Vehicle` asset data:

```
{
    "$class": "base.Vehicle",
    "registrationNumber": "JN6ND01S3GX194659",
    "licensePlate": "WPD 9321",
    "dateFirstAdmission": "2018-01-12T00:00:00Z",
    "dateAscription": "2018-01-13T00:00:00Z",
    "owner": "base.Registrant#9081237645",
    "make": "BMW",
    "model": "X5",
    "color": "Black",
    "maxMass": 2595,
    "maxSeating": 5
}
```

The following screenshot shows the request and the response of a successful retrieval:

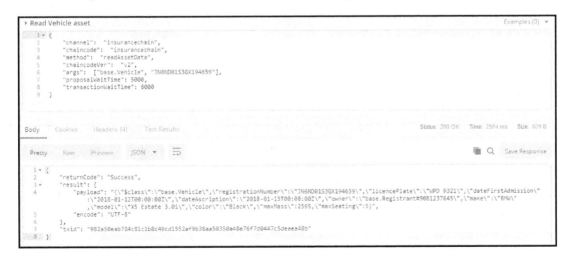

HTTP request for invoking the readAssetData transaction/function of the chaincode

If you enter a non-existing registration number, the response will contains an error message. The JSON payload contains the `resultCode` is `Failure` and the message that the vehicle can't be found in the chaincode state:

```
{
  "returnCode": "Failure",
  "info": {
    "proxyError": "Proposal not pass",
    "peerErrors": [
      {
        "peerId": "emergencyservices1peer0",
        "errMsg": "Sending proposal to emergencyservices1peer0 failed
because of: gRPC failure=Status{code=UNKNOWN, description=chaincode error
(status: 500, message: {\"Error\":\"Vehicle does not exist:
JN6ND01S3GX194651\"}), cause=null}",
        "verified": false
      }
    ],
  },
  "txid": "32aa88792fabca6c3e48d80efba5d937a5b7363e839613e70c7966..."
}
```

Faulty transactions are not traceable in the management console of the OBCS instance, as no peers will pass the proposal. If we navigate to the channel's ledger transactions, we can see the transaction of the invocation that was successful, as shown in the following screenshot:

| 5ed44eb1d9e29ffed9b5c71363792e9a6c91832d35fce8a6e18cf81d45da79be | Fri, 24 Aug 2018 14:55:09 GMT | insurancechain | Success |

Function name:	readAssetData
Arguments:	["base.Vehicle","JN6ND01S3GX194659"]
Validation Results:	VALID
Response:	200
Initiator:	emergencyservices: restproxy1
Endorser:	emergencyservices: peer0-1,acmeservices: peer1-1,axainsurance: peer0-1

Transaction invoking the readAssetData function appended to the ledger of the insurancechain channel

 Notice that the call shows the data used for the arguments. Data given as arguments is always visible to network administrators, so keep that in mind if you build something that is privacy-sensitive.

The code responsible for getting the stored asset data and returning the data to the client is shown in the following code snippet:

```
assetRef = fmt.Sprintf("%s#%s", assetClass, assetID)
valAsbytes, err := stub.GetState(assetRef)

if err != nil {
    jsonResp = "{\"Error\":\"Failed to get state for " + assetType + " with
id" + assetID + "\"}"
    return shim.Error(jsonResp)
} else if valAsbytes == nil {
    jsonResp = "{\"Error\":\"" + assetType + " does not exist: " + assetID +
"\"}"
    return shim.Error(jsonResp)
}
return shim.Success(valAsbytes)
```

The code creates the reference that the asset has stored in the chaincode state and uses the `stub.GetState` function to search for the asset. If something goes wrong or it does not exist, an error is returned, otherwise, the asset's data object is returned. The transaction reviewed in the preceding text can be used to verify or query an asset, and we will use it a few times moving forward to check the contents of an asset.

Reporting a new accident

Now that the demo assets are set up and we have verified that at least one of the assets is stored in the chaincode state database, we can execute the first functional operation. Let's imagine that an accident just happened and that the vehicle with the registration number JN6ND01S3GX194659 automatically reports the accident by calling the REST proxy of the lease company to which the car belongs, for example, AutoLease. The HTTP request calls the `{{AutoLeaseProxyHost}}/bcsgw/rest/v1/transaction/invocation` endpoint and invokes the `reportAccident` transaction/function.

The function expects a minimum of two arguments, namely the longitude and latitude, but it can also receive the date and time when the accident occurred and the registration number of the vehicle reporting the accident. Use the following JSON payload to report the accident:

```
{
    "channel": "insurancechain",
    "chaincode": "insurancechain",
    "method": "reportAccident",
    "chaincodeVer": "v2",
    "args":
```

```
["40.849496","-73.936206","2018-08-24T17:39:20.325Z","JN6ND01S3GX194659"],
   "proposalWaitTime": 50000,
   "transactionWaitTime": 60000
}
```

The longitude and latitude correspond to the intersection of Broadway and West 180th street in New York City. As explained in the previous chapter, when you send the request to the REST API of the chaincode and it includes a vehicle identification number, it will be checked to verify that the vehicle asset indeed exists. If the vehicle exists, the `AccidentReport` object is created and stored in the chaincode state. Finally, an event is transmitted and a response is sent to the client. The downloaded version of the chaincode contract returns the contents that are transmitted as part of the event in its response, as the REST proxy currently does not allow you to connect over WebSockets to listen to transmitted events.

If everything checks out, the response to the request is similar to the following payload:

```
{
   "returnCode": "Success",
   "result": {
     "payload": "{\"accidentId\":\"1535137974\",\"location\":\"40.849496,
-73.936206\"}",
     "encode": "UTF-8"
   },
   "txid": "244156f8995ecbe1001c49b21d43615822f07f9dd43e3111c86dee..."
}
```

You can verify what is created by retrieving the asset data of the accident report using the `readAssetData` transaction/function. The result will be similar to the following JSON payload:

```
{
   "$class": "accident.AccidentReport",
   "accidentId": "1535137974",
   "occuredAt": "2018-08-24T17:39:20.325Z",
   "status": "NEW",
   "location": {"$class": "accident.Location","longitude":
40.849496,"latitude": -73.936206},
   "involvedGoods": {"$class": "accident.Goods","vehicles":
["base.Vehicle#JN6ND01S3GX194659"]}
}
```

If you head back to the OBCS management console and look at the transaction, you will see that the `reportAccident` function has been endorsed successfully and that the location, date of accident, and the vehicle involved are all used to create the accident report, as shown in the following screenshot:

◢ 244156f8995ecbe1001c49b21d43615822f07f9dd43e3111c86deefdf3018218	Fri, 24 Aug 2018 16:47:20 GMT	insurancechain	Success

Function name:	reportAccident
Arguments:	["40.849496","-73.936206","2018-08-24T17:39:20.325Z","JN6ND01S3GX194659"]
Validation Results:	VALID
Response:	200

Transaction invoking the reportAccident function with the location, time of day of the accident, and the reporting vehicle

There are also a few error flows, for example, when the vehicle does not exist, or if the input arguments are not in the correct format or are missing. You can try them out yourself if you wish.

Updating the accident report

The emergency services information is still missing as they are yet have to respond to the accident. Let's imagine that the 34th precinct of the NYPD, located just a mile from the accident, is reporting on the accident. They will update the report twice. The first time will be to assign themselves as the responding emergency and rescue service, and the second time will be to record what happened and add the other vehicle involved to their report.

The first HTTP request "Update responding ERS" is again calling the REST proxy of the emergency services OBCS instance. The POST request to the `{{ErsProxyHost}}` `/bcsgw/rest/v1/transaction/invocation` endpoint sends the following payload.

The first argument is the ID of the accident, which will be different for every new accident, so this will be different for you as it's based on the Unix timestamp:

```
{
    "channel":  " insurancechain ",
    "chaincode":  "insurancechain",
    "method":  "updateReport",
    "chaincodeVer":  "v2",
    "args": ["1535137974", "NYPD 34th Precinct"],
    "proposalWaitTime": 25000,
    "transactionWaitTime": 30000
}
```

The chaincode function will check to see whether the accident with the given ID exists and whether the responding ERS is an existing Emergency Service. If everything checks out, the response to the request will have a similar response payload, as shown in the following code snippet:

```
{
    "returnCode": "Success",
    "result": {
        "payload": "{\"accidentId\":\"1535137974\",\"reason\":\"Emergencency
Services (NYPD 34th Precinct) responding to accident\"}",
        "encode": "UTF-8"
    },
    "txid": "d0326d53fb2a7320187bb8136b70d56c2f49dbc9072bfbb04bebc..."
}
```

The `payload` field contains the same JSON message that is transmitted via the `ReportUpdate` event. It contains the ID of the accident and the reason for the update. The second HTTP request "Update accident description and vehicles" is almost identical, but instead of only two arguments, this request includes four: the accident ID, the responding ERS, an accident description, and the other vehicle involved in the accident. The argument field has the following value:

```
"args":  ["1535137974", "NYPD 34th Precinct", "Nose to tail collision",
"1HTZR0007JH586991"]
```

This time, the chaincode function will check that the accident exists, the responding ERS is the same as the one already responding to the accident, and whether the other vehicle involved exists in the system. If everything checks out, the response to the request will be a similar to the following payload:

```
{
    "returnCode": "Success",
    "result": {
        "payload": "{\"accidentId\":\"1535137974\",\"reason\":\"Vehicle
1HTZR0007JH586991 added to report\"}",
        "encode": "UTF-8"
    },
    "txid": ad0049f094379f7e2be232fb6e539766688323aed821314bc651..."
}
```

Notice that the response is almost the same, only this time a different reason for the update is returned, as another vehicle is added to the report. When we look at the data of the `AccidentReport` asset, by invoking the `readAssetData` function of the chaincode, we see that the reporting ERS, the accident description, and the other vehicle involved are present in the asset data. This time, instead of using the `/invocation` endpoint, we use the `{{ErsProxyHost}}/bcsgw/rest/v1/transaction/query` endpoint. The difference between the `/query` and `/invocation` endpoint is that calling it doesn't result in a transaction that needs to be endorsed; it fetches the data from its local state database. The following screenshot shows the request and response of this `readAssetData` query:

HTTP request for invoking the readAssetData function to verify the updated accident report

The response displayed in the screenshot has the following JSON payload, containing the updated `AccidentReport` asset. Because we have updated the description and added the other vehicle involved, the status of the accident is changed to `RESOLVED`:

```
{
  "$class": "accident.AccidentReport",
  "accidentId": "1535137974",
  "occuredAt": "2018-08-24T17:39:20.325Z",
  "status": "RESOLVED",
  "location": {
    "$class": "accident.Location",
    "longitude": 40.849496,
    "latitude": -73.936206
  },
  "accidentDescription": "Nose to tail collision",
  "involvedGoods": {"$class": "accident.Goods",
    "vehicles": ["base.Vehicle#JN6ND01S3GX194659",
  "base.Vehicle#1HTZR0007JH586991"]
  },
  "respondingERS": "base.EmergencyServices#NYPD 34th Precinct"
}
```

As I mentioned before, there are some error flows programmed into the chaincode function.

For example, when the function is invoked and the ERS already-responding is not the same as the one shown when updating the report for the second time, you may get an error response similar to the following:

```
{
  "returnCode": "Failure",
  "info": {
    "proxyError": "Proposal not pass",
    "peerErrors": [
      {
        "peerId": "acmeservices1peer0",
        "errMsg": "Sending proposal to acmeservices1peer0 failed because
of: gRPC failure=Status{code=UNKNOWN, description=chaincode error (status:
500, message: Emergency Services already responding: NYPD 50th Precinct),
cause=null}",
        "verified": false
      },
      {...}
    ]
  },
  "txid": "1fe905fcd04dd3c4ab98fdb07757d3f2ad1a5601bfe4b1d188d680..."
}
```

The code responsible for the preceding error can be found halfway up the `updateReport` function, as shown in the following code block. It checks to see whether the responding ERS, given as an input argument to the function, is the same as the one already stored in the asset data:

```
// === Update reponsing ERS if not yet assigned
if accidentReport.RespondingERS == "" {
  accidentReport.RespondingERS = ersRef
  reason = fmt.Sprintf("Emergencency Services (%s) responding to accident",
respondingERS)
} else {
  return shim.Error("Emergency Services already responding: " +
respondingERS)
}
```

Now that we have updated the accident report and resolved it by adding all of the relevant information, we can proceed with the vehicle repair and insurance claim process.

Issuing a new insurance policy

Before we can request a quote for the necessary vehicle repairs, first we need to issue a missing insurance policy for one of the vehicles, as this policy is not part of the demo assets.

An insurer can use the `issuePolicy` transaction/function of the chaincode, as you might guess, to issue a new policy to the owner of a vehicle.

Examine the "Issue insurance policy to JN6ND01S3GX194659" HTTP request of the Postman collection. The request requires a total of 12 input arguments to create the new insurance policy successfully.

The 12 expected arguments are as follows:

- `authorizedBy`
- `validFrom`
- `validTo`
- `registeredVehicle`
- `countryCode`
- `insurerCode`
- `policyNumber`
- `vehicleCategory`
- `vehicleMake`
- `coverage`
- `policyholder`
- `issuedBy`

The `registeredVehicle`, `policyholder`, and `issuedBy` arguments reference existing assets in the chaincode state, namely `Vehicle`, `Registrant`, and `Insurer` assets. Another interesting argument is `coverage`, as this is a collection of country codes in which the vehicle is insured, which will be converted by the code into an array of strings.

This time, the insurer, AllSecur, invokes the function on its own REST proxy. For this reason, the request in Postman uses the `{{AllSecurProxyHost}}` variable in the endpoint. The body of the request has the following JSON payload arguments:

```
"args":   ["State of New York", "2018-08-01T00:00:00.000Z",
"2020-08-01T00:00:00.000Z", "JN6ND01S3GX194659", "USA", "AX203", "3459802",
"AF", "BMW", "US,CA,MX", "908123764", "AllSecur Insurance"]
```

The chaincode function first checks to see whether all 12 arguments are given and whether they are all in the correct format, such as the `validFrom` and `validTo` arguments. Then, it checks to see if the `Insurer`, `Vehicle`, and `Registrant` assets that are referenced indeed exist in the chaincode state. Using the data stored in the state, the code checks to see whether the vehicle is actually owned by the registrant to which the insurance policy is issued. The code for the last three checks is as follows:

```
// === Check if vehicle exists
vehicleAsBytes, err := stub.GetState(vehicleRef)
if err != nil {
  return shim.Error("Failed to get vehicle: " + err.Error())
} else if vehicleAsBytes == nil {
  return shim.Error("Given vehicle doesn't exists: " + vehicleRef)
}
// === Unmarshal vehicle asset
var vehicle Vehicle
if err = json.Unmarshal(vehicleAsBytes, &vehicle); err != nil {
 return shim.Error("Failed to unmarshal vehicle asset: " + err.Error())
}
// === Check if policy holder exists
holderRef := fmt.Sprintf("%s#%s", "base.Registrant", policyHolder)
holderAsBytes, err := stub.GetState(holderRef)
if err != nil {
  return shim.Error("Failed to get policy holder: " + err.Error())
} else if holderAsBytes == nil {
    return shim.Error("Given policy holder doesn't exists: " + holderRef)
}
// === check if vehicle is owned by policy holder
if vehicle.Owner != holderRef {
  return shim.Error("The vehicle is not owned by the newly assigned policy
holder")
}
```

When the chaincode function is successfully executed, it creates and stores the
InsurancePolicy asset in the chaincode state, and it will return its contents in the
response to the client as part of the payload field. The insurance policy that we just created
has the following JSON payload representation:

```
{
  "$class": "insurance.InsurancePolicy",
  "policyId": "USA-AX203-3459802",
  "autorisedBy": "State of New York",
  "validFrom": "2018-08-01T00:00:00Z",
  "validTo": "2020-08-01T00:00:00Z",
  "registeredVehicle": "base.Vehicle#JN6ND01S3GX194659",
  "countryCode": "USA",
  "insurerCode": "AX203",
  "policyNumber": 3459802,
  "vehicleCategory": "AF",
  "vehicleMake": "BMW",
  "coverage": ["US", "CA", "MX"],
  "policyHolder": "base.Registrant#908123764",
  "issuedBy": "base.Insurer#Allsecur Insurance"
}
```

The full HTTP request and response of the transaction is shown in the following screenshot:

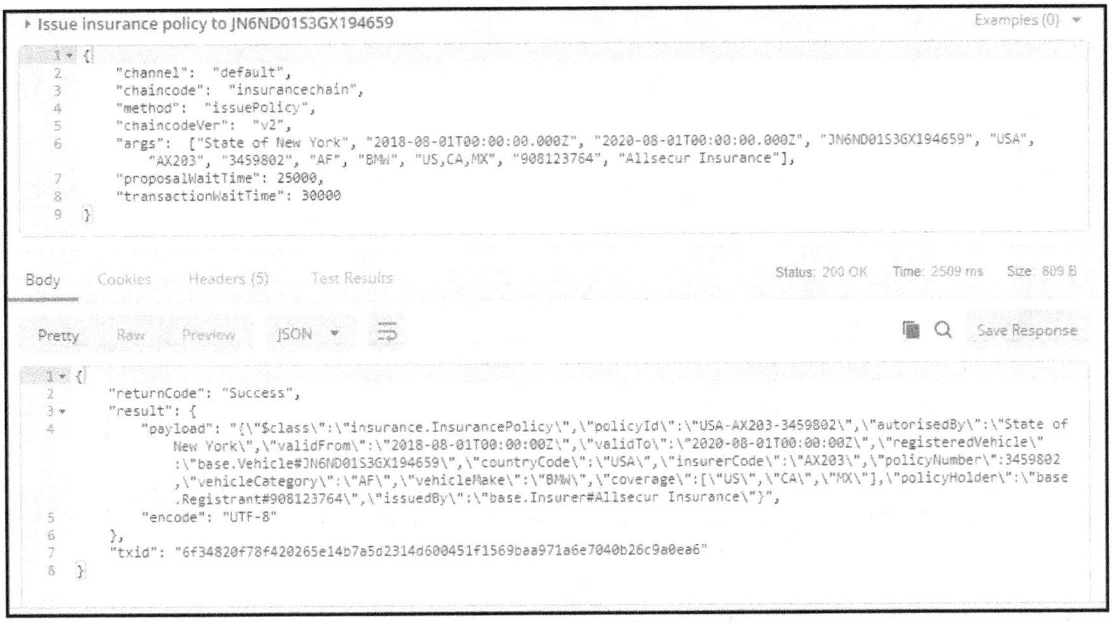
Issue insurance policy to JN6ND01S3GX194659
Examples (0)
{
"channel": "default",
"chaincode": "insurancechain",
"method": "issuePolicy",
"chaincodeVer": "v2",
"args": ["State of New York", "2018-08-01T00:00:00.000Z", "2020-08-01T00:00:00.000Z", "JN6ND01S3GX194659", "USA", "AX203", "3459802", "AF", "BMW", "US,CA,MX", "908123764", "Allsecur Insurance"],
"proposalWaitTime": 25000,
"transactionWaitTime": 30000
}
Body
Cookies
Headers (5)
Test Results
Status: 200 OK
Time: 2509 ms
Size: 809 B
Pretty
Raw
Preview
JSON
Save Response
{
"returnCode": "Success",
"result": {
"payload": "{\"$class\":\"insurance.InsurancePolicy\",\"policyId\":\"USA-AX203-3459802\",\"autorisedBy\":\"State of New York\",\"validFrom\":\"2018-08-01T00:00:00Z\",\"validTo\":\"2020-08-01T00:00:00Z\",\"registeredVehicle\":\"base.Vehicle#JN6ND01S3GX194659\",\"countryCode\":\"USA\",\"insurerCode\":\"AX203\",\"policyNumber\":3459802,\"vehicleCategory\":\"AF\",\"vehicleMake\":\"BMW\",\"coverage\":[\"US\",\"CA\",\"MX\"],\"policyHolder\":\"base.Registrant#908123764\",\"issuedBy\":\"base.Insurer#Allsecur Insurance\"}",
"encode": "UTF-8"
},
"txid": "6f34820f78f420265e14b7a5d2314d600451f1569baa971a6e7040b26c9a0ea6"
}

HTTP request for invoking the issuePolicy function to create a new insurance policy

When the chaincode function fails, for example, because the owner of the vehicle is not the one who was issued the insurance policy, then the response will contain the following error message in its response body:

```
"errMsg": "Sending proposal to allsecur2peer0 failed because of: gRPC
failure=Status{code=UNKNOWN, description=chaincode error (status: 500,
message: The vehicle is not owned by the newly assigned policy holder)}"
```

You can always verify that your transaction was successful by looking at the transaction details in the OBCS management console on the channel's ledger page:

⊿ 6f34820f78f420265e14b7a5d2314d600451f1569baa971a6e7040b26c9a0ea6	Sat. 25 Aug 2018 14:13:37 GMT	insurancechain	Success
Function name:	issuePolicy		
Arguments:	["State of New York","2018-08-01T00:00:00.000Z","2020-08-01T00:00:00.000Z","JN6ND01S3GX194659","USA","AX203","3459802","AF","BMW","US,CA,MX","908123764","Allsecur Insurance"]		
Validation Results:	VALID		
Response:	200		
Initiator:	allsecur: restproxy1		
Endorser:	axainsurance: peer0-1,acmeservices: peer1-1,autolease: peer0-2		

Transaction invoking the issuePolicy function with all 12 required input arguments

This newly-issued insurance policy is now attached to the first vehicle that was created when setting up our demo assets. This means that we can now request a quote for vehicle repairs on this first vehicle, as this request requires a valid insurance policy.

Requesting a quote for vehicle repairs

Let's take a different approach to this and the following HTTP requests in order to avoid this becoming an endless chapter, and also because it's fun to try out the other transactions on your own. Just examine the code of the chaincode and figure out what is happening.

In this and the following two sections, I will briefly go over the input arguments, the expected results, and some possible error flows. Imagine that the vehicle with the registration number JN6ND01S3GX194659 was damaged in an accident. This vehicle is owned by AutoLease, not personally by an individual, and it needs to be repaired as soon as possible. The lease company therefore submits a request for a quote to have the vehicle repaired using the `requestQuote` transaction/chaincode function.

We can use the HTTP request "Request a quote for vehicle repairs" which is available in the Postman collection to invoke this function of the smart contract. This HTTP request calls the REST proxy of the OBCS instance of AutoLease using the configured `{{AutoLeaseProxyHost}}/bcsgw/rest/v1/transaction/invocation` endpoint. Don't forget to set the environment variable to the correct host/port of the REST proxy.

The function expects exactly three arguments: the ID of the accident, the insurance policy ID of the vehicle owner, and a description of the damage. Our request contains the following argument values:

```
"args": ["1535137974", "USA-AX203-3459802", "Scratch on back bumper"]
```

With the ID of the insurance policy, a repair shop such as the New York branch of USA Automotive can access all of the information about the vehicle, its owner, and their insurance coverage to prepare the best estimate possible. Before the `QuoteRequest` asset is created and stored in the chaincode state, the code of the `requestQuote` function will check to see whether an accident report with the given ID exists, that the given `InsurancePolicy` exists and that it is still valid, and that the vehicle that is linked to the policy was actually involved in the accident. The code responsible for this check can be found in the the following code block:

```
// === Check if vehicle is involved in accident
vehicles := accidentReport.InvolvedGoods.Vehicles

// save the items in map
vmap := make(map[string]bool)
for i := 0; i < len(vehicles); i++ {
  vmap[vehicles[i]] = true
}

// Check if registered vehicle is involved in accident
var vehicleReg string
vehicleReg = insurancePolicy.RegisteredVehicle
if _, ok := vmap[vehicleReg]; !ok {
  return shim.Error("Insured vehicle is not involved in accident: " +
vehicleReg)
}
```

The code will also retrieve information about the vehicle in order to make the response payload be sent back to the client and transmitted as an event. The response body looks similar to the following:

```
{
  "returnCode": "Success",
  "result": {
    "payload":
{\"requestId\":\"1535212371\",\"vehicleMake\":\"BMW\",\"vehicleModel\":\"X5
\",\"damageDescription\":\"Scratch on back bumper\"}",
    "encode": "UTF-8"
  },
  "txid": "00c5927315a6635523dcafd27cb65c26350728b9de8398ecb38..."
}
```

Notice that, in the `payload` field, the ID of the new request (1535212371) is listed as well as the make (BMW) and model (X5) of the insured vehicle and a description of the reported damage. The vehicle data is retrieved using the reference stored in the insurance policy of the requester of the quote (`RegisteredVehicle`).

When the previous call is successful, we can call `readAssetData` with two arguments, the `vehiclerepair.QuoteRequest` class and the `1535212371` ID to retrieve the payload of the created `QuoteRequest`:

```
{
  "$class": "vehiclerepair.QuoteRequest",
  "requestId": "1535212371",
  "accidentReport": "accident.AccidentReport#1535137974",
  "vehicleInsurance": "insurance.InsurancePolicy#USA-AX203-3459802",
  "damageDescription": "Scratch on back bumper (2x0.1 inches)"
}
```

Offering a repair quote with estimates

The next HTTP request in the Postman collection, "Offer quote for vehicle repair", will propose a repair quote based on the submitted request of the previous HTTP request to the REST proxy. This time, the request is sent by one of the repair shops. Since they are not yet part of the blockchain network of peers, we can simulate this transaction using one of the REST proxies of the other member organizations.

The HTTP request invokes the `offerQuote` chaincode function, which expects exactly four arguments to offer a quote for vehicle repairs successfully:

- `requestId`
- `offerBy (RepairShop)`
- `json(estimates[])`
- `tax (%)`

The arguments are not all basic string values, as we have seen with all of the other function calls. The third argument, for example, expects a JSON payload that contains an array of estimates. Let's say that scratch removal costs $30.60 for refinishing, $100 for the labor, and that the taxes to be paid over the total cost is 11%. This will result in the following request arguments for this chaincode function:

```
"args":  ["1535212371", "USA Automotive NYC", "[{\"type\":\"REPAIR\",
\"description\":\"Scratch removal\", \"costOfRefinish\":30.6,
\"costOfLabor\":100.0, \"totalCost\":130.6}]", "11"]
```

The double quotes in the value of the third argument are escaped to keep the body of the HTTP request valid. After executing the request, the chaincode checks to see whether a QuoteRequest asset exists with the given ID, whether a repair shop with the given trade name exists, and that the JSON payload containing the estimates is valid. If there are multiple entries in the estimates array, the code will calculate the total costs of the repair by adding the amounts.

The following resulting payload is of a successful invocation of the preceding request, and it contains the ID of the request as reference, the ID of the created RepairQuote, and the total of all of the estimates:

```
{
   "returnCode": "Success",
   "result": {
      "payload":
"{\"requestId\":\"1535212371\",\"quoteId\":\"1535219101\",\"totalEstimate\"
:130.6}",
      "encode": "UTF-8"
   },
   "txid": "36862f38b775cee114d587cc4df0ab79f32133241a5a4c8524f..."
}
```

When the previous call is successful, we can call the readAssetData function with two arguments, the vehiclerepair.RepairQuote class and the 1535219101 id, to retrieve the payload of the RepairQuote created:

```
{
   "$class": "vehiclerepair.RepairQuote",
   "quoteId": "1535219101",
   "quoteRequest": "vehiclerepair.QuoteRequest#1535212371",
   "estimator": "base.RepairShop#USA Automotive NYC",
   "estimates": [{
      "$class": "insurance.Estimate",
      "type": "REPAIR",
      "description": "Scratch removal",
      "costOfLabor": 100,
      "costOfRefinish": 30.6,
      "totalCost": 130.6
   }
   ],
   "totalParts": 0,
   "totalLabor": 100,
   "totalRefinish": 30.6,
   "tax": 11,
   "total": 144.966
}
```

The following screenshot shows the recorded `offerQuote` transaction on the channel's ledger summary page:

TxID		Time	Chaincode	Status
◢ 36862f38b775cee114d587cc4df0ab79f32133241a5a4c8524fe7e6b9b9e6b91		Sat, 25 Aug 2018 17:45:01 GMT	insurancechain	Success
Function name:	offerQuote			
Arguments:	["1535212371","USA Automotive NYC","[{\"type\":\"REPAIR\",\"description\":\"Scratch removal\",\"costOfRefinish\":30.6,\"costOfLabor\":100.0,\"totalCost\":130.6}]","11"]			
Validation Results:	VALID			
Response:	200			
Initiator:	acmeservices: restproxy1			

Transaction invoking the offerQuote function including the JSON payload of estimates

Sending an insurance claim to the driver at fault

The last HTTP request available in the Postman collection is called "Send insurance claim," and it sends an insurance claim from the claimant to the driver at fault. The request is again very straightforward, as it only contains arguments that reference other assets present in the chaincode state. The `sendClaim` transaction/chaincode function expects exactly four arguments, including the ID of the accident report, the ID of the insurance policy of the claimant, the ID of the insurance policy of the at-fault driver, and the best repair quote received.

The request to invoke the `sendClaim` function of the chaincode is as follows:

```
{
    "channel": "insurancechain",
    "chaincode": "insurancechain",
    "method": "sendClaim",
    "chaincodeVer":   "v2",
    "args": ["1535137974", "USA-AX203-3459802"
            ,"USA-AS204-1042919", "1535219101"]
}
```

The request may be simple, however, the code of the chaincode function performs a lot of complex checks. Of course, it checks to see whether all of the reference assets exist in the chaincode state, and it also creates all of the objects in memory so that the code, for example, can check to see whether the vehicles associated with the given insurance policies were actually involved in the accident. If, in fact, the vehicle of the at-fault driver is not involved in the accident, the following error response is returned:

```
"errMsg": "Sending proposal to acmeservices1peer0 failed because of: gRPC
failure=Status{code=UNKNOWN, description=chaincode error (status: 500,
message: Insured vehicle of defendant is not involved accident:
base.Vehicle#1HTZR0007JH586991), cause=null}"
```

If the chaincode does not find any anomalies, the function finally creates the
InsuranceClaim asset, stores it in the chaincode state, and transmits the NewClaim event,
before returning the following result:

```
{
  "returnCode": "Success",
  "result": {
    "payload": "{\"claimId\":\"1535226697\",\"claimantPolicyId\":\"USA-
AX203-3459802\",\"defendantPolicyId\":\"USA-
AS204-1042919\",\"costOfRepair\",130.6}",
    "encode": "UTF-8"
  },
  "txid": "4df0ab79f32133241a5a4c8524f36862f38b775cee114d587cc..."
}
```

When the previous call is successful, we can call the readAssetData function with two
arguments, the insurance.InsuranceClaim class and the 1535226697 id, in order to
retrieve the payload of the InsuranceClaim created:

```
{
  "$class": "insurance.InsuranceClaim",
  "claimId": "1535219101",
  "dateOfClaim": "2018-08-25T19:55:12Z",
  "status": "NEW",
  "accidentReport": "accident.AccidentReport#1535137974",
  "claimant": "insurance.InsurancePolicy#USA-AX203-3459802",
  "defendant": "insurance.InsurancePolicy#USA-AS204-1042919",
  "codeOfRepair": "vehiclerepair.RepairQuote#1535219101"
}
```

This last request concludes all of the transactions programmed in our smart contract. You
can play around with the HTTP request and check to see what happens when you put in
some incorrect values or non-existing references.

The programmed contract is still not really a functional application, as many checks are still
missing. It also lacks the functions to create new assets, which are now created by the
setupAssets function, and it is missing the user-role based authorization to permit or
deny the execution of the chaincode function (which can be programmed into the
chaincode), but it certainly is a good start.

Monitoring executed transactions

In the previous sections, we tested all of the functions programmed in the smart contract (chaincode), and we have already seen a glimpse of how to monitor transactions using the management console provided by OBCS.

To conclude the testing phase, let's look at the complete ledger history. I will demonstrate this using the member organization instance of Acme Services. After logging into the management console, navigate to the **Channels** page and click on the name of the insurancechain entry. The channel's ledger details will now be shown, as seen in the following screenshot. In our case, we have 14 blocks created and a total of 12 user transactions within these blocks:

Ledger and transaction details of the insurancechain channel

Scroll through the list of blocks and notice that most of them have only one user transaction. The reason for this is that the configured generation time between blocks, by default, is 2,000 milliseconds, or 2 seconds (configured in the settings of the ordering service), and since our invocations are likely further apart, the transactions are not combined in the same block. In production, this would be different, of course, if you had multiple requests per second.

This configuration, called **Batch Timeout**, can be changed in the ordering service settings. To change the timeout, go to the **Network** page and click on **Ordering Service Settings**. This will show the following dialog popup, which allows you to increase or decrease the **Batch Timeout** value as well as the **Max Message Count** per batch:

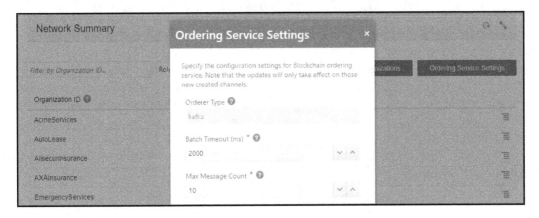

You can change the block generation timeout and Max Message Count per block in the Ordering Service Settings

Another fun thing that you can examine is the **Dashboard** page, as you can view the top channels and top peers of your OBCS instance. The following image shows a preview of Acme Service after executing all of the HTTP requests:

Dashboard overview showing channel and peer activity after executing the insurancechain chaincode functions

Summary

While we designed and developed our smart contract (chaincode) in the previous chapter, in this chapter we deployed and tested the chaincode on the blockchain network infrastructure that we set up in `Chapter 10`, *Introducing the Oracle Blockchain Cloud Service*.

In this chapter, we learned how to install the chaincode on the peers of the founder organization (Acme Service) and activated the first version on the `insurancechain` channel. To further demonstrate that chaincodes are versioned and that we can install a new version, we deployed the same chaincode under a different version and upgraded the chaincode on the `insurancechain` channel. After installing and upgrading the chaincode on the founder's OBCS instance, we installed the version v2 of the chaincode on all of the other member organizations. Since the chaincode was already activated on the channel by the founder, the chaincode was automatically instantiated (activated) for the members that previously joined the channel.

After activating the chaincode on the channel, we exposed the chaincode through the REST proxy so that an external application could use the REST API to call the transactions/functions programmed in the chaincode.

Once we enabled the chaincode in the REST proxy, we tested all of the available functions using the Postman collection provided, containing a set of HTTP requests. For each of the functions, I explained the request body sent in the call and the expected result, and I reviewed some of the possible failures that can be thrown by the code (for example, when data is missing or when values in the input arguments are invalid). For some of the created assets, we also verified that they were actually generated or updated in the chaincode store.

Finally, we looked at the full ledger history available via the management console provided by OBCS and learned how to influence block generation time.

In the next and final implementation chapter, we will extend the network by joining an existing Hyperledger Fabric organization (USA Automotive Services) to the existing business network. Remember, the difference between all of the other member organizations is that USA Automotive Services is not using OBCS, but rather their own on-premises installation of Hyperledger Fabric.

14
Configuring, Extending, and Monitoring Your Network

In Chapter 11, *Setting Up Your Permissioned Blockchain*, we set up our initial blockchain network as Acme Insurance Blockchain Services and joined four participating member organizations. In Chapter 9, *Building a Next-Generation Oracle B2B Platform* and Chapter 11, *Setting Up Your Permissioned Blockchain*, we looked at the use case of USA Automotive Services, who runs an existing Hyperledger Fabric network with their franchisors; and that we would later be adding this network to the **Oracle Autonomous Blockchain Cloud Service** (**OABCS**).

In this chapter, we will return to our blockchain network, and we are going to do exactly just that: join an external Fabric participant to the existing OABCS network. Furthermore, we will look at the possibility of configuring, optimizing, and monitoring peer nodes on the network. We will explore some of the management console pages that allow us to configure and monitor nodes, but we will also look at ways to integrate it with your **continuous integration** (**CI**) tooling. For example, you can interact with the BCS, using the Fabric SDK, to query channel and peer data and to monitor events.

The first part of the chapter, which covers extending the network, will follow the same style as the previous two chapters and apply a more hands-on approach to the instruction. The second part of the chapter, which covers the configuration and monitoring of the network, will be a walkthrough-style exploration.

In this chapter, you will learn how to do the following:

- Extend your OABCS network with external Fabric participants
- Configure and monitor your OABCS peer nodes
- Integrate existing CI tooling through the use of the Fabric SDK

Extending your blockchain network

Besides extending your network with other member organizations that use the Oracle Blockchain Cloud Service, it is also possible to add existing Fabric participants. These member organizations are not making use of OABCS; rather, they run their own Hyperledger Fabric nodes on-premises or in the cloud (for example, Amazon AWS, Microsoft Azure, and so on). In our case, USA Automotive Services runs the Fabric nodes on-premises.

In order for OABCS and Fabric participants to transact with each other, we need to join the member organizations using Fabric and make them part of the network of the founder organization. To achieve this, we need to perform the following tasks:

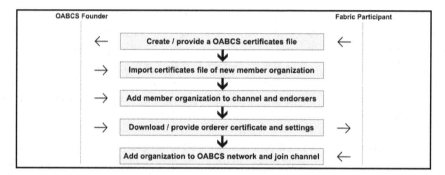

Creating a certificate file as a Fabric participant

Remember that in `Chapter 11`, *Setting Up Your Permissioned Blockchain*, we joined the other participants by exporting and importing the member organizations' certificates. This export resulted in a certificates file for each of the member organization, as shown in the following screenshot:

AXAInsurance_certificates.json	Date modified: 2-7-2018 13:19	
Type: JSON File	Size: 2,66 KB	
AllsecurInsurance_certificates.json	Date modified: 2-7-2018 13:19	
Type: JSON File	Size: 2,67 KB	
AutoLease_certificates.json	Date modified: 2-7-2018 13:18	
Type: JSON File	Size: 2,66 KB	
EmergencyServices_certificates.json	Date modified: 2-7-2018 13:17	
Type: JSON File	Size: 2,66 KB	

List of member organization certificates files exported in Chapter 11

For a member organization that uses Fabric to join an existing OABCS network, we must write a similar certificates file that contains its `admincerts`, `cacerts`, and `tlscacerts` information. This certificates file can then be imported by the founder to add the Fabric participant to the network.

In the current example, we are running a Hyperledger Fabric 1.1 network on-premises for the USA Automotive Services franchise. At the time of writing, version 1.2 of Fabric has already been released, but as OABCS uses the version 1.1 runtime, we are required to use that version in this book.

As part of `Chapter 12`, *Designing and Developing Your First Smart Contact*, we installed the necessary platform-specific binaries. So, to continue to build on what you accomplished in `Chapter 12`, *Designing and Developing Your First Smart Contact*, you can set up an on-premises Hyperledger Fabric network following the steps described in the Fabric tutorial *Building Your First Network*, which can be found at `https://hyperledger-fabric.readthedocs.io/en/release-1.1/build_network.html`. This will be the starting point of this section.

Before we can write the certificates file, we need to retrieve the Fabric certificates information. This information is stored in a couple of **PEM** (**Privacy Enhanced Mail**) files located in the MSP folder of the Fabric organization. Here is an example of where they are found, `/first-network/crypto-config/peerOrganizations/org1.example.com/msp/`.

The certificates file that we need to define must be written in a JSON format, and it has the following structure and fields:

```
{
    "mspid": "USAAutomotive",
    "certs": {
      "admincert": "-----BEGIN CERTIFICATE-----
\nadmin_certificate\nadmin_certificate==\n-----END CERTIFICATE-----\n",
        "cacert": "-----BEGIN CERTIFICATE-----
\nca_certificate\nca_certificate==\n-----END CERTIFICATE-----\n",
        "tlscacert": "-----BEGIN CERTIFICATE-----
\ntlsca_certificate\ntlsca_certificate==\n-----END CERTIFICATE-----\n"
    }
}
```

Field	Description
mspid	Specifies the name of the participating Fabric organization
admincert	Contains the content of the organization's Admin certificates file; for example, /msp/admincerts/Admin@{orgname}-cert.pem*

cacert	Contains the content of the organization's CA certificates file; for instance, `/msp/cacerts/ca.{orgname}-cert.pem*`
tlscacert	Contains the contents of the organization's TLS certificates file; for example, `/msp/tlscacerts/tlsca.{orgname}-cert.pem*`

List of mandatory fields of the certificates JSON file

When you copy the contents of a certificates file (`.pem`) into the JSON, remember to replace each new line with `\n` so that the contents are on one line as a concatenated string.

The following screenshot shows the contents of the original Admin certificate file and a portion of the certificates JSON file that OABCS requires to join a Fabric participant to the network:

Contents of both the Admin certificate and the OABCS certificates file

Before saving the file, don't forget to set the correct `mspid` value; that is, the name of the organization. The value can have a maximum length of 15 characters.

Importing the certificates file as founder

The next step is to upload and import the Fabric participant's certificates file using the console of the founder organization, Acme Services, to add the participant to the network. This is done in the same way as with the OABCS participants.

To do this, we need to log back into the administration console of Acme Services and navigate to the **Network** page. From this page, we can add the member organization by clicking on the **Add Organizations** button, as shown in the following screenshot:

Adding a Fabric organization to your existing business network

In the dialog box that appears, upload the certificates file for the Fabric participant that you want to add to the network. In the dialog shown in the following screenshot, you can click on the **Upload Organization Certificates** link and select the file that you want to upload. If the certificates file is valid, you will see the given `mspid` appear on screen:

Uploading and importing the certificates file of the new Fabric organization

If your certificates JSON file does not have all of the required arguments/fields, you will receive an error message mentioning that it contains an invalid argument, as shown in the following screenshot:

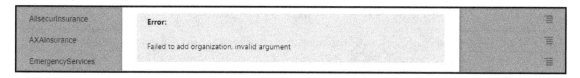

Error message when trying to import an invalid certificates file

If your certificates file is valid, the dialog will show a success message, as shown in the following screenshot. The dialog allows you to export the orderer settings that need to be transferred to the Fabric participant, or to close (**Finish**) the dialog.

In our case, click on **Export Orderer Settings** to keep the settings file safe for later use. Notice in the background that the organization is already visible in the list of participating organizations.

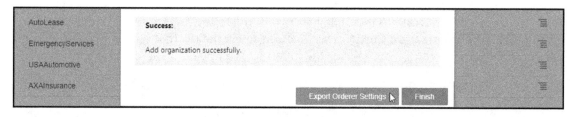

Success message when Fabric organization is correctly imported

Adding a member to an existing channel as founder

The next step is to add the new member organization to the existing insurancechain channel so that the network can interact with the new member organization and vice versa. While still logged into the console of the founder, navigate to the **Channels** page. Click on the **options** menu to the right of the insurancechain entry, and select the **Add Organizations to Channel** option, as follows:

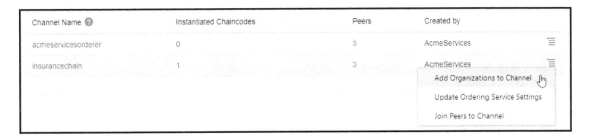

Channel option to add an organization to the channel

This will reveal a dialog popup, as shown in the following screenshot, in which you can see all organizations that are part of the channel and add organizations that are not yet part of the channel.

In our case, scroll down to the end of the list, check the box in front of the `USAAutomotive` organization's entry, and leave the **ACL** option on **ReaderWriter**. Add the organization by clicking on the **Submit** button. If the operation is successful, the dialog will show a success message for a short period of time and then close automatically:

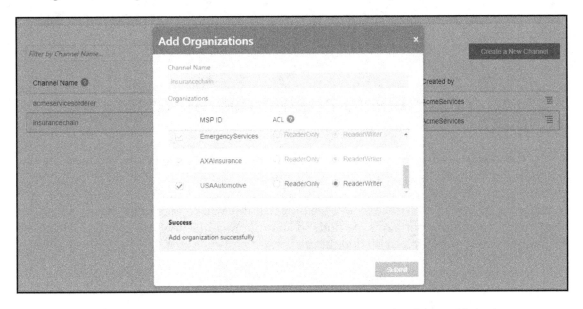

Dialog to add organizations, showing the success message after correctly adding the new organization to the insurancechain channel

You can check to see whether the organization is added to the channel by visiting the channel details and organizations. Click on the name of the channel and navigate to the **Organizations** section. If correct, the USAAutomotive organization is now listed with the existing organizations, as shown in the following screenshot:

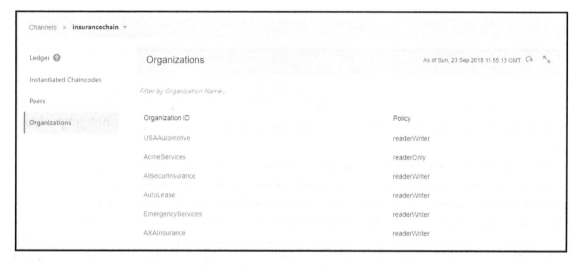

Channels > **insurancechain** ▾

Ledger ❓
Instantiated Chaincodes
Peers
Organizations

Organizations

Filter by Organization Name...

As of Sun, 23 Sep 2018 11:55:13 GMT

Organization ID	Policy
USAAutomotive	readerWriter
AcmeServices	readerOnly
AllsecurInsurance	readerWriter
AutoLease	readerWriter
EmergencyServices	readerWriter
AXAInsurance	readerWriter

List showing all organizations that joined the insurancechain channel

Adding a member to chaincode endorsers as founder

For the new organization to be part of the endorsement process, we need to add the organization to the endorsement policy of the insurancechain chaincode. The only restriction is that you can't currently update the endorsement policy of an already-instantiated version of a chaincode, but I expect that this will change in the future as Hyperledger Fabric supports this method. So, in order to add a new member organization to the list of endorsers, we can do two things:

- Deploy a new version of the chaincode, and instantiate it with the right endorsement policy. As a result of this action, other organizations must also deploy this version.
- Switch back and forth to a different version of the chaincode by upgrading the channel and changing the endorsement policy in the process.

In our case, we already have a version 1 and a version 2 of the `insurancechain` chaincode that are the same, so we can switch back and forth and change the endorsement policy in the process. In most cases, however, you would need to follow the first approach.

To upgrade the chaincode on the channel, navigate to the **Chaincodes** page. Click on the options menu to the right of the `insurancechain` entry in the list of installed chaincodes, and select the **Upgrade** option. In the dialog that pops up, select the **Version Source** and existing **Version** - that is, **v1**- and click **Next**. The following screenshot shows this first step of the upgrade wizard:

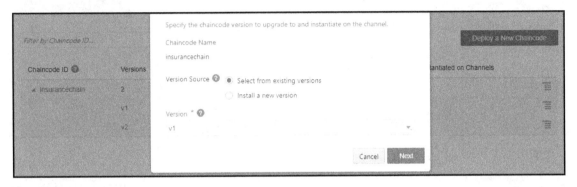

Upgrade back to the previous version of the chaincode, or install a new version

In the second step of the upgrade of the chaincode, select all of the peers and leave everything empty (default behavior). Click **Next** to revert the chaincode on the channel to the old version.

Do this process one more time, and switch back to version 2 of the chaincode. However, this time in the second step of the wizard, add all organizations to the endorsement policy section. Also, configure the requirement that four out of the six organizations need to endorse transactions. While only three were required for endorsement in the previous chapter, we want a majority of the organizations to endorse transaction, and with the newly-added organization, three organizations is no longer a majority.

The following screenshot shows our new endorsement policy:

New endorsement policy for version 2 of the chaincode

Adding yourself to the network as a Fabric participant

The last step of the process is for the Fabric participant to add themselves to the existing network. This can be achieved by following these tasks:

- Retrieve the orderer settings file from the founder
- Compose the orderer certificate PEM file based on tlscacert information
- Add the Fabric participant to the network

Retrieving the orderer settings file

As we have exported the ordering settings file before, we can send it to the Fabric organization that wants to join the network; in this case, USA Automotive Services. For example, you can send this file via email or a shared cloud storage (for example, Dropbox).

Composing the orderer certificate PEM file

As a Fabric participant, we need to compose the orderer certificate, based on the information in the orderer settings file, in order to be able to join the network. Open the settings file, and note that it uses JSON for its structure, which includes the certificates and connection information of the ordering service managed by OABCS.

The contents of the orderer settings file is shown here:

```
{
    "mspid": "AcmeServices",
    "tlscacerts": "-----BEGIN CERTIFICATE-----
\nMIICZjCCAg2gAwIBAgIQYaE18EUOf7aftpx94MmnVTAKBggqhkjOPQQDAjCBhDEL\nMAkGA1U
EBhMCVVMxEzARBgNVBAgTCkNhbGlmb3JuaWExFjAUBgNVBAcTDVNhbiBG\ncmFuY2lzY28xIDAe
BgNVBAoTF2FjbWViY3Mub3JhY2xlY2xvdWQuY29tMSYwJAYD\nVQQDEx10bHNjYS5hY211YmNzL
m9yYWNsZWNsb3VkLmNvbTAeFw0xODA2MjcxNTE5\nMTNaFw0yODA2MjQxNTE5MTNaMIGEMQswCQ
YDVQQGEwJVUzETMBEGA1UECBMKQ2Fs\naWZvcm5pYTEWMBQGA1UEBxMNU2FuIEZyYW5jaXNjbzE
gMB4GA1UEChMXYWNtZWJj\ncy5vcmFjbGVjbG91ZC5jb20xJjAkBgNVBAMTHXRsc2NhLmFjbWVi
Y3Mub3JhY2xl\nY2xvdWQuY29tMFkwEwYHKoZIzj0CAQYIKoZIzj0DAQcDQgAEXjJQv3mMvt33D
Fri\nPt8MQK3/W5P+A1hdRxxz1t8nxBMA8XDxoQmLrJVf6331JbuOZ6a1U4WXcHFnYgqN\nuQsO
EqNfMF0wDgYDVR0PAQH/BAQDAgGmMA8GA1UdJQQIMAYGBFUdJQAwDwYDVR0T\nAQH/BAUwAwEB/
zApBgNVHQ4EIgQgzcanqxKFSrIrG67dZ850h3Hh+EJTutVW0GhL\nbRURWkIwCgYIKoZIzj0EAw
IDRwAwRAIgAU+JzGFRwUcUHDjzndXNXWToYeBnqA5j\nnmi4JxHMQP2gCIFzM0+rM53MvjuGeANn
38Z/UNr3+1Fd68ihYlK6B4j5w\n-----END CERTIFICATE-----\n",
    "ordererSeviceInfo": [
      {
        "address": "192.168.99.101",
        "port": 7000,
        "native": true,
        "restport": 8080
      }
    ]
  }
}
```

We need to extract the `tlscacerts` information and create a new file called `orderer.pem`. Copy the information and paste it into the `orderer.pem` file. You must replace all instances of \n with the newline character. The `orderer.pem` file must look similar to the following:

```
-----BEGIN CERTIFICATE-----
MIICZjCCAg2gAwIBAgIQYaE18EUOf7aftpx94MmnVTAKBggqhkjOPQQDAjCBhDEL
MAkGA1UEBhMCVVMxEzARBgNVBAgTCkNhbGlmb3JuaWExFjAUBgNVBAcTDVNhbiBG
cmFuY2lzY28xIDAeBgNVBAoTF2FjbWViY3Mub3JhY2xlY2xvdWQuY29tMSYwJAYD
...
-----END CERTIFICATE-----
```

Save the file and keep it close by, as we will need it in a moment.

Adding the Fabric participant to the network

The first thing that we need to do is navigate to the Fabric network directory. If you are using the example network from the tutorial from the previous chapter, you need to navigate to the `first-network` folder within the `fabric-samples` folder. If the network is not running yet, start the network by executing this command in a Terminal shell:

```
./byfn.sh -m up
```

The preceding command will compile Golang chaincode images and spin up the corresponding containers. In our case, we are not interested in the existing Hyperledger Fabric network, but will join org1 (USAAutomotive) to the OABCS network.

Before we start, let's look back at the orderer settings. The orderer address is `192.168.99.101` and the port is `7000`. We need these two values in the following commands as we execute them. Also, copy the `orderer.pem` file to the root directory of the `first-network` folder. The other thing that we need to know is the *channel* to join, which in our case is `insurancechain`.

First, fetch the channel's genesis block with the following command:

```
../bin/peer channel fetch 0 insurancechain.block -o 192.168.99.101:7000  -c
insurancechain --tls --cafile orderer.pem --logging-level debug

 2018-09-23 16:46:10.296 UTC [channelCmd] InitCmdFactory -> INFO 003
Endorser and orderer connections initialized
 2018-09-23 16:46:10.302 UTC [channelCmd] readBlock -> DEBU 00a Received
block: 0
 2018-09-23 16:46:10.302 UTC [main] main -> INFO 00b Exiting.....
```

This will download the genesis block (#0) data of the `insurancechain` channel from the orderer, which contains the configuration transaction to join the channel. Even though the peer command is used, it is not performed on a peer, as it connects to the orderer to perform this function. More information about this command can be found in the documentation at `https://hyperledger-fabric.readthedocs.io/en/release-1.1/commands/peerchannel.html#peer-channel-fetch`.

Second, join the channel with the following command:

```
peer channel join -b insurancechain.block -o 192.168.99.101:7000 --tls
 --cafile orderer.pem --logging-level debug
```

```
2018-09-23 16:55:26.711 UTC [channelCmd] InitCmdFactory -> INFO 003
Endorser and orderer connections initialized
2018-09-23 16:55:26.771 UTC [channelCmd] executeJoin -> INFO 006
Successfully submitted proposal to join channel
2018-09-23 16:55:26.771 UTC [main] main -> INFO 007 Exiting.....
```

The peers of the organization are now joined to the channel. Up until this point, we have not installed and tested the chaincode, as this is out of scope for this chapter and this book. We will not explore this procedure in detail. In future, blogs will be published about this subject. In short, you have to call the following command to install and test the chaincode, where `CC_SRC_PATH` is the folder that contains the chaincode:

```
peer chaincode install -n insurancechain -v 2.0 -l "golang" -p
${CC_SRC_PATH}
```

You can invoke the chaincode with this command:

```
peer chaincode invoke -o ${orderer_addr}:${orderer_port} --tls true --
cafile orderer.pem -C insurancechain -n insurancechain -c
'{"Args":["invoke","a","b","10"]}' --logging-level debug
```

Using the following command, you can query the chaincode:

```
peer chaincode query -C insurancechain -n insurancechain -c
'{"Args":["query","a"]}' --logging-level debug
```

Configuring your blockchain network

As mentioned at the beginning of this chapter, as well as in previous chapters, you can configure your network using the management console without scripting the changes yourself. In this section and its subsections, we will explore some of the ways in which we can configure and optimize our network. We can, for example, change the settings of the ordering service and the configuration of peer, orderer, and **Certificate Authority** (**CA**) node. Let's explore the configuration of the nodes using our founder instance (Acme).

 Disclaimer: Keep in mind that these configuration screens and dialog windows can change as the OABCS matures in the future. These screens and dialog windows are based on the GA version. Always check the online documentation (`https://docs.oracle.com/en/cloud/paas/blockchain-cloud/`) of OABCS whenever it looks different to you.

Ordering service

In *Chapter 11*, *Setting Up Your Permissioned Blockchain*, we configured our founder network to use Kafka as the type for our orderer. Compared with SOLO, it is the best type for running a production blockchain based on Hyperledger Fabric, as it supports clustering and partitioning. Once the network is created, you can't change the ordering type back to SOLO, but you can alter its settings and configuration.

Changing the settings of the ordering service

We can change the settings of the ordering service by navigating to the **Network** page. On this page, all organizations are listed that are part of the network, and it allows us to add organizations and update the ordering service settings. Click on the **Ordering Service Settings** button to display the current settings, as shown in the following screenshot:

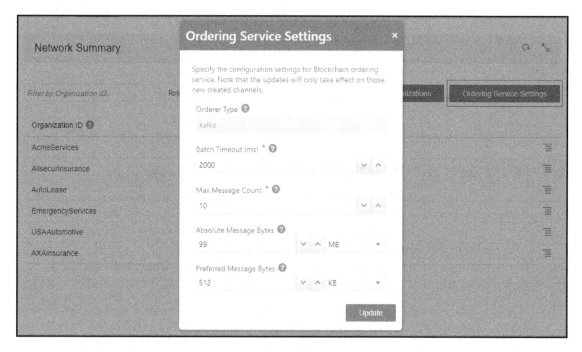

Update the settings for the ordering service

Let's go over the setting fields that we can change in this dialog window:

- **Orderer Type**: This field displays your instance's orderer type. Kafka for production and SOLO for development.
- **Batch Timeout (ms)**: This field specifies the amount of time in milliseconds that the system should wait before creating a batch. This can be a number between 1 and 3,600,000. By default, this is set to 2,000 milliseconds (2 seconds). If you don't have a lot of transactions, you can set the batch time to a higher value so you don't always have one transaction per block.
- **Max Message Count**: This field specifies the maximum number of messages to include in a batch. This can be a number between 1 and 4,294,967,295. By default, it is set to 10 messages. Even though you can set a batch timeout to a very low or very high setting, you can limit the number of messages processed per batch.
- **Absolute Message Bytes**: This field specifies the maximum number of bytes allowed for the serialized messages in a batch. Serialized messages are the result of marshaling an object in Golang or Node.js to JSON to be stored on the blockchain ledger. By default, the value is 99 MB. If, for example, your blockchain handles large messages, you can tweak this setting, starting from 1 byte even up to gigabytes.
- **Preferred Message Bytes**: This field specifies the preferred number of bytes allowed for the serialized messages in a batch. A message can still be larger than this byte size, resulting in a larger batch. Nonetheless, the batch size will be equal to or less than the number of bytes specified in the **Absolute Message Bytes** field.

We can also change the configuration of the actual orderer node itself. The preceding settings affect the runtime operations, whereas the configuration affects the network.

Changing the configuration of the orderer node

As explained in `Chapter 10`, *Introducing the Oracle Blockchain Cloud Service*, an orderer node collects transactions from the peer nodes, bundles the transactions in batches, and submits the batches to the blockchain ledger as a block. The node's configuration determines how it performs and behaves on the network.

We can change the configuration of the orderer node by navigating to the **Nodes** page. On this page, all nodes are listed that are part of the instance of the organization and it allows us to add nodes, export and import peers, and also to change the configuration of the orderer node. Click on the options menu at the right side of the Orderer node entry in the list. To find the orderer entry easily, you can filter on its type. In the collapsed options menu, as shown in the following screenshot, select **Edit Configuration**:

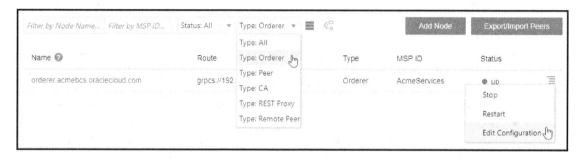

Filter on the orderer type, and edit the nodes configuration

This action will display a dialog window in which we can review and change the node's configuration. The dialog shows information such as its ID, the port to which it listens, and the location of the ledger on disk. The latter item can't be changed, but it allows administrators to change the log level and some advanced attributes, though they are mostly the same as in the ordering service settings, because these fields are linked.

The following screenshot shows the dialog window for editing the configuration of the node:

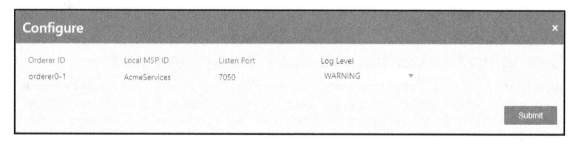

The configuration attributes of the orderer node

Let's go over the attributes we can review/change in this dialog window:

- **Orderer ID**: This attribute specifies the identifier or name that OABCS assigned to the node when it created it. In the current version, the default value is `orderer<number-partition>`, which can't be modified.
- **Local MSP ID**: This attribute specifies the assigned MSP ID for the member organization; `AcmeServices`, in this case, which can't be modified.
- **Listen Port**: This attribute specifies the listening port assigned to the node, which can't be modified.
- **Log Level**: This attribute specifies the log level that you want to use for the node. During development, you can set it to DEBUG or INFO, but in production it is best to set it to ERROR. When something happens on the node and it wants to write messages to the log file, it will check this settings first.

CA node

The CA node of the network keeps track of enrolled identities and certificates on the network. We can change the configuration of the CA node on the same **Nodes** page. Filter the list on type – CA, in this case, and click on the options menu at the right side of the entry in the list. Again, in the options menu, select the option to **Edit Configuration**. This action will display a dialog window in which we can review and change the node's configuration. It includes the ID of the Fabric CA, the **Listen Port**, the **Max Enrollments**, and the **Log Level** attributes, as shown in the following screenshot:

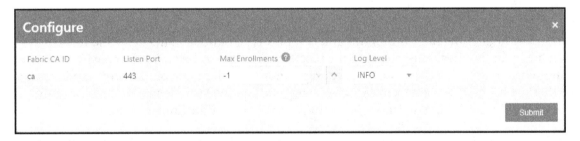

The configuration attributes of the CA node

Let's go over the attributes we can review/change in this dialog window:

- **Fabric CA ID**: This attribute specifies the identifier or name that the OABCS instance assigned to the node when it was created, which can't be modified.
- **Listen Port**: This attribute specifies the listening port assigned to the node, which can't be modified and is specific to your organization.
- **Max Enrollments**: This attribute specifies an attribute to determine how many times the CA server allows a secret password to be used for enrollment on the network. The value should be 5 or less.
- **Log Level**: This attribute specifies the log level that you want to use for the node. During development, you can set it to **DEBUG** or **INFO**, but in production it is best to set it to **ERROR**.

Following are the options you can consider:

- Use **-1** to allow for a password to be used an unlimited number of times for the enrollment of new peer identities and certificates
- Use **0** to disable enrollment of new identities and certificates so that no new registrations are allowed
- Use **1** so that and enrollment ID's can only be used once

More information about the Fabric CA can be found in the documentation at `https://hyperledger-fabric-ca.readthedocs.io/`.

Peer nodes

The peer node is the most important and complex type of node in the network. It reads, endorses, and writes transactions to the blockchain ledger. A network can consist of one or more peer nodes. We can change the configuration of a peer node on the same **Nodes** page. Filter the list on type – for example, Peer – and click on the **options** menu at the right side of one of the entries in the list. In the options menu, select **Edit Configuration**.

This action will display a dialog window in which we can review and change the node's configuration. For this peer node, we can configure a lot of advanced attributes in four different categories: Gossip, Leader Election, Event Service, and Chaincode, and it also includes also some general attributes, as shown in the following screenshot:

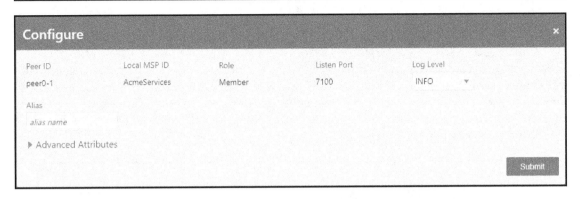

The general attributes of a peer node

Let's go over the general attributes we can review/change in this dialog window:

- **Peer ID**: This attribute specifies the identifier or name that the OABCS instance assigned to the node when it was created, which can't be modified.
- **Local MSP ID**: This attribute specifies the assigned MSP ID for the member organization – in this case, `AcmeServices` – which can't be modified.
- **Role**: This attribute specifies the peer's role, which can be **Member** or **Admin**. In most cases, this displays the value **Member**. The role is used by the chaincode's endorsement policy, which specifies the MSP that must validate the identity and role of the signer peer. The admin role is assigned to protect sensitive operations further and to make sure that those operations are endorsed by specific peers. However, this is not supported in OABCS at the time of writing, and the role can't be changed.
- **Listen Port**: This attribute specifies the listening port assigned to the node, which can't be modified and is specific to your organization.
- **Log Level**: This attribute specifies the log level that you want to use for the node. During development, you can set it to **DEBUG** or **INFO**, but in production, is best to set it to **ERROR**.
- **Alias**: This attribute lets you specify an alias for the node to make it easier to identify.

Gossip attributes

By collapsing the **Advanced Attributes** section of this dialog window and selecting the **Gossip** tab, we can control the behavior of the gossip protocol used to propagate messages between peers. Normally, you would not change this without knowing what you are doing, so to give you an idea what the impact is of changing one of these configuration properties, I'll briefly explain the most important ones in the following subsections. The following screenshot shows all gossip-related attributes:

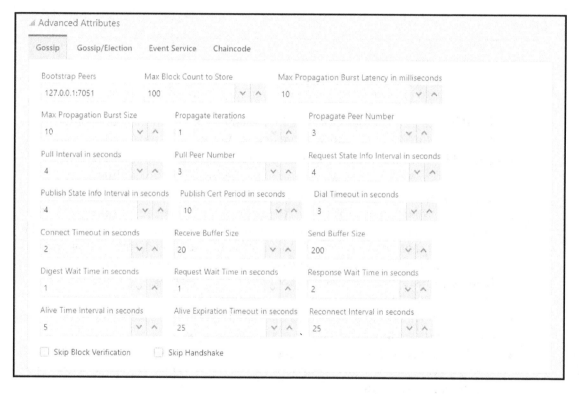

The gossip attributes of the peer node

Let's go over the most important gossip attributes we can change in this tab:

- **Bootstrap Peers**: This attribute specifies the service endpoint (address and port) that the peer uses to contact other peers during startup. Each peer in the same organization must match the same endpoint.
- **Max Block Count to Store**: This attribute specifies the maximum number of blocks to store in memory. The default value is 100, but it can be tweaked to save memory.

- **Max Propagation Burst Latency**: This attribute specifies the number of milliseconds between message pushes among peers. (The default is 10.)

- **Request State Info interval** and **Publish State Info interval**: These attributes specify how often (in seconds) to pull or send state information messages from or to the peers.

- **ReceiveBuffer Size** and **Send Buffer Size**: These attributes specify the size of the buffer for received messages and sent messages; that is, the number of messages to buffer.

- **Alive Time interval**: This attribute specifies the number of seconds between checks whether peers are still alive by sending alive messages. (The default is 5.)

Of course, there are more attributes, most of which control different kinds of timeouts. For the full list, check the Oracle documentation at `https://docs.oracle.com/en/cloud/paas/blockchain-cloud/user/peer-node-attributes.html`.

Election attributes

By selecting the **Gossip/Election** tab, we can control the behavior of the leader election. A leader peer receives blocks and distributes them to the other peers within its cluster.

The following screenshot shows all of the election-related attributes:

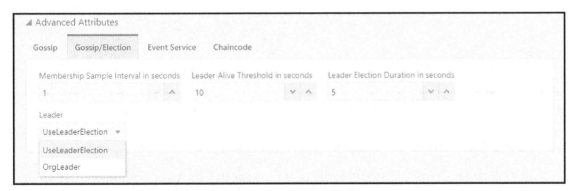

The gossip/election attributes of the peer node

Let's go over the election attributes that we can change on this tab:

- **Membership Sample Interval**: This attribute specifies the number of seconds between each time the peer checks its stability on the network.

- **Leader Alive Threshold**: This attribute specifies the number of seconds to elapse for other peers in the cluster to declare they are alive, before the peer determines its next leader election.
- **Leader Election Duration**: This attribute specifies the number of seconds to elapse after the peer sends the proposed message and declares itself leader.
- **Leader**: This attribute specifies the mode to use to determine a leader. Select **OrgLeader** to use the static leader and make the peer the organization leader, or select **UseLeaderElection** to use a dynamic leader election and let every peer choose a new leader randomly.

More information about leader election can be found in the Fabric documentation at `https://hyperledger-fabric.readthedocs.io/en/latest/gossip.html#leader-election`.

Event service attributes

By selecting the **Event Service** tab, we can control the behavior of events. The event service allows external applications to listen to events using web sockets. The service runs on its own port to which applications can connect. The following screenshot shows the event service-related attributes:

The event service attributes of the peer node

Let's go over the event attributes that we can review/change on this tab:

- **Port**: This attribute specifies the port number to which applications can listen in order to receive events. This port is assigned by OABCS and can't be modified.
- **Buffer Size**: This attribute specifies the maximum number of events that the buffer of the peer can contain. If the number of events generated is larger than the buffer size, then the system won't send these events.
- **Timeout**: This attribute specifies the maximum time (in milliseconds) allowed for the business network to send an event. This means that the event payload needs to be small, else it will be rejected.

More information about the Fabric's peer-channel event services can be found at `https://hyperledger-fabric.readthedocs.io/en/latest/peer_event_services.html`.

Chaincode attributes

By selecting the last tab, **Chaincode**, we can control the behavior of deployed smart contracts (chaincodes). We can, for example, control the startup and execution timeout of containers. The following screenshot shows the chaincode-related attributes:

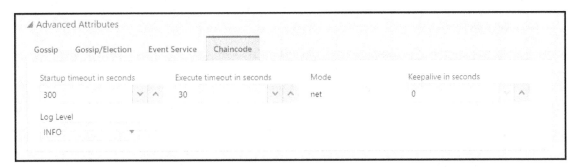

The chaincode attributes of the peer node

Let's go over the chaincode attributes that we can review/change on this tab:

- **Startup timeout in seconds**: This attribute specifies the maximum time to wait (in seconds) between the start of a chaincode container and the registry checking to see whether it's alive.
- **Execute timeout in seconds**: This attribute specifies the maximum time to attempt (in seconds) the execution of a chaincode before timing out.
- **Mode**: This attribute specifies the system that runs the chaincode. Currently, this attribute always has the value **net**.
- **Keepalive in seconds**: This attribute specifies the maximum amount of time (in seconds) to keep the connections between a peer and the chaincode alive. This is useful when you use a proxy to communicate over the network.

Monitoring your blockchain network

In the previous chapter, we intensively tested our smart contract and reviewed how we can monitor transactions, so we won't go over this again. However, there are some small details left to discuss.

In this section and its subsection, we will look at the ways in which we can monitor the state of the network and its infrastructure, from both within and outside the console, and explore how external application of CI tooling can interact with the blockchain network.

Checking the log files of nodes

You can easily check the current log for the health of a peer and chaincode executions. Let's demonstrate this with one of the peers of Acme services. Imagine that we have just invoked some chaincode and made some errors along the way while invoking the available chaincode functions.

First, navigate to one of the peers that you want to inspect; for example, **peer0-1**. We can navigate to that peer node via the **Nodes** page. From there, we can directly monitor its health, as this is provided by default. The following screenshot shows the current health of the peer node and the user transaction it endorsed:

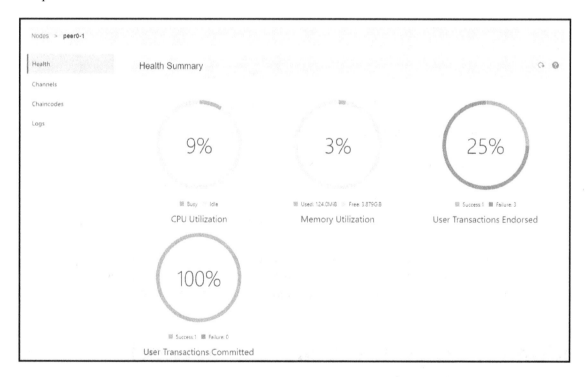

The current health of peer node 0-1

From the page we saw in the previous chapter, we can examine the channels that it has joined and also the chaincodes that are installed on the peer node. In this case, however, we are interested in the **Logs** page. On this page, seen as follows, we can view and download the available log files:

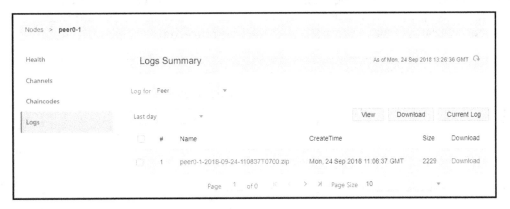

View and download log files stored for peer node

To view a specific log file, you need to click on the name of the ZIP file, or check the box in front of the entry, and click on the **View** button. In both cases, a dialog window pops up and shows the contents of the log file. To view the current log file quickly, you can click on the **Current Log** button, as seen in the following screenshot:

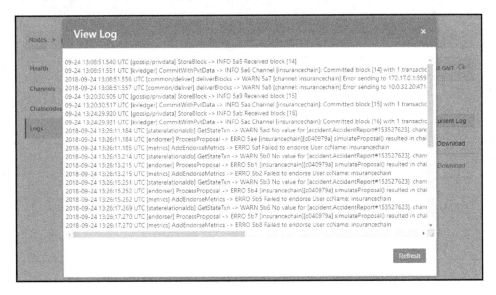

Contents of the current log file of a peer

To refresh the log files, just click on **Refresh**. To close the dialog, click the close button (**x**) in the top-right corner. On the page itself, you can switch between the log files for the Peer or the log files of the installed Chaincode.

When switching to the Chaincode logs, the UI changes a bit, as you need to choose the chaincode and the version of which you want to retrieve the logs. In the following screenshot, we can see the logs for **V2.31** of the **insurancechain** chaincode:

Switching to Chaincode view to see logs containing the execution logs

Again, from here you can view and download archived logs or view the current log. The log shows all invocations of the chaincode and the log messages produced by the chaincode itself. The following screenshot shows the contents of one of the archived chaincode logs:

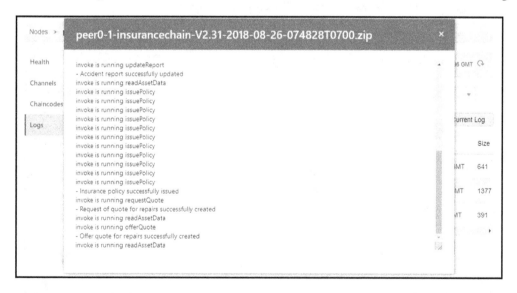

Contents of archived insurancechain v2.31 chaincode log file

For the sake of our examples, this log visualization works, but in a real, much more complex environment, it would be insufficient and it's better to turn to a log aggregation tool, such as *Splunk* and Elastic's *Elasticsearch* and *LogStash*.

Logs are archived if the peer is idle for a period of time, or if the log buffer reaches a certain size, so you can have multiple files per day. Unfortunately, at the time of writing, there is no API to download the log files or a solution to integrate them with some type of log agent to collect them.

Things we can/can't monitor from the platform's perspective

As you learned in the previous chapter, we can monitor a lot within the management console of the platform. For most of the components, there are one of more views to see its health and usage. The following list shows what components we can monitor from the platform's perspective:

- **Dashboard**: Shows a summary of the number of channels, peers, orderers, chaincodes, and participating organizations
- **Dashboard**: Shows the overall health and utilization of nodes and channel and peer node activity
- **Network page**: Includes a diagram showing the relationships between organizations and nodes
- **Channel details page**: Includes the transactions committed to the ledger per block, which can be inspected individually
- **Channel details page**: Shows the instantiated chaincodes, joined organizations, and peers on the channel
- **Chaincode details page**: Shows a summary of the installed version and peer version the peers and channels on which they are installed and instantiated so that they can be inspected
- **Nodes page**: Shows a summary of the different types of nodes that are part of the network and a diagram showing the relationships between peers and channels
- **Node details page**: Includes the CPU and memory utilization of a specific node, and you can inspect its logs
- **Peer node details page**: Besides CPU and memory utilization, also includes the endorsed and committed user transactions
- **REST proxy details page**: Includes transaction metrics per user that invoked the available REST APIs

The following screenshot shows the details page of a REST proxy node:

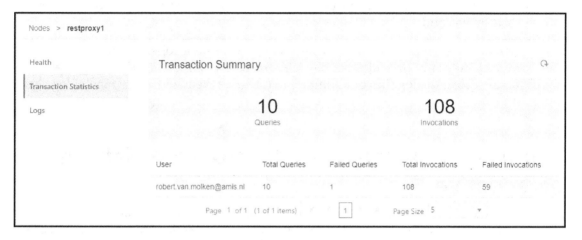

Summary of transaction invoked on one of the REST proxies

So, what can't we monitor from the platform's perspective (at the time of writing)? Initially, not much, in my opinion; but that when you look at what the Hyperledger Fabric SDK supports (discussed in more detail in following section) – here are a couple of details:

- The platform does not/can't listen to custom events or events (block and transaction) in general. Both in the management console and in the logs, events are not traceable and you can't monitor to see whether events are published by a chaincode.
- Searching on a transaction by its ID, or a specific block by its ID or by its hash in the UI. Search capabilities of the ledger data are missing in general.

Integrating applications using Fabric SDK

As OABCS uses Hyperledger Fabric at its core, we can also interact with all the nodes using the Fabric SDK. So, in this final section of the chapter, we will explore the capabilities of the SDK to enable you to interact with the ledger and the available metrics, and to integrate this functionality into your existing CI/monitoring tools. I won't go into much detail, as this would deserve a separate chapter in and of itself, and it is out of scope for this book. Nonetheless, I will point you in the right direction to explore this yourself.

Oracle allows you to use the Fabric SDK to interact directly with the blockchain ledger without using the REST proxy. The REST proxy only exposes user-installed chaincodes and no system chaincodes. With the SDK, you can interact with the blockchain network on behalf of users. For example, you can do the following:

- Create a new channel
- Install a chaincode on a peer and instantiate it on the channel
- Submit transactions and query the latest application state
- Use various query capabilities to retrieve block and transaction data
- Monitor events (block, transactions, and custom events)
- Register and enroll a new user

The SDK is available in three flavors: Node.js, Go, and Java. I myself prefer the Node.js SDK as it is one of the is best documented among these, and it can be found at `https://fabric-sdk-node.github.io/`. Furthermore, it integrates easily with web applications, the learning curve is less steep, and there are a lot of examples on the web.

Security is enforced with digital signatures, and all requests made to Fabric must be signed by users with the appropriate certificates. The only catch here is that to communicate with OABCS, you can't use the Fabric Node.js and Java SDKs available on GitHub out of the box—the SDK needs to be rebuilt to connect successfully to the OABCS orderers and peers, as there is an incompatibility between an OCI infrastructure component and the SDKs provided with Fabric.

You can download the instructions for all SDKs from the **Developer Tools** page of your OABCS instance, as shown in the following screenshot:

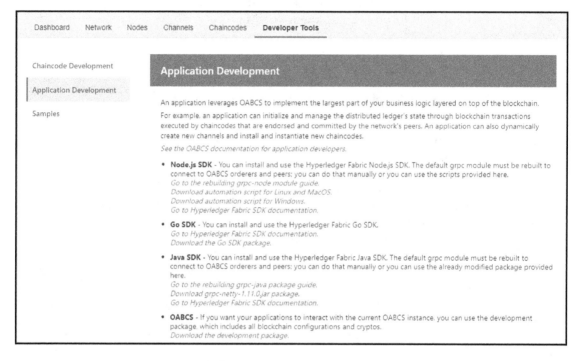

Developer tools tab available on your OABCS instance

In general, for each of the SDKs, there are two methods of updating the Hyperledger Fabric SDK to work with OABCS:

- Using the automated Oracle scripts to download and install the SDK, which patch the code as it installs
- Manually, by changing the gRPC security code and rebuilding the module

For the Fabric Java SDK, there is an updated `grpc-netty-1.xx.0.jar` file that you can download, which is referenced by the Java SDK. This file needs to be put in the classpath, whereas for the Node.js SDK, you can download the `npm_bcs_client.sh` script to replace the standard `npm install` operations that you would perform to download and install the Node.js Fabric client package. Let's look at commands in this shell script to see what is actually patched.

In the `main` function, we can see the following operations being executed:

```sh
#!/bin/sh
WORK_DIR="${PWD}"
NPM_GLOBAL=0
NPM_PACKAGE=fabric-client
NPM_PACKAGE_VER=@1.1.2
NPM_ROOT_DIR=""

main() {
  ...
  if [ "$NPM_GLOBAL" -eq 1 ]; then
    BASE_DIR="${NPM_ROOT_DIR}""/$NPM_PACKAGE/node_modules/grpc"
    declare -r npm_option="--global --ignore-scripts"
  else
    BASE_DIR="./node_modules/grpc"
    declare -r npm_option="--ignore-scripts"
  fi

  npm install "${npm_option}" $NPM_PACKAGE$NPM_PACKAGE_VER
  edit_code
  rebuild_code

  cd "${WORK_DIR}"
  npm install
}
```

The code in the `main` function checks to see whether the user wants to install the module as global or only local to the working folder and sets the correct `BASE_DIR`, . More importantly, however, it declares the right `npm_option` to ignore compilation scripts of the gRPC module. It then installs the unpatched code of `fabric-client`.

After the preliminary installation, it calls the `edit_code` function, which calls the `edit_fabric_client` function, as shown in the following code block:

```
edit_fabric_client()
  {
    declare -r
file="${BASE_DIR}""/deps/grpc/src/core/lib/security/security_connector/secu
rity_connector.cc"

    sed -i".orig" "s/if (p == nullptr) {/if (false) {/; s/if
(\!grpc_chttp2_is_alpn_version_supported(p->value.data, p->value.length))
{/if (p \!= nullptr \&\&
\!grpc_chttp2_is_alpn_version_supported(p->value.data, p->value.length))
{/" "${file}"
  }

  edit_code() {
```

```
    if [ "$NPM_PACKAGE" = "fabric-client" ]; then
      edit_fabric_client
    fi
  }
```

The `edit_fabric_client` function alters `ssl_check_peer` and updates the code to add APLN support. The reason why this is needed is because Oracle's OCI uses HTTP/2 over TLS and this mandates the use of ALPN to negotiate the use of the h2 protocol by the `gRPC` module. After finishing this function, the code in the `main` function continues and rebuilds the code using the `rebuilt_code` function:

```
rebuild_code() {
    if [ "$NPM_GLOBAL" -eq 1 ]; then
      cd "${NPM_ROOT_DIR}""/""${NPM_PACKAGE}"
    fi

    npm rebuild --unsafe-perm --build-from-source
  }
```

This function rebuilds the code from the patched source code. The main function then continues and installs the `fabric-client` SDK as normal. After a successful installation, you can start programming with the Fabric Node.js SDK.

More information about the manual patching of the SDKs and the development of applications using the SDKs can be found in Oracle's documentation at `https://docs.oracle.com/en/cloud/paas/blockchain-cloud/user/developing-applications-using-hyperledger-fabric-sdks.html`.

Summary

In this final implementation chapter, we learned how to extend, configure, and monitor our blockchain network. First, we extended our blockchain network by joining an existing Hyperledger Fabric organization, USA Automotive Services. In the process, as an existing Fabric participant, we wrote an OABCS certificates file and included the contents of the MSP certificates (`admin`, `ca`, and `tlsca`). Next, as the OABCS founder, we imported this certificates file into the network and added the new organization to the insurancechain channel. Finally, we connected the Fabric organization to the ordering service of the OABCS network and joined the insurancechain channel.

In the second part of the chapter, we looked at how to configure our blockchain network and its capabilities in order to optimize different kinds of nodes in the network. For each type, we reviewed the attributes and looked at those that we could modify in the future.

In the third part of the chapter, we looked at how to monitor our blockchain network. We explored the various log files of one of the peers, and I explained how you can let applications interact with the blockchain ledger using the Fabric SDKs.

In the next chapter, which starts of, *Part IV, Real-World Industry Case Studies,* we will look at the impact of blockchain in the financial services sector and explore some real-world use cases in this industry.

Part IV

Real World Industry Case Studies

15
Blockchain Across the Financial Services Industry

The previous chapter concluded Part III of this book, *Implementing a Permissioned Blockchain*, which used the knowledge you gained in Part II, *Blockchain Core Concepts and Terminology*, to review a recognizable use case and implement it using the Oracle Blockchain Cloud Service. We created our own permissioned blockchain and developed our first smart contracts, also known as chaincode. This chapter begins Part IV of this book, *Real World Industry Case Studies*, which will examine three different industries and their approach toward implementing blockchain in day-to-day (critical) applications. The first industry that I will cover is financial services, followed by transportation, and then finally healthcare.

In this chapter, we are going to focus on financial markets and services and how blockchain is impacting, or going to impact, this sector. We will examine the reasons why blockchain is a viable technology to use in this sector, and which companies are already rolling out new platforms based on this technology. We will go over some real-world use/study cases and highlight some interesting projects that use blockchain behind the Oracle Blockchain Cloud Service.

In this chapter, you will learn about the following topics:

- What impact does blockchain have on financial services?
- Why is blockchain a viable technology for this industry?
- Real-world use case: Cryptocurrencies ATM and Payment Gateway
- Real-world use case: **MonetaGo**—Secure, fraud-proof factoring of invoices

Impact on financial services

We have already seen how blockchain is disrupting financial markets through the rise of thousands of cryptocurrencies. (As of September 2018, more than 1,910 currencies are registered with `coinmarketcap.com`). The top 100 cryptocurrencies together have a market cap of $70 million or more. This list is led by Bitcoin, with a market cap of $127 billion and rising. Only a handful of currencies can be used online or even in some retail stores, and most only hold a virtual value based on supply and demand, which can be influenced by many factors. Millions of people already own one or more cryptocurrencies, and as the adoption of cryptocurrencies increases, there will come a time when you can actually buy something with it.

The growth of cryptocurrencies has already had an impact on the country of Venezuela, as it became one of the biggest crypto markets in the world due to the hyperinflation of its national currency, the Venezuelan bolivar. The bolivar's value had depreciated rapidly since 2014, so Venezuelans needed to fill the void and started exchanging their money for bitcoins (`https://cointelegraph.com/news/how-venezuela-came-to-be-one-of-the-biggest-markets-for-crypto-in-the-world`). The government even developed and issued their own cryptocurrency, the **petro**, in February 2018, which initially was tied to the cost of one barrel of oil. Luckily, as of April 2018, it no longer serves as a currency (`https://www.aljazeera.com/news/2018/02/venezuela-petro-cryptocurrency-180219065112440.html`), as its primary goal seemed to be to exploit loopholes in international regulations and sanctions toward the dictatorship, and it is widely seen as a major fiasco.

The impact of blockchain on the financial services versus financial markets

In my opinion, we will see significant differences in the financial sector over the next three to five years. Fundamentally, this industry is facilitating the trusted exchange of value between untrusted parties. These financial services companies bear the enormous responsibility of brokering trust, as we saw in Chapter 9, *Building a Next-Generation Oracle B2B Platform*, and they carry a significant risk, which is the reason why this industry is reliant on costly intermediaries, error-prone reconciliations, and even manual processes. Financial institutions are looking to blockchain to enable more efficient ways to do cross-organizational collaboration by eliminating intermediaries (for example, insurance brokers such as Acme Services).

Blockchain is a viable technology for this industry, as it addresses multi-party business processes and value exchange without complex EDI transactions and shared data schemes that each party needs to implement themselves. The core technology provides a secure distribution of the shared ledger as a replacement of traditional EDI messaging. Smart contracts, on the other hand, act as a shared application / tool to govern changes to the underlying ledger and state database in accordance with the agreed-upon business rules. It allows for more efficient collaboration between organizations, as every participating member of the network holds a record of every transaction that is governed in the same way by the shared smart contract.

In my view, blockchain offers a number of key benefits for financial services, such as cost reduction (fewer errors, cutting out the middleman), improved business outcomes (single point of truth), and reduced responsibility and risk (no offline reconciliation) to disrupt their business models. To give you an idea of some of the day-to-day operations already being transformed by blockchain technology in this industry, look at the following diagram:

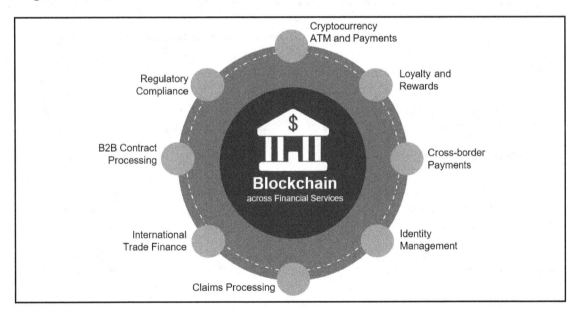

In the following sections, we take a closer look at two of them; international trade finance and cross-border payments.

International trade finance

Blockchain is helping to manage the financial risk of international trade for both the importing and exporting parties. In situations where there is a lack of trust between trading partners, it can guarantee that payments will only take place once the goods are exchanged according to the agreed-upon rules.

Current state and inefficiencies

- A lack of end-to-end transparency in the supply chain.
- Paper data is difficult to verify (error prone, manual labor), which leads to multiple versions of the truth and major fraud, compliance, and audit risks.
- The lengthy processing time between the manufacturing of goods to when payment is received, for example 30–90 days after delivery, ties up the working capital of a business. (Working capital is calculated as current assets, for example, inventories and liquid assets, minus current liabilities, for instance, creditors).
- EDI messages need to be reconciled, and this normally takes place overnight.
- For everybody to understand the information, an international character set, for example, Roman characters, is required. This means that a significant amount of translation takes place at trading points.
- Compliance costs for using trade service providers limit the number of small and medium-sized businesses that can participate in international trade.

As I explained in the use case described in `Chapter 9`, *Building a Next-Generation Oracle B2B Platform*, blockchain is solving most of these problems by streamlining trade finance, enabling real-time tracking and management of assets and documents. It can disintermediate third parties and accelerate settlement by making the exchange of data much easier and enabling direct interaction between import and export banks.

Blockchain can automate, for example, a letter of credit or the creation and management of credit facilities all through the power of smart contracts. Because every transaction is stored on a distributed, shared ledger, it improves end-to-end visibility of the transactions in real-time to enable better regulatory and customs oversight by officials.

Cross-border payments

Blockchain enables the near real-time transfer of funds between the sender and the recipient, thereby avoiding intermediary bank charges. This technology is starting to have a major impact on domestic payments and international monetary transfers. In my view, it is crucial that everyone understands some of the implications of this capability.

Current state and inefficiencies

- The system of international payments is a slow, closed, and compartmentalized system, similar to the systems of communication (email) in the 1980s. You can only send transactions (or messages) to users of the same (messaging) system.
- Cross-border transfers involve a number of banks and most likely a number of currencies before the money can be collected by the recipient, significantly increasing the amount of cross-checking of data at each stop and resulting in longer transaction processing times, increased unit costs, and a higher risk of error.
- Payments generally take more than a day and are only processed during the business hours of the banking agencies involved. Third-party intermediaries, such as Western Union, are faster, but very expensive.

As you have learned in reading this book, blockchain technology can cut out the traditional middleman, speeding up and simplifying the process. Moving toward near real-time transaction settlement will increase liquidity, operational costs, and overhead as well as profitability.

The following diagram illustrates a traditional cross-border payment process:

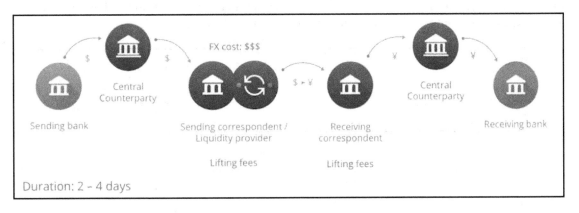

Traditional cross-border payments can take 2–4 days (Image courtesy of Ripple)

We now see the birth of new payment models, such as micropayment via the Lightning Network (`https://lightning.network/`) or the IOTA network (`https://www.iota.org/`), offering instant transactions and large scalability, forcing companies such as Western Union and SWIFT to change their business model, or else they may become obsolete.

Another big company in this area is **Ripple** (`https://ripple.com/`). Besides having its own cryptocurrency, Ripple offers an internet protocol whose purpose is to facilitate the supply of funds among its members. The protocol is called **RTXP** (**Ripple Transaction Protocol**), and it defines a set of rules to perform transactions on the internet instantly and free of charge. Members can conduct transactions, as shown in the following diagram, in any currency, cryptocurrency, raw material (such as gold and silver), or any other unit of value:

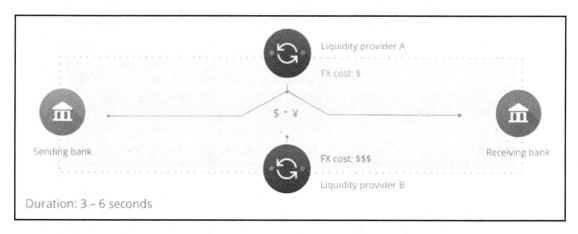

Transactions via RippleNet take 3-6 seconds to be processed (Diagram courtesy of Ripple)

The **RippleNet** blockchain connects banks, payment providers, digital assets, and corporations in order to provide cross-border payments to their customers. The following image illustrates some of the members of RippleNet, including American Express:

Some of the members of RippleNet

Use case – ATM and payment gateway

As promised, let's look at some real-world use cases of blockchain. In this section, we will look at the fastest growing cryptocurrency ATM by **General Bytes**, and also, at **PayIOTA**, a payment gateway that helps merchants accept IOTA (micro) payments.

Cryptocurrency ATM

In 2014, the company **General Bytes**, headquartered in Czechia, started selling its first Bitcoin ATM. It was the first Bitcoin/crypto machines company to incorporate **NFC** (**near field communication**) into their hardware to allow for contactless interaction. At the time of writing, there are around 1,900 machines sold to more than 53 countries, supporting dozens of cryptocurrencies. General Bytes is not the only Crypto ATM company, as **Coin ATM Radar** (https://coinatmradar.com/) reports that they have more than 3,700 crypto ATMs deployed all over the world. Even in a small country such as the Netherlands, there is already a crypto ATM available at 23 locations.

General Bytes offer two machines, the **BATMTwo** and the **BATMThree**, in different configurations. The cost of these machines ranges from as low as $3,000 up to $9,500 USD for the largest / top-of-the-line model. The BATMTwo is only unidirectional, which means that you can only buy cryptocurrency with the machine but not sell it. To buy and sell cryptocurrency with/for fiat currencies, you need the **BATMThreeM+** version or higher, as shown in the following image.

The General Bytes BATMThree cryptocurrency ATM

The machine features bi-directional transactions. This means that the ATM can convert cash into over 30 different cryptocurrencies, but it can also convert cryptocurrencies into cold hard cash. The cryptocurrencies supported include BTC (Bitcoin), BCH (Bitcoin Cash), ETH (Ethereum), LTC (Litecoin), DASH, XMR (Monero), and DOGE (Dogecoin). The machine has NFC card support for contactless payment capabilities. The ATM can issue you an NFC card containing the Bitcoin private key. You can use this card later as a Bitcoin wallet to receive and send Bitcoins by placing the card on an NFC reader.

For more information about this cryptocurrency ATM, check their website at `https://www.generalbytes.com/batmthree/`.

PayIOTA – Payment gateway

Earlier in this book, I introduced IOTA and its Tangle consensus algorithm. Because of the way the network proves transactions (using a directed acyclic graph protocol), it allows for fee-less micropayments.

> *In order to participate in this network, a participant simply needs to perform a small amount of computational work that verifies two previous transactions.*

Once the IOTA network was operational, a collection of supporters around the world helped build **PayIOTA** to unlock fee-less transactions. PayIOTA (`https://payiota.me/`) is a payment gateway that helps web merchants accept IOTA payments easily on their websites with no additional fees. Currently, all payment providers ask for a fee with every transaction. These fees are paid by the web merchant, or the customer is changed for the transaction. PayIOTA is currently available as a Woocommerce plugin for WordPress, as shown in the following screenshot, and for a few more e-commerce platforms:

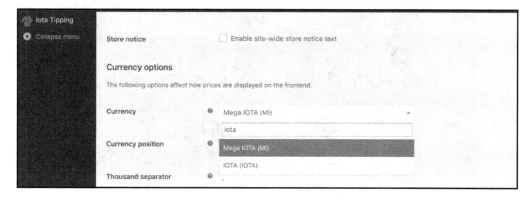

Configuration of the PayIOTA Woocommerce plugin for WordPress

Use case – MonetaGo – bill discounting

Throughout this book, you learned a lot about Hyperledger Fabric and the Blockchain Cloud Service of Oracle. So, it would be great to discuss the first blockchain production network using Fabric. In April 2018, a company called **MonetaGo** (`https://monetago.com/`) went live with a blockchain that provided secure, fraud-proof factoring of invoices for micro, small, and medium-sized enterprises in India.

You might ask, "What does factoring mean?" Let me explain this term.

Invoice factoring is a financial transaction and a type of financing option available to businesses that invoice business (B2B) or government agencies. Factoring provides short-term working capital to businesses in exchange for selling their accounts receivable (invoices) and assigning those invoices to a third party, called a factor. In return for a discount, the factor advances the business roughly 80% of the invoice's value. Once the invoice is paid, the factor pays the remaining 20% minus the discounts/fees. Businesses can use these services if their cash flow is insufficient, but they still have a large number of unpaid invoices that need to be paid by other partners.

MonetaGo implemented the use of a blockchain that joins three existing platforms that offer **Trade Receivables Discounting Systems** (**TReDS**) in India. All three platforms still work independently, but they are interlinked using the Hyperledger Fabric blockchain and they share data. The following diagram shows the idea behind MonetaGo:

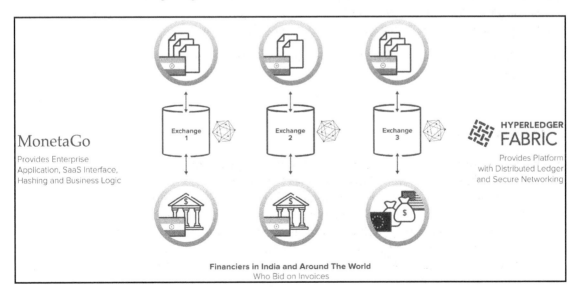

MonetaGO provides a platform of real-time exchanges for the secure, fraud-proof factoring of invoices

The reason for building this platform, explains Jesse Chenard, chief executive officer and founder of MonetaGo, is that many small business owners like to sell their open invoices at a discount to a factor so that they don't have to worry about collecting on them. This can be a quick way for a business to get back some working capital. Many firms are still very small in India – too small for banks to bother with, as they could earn more processing invoices from larger enterprises. Doing so puts extra strain on developing economies such as India, where most businesses are small.

Reportedly, the factoring of invoices in India delivers $219 billion to micro, small, and medium-sized enterprises, which leaves another $188 billion of invoices that no one else wants. The Reserve Bank of India stepped in and licensed three exchange organizations to provide an online marketplace for factoring, known as the TReDS. Through these exchanges, financiers bid on sets of invoices with lower risk, while sellers benefit from better prices and faster payments. The risk with three active exchanges is that buyers and sellers could register on all three platforms, raising the chances of the same bill getting discounted twice. This will not happen once blockchain is implemented, as invoices are shared between exchanges.

MonetaGo used Hyperledger Fabric for all of the basic functions of the network – the ordering system, certificate authority, and blockchain. On top of that, it created a smart contract with the required business logic, applications, interfaces, and security. The interfaces include an API for large exchanges to integrate directly into on-premises systems and a SaaS adapter for smaller participants to use over the web. Exchanges only pay a transaction fee on a pay-as-you-go plan with no up-front costs, so there is no need for any cryptocurrency as the API management layer manages the fees.

Read more about this use case on the Hyperledger Fabric project page at `https://www.hyperledger.org/resources/publications/monetago-case-study`.

Summary

In this first of three industry-specific chapters, we explored the impact and real-world use cases of blockchain in the financial services sector. I started the chapter by explaining the impact that can already be seen on financial markets and services, and why blockchain is a viable technology for the financial services industry, as it addresses multi-party business processes and value exchange without complex transactions and shared data schemes. I then went over some of the key benefits for the financial services sector and how blockchain is already disrupting day-to-day operations in international trade finance and cross-border payments.

Next, we explored two (technically three) real-world use cases of blockchain in the financial services industry. The first use case told the story of the BATM machine, which allows you to buy and sell cryptocurrencies with a fiat currency, and a payment gateway for web merchants to utilize IOTA for micropayments.

The second use case told the story of MonetaGo, a blockchain built with Hyperledger Fabric that connects three TReDS in India for factoring invoices. The blockchain prevents fraud, as exchanges are informed about all the invoices received. When more than one exchange receives the same invoice, they can detect this on the blockchain and indicate it as fraudulent.

In `Chapter 16`, *Blockchain Across the Transportation Industry*, we will again look at the impact that blockchain has already had on the transportation industry and explore some more examples and real-world use cases.

16
Blockchain Across the Transportation Industry

In the previous chapter, we reviewed the impact of blockchain across the financial services industry and how it is already affecting day-to-day operations. In this and the next few chapters, we will follow a similar outline. Presently, we are going to focus on the transportation (and logistics) industry and how blockchain is already impacting or going to impact this industry, why blockchain is an even more viable technology to use in this sector than in financial services, and which platforms and alliances are already being developed/formed. We will also go over some real-world use/study cases.

The following diagram shows some of the use cases in the transportation industry:

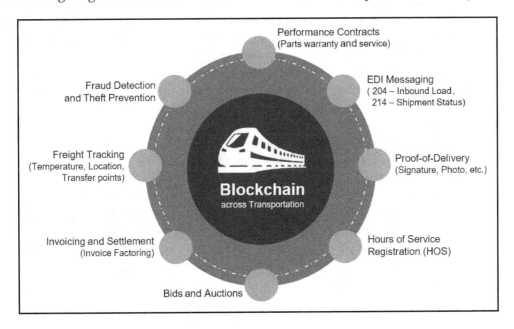

Eight everyday use cases of blockchain in the transportation and logistics industry

In this chapter, you will learn about the following topics:

- What is the impact of blockchain on the transportation sector?
- Why is blockchain a viable technology for this industry?
- Real world use case: **SkyCell**—refrigerated air freight
- Real world use case: **TradeLens**—Maersk shipping solution
- Real world use case: **BiTA**—transport alliance

Impact on transportation and logistics

Just like the financial services industry, the transportation and logistics industry uses a combination of paper and electronic (EDI) messages in day-to-day operations. As a result, the industry has been plagued by issues involving dispute resolution, administrative inefficiencies, and order tracking for decades. Let's explore some of these issues:

- Every day, there are billions of dollars (`https://www.fleetowner.com/ electronic-security/blockchain-trucking-what-about-middlemen`) tied up in disputes over payments. On average, a company has to wait 42 days before receiving payment on an outstanding invoice.
- Processing and administration costs have risen to around one-fifth of the overall costs of the transportation industry, due to the fact that companies rely on paper transactions (`http://www.dcvelocity.com/articles/20160116-maersk-ibm-launch-first-blockchain-joint-venture-for-trade-transportation/`).
- Sensitive shipments (for example, pharmaceutical or medical) experience temperature deviations, which leads to products never making it past customs, due to them exceeding the acceptable temperature ranges, making them unusable.
- Most logistics/trucking companies have small fleets (six trucks or less). So for large loads, the industry struggles to match the demand (shippers) with the supply (carriers) (`https://techcrunch.com/2018/03/02/blockchain-will-work-in-trucking-but-only-if-these-three-things-happen/`).
- In the U.S., the average number of cargo thefts is 54 incidents a month. In 2017, there were 649 reported cargo theft incidents. One of the most common approaches to stealing cargo is the use of counterfeit documents to collect packages (`https://portaldagestaoderiscos.com/wp-content/uploads/2018/02/2017_annual_us.pdf`).

The traditional transportation industry is built around centralized points of authority that oversee the movement of shipments and the purchase of vehicle parts or other assets (such as train tracks, railroad switches, light switches, and so on) and their secure delivery. Every step in the process runs through these centralized channels, and thus is subject to misinterpretation, tampering, or event alteration.

Blockchain is a viable technology for this industry, as it enables more efficient and cost-effective business operations. With a blockchain-enabled platform, it becomes easy to share the original shipping/packing documents using a distributed ledger, making physical paperwork largely unnecessary and reducing the counterfeiting of documents, as the originals are stored in a blockchain. A warehouse can, for example, check to see whether the paperwork of the collecting party contains the same information as that which is stored in the ledger.

A simple shipment of a container from one part of the world to another can pass through many different organizations, requiring hundreds of separate communications. Any hiccup could cause the container to be held up or lost. Blockchain technology allows multiple businesses to exchange traditional EDI messages for invoices, shipment status reports, orders, and trailer manifests with each other without the involvement of a centralized organization or middleman. It can even replace these traditional EDI messages using smart contracts, as companies can program the whole data model in code. A smart contract can make approvals and the clearing of customs faster and more efficient.

Another problem that blockchain addresses in this industry is the rising demand for same-day or even one-hour delivery services. Traditional technologies are not able to scale to address this issue. For example, the technology behind blockchain already provides a scalable and immediate solution for the tracking and authentication of diamonds (Everledger, `https://www.everledger.io/`).

Let's look at some of the day-to-day operations already being transformed by blockchain technology in this industry.

Freight/fleet tracking

Blockchain offers a solution for real-time updates on the location of your freight, including trucks and containers. With the rise of same-day and one-hour deliveries, blockchain technology offers a platform that can easily scale as the average number of updates grows over time.

Current state and inefficiencies

- The tracking of in-transit freight or a fleet of trucks is not new. For many decades, organizations have been using technologies such as GPS to track freight-hauling assets.
- In the past, location updates were provided by phone and fax machines. These were later replaced with automated systems using EDI messaging and APIs.
- These automated systems belong to many different companies, so organizations normally won't have end-to-end visibility of the circulated data.
- The more systems that are involved, the bigger the chance of data being misinterpreted, altered, or tampered with, with or without the owner's knowledge.
- 70% of traditional systems can't scale well and have a high probability of choking as the amount of data becomes unwieldy. This causes turmoil in the global supply chain. Trust in the validity of the updates decreases if some of them are lost.

As you have learned throughout the course of the book, with blockchain, the entire network contributes to validating the data that is updated on the ledger, which brings trust to the entire ecosystem of participating members. With the use of smart contracts, the business rules that are programmed into the automated system can be easily migrated. Instead of every system implementing its own rules, a smart contract consolidates and simplifies the rules in one place. The contract and its associated data is then stored in a decentralized manner. All of the existing systems of a participating member connect to a single source of truth which simplifies the integration of data.

Because of the distributed shared ledger, the same information is available to all companies at the same time, giving the original supplier, all carriers, and the recipient end-to-end visibility of the transaction (that is, transfer of goods).

Performance contracts

Blockchain enables businesses, such as the Dutch organization ProRail and the German company Deutsche Bahn, to use subcontractors to perform maintenance on their railway assets, to manage their performance, and to reward them when issues are fixed on schedule. Blockchain technology is changing the way that trust is built between these companies by creating a decentralized audit log of all asset state changes and consumption information.

Current state and inefficiencies

- Subcontractors depend on a central registry of asset information and the status of those assets to execute their work.
- Users of the system are very dependent on the accuracy and timeliness of the information.
- Updating the information in this system is very time-consuming, because of incomplete and incorrect data.
- There are multiple parties that can alter the same source/asset. During such alterations, all others are locked out from working with the asset and it cannot be modified. If the asset is being maintained, it can sometimes remain in a locked state for a long period of time, which can result in conflicts about the correctness of the asset status and information.
- Changes being made to the structure of an asset's information by a subcontractor (for instance, adding a sensor field) takes a long time, as they are managed by the central system owner. In reality, however, the subcontractor has more and better information.
- Audit logs of events on assets are often difficult to retrieve, especially when transferring assets from one subcontractor to another as the contract period ends. Without correct audit logs, it may seem as though an asset is still defective, when in fact the subcontractor has already fixed the issue, resulting in a lower (or no) financial payout.
- Performance contracts cover a certain geographical area and have a duration of four years. After the four years are up, a subcontractor needs to bid for a new four-year contract. If the subcontractor does not win the bid, it needs to transfer all of its working assets to the new subcontractor, resulting in less maintenance (or possibly none) in the last year of the contract of the existing subcontractor, as it is uncertain that it will win the next bid. The new subcontractor is then responsible for repairing the assets when they break down.

By switching to blockchain, organizations (for example, ProRail) can offer a platform on which subcontractors have access to a decentralized ledger with all railway assets, a full audit of all alterations/state changes of each asset, and an overview of the real-time status and consumption information of an asset. This allows subcontractors to make valuable additions and alterations to asset information using smart contracts.

ProRail can track the state changes of an asset and how much time it takes for a subcontractor to fix defects. With the platform, subcontractors are better incentivized when they do a great job, but they can be fined when they don't.

Use case – SkyCell (refrigerated air freight)

Some of the most valuable drugs being produced are temperature-sensitive biopharmaceuticals (for instance, cancer treatment drugs). The **World Health Organization (WHO)** has estimated that two-fifths of vaccines shipped worldwide degrade due to temperature variation during transport. Most temperature deviations occur on airport tarmacs, which affects the quality of biopharmaceutical shipments. Logistics personnel often plan ahead when under time constraints and park pallets on the tarmac next to the aircraft, sometimes hours before departure.

There, they can be exposed to very low temperatures (-40° Celsius/-40° Fahrenheit) or very high temperatures (49° Celsius/120° Fahrenheit).

SkyCell, a tech firm based in Switzerland, created an IoT and blockchain-enabled refrigerated container for air freight, especially for biopharmaceuticals, as this competing in this market is an order of magnitude more expensive than traditional drug factories ($200-500M instead of $20-50M).

> *Biopharmaceuticals are exceptionally sensitive to changes in pH, temperature, and environmental contaminants. Even slight changes can alter the chemistry of the protein under production, rendering it ineffective or even dangerous.*
> (https://www.freightwaves.com/news/blockchain/skycellblockchaincoldchain)

The air freight containers (https://skycell.ch/products.html) shown in the following diagram are built using insulation that is kept cold by a special rechargeable, passive technology, so there is no need for dry ice. Each container is equipped with IoT sensors that monitor temperature, humidity, and geolocation, all connected to a data cloud.

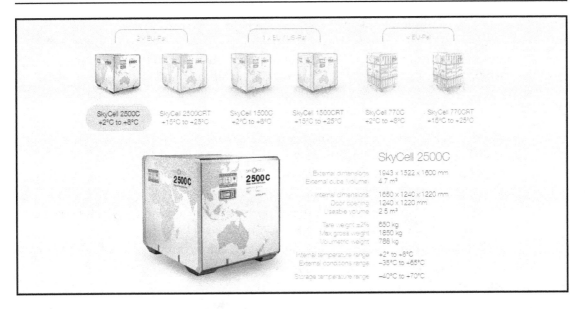

SkyCell's line of air freight containers

SkyCell offers monitoring software (`https://skycell.ch/software.html`) that is based on blockchain technology and an infrastructure of IoT sensors and gateways. The monitoring software records various types of documentation, such as bills of lading and customs forms, for each container on the blockchain ledger in order to provide an acceptable level of supply chain visibility and security. With the SaaS application, you can track your container worldwide. No container is cleared for use unless the software indicates that the container is still in perfect condition before take-off.

For more information about SkyCell's platform, you can read their whitepaper at, `https://smartcontainers.ch/en/assets/20180502_smartcontainers_whitepaper_v2.pdf`.

Use case – TradeLens (shipping solution)

In April 2018, **Maersk**, an integrated container company working to connect and simplify its customers' supply chain, announced that it was going to launch a shipping supply chain platform in conjunction with IBM. This announcement was further advanced in August 2018, when they announced the creation of **TradeLens** (`https://www.tradelens.com/`).

TradeLens, an open and neutral blockchain-enabled shipping solution designed to promote more efficient, predictable, and secure exchange of information across the global supply chain, is the result of a collaboration agreement between Maersk and IBM. It brings together various parties in order to support information sharing and transparency. As part of the early adopter program, 94 organizations are actively involved or have agreed to participate. The TradeLens ecosystem currently includes the following:

- More than 20 ports and terminal operators across the globe, including the ports of Halifax and Rotterdam and terminals in Singapore and Hong Kong
- Customs authorities in the Netherlands, Saudi Arabia, Singapore, and Australia, and customs brokers such as Güler Dinamik
- Beneficial cargo owners (that is, the importer of record, who physically takes possession of the **cargo** at the destination)/non-vessel owning carriers
- Freight forwarders and transportation and logistics companies
- Global container carries, such as Hamburg Süd, Maersk Line, and Pacific International

TradeLens uses the Hyperledger Fabric blockchain technology as the foundation of its digital supply chain. As we have learned previously, it empowers multiple trading partners to collaborate by establishing a single shared view (single source of truth) of all transactions without compromising details, privacy, or confidentiality. One key benefit of TradeLens is that shippers, shipping lines, freight forwarders, port and terminal operators, inland transportation companies, and customs authorities can interact more efficiently through real-time access to shipping data and documents, including IoT and sensor data (for example, temperature control and container weight). Other key benefits of TradeLens are shown in the following diagram:

The key benefits of the TradeLens shipping solution

TradeLens uses smart contracts to enable digital collaboration between the parties involved in international trade. One of the types of smart contracts is called the trade document module, and it enables importers/exporters, customs brokers, and trusted third parties, such as customs, to collaborate in cross-organizational business processes and information exchanges.

Currently, there are 174 million shipping events captured on the platform. Events captured include the arrival times of vessels, the arrival of containers at gates, and documents such as customs releases, invoices, and bills of lading. A video of the TradeLens solution can be seen on YouTube at: `https://youtu.be/thLZacM2z3k`. The platform includes many different parties in the ecosystem, and thus different use cases, as shown in the following diagram:

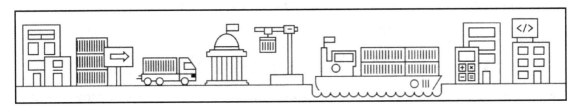

Let's look at the key operations they can perform with the platform:

- **Non-vessel carriers** can eliminate the need to manage much of the information related to their shipments manually. They also get complete, trusted information about shipments to validate fees and surcharges efficiently.
- **Freight forwarders** can improve their competitiveness by reducing costs and increasing their focus on higher-value services (for instance, compliance), and gain easy access to historical and current data in order to plan logistics more effectively.
- **Inland transportation** can speed up pick-up and drop-off processes with real-time information updates for all parties, and they can improve equipment utilization.
- **Customs** can access more complete information earlier and with greater provenance in order to make more informed decisions about inspections and to gain visibility of the entire container shipment lifecycle.
- **Ports and terminals** can reduce the cost of connecting to logistics partners using a standard industry platform. They can also improve their utilization of assets and reduce queues with quicker, more reliable ETAs for all port participants.
- **Ocean carriers** can prevent incorrectly-declared cargo with a clear audit trail and immutable records of source documents, which results in better safety and simplifies compliance with regulatory audits.

- **Financial services** can eliminate discrepancies on insurance policies and letters of credit. They can also reduce the costs associated with sending people across the globe to verify events and information integrity in person, as it can now be done digitally.
- **Developers** can access a single, open platform for application development and integration, and they are able to commercialize their own custom trade applications.

In the weeks after the launch of the early adopter program, criticism arose as some large shipping and logistics companies raised concerns. Some thought that blockchain does not solve the current issues with global trading, and that API connectivity drives value in terms of linking trading partners, carriers, and logistics companies in a real-time manner. A good article about such criticism can be found at: https://goo.gl/g1DX4U.

Use case – BiTA (Transport Alliance)

Most projects discussed up until this point were commercialized by one company (or start-up), which eventually can result in platform silos (without any compatibility with other blockchain-based SaaS application/platform vendors). In my view, most of these projects are making the same mistakes as we witnessed 10 years ago, when every company made custom solutions for each of their customers, instead of designing to industry standards or using standard applications that could be easily customized.

Today, this is something that most prominent leaders in the trucking industry are trying to prevent. In light of that, they have set up a consortium, called the **Blockchain in Transport Alliance** (**BiTA**). Founded in August 2017, the consortium is forging a path toward industry standards for blockchain use within the trucking industry. All companies within BiTA are working together to develop a standard framework, educating the market on blockchain applications and encouraging their use through exemplary implementation. The need for such standards is very real, as explained by Ken Craig from McLeod Software (a BiTA member):

> *Blockchain provides another aspect of interoperability and visibility within the supply chain, much like EDI, application program interfaces, or web services... However, blockchain, without its own truly interoperable standards, will develop into nothing more than a new process that mimics the difficulties surrounding the use of EDI.*

The first set of standards are scheduled to be published in November 2018 at the BiTA Fall Symposium (https://www.freightwaves.com/news/blockchain/bita-announces-timeline-for-standards).

The standards will continue to be developed as more members join the discussion surrounding issues such as chain of custody, freight payments, and asset maintenance.

For more information on BiTA, you can check out their website at: `https://bita.studio` or view their presentation deck at: `https://static1.squarespace.com/static/` `5ad61846e749405faa26ee91/t/5baa4cc9f9619a770c20dde5/1537887436064/BiTA_Deck_` `20180925.pdf.`

Summary

In this second industry-specific chapter, we reviewed the impact and real-world use cases of blockchain across the transportation and logistics sector. We explored the kinds of issues that the transportation industry needs to address and how blockchain can help solve them.

I explained that blockchain is a viable technology for this industry, as it enables more efficient and cost-effective business operations. For example, it is easy to share original shipping/packing documents using the distributed ledger, which reduces the counterfeiting of documents. We then looked at some key benefits for the transportation industry and how blockchain is transforming day-to-day operations by studying two examples: freight tracking and optimizing performance contracts.

Furthermore, we explored three real-world use cases in the transportation and logistics sector. The first use case told the story of SkyCell and its refrigerated air freight container. This container is a combination of an IoT-enabled freight container and a blockchain platform manufactured specifically for transporting biopharmaceuticals, which connects to their standard SaaS application in the cloud for remote monitoring and prevention.

The second use case told the story of TradeLens, a shipping solution from Maersk and IBM designed to improve the global supply chain of ports, freight forwarders, ocean carriers, customers, and many other parties. I explained the solution that TradeLens has developed, and for each of the types of TradeLens users. I reviewed the specific key benefits.

Finally, the third use case was not really a blockchain-enabled solution. Rather, it introduced the BiTA consortium, an organization that is developing standards for the trucking industry regarding the use of blockchain. Thus, instead of building a platform, as Maersk has done, they define open standards that trucking companies can use to implement their own blockchain solutions.

In `Chapter 17`, *Blockchain Across the Healthcare Industry*, we will examine how blockchain is having an impact on, and transforming, the healthcare industry.

17
Blockchain Across the Healthcare Industry

In the previous chapter, we examined the impact of blockchain across the transportation industry and how it is affecting day-to-day operations in the shipping supply chain and the railway and trucking sector. In this chapter, we are going to focus on the healthcare (and pharmaceutical) industry and how blockchain is currently affecting, or going to affect, this industry. Following the same outline as the previous chapters, we explore why blockchain is a viable technology to use in this sector, and which use cases and platforms are already being implemented/developed. We will go over a few of the real-world use/study cases illustrated in the following diagram:

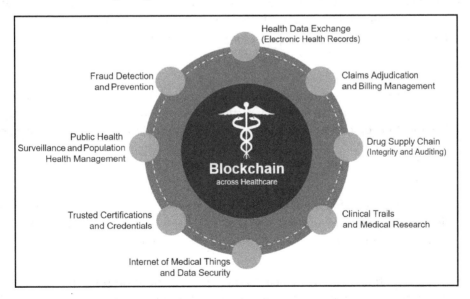

Eight everyday use cases of blockchain in the healthcare and pharmaceutical industry

In this chapter, you will learn about the following topics:

- What impact does blockchain have on the healthcare industry?

- Why is blockchain a viable technology for this industry?

- Real-world use case: **MedicalChain** – electronic health records

- Real-world use case: **Nano Vision** – gathering molecular-level data

Impact on healthcare

Compared with the industries previously discussed, healthcare is the one with the most potential to be disrupted by blockchain. Although it has the most exciting and advanced real-world use cases to enhance its operations, blockchain will not be a cure-all for the entire industry. Let's look at some of the issues associated with the current healthcare system.

- The healthcare industry is drowning in data – clinical trials, medical research, patient medical records, complex billing, sensor data of medical equipment, and more (https://www.forbes.com/sites/bernardmarr/2017/11/29/this-is-why-blockchains-will-transform-healthcare/#233b74e1ebe3).

- Federal rules and regulations are making patient health management processes tedious, lengthy, and often very difficult. As a result in many cases, it's not feasible to keep these processes intact as is and still provide effective patient care (https://hackernoon.com/blockchain-in-healthcare-opportunities-challenges-and-applications-d6b286da6e1f).

- The growing gap between providers and payers is one of the major issues in delivering quality healthcare services. In most cases, dependence on a middleman in the supply chain makes it even worse.

- Critical (patient) medical research data and information remains scattered across different departments and systems. In times of need, crucial data may not be accessible and handily available.

- The number of players in the healthcare system is nearly infinite. Moreover, numerous players do not have a system in place for smooth business process management. This leads to insufficient information exchange.

- The misuse of available data and misleading information is preventing organizations from delivering appropriate patient care and high-quality services.

As noted above, blockchain cannot cure the entire industry's woes, as this requires all parties to come together and overcome collaboration and governance issues. Nevertheless, with blockchain, the industry can move a long way forward. The technology provides the tools to improve patient care quality successfully by enabling better data sharing, data security, and multi-level authentication and fraud prevention.

According to a study by IBM, already around 16% of healthcare executives are said to have plans to implement a blockchain solution in their line of work this year (that is, 2018), whereas another 56% are expected to adopt blockchain by 2020 (https://www.ibm.com/blogs/blockchain/2018/05/blockchain-rx-a-cure-for-healthcare-and-life-sciences/).

Blockchain is a viable technology for the healthcare industry because it can provide a brand new model for **healthcare information exchanges** (**HIE**) by distributing the information more efficiently and making **electronic medical records** (**EMR**) more cryptographically secure. It can support the entire lifecycle of these records, and it eliminates redundant administration, which reduces friction and the costs of current intermediaries associated with health information exchange.

The following diagram illustrates the current healthcare system in the U.S., so you can imagine how difficult it is to share information without it being misinterpreted or lost during transfer:

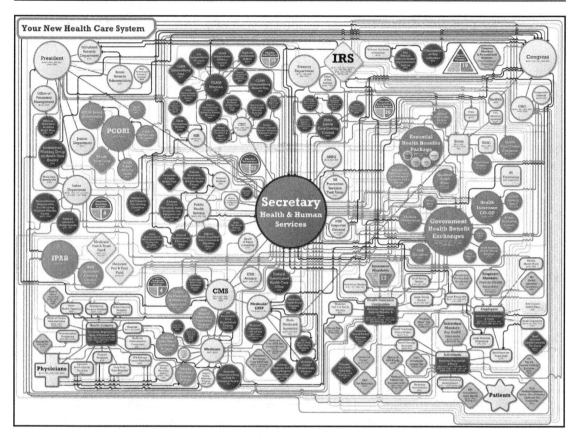

The complexity of the U.S. healthcare system in the absence of using blockchain (https://visual.ly/community/infographic/politics/your-new-health-care-system)

As I explained previously, I see the role of blockchain in the enterprise as the new B2B platform. Certainly for the healthcare industry, this is a major advancement. In many cases, information is sent in the form of EDI messages to parties via B2B brokers and third-party intermediaries. The EDI messages use healthcare standards, such as **Health Level 7 International (HL7)** and **fast healthcare interoperability resources (FHIR),** which are complex, and printing these standards on paper would consume thousands of pages. Every party in the chain needs to implement these standards in their own system, which can lead to human errors and inconsistencies in handling the messages. A good article about HL7 and blockchain can be found at:

https://medium.com/@Connected_Dots/hl7-fhir-multiple-standards-and-formats-one-healthcare-blockchain-f1153f79c1fb.

Connecting these fragmented systems using a blockchain platform and making medical information accessible through smart contracts will give better insights into the data, making it easier to assess the value of care provided to patients without compromising privacy and data security. For example, the HL7 standard can be converted into a smart contract that enables everybody to use the same implementation. The following statistics emphasize the fact that the current healthcare system has to change:

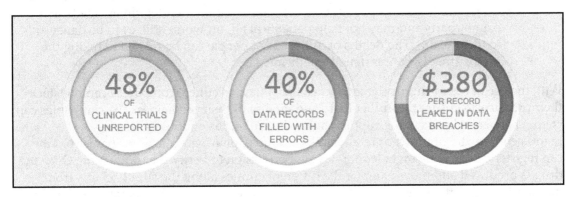

Some of the issues that the healthcare system is facing when sharing data between providers and payers

Is blockchain the right technology / tool for the job? We will have to see, as not every issue in this industry can be fixed with just technology. Nevertheless, we can already see some of the day-to-day operations in this industry being affected by the technology.

Drug traceability and anti-counterfeiting

Blockchain offers a solution for securely logging and timestamping transactions, which can be utilized for drug traceability as it makes it easy to track a product and ensure that its information has not been altered when saved inside one of the blocks. Pharmaceutical companies would then have proof that the drugs manufactured by them are authentic.

Current state and inefficiencies

- Counterfeiting of drugs, along with the manufacturing of fake drugs in the supply chain, constitutes an annual loss of billions of dollars. According to a report by the **Health Research Funding Organization** (**HRFO**), nearly 10–30% of drugs manufactured by developing countries are not original.
- Counterfeited drugs produce different effects than their legitimate medicinal counterparts and may not help patients at all, or, worse still, even be dangerous to their health. The deaths of hundreds of people can be related to taking the wrong (that is, counterfeited) medicine.

With the use of consortium/private blockchains, pharmaceutical companies can register their products to ensure the authenticity and quality of their medicines. The companies can choose between players in the supply chain who will act as endorsers, be they manufacturers, distributors, or retailers. For example, pharmaceutical companies or labs can register drugs, with a wholesaler having permission to verify the transaction. Once the drug is produced and moves among the different entities along the supply chain, from manufacturing all the way to the retailer, every transfer point and its operational data is recorded on the blockchain. Having data transparency firmly rooted in the blockchain makes it extremely easy to track the whole path of the drug back to its origin, helping to eradicate the circulation of counterfeit drugs.

Companies such as **OriginTrail** (`https://origintrail.io/`) and **Block Verify** (`http://www.blockverify.io/`) are working hard to get their platform ready for launch in 2019. Block Verify is specifically aiming at delivering an anti-counterfeiting solution where products are securely labelled with a *Block Verify* tag. This tag is verified all along the supply chain, making it even more transparent. Retail locations can use mobile devices for verification so that they can be assured that the goods they receive are genuine.

Cybersecurity and data security

According to a study from the Ponemon Institute, the healthcare industry faces a number of immediate challenges around cyber and data security. Not all can be met with blockchain technology, as it will do little to counter phishers seeking credentials or the authorization to steal patient data, important financial documents, unsecured mobile devices (BYOD), and medical devices. However, it can fundamentally change the way the industry stores health data and controls access to information.

Check out the study from the Ponemon Institute for information on cybersecurity-related challenges in the healthcare industry: `https://cdn2.esetstatic.com/eset/US/resources/docs/white-papers/State_of_Healthcare_Cybersecurity_Study.pdf`.

Current state and inefficiencies

- Between 2015 and 2016, 48% of healthcare organizations suffered a data breach incident involving the loss or exposure of patient information. The industry reported that 140 million patient records were breached.
- A total of 79 percent of the security threats in the healthcare industry are related to system failures. System downtime and the unavailability of patient information can put patients' lives at risk.
- The majority of healthcare organizations say that legacy systems and new technologies, such as cloud-based data storage and IoT, pose a greater risk to patient information than employee negligence.

Blockchain will transform the day-to-day operations of information security administrators in the coming years, as the technology offers a solution to system downtime. Since blockchain provides a distributed network of nodes, information is no longer stored on a single system and thus it can withstand DDOS attacks. The private nature of a consortium blockchain provides access control only to known users using public-key cryptography and certificates. As such, this addresses a rapidly approaching threat: integrity-based attacks. Blockchain makes it almost impossible for malicious insiders or external actors to modify data without being noticed, for example, by adding or removing drug allergy information, as all changes are tracked.

The smart contracts that can be developed and run on the blockchain network will be the gatekeeper for accessing and modifying data. Using role-based or attribute-based authorizations, the smart contract can permit or deny access to certain information on the blockchain. When you add patients as a part of the blockchain network, they are able to approve or deny any sharing or changes to their data, ensuring a higher level of privacy and greater consumer control.

While current health information exchanges may already be operating this way, and some may already implement highly-available/redundant systems in their architecture, blockchain includes some important differences right out of the box. Of course, the most important one is the validation of changes/transactions. Furthermore, blockchain provides the needed data encryption to secure sensitive information so that it can't be read by unauthorized actors, as every transaction can be encrypted using a patient's public key and may only be unlocked with the patient's private key.

Use case – MedicalChain (health records)

I already briefly mentioned MedicalChain in a previous chapter when illustrating the potential of data sharing using blockchain technology. The reason I'm discussing this project once again is because of the changes that it has undergone, its current impact on the healthcare industry, and because it uses Hyperledger Fabric as its blockchain framework.

MedicalChain is the first healthcare company that started to use blockchain and smart contracts in order to build a decentralized platform that enables secure, transparent, and an auditable exchange and use of medical data. Their blockchain-enabled platform creates a user-focused electronic health record while maintaining a single source of truth / view of the user's data.

MedicalChain enables users to approve conditional access to their personal data for different healthcare professionals, such as doctors, hospitals, and pharmacists, as they deem appropriate. Every interaction with the medical data is recorded on the distributed ledger in an auditable, transparent, and secure way. The platform facilitates the storage and utilization of these records to deliver a new telemedicine experience, and it enables others to build applications that complement and improve on the user experience. As it is built on Hyperledger Fabric, MedicalChain enables varying access levers so that users control who can view their records, how much they can see, and for how long they can view them. Before looking at the platform in depth, let's review what it is trying to solve.

Check out the white paper by MedicalChain for information on current healthcare system inefficiencies: https://medicalchain.com/Medicalchain-Whitepaper-EN.pdf.

Current state and inefficiencies of health records

- Legacy systems are very slow and a burden to work with for some professionals. Often, these systems are vulnerable and provide limited access for the patient.
- As already mentioned, health services and organizations are fragmented. Data is siloed in legacy systems and difficult to share. Most of these systems use varying formats and standards that are incompatible with each other. As a result, there is no single version of the truth as stakeholders keep their own records.
- As medicine is becoming more democratized and patients are further empowered, there is a reasonable chance that they will tend to seek a second opinion. With patient mobility, patients can switch their caregiver. Likewise, there is also the need for information mobility, which is currently lacking.

- Electronic patient / health records are currently stored in centralized databases, which increases their security footprint and requires trust in a single entity / authority. Moreover, current healthcare systems cannot ensure security and data integrity, regardless of controlled access requirements, as it can be manipulated without external validation.
- Common healthcare fraud incidents involve perpetrators who take advantage of patients by entering false health information (such as diagnoses and conditions that patients do not have). As a result, fraudulent insurance claims can be submitted for payment.

Key features of the platform

Let's go over some of the key features of the MedicalChain platform that demonstrate the power of the blockchain. The first key feature is that it provides a platform for multiple participants: practitioners, patients, and research institutions. Thus, instead of having fragmented records for the same patient held at different institutions or practitioners, there is only one source of truth.

The practitioner or institution is no longer the owner of the records — the patient is now the owner of their own medical records and has full access to and control of the data. Another strong feature of the platform is data security, as the system uses a double-encryption mechanism on top of the already permissioned blockchain.

Dual-blockchain system

MedicalChain is based on a dual-blockchain implementation, and it uses a combination of Hyperledger Fabric and Ethereum. Fabric controls access to the health records and implements rule-based authorization and the business logic using smart contracts. Ethereum is used for their ERC20 token (cryptocurrency), which users can use for the underlying application and services offered by the platform.

Multiple participants and permissions

As the healthcare system involves a plethora of different actors, identity management and access to data needs to be implemented by design. Using Hyperledger Composer, the MedicalChain platform implements a dynamic system that identifies actors and gives them the appropriate scope over a health record, while at the same time taking the patient's permission into account.

There are three main participants in the healthcare system:

- A **practitioner**, for example, can read or write on permissioned records (EHRs), or they can request permission for other practitioners/institutions to have access.

- A **patient** can read their EHR, giving or revoking the permission of a practitioner or institution to read or write an EHR or a portion of it, and write certain attributes to the EHR (for instance, weekly exercise or permissible alcohol consumption).

- A **research institution** can read permissioned EHRs, for example, to research population health or the spread of diseases.

For permissions, the platform uses an **access control language** (ACL), which spells out access to the data model and transactions implemented in the smart contract(s) used by the platform. By defining these ACL rules, they are able to control to which resources participants have access. One example of these access rules is shown below:

```
rule PractitionerCanReadPatientIfAuthorize {
  description: "Allow Practitioner access to granted patients"
  participant(p): "org.acme.medicalchain.Practitioner"
  operation: READ
  resource(r): "org.acme.mediclchain.Patient"
  condition: (r.authorized.indexOf(p.getIdentifier()) > -1)
  action: ALLOW
}
```

Data is cryptographically encrypted

As you have learned in this chapter, data security is the most important part of this particular industry. To ensure the privacy of health records, MedicalChain is using symmetric key cryptography (https://en.wikipedia.org/wiki/Symmetric-key_algorithm). The platform encrypts the record and stores it in a datastore with the appropriate regulatory jurisdiction. The symmetric key will be encrypted with the public key of a 2048-bit key pair for each of the entities that are given permission to access the patient's record. Thus, every time the record is decrypted with the owner's private key and stored, the symmetric key is encrypted with the new key of the authorized user (that is, the practitioner or institution).

In case access is removed from a record for a previously authorized user, the full symmetric key is decrypted using the private key of the patient and the EHR is decrypted using the symmetric key.

As the record is now fully decrypted, it can be re-encrypted with a new symmetric key, which itself is encrypted with all of the public keys of the remaining authorized users.

The following diagram shows the process that takes place when a user is authorized to access the record and requests access. The private key of the requesting user is used to decrypt the symmetric key for the EHR, which is then used to decrypt the patient's EHR; as demonstrated in the following diagram:

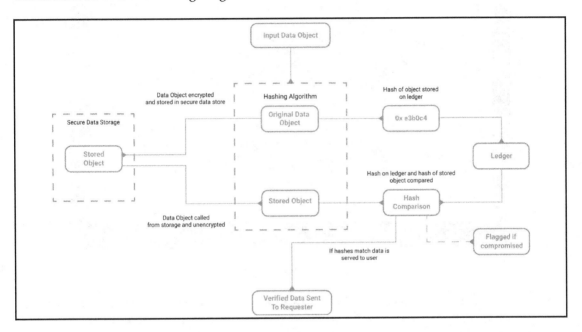

Process that takes place when an authorized user requests access to a health record

Platform services

MedicalChain also offers several services to all participants. One of their flagship services is the **Telemedicine** consultation platform. It provides direct utilization of health records by allowing patients to communicate with doctors and share their data during online consultations, known as *telemedicine*, employing a webcam interface. MedicalChain not only provides such an interface, but it is also integrated with the health record system and enables live interaction with the patient's records, as shown in the following screenshot.

During the consultation, patients can grant access to their records, allowing for a better and more valuable user experience:

User interface of MedicalChain Telemedicine's consultation platform

MedicalChain will also connect research institutions with patients who are willing to have their personal healthcare data used in studies throughout the marketplace. Every study lists how their data is being used and what data will be required. In most cases, data can be made anonymous to ensure the privacy of anyone involved. In return, a participant is compensated in **MedTokens**, the ERC20 token used by the platform services. It lets patients monetize their health data, and, in return, power the next generation of medicine.

Use case – Nano Vision (cure development)

The second example that I want to address briefly is a platform called Nano Vision (`http:/ /nanovision.com`). The goal of this platform is to decentralize the funding of medical research and to enable scientists to share their research and collaborate on an open, global scale. It enables everyday consumers to fund medical research (for example, direct funding of potential cures) that are important and matter to them.

What really makes this platform different, however, is the collection and processing of molecular data, a subset of biological information, in real time to accelerate the development of cures.

Before looking at this platform in more detail, let's examine what it is trying to solve.

Current inefficiencies of medical research

- Hundreds of billions of dollars are wasted in the industry on paperwork, primarily administrative in nature.
- Funding for important government or large foundation research continues to decline, as drug companies prioritize maximizing profits rather than solving difficult health problems.
- Research papers are not shared to foster broader breakthroughs and become siloed.
- Almost all clinical trials end in failure, costing nearly a billion dollars each. Meanwhile, the industry is still fighting cancer with chemotherapy.
- Large companies such as Pfizer are dropping important research on Alzheimer's while giving priority to more lucrative drugs with lower risks, such as Viagra.

Nano Vision is still developing the platform, but let's explore what they are working on at present. Just like MedicalChain, Nano Vision uses a dual-blockchain approach; Ethereum for the cryptocurrency and a distributed ledger technology developed by Nano. The platform aims to prevent diseases, detect threats, improve diagnostics, and find new therapies.

The Nano Sense chip

This chip, developed in partnership with ARM, enables the real-time streaming of molecular data. This data can be used to recognize and analyze health threats caused by pathogens and other living organisms. The chip takes advantage of the progress that is being made in nanotechnology, optics, artificial intelligence, blockchain authentication, and edge computing in order to access and analyze the data in real time, increasing the amount of available data by an increased order of magnitude. These chips are deployed in so-called **Nano Bot** devices in order to sense and detect molecular and environmental data and alerts in real-time. More information about this chip can be found in the following article: `https://prn.to/2p5ULC0`.

Nano Cure Chain and marketplace

The platform uses blockchain to secure and write all data to its correct, original source. On top of the blockchain, a marketplace is built where contributors are compensated with the platform's **Nano Cure** coins. This means that when the contributed data is used to develop a critical health solution, the contributor will get credit and can receive compensation for their contribution. You can compare this to royalties received by musicians as compensation for the use of their music. The coins will keep the platform running through its lifecycle and will fund important research in the future.

The AI/ML inference engine

The last and maybe most important technology used by the platform is its **Artificial Intelligence** and **Machine Learning** (**Inference**) **engine**. By forming the largest and most continuously growing dataset / collection of biological data, it will enable the engine to identify trends and draw conclusions using artificial intelligence and machine-learning algorithms. The idea of the engine is to give scientists an entirely new tool to research and create life-saving solutions.

Initial health threat targets

In partnership with teams from several leading institutions in the areas of research, academia, and healthcare, Nano Vision is planning to accelerate the collection of data and the population of key research associated with infectious diseases, such as tuberculosis, Zika and dengue, oncology research and the treatment of cancer, and neurology research and the treatment of Alzheimer's disease. The following diagram shows all of the planned Nano Vision research:

INITIAL HEALTH THREAT TARGETS

Worldwide infectious diseases	Oncology research and treatments for:	Bacteriology research and treatments for:
· Tuberculosis	· Pancreatic cancer	· Methicillin-resistant
· Zika	· Brain cancer	Staphylococcus
· Malaria	*Virology research and*	aureus (MRSA)
· Dengue	*treatments for:*	· Clostridium difficile
· Chagas	· Hepatitis B & C	(C. Diff)
Research and	· Influenza A & B	*Neurology research*
treatments to combat	· Respiratory	*and treatments for:*
antimicrobial	Syncytial Virus	· Alzheimer's disease
resistance (AMR)		

List of initial research planned for the Nano Vision platform

Summary

In this third and final industry-specific chapter, we reviewed the impact and some of the most advanced real-world examples of the use of blockchain across the healthcare industry. We explored the kinds of challenges this industry faces and how blockchain can help conquer these challenges. Because of the complexity of this industry, not all things can be solved with blockchain, such as the prevention of cyber and phishing attacks, but blockchain can handle those threats much more easily than traditional systems.

The chapter provided some examples of how blockchain can serve as a viable technology for a variety of day-to-day operations in the healthcare sector. For instance, it can be a solution for both drug traceability and as an anti-counterfeiting platform. We also looked at how blockchain improves cybersecurity and the security of privacy-sensitive data such as electronic health records (EHRs).

Next, we explored two real-world use cases in the healthcare industry. The first use case told the story of MedicalChain and its platform for securely sharing patient health data among practitioners, patients, and research institutes. Solving the fragmentation of legacy systems and providing tools to encrypt and decrypt data safely empowers the patient to share just the amount of data that they want the practitioner to know.

The second use case told the story of Nano Vision and the Cure Platform, a highly-advanced Artificial Intelligence and Machine Learning platform for researching cures based on captured biomolecular data. It includes a combination of a hardware chip, distributed ledger technology, and an intelligent research engine.

In the next and final chapter of the book, `Chapter 18`, *Future Industry and Technology Directions*, we will examine a number of other industries that happen to be disrupted by blockchain technology. It also wraps up the book, where we will look back at what we have learned.

18
Future Industry and Technology Directions

Welcome to the last chapter of this book, and thank you so much for your attention. Hopefully, you've learned the essentials that you had hoped to get from this book.

This book was intentionally split into four parts. Part I addressed the implications of blockchain by introducing the technology and how it will affect your organization. Part II took a deep-dive into the core concepts and terminology. Furthermore, it explained all of the bits and bytes of the technology. Part III focused on implementing your own permissioned blockchain. Finally, Part IV explored some industries that are already being affected by the technology.

In this final chapter, we will take a look at future directions of some more industries that are on the verge of being affected by blockchain technology, the future of the technology itself, and how you can continue your blockchain studies after you finish this book. Will blockchain technology still be the same in 10 years, or will it evolve in something different? Read on…

Future industry directions

Instead of examining the impact of blockchain on another particular industry and exploring what day-to-day operations are already being transformed, this chapter will assess two industries that are looking into using blockchain, including the energy and the food and agriculture industries.

A great source of real-world use cases is this video: https://www.youtube.com/watch?v=G3psxs3gyf8 ("19 Industries the Blockchain Will Disrupt"). For now, let's explore three of these industries that, in my opinion, will benefit the most from blockchain technology.

Energy industry

The energy industry is one of those that has great potential for being disrupted by blockchain in the next year. Over the past year, roughly 120 energy-related blockchain start-ups were formed and collectively raised a total of $324 million. These companies are exploring the cost-saving benefits of blockchain technology. Moreover, these companies are forming consortiums to discuss future applications instead of building something custom on their own with the added risk of building the same solution. Most companies are focusing on two realms in which to innovate with blockchain technology: the electricity grid and incumbent commodities such as oil and gas. Some good research papers can be found at: `https://www.pwc.com/gx/en/industries/assets/blockchain-technology-in-energy.pdf` and `https://www.greentechmedia.com/research/report/blockchain-for-energy-2018#gs.ZQfYnbo`.

Peer-to-peer trading and microgrids

In a study by GTM Research, "Blockchain for Energy, 2018," it is noted that 59% of blockchain projects in the energy sector focus on building a peer-to-peer grid network. With the increase in renewable power generation initiatives, the need for a stable system on local, national, and European levels is the key objective of power grid management. A direct peer-to-peer trading platform could be built using blockchain technology and even enable **virtual power plants** (**VPP**), consisting of clusters of electricity generators, as well as load and storage systems that are pooled in an intelligent manner and are jointly controlled by the system.

Current state and inefficiencies

- Units (or lot sized) in energy and commodity trading are standardized and defined according to size, quality, and quantity. In the current market, these criteria are needed to overcome transaction costs.
- Actors that can't offer their goods to match the standardized criteria are not able to sell in wholesale power markets.
- Actors who can't sell are forced to use third-party intermediaries, such as brokers or banks, to draft specific trade contracts.

Blockchain can disrupt the traditional model, as it can reduce transaction costs by creating a more connected market of smaller actors through standardization of data sharing via smart contracts and the automatic execution of trade orders.

This concept helps facilitate a distributed network of entities and maybe even individuals who buy and trade excess energy among themselves, decreasing transaction costs dramatically, bypassing third-party intermediaries, and allowing for smaller sized lots. In more and more countries, the cost of renewable energy is becoming equal to or lower than traditional retail energy sources (this is also known as *energy parity*). Such a peer-to-peer trading platform gives individuals the ability to produce their own energy at home or to trade it with their neighbors and peers at a lower price than retail energy sources. Blockchain can create connected communities or **microgrids**, which in theory can be self-sustaining apart from the existing national grid. The Australia based company, **Power Ledger** (https://www.powerledger.io) is developing such a platform, although currently microgrids only exist as a layer on top of the national grid.

The system behind Power Ledger allows its users to choose the source of their electricity, become part of an economy where households that generate electricity can trade with their neighbors, and get a fair return on their personal investment while providing stable and affordable energy. Power Ledger not only offers a microgrid trading platform, but also peer-to-peer trading, electric vehicle metering and settlement, and VPPs. Power Ledger has published a very interesting and extensive whitepaper, which can be found at: https://cdn2.hubspot.net/hubfs/4519667/Documents%20/Power%20Ledger%20Whitepaper.pdf, and more general information about microgrids can be found at: http://www.supersmartenergy.com/potentiality-of-microgrid-across-globe-in-india/.

This diagram shows how microgrids work together:

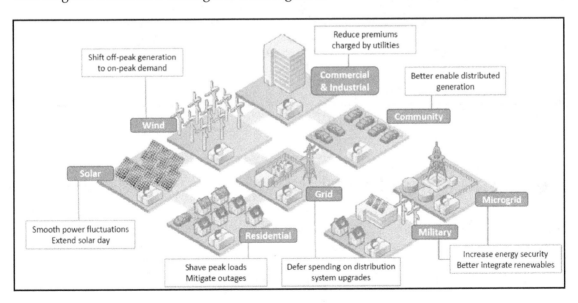

Several types of microgrids working together

Technically, microgrids use a hybrid public and consortium blockchain approach – Ethereum for its public layer and **EcoChain** for its consortium and application layers. The public layer provides a mechanism for interfacing and transacting with the consortium layer through their **POWR** (Ethereum CR20) tokens.

The consortium layer uses the EcoChain blockchain, a private proof-of-stake, low-power blockchain developed in-house by a company with the same name from the Netherlands. The following figure shows the architecture that you can find in Power Ledger's whitepaper:

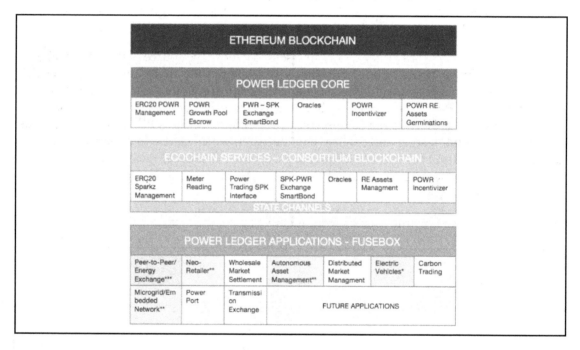

The ecosystem of Power Ledger is built upon a number of technology layers

Food and agriculture industry

The food and agriculture industry can clearly benefit from blockchain technology. This industry has a lot of the same day-to-day operations as the transportation and healthcare industries: improving supply chain efficiency, fraud prevention (because of false product certification and counterfeit products), and the integrity and traceability of food and fresh produce. Let's look first at some of the agricultural issues in developing countries.

Current state and inefficiencies

- Around one-third of all food produced worldwide is wasted. In wealthy countries, it is mainly wasted on the consumer side; but in most of the world, it happens in the production and distribution of the food and produce.
- Due to global warming's effect on climatic conditions, the industry needs to cope with erratic weather such as inadequate rainfall and long heat waves, resulting in a lack of available water for irrigation and frequent crop failures.
- Due to an unsatisfactory fall in prices, most farmers are unable to sell their produce in normal markets. In some markets, a middleman is needed, who takes a share of the profits. Farmers, in turn, get lower prices for their crops, and with the lack of transparency in the supply chain, it is hard to verify the fairness of prices.
- Due to inadequate storage facilities, such as cold storage, a lot of produce is damaged, resulting in the inability to sell produce at a reasonable price.
- In developing counties such as India, 60% of farmers don't have access to credit systems, which increases dependency on money lenders who charge high interest rates, resulting in the farmers' inability to repay loans and their indebtedness (`https://medium.com/@Zebidata/how-blockchain-can-revolutionize-the-agriculture-industry-691d630dac61`).

The problem with this industry, and most certainly in developing countries, is that most of the business is conducted on paper. Even on a global scale, this is no exception. In this industry, you need to deal with a lot of actors and regulations, such as import/export laws, banks, auditors, and spilling a lot of paper and ink faxing things around in order to exchange information. There is no standardization and the lack of it slows everything down, as the information is harder to gather and process/analyze.

There have been systems, such as GS1 (`https://www.gs1.org/standards`), created to standardize the global supply chain, but companies still have to implement this redundantly, and it doesn't really provide a working solution. This is where blockchain comes in, resulting in different projects such as Agriledger (`http://www.agriledger.com/`), Provenance (`https://www.provenance.org/`), and Blockgrain (`https://blockgrain.io/`), as well as projects from large companies such as Walmart (`https://newfoodeconomy.org/blockchain-food-traceability-walmart-ibm/`), Coca-Cola (`https://www.reuters.com/article/us-blockchain-coca-cola-labor/coca-cola-u-s-state-dept-to-use-blockchain-to-combat-forced-labor-idUSKCN1GS2PY`), and CarreFour (`http://www.carrefour.com/current-news/carrefour-launches-europes-first-food-blockchain`).

Most of these projects use Hyperledger Fabric as their blockchain, and each focuses on a different area. However, they all aim to standardize their market.

Notable platforms to watch

Instead of picking one example, I'm going to explore some of the notable projects currently under development. Some of them I'll just mention briefly, but all are worth watching.

Agriledger/AgUnity

The **Agriledger** platform from **AgUnity** (`https://agunity.com`) uses blockchain technology to create trust for small farmers in developing countries. They focus both on providing access to regional and international markets as well as capital for small farmers (who reportedly supply around 80% of the food consumed in their countries). The system is built so that it can run off a smartphone using a mobile app. The AgUnity app records all details of the farmer's crops and transactions, and it locks those details to the blockchain via the use of a QR code.

More information on the Agriledger project can be found in this article at `https://www61-bit.com/agunity-blockchain-agtech/`.

Foodshed

Foodshed (`http://www.foodshed.io`) is a platform that focuses not on a regional or global market, but on local food markets. It tries to solve the inefficiencies of local food distribution and the accessibility of local food markets. Foodshed is a platform that can connect farmers and buyers within a 250-mile/400-kilometer radius, as shown in the following diagram, making it easier for small farmers to sell food/fresh produce and for buyers to get cheaper food/fresh produce.

Other key features of Foodshed include tracking and tracing of food in real-time and the implementation of route optimization to cut down on shipping costs for farmers. Foodshed is a single platform that contains both a mobile marketing app and a logistics platform for accessing urban markets and responding to local demand and opportunities:

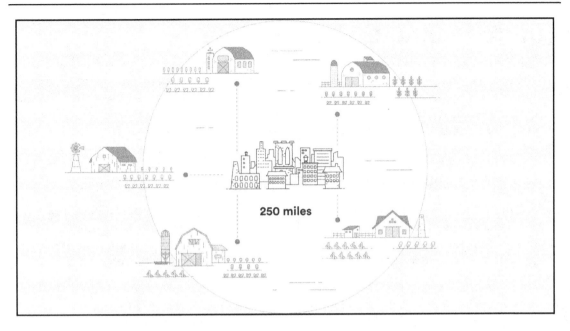

Foodshed connects farmers and buyers within a 250-mile/400-kilometer radius

Foodshed integrates blockchain technology into the platform to provide traceability of goods, so that buyers know when the food was harvested, where it came from, who handled it, and what procedures were followed. Because of this, both buyers and public health officials are able to address food safety issues relating to registered transactions.

Provenance

Provenance (`https://www.provenance.org`) is one of the better well-known blockchain projects for the food supply chain, and it uses Hyperledger Fabric. It is backed by Unilever for tracking tea (`https://www.supplychaindive.com/news/unilever-blockchain-tea/513365/`) in Melawi. The primary focus is on making supply chains more transparent and supporting the increased demand on environmentally friendly products. Provenance uses their platform for specific use cases, such as the traceability of Indonesian fish, increasing the integrity and interactivity of digital certification (for example, organic soil), even on a smaller scale, from coconuts to fashion products. Some key components of the platform include a traceability system that confirms identities and product attributes, storing everything securely in the blockchain and linking the digital world to the physical world through labeling and smart tags.

More information about Provenance can be found in their whitepaper at `https://www.provenance.org/whitepaper`.

Future technology directions

It might be too early to think and write about the future of the technology, as real-world production systems are just being released or are still in development. One thing for sure, though, is that blockchain technology certainly has a future in the enterprise. After 10 years of being known as the technology behind Bitcoin and other cryptocurrencies, blockchain technology has matured and more and more production platforms are being commercially released and used by end users. Now we are seeing a new series of services starting to emerge that are built on top of established blockchains, also known as **layer 2 blockchain** services, which promise big gains in scalability, interoperability, and functionality.

Layer 2 blockchain services include the **Lightning Network** and the **Raiden Network**. These services offer instant transactions with no fees and processing as fast your application can submit them. Another major development is IOTA's Tangle network, designed to be the lightweight network for the IoT and better suited for micro and nanopayments.

Another next step for blockchain technology will be to incorporate it with other technologies in order to be able to query the massive amounts of data stored in future blockchains.

The defining feature of a layer 2 blockchain service is that computations are moved off-chain in order to make transactions more private or to save computing resources. Rather than having every node in the blockchain network execute the same scripts or smart contract functions, it is implemented in a more simplified manner and only requires a few computers to be involved in the transaction. You still get the same level of security protection as with on-chain transactions, as a Layer 1 blockchain acts as the anchor of trust.

The same layering also occurred with the World Wide Web in the 1990s, where the second layer solution (HTTP, Hypertext Transfer Protocol) transformed the internet from a clunky network (only using TCP/IP, Transmission Control, and Internet Protocols) into a global phenomenon, giving rise to a host of web-based applications and online services.

The technology is still in its early phases, and it requires new security and trust solutions. One key problem to figure out is how to ensure that transaction histories are kept in sync and validated by the "on-chain" consensus algorithms. Moreover, whereas HTTP was universally adopted as a standard, there is a great deal of competition in the blockchain ecosystem.

Lightning Network

This network was originally designed to make Bitcoin transactions fast and scalable, but it already supports interoperability with other blockchains and is powered by smart contracts. The Lightning Network, as the name suggests, is a network for instant/lightning-fast blockchain payments without worrying about and waiting on block confirmation times. It enforces security through the use of smart contracts without creating an on-chain transaction for individual payments.

The Lightning Network is expected to be capable of millions to billions of transactions per second across the network. This capacity can't be met by any legacy payment systems, such as Visa, which can only handle around 1,670 payments per second. This vast capability is made possible by transacting and settling off-chain. It also offers low-cost transactions, which enables instant micropayments. The network works across blockchains as well, meaning that it is possible to conduct transactions across different blockchains without the need to trust in third-party custodians.

Since it is a layer 2 solution, this means that it is dependent on the underlying technology of the blockchain, which in the case of the Lightning Network is the Bitcoin (layer 1) network. It uses the same transaction format and native smart-contract scripting language to create a new layer of services on top of the blockchain.

With the Lightning Network, participants can create bidirectional payment channels. The user-generated channels securely send payments back and forth in a trustless fashion between two participants. The two parties that wish to transact need to set up a *multisig* wallet with each other, meaning that it requires more than one signature to conclude a transaction. This wallet holds the required cryptocurrency and its address is saved onto the blockchain.

Once the payment channel is set up, the two parties can conduct an unlimited number of transactions without touching the information stored on the blockchain. With every transaction, both parties sign an updated balance sheet to reflect the amount of cryptocurrency stored in the wallet. When the two parties are finished transacting, they close the channel, which results in the updated balance being registered on the blockchain. You can even program a smart contract that sends a payment every x amount of time, as long as the channel is open.

You don't even have to set up a direct channel to transact using the Lightning Network. You can send payments to someone via channels that are set up by people connected to you.

The following diagram shows the number of open/connected channels at a certain time:

Graph of open and connected channels on the Lightning Network

This graph is generated using the Lightning Network Explorer at `https://explorer.acinq.co/`.

Raiden Network

The Raiden Network is the equivalent of the Lightning Network, but it works specifically as an infrastructure layer on top of the Ethereum blockchain. It is a network of nodes in which nodes can establish payment channels with other nodes. The payment is routed through the network via multiple nodes, but a single node can only communicate with its direct neighbors. The security built in to the Raiden Network is that each of the nodes has to hold the balance of the amount being moved. You can imagine that the higher the amount that you want to transfer, the harder it is to find a path through the network.

The use case of the Raiden Network is for transferring small amounts of Ether almost instantaneously and in a reliable way. To learn more about how the Raiden Network works, read the Raiden 101 document at `https://raiden.network/101.html`.

The Raiden Network allows for the transfer of ERC20 tokens among participants without the need for the global consensus of the Ethereum main net. This is achieved by using signed and hash-locked transfers, also called *balance proofs*.

A *hash-lock* is a type of obstacle that restricts the spending of an output until a specified piece of data is publicly revealed. This concept is also known as *payment channel technology*. As part of the Raiden Network, these payment channels allow for unlimited, bidirectional transfers of tokens between two participants.

IOTA Tangle network

I have previously mentioned IOTA in this book and explained how the network works. Instead of being a layer 2 solution, it was built with the same concept from the start in 2015/2016. IOTA developed the **Tangle** network, which is the data structure behind the IOTA network, and instead of it being a blockchain, it is a particular type of directed graph that holds transactions, as shown in the following diagram:

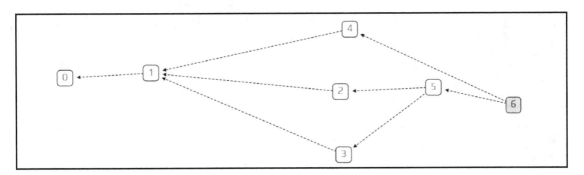

Example of the Tangle data structure

Each transaction is represented on the diagram as a vertex in the graph. When a new transaction is added to the Tangle Network, it picks two previous transactions to approve, adding two new edges to the graph. The newly-added and unapproved transaction is called a *transaction tip*. The technology behind IOTA will pick the best two tips to approve.

So, instead of having blocks that are chained together, each block contains multiple transactions. The Tangle Network does not have the notion of blocks, but rather chains the transactions together. This makes the network much faster than traditional blockchains, as the approver does not need to know about all transactions – only the ones assigned to the approver need to be approved. This means that you do not need to have gigabytes of data stored on your computer in order to approve transactions.

A very clear explanation about the Tangle Network technology can be found on the blog of IOTA, starting with the first illustrated introduction at `https://blog.iota.org/the-tangle-an-illustrated-introduction-4d5eae6fe8d4`.

How do I remain current on blockchain developments?

We are now nearly at the end of this chapter and of this book. But how can you remain current on blockchain developments and on its future? For this, I have registered the URL `https://implementblockchain.tech`. This website is dedicated to supporting this book, where you will find new blog articles, hands-on labs, and a full rundown on how to design, develop, secure, and implement smart contracts.

Other websites that I have referenced throughout this book and highly suggest that you keep monitoring are listed in the following table. This list will be updated in the future on the preceding website. Note: sources are listed randomly:

Source	URL
Oracle Blockchain	`https://www.oracle.com/cloud/blockchain/`
Autonomous Blockchain	`https://cloud.oracle.com/en_US/blockchain/`
Hyperledger Fabric	`https://www.hyperledger.org/projects/fabric`
Hyperledger Fabric	`https://hyperledger-fabric.readthedocs.io/`
Ethereum	`https://ethereum.org/`
Ethereum Solidity	`https://solidity.readthedocs.io/`
IOTA	`https://blog.iota.org`
Coindesk Beginner's Guide to Blockchain	`https://www.coindesk.com/information/`
Hackernoon Blockchain Learning	`https://hackernoon.com/index-of-best-blockchain-crypto-learning-resources-3351907ca6cd`
ConsenSys	`https://medium.com/@ConsenSys`
Forbes	`https://www.forbes.com/crypto-blockchain`
Blockonomi	`https://blockonomi.com/tag/blockchain/`
Techcrunch	`https://techcrunch.com/tag/blockchains/`
YouTube Playlist	`https://www.youtube.com/playlist?list=PLIVskXGUATGywfDVDfuE8WTwdI53sbWzq`
Slideshare	`https://www.slideshare.net/RobertvanMlken/clipboards/blockchain-week-in-review`
GitHub	`https://github.com/robertvanmolken/blockchain-across-oracle`

Summary

You have reached the end of my book. I really appreciate you taking the time to learn about this technology, and I hope that you got everything out of the book that you were expecting. In this last chapter, we looked at two more industries that are on the verge of being affected by blockchain: the energy and the food and agriculture industries. The energy industry has the greatest potential, but it is still looking at exactly how to implement it. Currently, we only see implementation in the supply chain.

Next, I discussed the future of blockchain technology and the layer 2 services currently being developed on top of blockchain to make it faster and more scalable. We looked at networks such as the Lightning Network, the Raiden Network, and IOTA, which provide this new layer.

Finally, I mentioned that I'm continuing my work and have registered a website, `https://implementblockchain.tech`, where I will be publishing new articles, hands-on labs, and maybe even videos. Moreover, the chapter contained a list of useful resources to check if you want to learn more about blockchain.

> *I hope that you enjoyed the book, and good luck implementing blockchain in your own line of business or organization. You can always find me on social media accounts such as Twitter (`@robertvanmolken`) and LinkedIn – With kind regards, Robert van Mölken.*

Other Books You May Enjoy

If you enjoyed this book, you may be interested in these other books by Packt:

Mastering Blockchain - Second Edition
Imran Bashir

ISBN: 978-1-78883-904-4

- Master the theoretical and technical foundations of the blockchain technology
- Understand the concept of decentralization, its impact, and its relationship with blockchain technology
- Master how cryptography is used to secure data - with practical examples
- Grasp the inner workings of blockchain and the mechanisms behind bitcoin and alternative cryptocurrencies
- Understand the theoretical foundations of smart contracts
- Learn how Ethereum blockchain works and how to develop decentralized applications using Solidity and relevant development frameworks
- Identify and examine applications of the blockchain technology - beyond currencies
- Investigate alternative blockchain solutions including Hyperledger, Corda, and many more
- Explore research topics and the future scope of blockchain technology

Tokenomics

Sean Au, Thomas Power

ISBN: 978-1-78913-632-6

- The background of ICOs and how they came to be
- The difference between a coin and a token, a utility and a security, and all the other acronyms you're likely to ever encounter
- How these ICOs raised enormous sums of money
- Tokenomics: structuring the token with creativity
- Why it's important to play nicely with the regulators
- A sneak peak into the future of ICOs from leaders in the industry

Implementing Oracle API Platform Cloud Service

Andrew Bell, Sander Rensen, Luis Weir, Phil Wilkins, Phil Wilkins

ISBN: 978-1-78847-865-6

- Get an overview of the Oracle API Cloud Service Platform
- See typical use cases of the Oracle API Cloud Service Platform
- Design your own APIs using Apiary
- Build and run microservices
- Set up API gateways with the new API platform from Oracle
- Customize developer portals
- Configuration management
- Implement Oauth 2.0 policies
- Implement custom policies
- Get a policy SDK overview
- Transition from Oracle API Management 12c to the new Oracle API platform

Leave a review - let other readers know what you think

Please share your thoughts on this book with others by leaving a review on the site that you bought it from. If you purchased the book from Amazon, please leave us an honest review on this book's Amazon page. This is vital so that other potential readers can see and use your unbiased opinion to make purchasing decisions, we can understand what our customers think about our products, and our authors can see your feedback on the title that they have worked with Packt to create. It will only take a few minutes of your time, but is valuable to other potential customers, our authors, and Packt. Thank you!

Index

CPSIA information can be obtained
at www.ICGtesting.com
Printed in the USA
BVHW010817091118
532658BV00006B/78/P